Simon & Schuster
1230 Avenue of the Americas
New York, NY 10020

For my grandparents,
who gave me an education

Who is wise? The one who learns from everyone.

—*Pirkei Avot*

CONTENTS

PROLOGUE

••

W hen I first met Lin-Manuel Miranda to discuss this project, he was trying to help his four-year-old log on to Disney Plus.

It was a clear, wintry day in 2022, and he'd invited me to the Drama Book Shop, a shrine to playwriting in Midtown Manhattan's theater district that had given him and his friends a basement space after college to work on the show that became his first Broadway musical, *In the Heights*. Between substitute teaching and dancing at bar mitzvahs to pay his rent, he'd pop down to the bookshop basement and figure out a song on its creaky piano. He now owned the bookshop with one of his earliest collaborators on that show. He pointed out a perk of ownership—"Free coffee!"—when we filled our cups at the café and found a table to chat.

But before we did that, he had to help his son crack the Disney app. The little guy wanted to watch *Encanto*.

I had to suppress a laugh. If anyone should have Disney Plus streaming without a hitch, it ought to be the songwriter who supplied its most beloved content. The Broadway smash *Hamilton* more or less launched Disney Plus when the show's live film version was released on the service in 2020, quickly becoming its most-streamed title. Disney's *Encanto*, for which Lin-Manuel wrote the songs, was the most-streamed movie in the world in 2022, bested the next year by Disney's *Moana*, also with songs by Lin-Manuel. Numbers like "We Don't Talk About Bruno" and "Surface Pressure" from *Encanto* became so popular that *Billboard* named

Lin-Manuel its 2022 songwriter of the year, ranked higher even than Taylor Swift. In addition to his multiple Tony, Grammy, and Emmy Awards, the Pulitzer Prize, and the MacArthur "genius grant," Lin-Manuel had arguably created the soundtrack to the post-pandemic world. He redefined musical storytelling by synthesizing his Latino heritage with his love of hip-hop, Broadway, and every other form of pop culture he'd encountered, the rare theater artist to become a household name.

And yet that didn't mean the iPad app worked better for his family than for anyone else's. It had been a crazy year, Lin-Manuel told me after he'd gotten his son logged on. With studio release calendars reshuffled by the pandemic, he'd had four movies come out in the past eight months. In addition to *Encanto*, there was the film version of *In the Heights*, an animated musical for Sony called *Vivo*, and his directorial debut on Netflix, a film based on *Rent* composer Jonathan Larson's autobiographical musical *Tick, Tick . . . Boom!*. Even for an artist who famously writes like he's running out of time, it was a lot.

But now, he said, his calendar was finally clear. He had nothing going on except helping his older son get ready for school. And cowriting a concept album based on the 1979 movie *The Warriors*. And composing the songs for the *Lion King* prequel, *Mufasa*. And finishing a new musical with one of his composer heroes, John Kander. And polishing the score for a live-action remake of *The Little Mermaid* with another of his heroes, Alan Menken. And working out a performance with Andrew Lloyd Webber to celebrate the queen's jubilee.

When he talked about these projects, he didn't seem burdened or overwhelmed. He looked giddy. In a gray overcoat, sweater, and jeans, with a scruffy pandemic goatee, he could barely sit still. After leading me down to the Drama Book Shop basement, he started playing tunes on an old piano, popping up to illustrate dance steps, then whipping out his laptop to show me video clips. Unlike his early days in that basement, he no longer had financial worries. With the success of *Hamilton*, he said, he had the freedom to pursue projects that met his main criterion: "I like to work on things I'll learn from."

It was that appetite for learning that had drawn me to Lin-Manuel. As a theater professor and an arts journalist, I'd written about his career before. Trained as a Shakespeare scholar, I wondered who our Shakespeares might be today—artists telling national stories in innovative dramatic forms—and in 2016, the head of New York's Public Theater, Oskar Eustis, suggested I check out the guy who'd just created a hip-hop musical about the American Revolution. For the *New Yorker*, I covered the 2017 opening of *Hamilton* in London, and I traveled to Puerto Rico for the *Atlantic* in 2019 when Lin-Manuel took *Hamilton* there on a fundraising tour after Hurricane Maria. I wrote about his contributions to *Moana* and *Mary Poppins Returns*—sometimes appreciatively, sometimes critically. And every time I heard him speak, what struck me, besides his exuberance, was his interest in trying things that would help him learn new skills. For a songwriter who'd already found so much success, he seemed almost insatiable in his desire to expand his tool kit.

His collaborators noticed it too. "Lin is the best in the world at what he does because he's continually challenging himself," Jared Bush, the screenwriter for *Moana* and *Encanto*, told me. "He has this constant desire to keep improving, stretching, and learning." And that desire, his longtime friends say, has characterized his approach to creativity for years. "Without diminishing his talent, I don't think of him as a genius," says Owen Panettieri, his college friend and vice president of Lin-Manuel's company 5000 Broadway Productions. "It's a bit of a disservice to say, 'Oh, he's just brilliant,' or 'Oh, he has this gift.' Maybe there's some truth to that, but I don't believe that's the key to his success over decades. If you really want to create art that's lasting, there's work and there's sacrifice, and there's also a commitment to openness and learning. He works really hard, and he continues to learn, and that, more than anything, is what helps."

Comments like that intrigued me. I wanted to find out what Lin-Manuel had learned. I knew the output; I was curious to figure out the input. And doing so, I suspected, might help me reach a different understanding of creativity. Many of us assume that some people come into the world as inherent creators, and we imagine masterpieces springing, fully formed, from the brains of those unique geniuses. If any work seemed to illustrate that idea, it would surely be *Hamilton*. Lin-Manuel was the originator, the lyricist, the composer, the scriptwriter, and the star, motoring through brilliant raps on Broadway that changed the way America tells its origin story. If you encountered Lin-Manuel only as Alexander Hamilton, you might think he was a born genius.

And yet I soon learned that was not how most people who knew Lin-Manuel as a child would have described him. Though he had the promise to test into a Manhattan public school for gifted children, he wasn't considered the best writer in his cohort, or the best composer, or the best musician. He was kind, enthusiastic, smart, and imaginative, and he had charisma onstage, if not particular singing talent. He enjoyed making up songs with his toys, but so do lots of children. Coming up with a ditty like "The Garbage Pail Kids are in town!" in preschool doesn't guarantee that three decades later you'll come up with a line like "I'm past patiently waitin'. I'm passionately smashin' / Every expectation, every action's an act of creation!" He had to learn how to become an artist.

What people did recognize in Lin-Manuel back then was a burning desire to create art and a limitless curiosity about ways to do it better. He sat up close to his elementary-school bus driver, an aspiring rapper from the Bronx who taught his passengers to repeat bars from early hip-hop groups like the Sugarhill Gang and the Geto Boys. He memorized tracks from his sister's '80s cassette tapes so he could lip-synch to them at the school talent show, and he watched Disney animated musicals over and over until he could perform the soundtracks for his classmates. He apprenticed himself to the older high-school students who directed plays and wrote original scripts so he could learn to direct and write as well. And he embraced the messy process of making things—movies, plays, musicals—as stages in his growth rather than referenda on his ability. Masterpieces didn't turn up in his hands overnight. When it opened in 2015, *Hamilton* was the eighth musical that the thirty-five-year-old creator had written, if you counted his scripts back through college and high school. *Hamilton* itself required seven years of development. It took Lin-Manuel a long time to become a genius.

That process of learning to create was also a process of learning to draw on all the different parts of his identity. Lin-Manuel grew up between cultures. Both his parents came to New York from Puerto Rico and raised him and his sister in a largely Spanish-speaking immigrant neighborhood at the northernmost tip of Manhattan. At Lin-Manuel's elementary school, which drew from communities all over the island, many of his classmates couldn't pronounce his name. He became Lin at school and Lin-Manuel at home. He spent summers with his grandparents near San Juan, but he didn't speak Spanish well enough to fit in with the other kids. He was too much of an outsider in Puerto Rico, too Puerto Rican on the Upper East Side. It wasn't until he got to college that he met other children of the Caribbean diaspora and felt like he didn't have to code-switch anymore. It was the late 1990s, the era of the Latin crossover boom in pop music, and for the first time, he tried writing salsa and merengue tunes. He had to learn how to make art that reflected his fully hyphenated self and how to create opportunities for people, like himself, who hadn't felt represented in a lot of mainstream media. It took hard work to grow into the name Lin-Manuel Miranda.

This slowly unfolding genesis wasn't a solo act. He benefited from devoted parents, from schools that allowed him to try creative projects and supported his experiments, from many influential mentors who gave him opportunities to demonstrate his potential, and from creative partners who improved his ideas. Early on, Lin-Manuel figured out that he could create better work by collaborating with his talented classmates. He enlisted his friends to help him make movies on the weekends at his house. He recruited the best musicians to play the scores for his musical projects. He found better actors and singers than himself to star in his scripts. And he handed his drafts over to directors who could strengthen his initial impulses. Over and over—in high school, in college, as a young professional—he gathered artists around him to execute something that none of them could make alone. He'd realized, in other words, that artistic genius is a team sport.

He also learned how to become a valued collaborator. Every skill that his Broadway and Disney partners praise him for now—that he's infectiously enthusiastic and upbeat, that he's ready to support the best idea no matter who comes up with it, that he's willing to cut his own material when it doesn't work, that he's always lifting up his fellow artists—is something he figured out how to do, through trial and error, in his early years. For that, he credits his mentors—not only the elementary-school music teacher who cast him in his first play and the college thesis adviser who put up with his idea for an original musical, but peers like the high-school girlfriend who showed him how to support his fellow actors, and the singers in his a cappella group who taught him how to turn melody into harmony. When he won his first Tony Award, he thanked his eighth-grade English teacher, Dr. Rembert Herbert, for telling him that he was a writer.

There was luck involved too. Lin-Manuel had the good fortune to come of age in New York in the 1990s, when hip-hop was becoming mainstream, Latin pop was finding English-language listeners, Disney movies were rediscovering musical-theater structures, and Broadway was returning to the sounds of the contemporary airwaves. He emerged on the professional scene at the same time as Barack Obama, when immigrant stories and the promise of multiethnic identities drove the American narrative. But he also developed the skills to transform everything he absorbed into material for his own stories and to attract the collaborators who could help him share those stories with an audience at the right time. It wasn't obvious that anyone needed to find the overlapping center of the Venn diagram that included Jonathan Larson, *The Little Mermaid*, Marc Anthony, and the Notorious B.I.G. until Lin-Manuel gained the confidence to map all his influences onto an American musical.

In the basement of the Drama Book Shop, I gave Lin-Manuel my pitch. I wanted to write a book about his education as an artist, focusing on the range of teachers—friends, relatives, classroom instructors, mentors, professionals—who helped him learn how to do what he now does so well.

He agreed.

During the next two years, I met with Lin-Manuel over a dozen times to learn the story of his first forty-two years—not womb to tomb, of course, but something like womb to *Tick, Tick . . . Boom!*. As I interviewed over a hundred and fifty of his teachers and collaborators, from his elementary-school bus driver to Andrew Lloyd Webber, I started to piece together a fuller picture of his education. I visited his family in Puerto Rico, toured the campuses that nourished him at Hunter College High School and Wesleyan University, and looked through the elementary-school projects and report cards that his mother had saved in her Upper Manhattan home. I also pored through early scripts, rough recordings, and grainy videos of sixth-grade musicals, high-school one-acts, college projects, and pre-Broadway experiments. No journalist had seen these unpublished pieces beyond the glimpses Lin-Manuel occasionally posted on his Twitter account, but they provided a key to unlocking his growth as an artist. Over and over, I found that it was those early encounters, those initial, fumbling forays, those persistent, driving questions that shaped what Lin-Manuel went on to create in his professional career, even as he continually expanded his skill set to address those questions.

Just as frequently as they used the word *genius*, friends, collaborators, and teachers described Lin-Manuel as a *sponge*—for ideas, for learning, for technical knowledge, for pop culture, for American art in all its forms. There, I thought, was a metaphor that anyone could apply, that didn't require special gifts to demonstrate. Perhaps Lin-Manuel's story—viewed not as a blueprint but as a mindset—could inspire my own students. What can you absorb? What can you filter from your environment? What can you soak up and then turn into your own? How can you approach the world around you as a space for learning, for collaboration, for bringing all of yourself to fruition?

The stories I heard about Lin-Manuel weren't all triumphal narratives. He wrote songs that had to be scrapped. He wrote entire shows that didn't work. He spent years on projects that stalled out, that studios abandoned, that met an indifferent or even hostile reception. He got upset with his collaborators and had to apologize. He made mistakes—sometimes, as his reach and renown grew, on a national scale. On a few occasions, his timing aligned perfectly with a broader cultural wave; at other moments, he found himself out of step. He had to learn not only how to become an artist but how to become a leader—even, at times, the public face of policies and choices that he felt were thrust upon him. And he had to learn when to step aside, when to redefine what he calls his lane, and when to boost other voices above his own.

At that initial meeting, Lin-Manuel made one request of me. His father, Luis, had garnered a lot of attention as a high-profile political consultant, and though both parents were irrepressible champions of their son's work, he didn't feel that his mother, Luz, had received enough credit for being his primary teacher. As a child psychologist, she was the one who had helped him process his often overwhelming emotions and learn how to channel them into art. He asked if I would interview her first.

I agreed.

1

THE TOP OF THE WORLD

• •

*L*in-Manuel didn't like to practice piano. He enjoyed making up songs, tinkering on the upright outside his sister's bedroom, even though no one would listen to his originals; his sister, Cita, was too busy, and his parents were always at work. But the lessons from his piano teacher didn't excite him. At age six, he'd been taught only the first five notes of the C major scale. It wasn't fair. His sister was six years older, so she got to use all the keys. Cita, who practiced methodically, could play fancy pieces by Kabalevsky and Mozart. He was stuck with kiddie songs like "Camptown Races" and "Salizar, the Siamese Cat." The only piece he relished was "Pop Goes the Weasel." That one leaped up to the sixth note for an exciting "Pop!" And he figured out that if he started playing it two white keys below C, down in A minor, its chipper mood vanished, and the song sounded deliciously scary.

To get Lin-Manuel to his piano lessons, his Abuela Mundi took him two stops on the subway from their northern Manhattan neighborhood down to 181st Street. When they rode the escalator out of the station, they could see the gray towers of the George Washington Bridge looming above the brick buildings. His teacher, a friendly woman with curly hair and big glasses, was a little disappointed that he didn't practice, but she wanted to support him. After he ran through the assigned pieces, she let him try out his original tunes, and she gave them sophisticated-sounding names, like "Tarantella."

Soon it was time for Lin-Manuel to perform at his first piano recital.

On the appointed day, he dressed up in a white button-down shirt tucked into blue slacks. He climbed up onto the bench in front of the black grand piano. As instructed, he played "Camptown Races." And when he finished, the audience clapped.

Lin-Manuel looked up. No one had told him that applause came with playing the piano. That was a pleasant surprise.

"I know another one!" he announced. He played the second piece in his repertoire. The audience clapped some more.

"I know another one!" he said again. He played a third piece.

After the fourth piece, his teacher pulled him off the bench.

He'd gotten a taste of something addictive. "Music became a route to applause," he later reflected. "I realized cool things could happen if I kept at this."

Everyone in the Miranda family tells the tale of this piano recital. It's become an origin story—the moment when the future global entertainer stepped into the spotlight. (Lin-Manuel even called one of his music-production companies I Know Another One, Inc.) It wasn't the debut of a piano prodigy; he wasn't Stevie Wonder, dazzling audiences on the keyboard as a child. His sister was the skilled pianist. But he, the younger child, had the appetite for attention. And once he experienced that thrill, he couldn't wait to feel it again.

Performing also offered a way to channel the emotional vulnerability and identity divisions that characterized his childhood. His performances hadn't always met with acclaim. In preschool, he learned to read before some of his classmates; when he opened a book at recess, the other boys threw sand in his mouth. "I don't want to go back to school," he told his mother. If he saw the school letterhead, he burst into tears.

He was a sensitive, empathetic child. He cried when he saw a news report about the famine in Ethiopia in the early 1980s. He cried when he saw an unhoused person on the street. Even the chord changes in Paul Simon's "Bridge over Troubled Water" made him cry. "Mommy, that song is too sad," he'd say. "You have to change it."

Luz Towns-Miranda knew what to do. "I'm a psychologist, so part of my job is helping my kids navigate the world and their emotions," she says. "I wanted to let him know it was okay to feel what he was feeling."

She got Lin-Manuel a picture book that set out a psychological framework for handling feelings, a system called transactional analysis, in child-appropriate terms. "Your feelings are as real as your big toe," *T.A. for Tots* explained next to an illustration of a sniffling turtle. "If you are not happy, you have a right to feel your unhappiness and talk about it." The book described "cold pricklies" that made you feel bad and "warm fuzzies" that made you feel better. To counteract the cold pricklies at Lin-Manuel's preschool, Luz made sure that her son got plenty of warm fuzzies at home: a relaxation exercise, a song at bedtime. She'd grown up with Al Jolson tunes and would sing him "April Showers" and "California, Here I Come" until he fell asleep.

Luz decided to become a psychologist when she was thirteen. She wanted to know why people behaved the way they did. Her Mexican-American father, an engineer in the merchant marine, came home to their New Jersey suburb for only two days every two weeks. Her mother had grown up on a farm in Puerto Rico without electricity, one of thirteen children, unable to go to school past third grade because she couldn't afford the necessary shoes; as a homemaker in East Brunswick, she taught herself English by reading the *Daily News*. Luz, one of six siblings, helped her mother with the groceries, the laundry, the ironing, the childcare. But she wanted out.

She enrolled at Rutgers and moved out of her parents' house, supporting herself by working two or three jobs at a time to cover rent and tuition. Then, as a sophomore, she was diagnosed with thyroid cancer. After surgery, she says the doctors told her, "If it doesn't come back in two years, you'll be fine. If it does, we'll make you as comfortable as possible."

As she faced this life-threatening prospect, she knew that she wanted to become a mother and a psychologist. When she was still alive two years later, she got pregnant. ("It was a distraction from thinking about death," she says.) The Supreme Court had just decided *Roe v. Wade*, so she knew she had options, but she wanted the child even though the father wasn't involved. She graduated from college in 1973, and that fall, little Luz was born—Lucecita, or Cita for short.

Luz had met her first goal of becoming a mother; now it was time for her second goal. When Cita was three, Luz got into New York University's doctoral program in psychology, recruited for a new initiative to diversify the program by attracting top Black and Hispanic students.

Luis A. Miranda Jr., a third-year doctoral student from Puerto Rico, interviewed her for admission. He arrived late; he'd been at a protest. He asked Luz out on a date—a trip to Washington, DC, to march outside the Supreme Court in support of affirmative action. (The court was hearing arguments in the Bakke case about racial criteria for university admissions.) For their second date, back in New York, they danced to a Puerto Rican protest band.

Luis was sprightly and compact with a thick black mane of hair and a bushy mustache. Luz was petite with sparkling brown eyes, dark curly hair, and a mischievous smile. Three months later, they got married. After a ceremony in New Jersey, they had a short honeymoon: dinner at Tavern on the Green, a new musical called *Runaways* at the Public Theater, and a night at the Plaza.

Luis soon legally adopted Cita. "You're the best daddy I ever had," she told him. The family moved into an NYU apartment in Greenwich Village that had a view of the Twin Towers. Cita got her own bedroom with a princess canopy bed.

Luz wanted to work with children, and when she finished her coursework, she took an internship with the Jewish Board of Family and Children's Services. Then in 1979, she found out, to her surprise, that she was pregnant again. Luis asked his own childhood caretaker from Vega Alta, a stout, older woman named Edmunda Claudio—Mundi for short—to come to New York to help them out. Living space was tight. A bunk bed for Cita and Mundi replaced the canopy bed; a futon next to a crib served Luz and Luis and the baby. After Lin-Manuel was born, on January 16, 1980, Luz started to look for a new home.

She spotted an ad for a rarity in New York: an affordable house on a pretty cobblestoned street facing a forested park. It had an upstairs and a downstairs apartment, a driveway, and a finished basement. Where could such a marvel exist? In Inwood, just above Washington Heights, at the very northern tip of Manhattan. The neighborhood had become home to Jewish and Irish immigrants at the start of the twentieth century, then, after World War II, to Puerto Ricans, Cubans, and Dominicans. When the Mirandas made an offer to the elderly Jewish couple who owned the house, the Irish tenants upstairs told Luis, "You won't have to worry about us. We're not living with *spics*."

The Mirandas got the house for seventy-five thousand dollars; thanks to loans from relatives, they could make the down payment. They moved upstairs and sublet the downstairs apartment.

Cita attended Greenwich Village Neighborhood School by their old apartment at NYU, and when Lin-Manuel was four, he joined her there for preschool. It took an hour on the A Train to ride two hundred blocks south from Inwood. On the subway map, it looked as though they lived at the top of the world. On the uptown ride back home from West Fourth Street, Cita and her brother played a game, guessing where the last white passenger would get off: Fifty-Ninth Street? Or 125th Street? Often, by the time they arrived at their stop, the second-to-last one, just before 207th Street, Lin-Manuel had fallen asleep in Mundi's lap. After a day getting bullied in the sandbox, he was worn out.

His father tried to toughen him up. To teach Lin-Manuel how to defend himself, he pulled out Rock 'Em Sock 'Em Robots—a toy with battling plastic figures—for a boxing lesson. "New York is a tough city," he said. "I came from somewhere else, and I had to fight my way to survive it."

Luis was scrappy, driven, indomitable. Born in a hill town in Puerto Rico where his father ran the credit union and his mother owned a travel agency, he dreamed of a life beyond Vega Alta. He finished high school in two years and graduated from the University of Puerto Rico in three with a double major in psychology and political science. His favorite movie was *The Unsinkable Molly Brown*, about a small-town kid, undaunted by local bullies, who made it big.

In 1974, nineteen-year-old Luis was accepted to NYU's doctoral program in psychology; he went, leaving behind a promising job at Sears and admission to law school in Puerto Rico. But he eventually grew frustrated with the pace of clinical psychology, abandoned his doctoral studies, and returned to community organizing, fighting for better schools and health services for the immigrants who lived in Inwood. (He'd been a student activist with the Puerto Rican Socialist Party.) Though Luis frequently criticized Mayor Ed Koch for neglecting Latino communities, Koch appointed him special adviser for Hispanic affairs in 1986. "Koch loved him because he was authentic, and he was as brash as Koch was," his colleague Lorraine Cortéz-Vázquez explained.

But Lin-Manuel didn't share his father's combative spirit. The boxing lessons fizzled. "No fighting," Lin-Manuel would say when Luis got out the toy.

Luz thought it was intolerable that other kids tormented her son because he could read. She wanted to switch him to another school midyear.

"But it's a good school," Luis insisted. "You take shit, and you plow through it."

That wasn't Luz's philosophy. "I'll be damned!" she replied. "He's not going back!"

So they found Lin-Manuel a nursery school uptown in Washington Heights where his ability to read was celebrated. The other kids clamored for him to decipher the inscription on a plaque at their playground near the George Washington Bridge. "Okay, but I'm not good at *big* words," he told them. He made friends and invented silly songs inspired by his new Garbage Pail Kids trading cards: "The Garbage Pail Kids are in town! Oh, they're so ugly you wouldn't wanna see them."

His preschool teacher lived down the street; she drove him and his classmates to Uptown Nursery each day. He was closest to the daughter of friends of his parents, a girl named Allie. They played together all the time. They pretended they were boyfriend and girlfriend. Whenever he saw her, he gave her a kiss.

One morning that spring, his mother woke him up. She had been crying. She had to tell him something terrible: There had been an accident. Allie had drowned. He would never see her again.

Sobbing, Lin-Manuel rode to preschool in his teacher's car. At each stop, he heard his teacher whispering to the parents that Allie was dead. He felt as though he were getting the unfathomable news fresh again and again. The next few months were gray, lifeless. "It took him a while to process that," Luz says. "Whenever anyone asked if he had a little girlfriend, his face would fall, and he would say, 'My girlfriend died.'" A fear of death began to haunt him.

Both of his parents worked hard, seven days a week, taking on extra jobs to ensure that their kids could ultimately get a debt-free college education. Luis slept barely five hours a night. While he rose in Latino political circles, Luz ran a children's clinic at Bronx-Lebanon Hospital and started training other family doctors. They both organized immigrant parents in their Inwood school district, dragging their kids along to contentious school-board meetings. As Luis put it, "We were a struggling middle-class family in a struggling working-class neighborhood."

During the week, Mundi was the kids' primary caretaker. Lin-Manuel called her Abuela Mundi even though she wasn't really his grandmother. "I could do no wrong in her eyes," he recalled. "She gave me unconditional love." She'd pick him up from Uptown Nursery and buy him Now and Later candy while she scratched off her lottery tickets. Every morning, she brought Luis a cup of coffee. "She was very old-school," Cita says. "My brother was the prince. My father was the king. My mom and I were just there."

Education was the parents' department. While living in NYU housing, Luz had seen other grad students trying to get their kids into Hunter College Elementary School. A selective public school for intellectually gifted students associated with the teacher-training program at Hunter, it offered the equivalent of a private-school education for free to the lucky Manhattan few who tested in. With his strong verbal skills, Lin-Manuel did well on the cognitive test. At the in-person visit, he felt nervous entering the Hunter campus, a giant brick edifice on the Upper East Side. He didn't want to part from his mother, though he soon warmed to the other children, even sharing his crayons with a fellow applicant.

He got in. For Lin-Manuel, having forty-five classmates who were also exceptionally verbal, bright, and creative made Hunter both exciting and intimidating. The kindergarten teacher challenged the kids to create their own paintings in the style of Georgia O'Keeffe. By third grade, the students were writing their own novellas. (Lin-Manuel composed a rhyming tale of Garfield, his favorite comic-strip character, traveling in a time machine.) "We could not believe the sensitive, insightful, smart conversations that these six- and seven-year-olds would have with each other," Luis says.

Some school days concluded with a playdate, a chance for Lin-Manuel to mess around with He-Man action figures or watch Disney Afternoon shows at a friend's Upper West Side apartment. (Few students wanted to make the hour-long schlep up to Inwood.) Others days ended with Lin-Manuel experiencing a headache or a stomachache. "Inside of me is a volcano / and when it erupts I throw up," he confessed in an early poem. It could be daunting, even stomach-churning, to be surrounded by so many brilliant kids. One day in the cafeteria, he approached a curly-haired boy in his grade who was rumored to have mastered the impossible word from *Mary Poppins*. "Hey," Lin-Manuel said, "I hear you can spell *supercalifragilisticexpialidocious*." The boy, Arthur Lewis, looked up and replied, "Backwards or forwards?"

Luz could tell when her son was overwhelmed, and she'd return to their bedtime ritual: a relaxation exercise, a breathing exercise, a lullaby. "There were lots of reasons to feel 'less than' or 'not as good as,'" Luz says. "I always felt it was important for Lin-Manuel to understand that whatever he was doing was okay. Whatever went on, we would find a way to help him or fix it." Luis recognized the parental division of labor. "I've always said to my kids: 'If you need shit done, go to me. If you need feelings to be processed, go to Luz.'"

Writing did not come easily to Lin-Manuel. "I would give these very flowery answers when I'd speak, and then I would do the bare minimum when I had to write it down," he says. (On an elementary-school standardized test, he received a particularly low score in a category called "language expression.") The physical act of gripping his pencil and writing caused him pain. A diagnosis of dysgraphia clarified the problem: a gap between what he was thinking and what he was able to write. Luz supported him, taking down his words as he dictated them until he learned to use a computer keyboard. "I am a very bad poet / and soon everyone will know it," he typed in an early attempt at rhyming verse.

The word that most perplexed Lin-Manuel's classmates at Hunter was his name. The non-Latino students couldn't pronounce it. Was it Lin-*Manual*, like a set of instructions? Some version of Leonard? Linard? Growing up in Inwood, he heard Spanish all around him. Mundi spoke Spanish exclusively, and there were enough Puerto Rican and Dominican bodega owners that Mundi could make her neighborhood rounds without difficulty. Luz, who'd moved to the mainland from Puerto Rico when she was two, spoke mostly English but switched to Spanish around Mundi, and Luis went back and forth. Cita was fluent in Spanish, too, having been cared for in early childhood by Luz's Spanish-language-dominant mother.

Hunter was different. Most of Lin-Manuel's classmates were white, the children of affluent parents who lived close to Hunter on the Upper East Side or crossed Central Park from the Upper West Side. Hardly anyone else traveled the seven miles from 207th Street down to East Ninety-Fourth and Park Avenue. When Lin-Manuel heard Spanish around his Hunter classmates, it usually came from their nannies. "The culture shock most people get in college, I experienced when I was five," he says.

At first, he had fun playing with the linguistic contrast between Hunter and Inwood. "Want to hear my name in English?" he'd ask his mom. In a dull voice, he'd intone: "Lynn-Man-well Murr-ann-duh." Then he'd say, "Want to hear it in Spanish?" With a lilt, he'd sing: "*Leen*-Mahn-*well* Meer-*ahn*-dah!" Soon, though, he grew accustomed to using separate names in separate places. "It was code-switching," he says. "I'm Lin-Manuel at home and Lin at school."

He knew his name was unusual. His father had encountered it in the late 1960s in Vega Alta when he became involved in the independence movement. His uncle had helped to found the Puerto Rican Independence Party, and when Luis joined the cause, he started to read anti-colonial literature. A piece by Puerto Rican poet José Manuel Torres Santiago about the war in Vietnam particularly moved Luis. In the poem, "Nana Roja Para Mi Hijo Lin Manuel," a revolutionary lullaby, a father addresses his son, who has a Vietnamese first name and a Spanish surname: Lin Manuel. Worried that his son's life will be sacrificed in another foreign war, the father envisioned young Lin Manuel growing up to join him in "la guerra justa contra los asesinos yankis" ("the just war against the Yankee killers"). Luis made an adolescent resolution: If he had a son, his name would be Lin-Manuel.

"That name was special because it was the dreams and aspirations of a Puerto Rican dad," Luis says. His dream was to instill his own work ethic in his children. "I never knew what my kids were going to do with their lives, but I knew that whatever it was, they would need to approach it with love and lots of energy, and they would need to excel."

Over summer vacations, Lin-Manuel and Cita went to visit their grandparents in Vega Alta. Lin-Manuel was known around town as "Luis the expat's boy"—"el nene de Luisito, que se fue a Nueva York." Luis A. Miranda Sr., nicknamed Güisin, was a quiet, old-fashioned man who watched *Gunsmoke* and kept a dime-store cowboy novel tucked in his pocket, but he doted on his sensitive grandson. He took Lin-Manuel to movies and baseball games, bought him French fries, drove him to the arcade in San

Juan and gave him ten dollars in quarters to play; he even built him a swimming pool in the backyard.

But it wasn't quite a joyful homecoming. Abuelo Güisin and Abuela Eva, beloved pillars of the Vega Alta community, worked all day at the town credit union and travel agency, so the kids were often left to amuse themselves. Cita, six years older than Lin-Manuel, spoke Spanish well enough to make friends and head off on her own. Lin-Manuel's Spanish wasn't as good. When he tried to speak in his Nuyorican accent, the other kids laughed at him. As he put it: "In my neighborhood, I'm the kid who goes to the fancy school. In Puerto Rico, I'm the kid who speaks Spanish with a kind of messed-up gringo accent. At school, I'm the kid who lives all the way uptown."

The benefit of straddling cultures came from the range of music he encountered. He always responded to rhythm. Luz remembers going to a club on New Year's Eve when she was nine months pregnant with Lin-Manuel. "The music starts, and the baby starts kicking," she says. "The music stops; the baby stops kicking. The music starts, and he's up and dancing inside! We had to leave the club." As a toddler, he'd bop up and down as she played a mix of Latin albums and Broadway cast recordings, salsa acts like El Gran Combo and Héctor Lavoe alternating with *My Fair Lady* and *Man of La Mancha*, which she'd seen on a high-school class trip.

Driving Lin-Manuel to her parents' house in East Brunswick, Luz sang along to her favorite music from her 1960s adolescence: *Camelot*, the Mamas and the Papas, and the Moody Blues. As for Luis, growing up in Vega Alta, he annoyed his John Wayne–loving father by insisting on watching *The Sound of Music* over and over; he loved the telenovela-style story of a governess marrying her employer, and he cheered for the moral conviction of a family that sang against the Nazis.

Once Lin-Manuel learned how to use a tape deck, he started making his parents personalized mixtapes as gifts for Mother's Day and Father's Day, stringing together medleys of songs he knew they'd like. He sometimes added in his Garbage Pail Kids song, too, which he'd recorded on his yellow Fisher-Price cassette deck. His parents took him to see *Les Misérables* on Broadway when he was seven; he fell asleep midway through, but the cast album entered their family's rotation, and he noticed that his mom cried every time she heard "Bring Him Home," a prayer for a young man's safety. He learned he wasn't the only one who cried at music; the right song could move a grown-up too. And on a mixtape, all the parts of his identity could play together on a unified emotional journey: Puerto Rican protest songs and Broadway ballads could share the same cassette.

Cita offered him her own music instruction—'80s pop, like Genesis and Cyndi Lauper, and early-'90s hip-hop, like De La Soul and Black Sheep. In first grade, Lin-Manuel memorized a track, "Land of Confusion," from one of her Genesis tapes and signed up to lip-synch it at the Hunter talent show, chasing the applause he'd discovered at his first piano recital. Cita dressed him in a turquoise Benetton cardigan over a white turtleneck, and, to complete the look, a pair of aviator sunglasses. When he was called to the Hunter auditorium stage, he donned the sunglasses with an eyebrow wiggle, then dropped them as he bopped to the song. As he left the stage, he heard cheers from the audience. He turned back and smiled.

At first, Cita and her little brother weren't a team. She resented the intruder in the family who'd made her lose her princess canopy bed and forced her to share a room with Mundi, who was so possessive of the baby that Cita couldn't get near him. As they grew up, their temperaments diverged. Cita clicked with science and math, while he preferred words. As the older child, she had to endure endless lectures from her father on living up to her potential, while Lin-Manuel realized that if he just said, "I'm sorry, Daddy, you were right," he could slip away to his room. "I remember seeing my sister get into fights that in my head were avoidable," he says. "When my parents were around, she felt the double standards at play: I'm younger, I'm the boy, I get favorable treatment. But when it was just the two of us, we were good."

One year, Cita and her friends went trick-or-treating as the Go-Go's, an '80s girl group, and she helped Lin-Manuel don a white sheet with two holes so they could go as "the Go-Go's . . . and a ghost." She stayed up late on Christmas Eve to build him a He-Man play set, even though Santa got the credit. She brought her brother to see early hip-hop movies like *Beat Street*, a drama about a breakdance crew in the South Bronx, and *Disorderlies*, featuring the subversive antics of the rap trio the Fat Boys. "She took him under her wing," her mother says.

Lin-Manuel was delighted. He'd pretend he was a DJ, scratching his

Dr. Seuss record on his toy Fisher-Price phonograph. The sounds and rhythms of rap verses appealed to him. Even watching cartoons, he thrilled to a playful rhyme in the theme song to *Darkwing Duck*: "When there's trouble you call DW!"

Hip-hop had been born in the Bronx, just across the Harlem River from his neighborhood, six or seven years before him; it felt, in a way, like another big sibling. He turned out to have a direct conduit to its origin. When he started commuting to Hunter, his parents signed up for a little yellow school bus that shuttled students from northern Manhattan to the public magnet schools on the Upper East Side. The bus service was run by the Bakers, a Black family from the Bronx. "Lin used to read a book on the bus," the father, Billy Baker, says. "He was a quiet little guy with cute chubby cheeks." Billy's son Duane was an aspiring rapper, and when Duane was old enough to drive the Baker bus, he tested his material on Lin-Manuel and the other kids. Lin-Manuel sat rapt.

During the forty-minute drive down the Henry Hudson Parkway from Inwood, Duane taught the captive Baker bus crew his favorite bars. He made Lin-Manuel memorize the lyrics to "Beef" by Boogie Down Productions, a rapping diatribe against the meat industry. "'Beef, what a relief! When will this poisonous product cease?'" they would shout. Geto Boys' "Mind Playing Tricks on Me," a cautionary tale of anxiety and drug-induced paranoia, was another standby. "They were all kind of educational raps," Lin-Manuel says.

The Baker family was enmeshed in the emerging hip-hop scene. Billy Baker had grown up with Big Bank Hank, a rapper in the Sugarhill Gang, the group that helped bring hip-hop from the streets to the radio when their 1979 single "Rapper's Delight" became the first rap song to hit the *Billboard* Hot 100. Billy had gotten married at Hank's house, and he used to drive the early rap crews around the neighborhood. "I had a van to take their equipment to the park," he says. "That's how hip-hop began in the Bronx—they stole electricity from the lamppost and did free concerts."

On the Baker bus, Duane taught Lin-Manuel "Rapper's Delight." What could have been a slog in traffic became an education. The bus's downtown path mirrored the spread of hip-hop from Black protest music in New York's northern borough to the burgeoning entertainment soundtrack for kids everywhere.

Arriving at school revved up on Duane's rap tutorial, Lin-Manuel gained more confidence performing in the classroom. His fourth-grade teacher noticed that "after some initial nervousness," he started to let his sense of humor and creativity come through in his assignments; for instance, he wrote a "Jack and the Beanstalk Rap." Building on his success, he and a classmate crafted an illustrated sci-fi story where robots fell in love. The *Romeo and Juliet* narrative was about bridging different backgrounds; one robot came from the rap world of Run-DMC, the other from the musical-theater world of Jean Valjean, the prisoner given the number 24601 in *Les Misérables*. They called their story "DMC Meets 24601."

When Lin-Manuel was in fourth grade, his worlds started to converge even more when he saw Disney's 1989 animated musical *The Little Mermaid*. As the big calypso number "Under the Sea" began, he couldn't believe it: He was hearing the sounds of the Caribbean—steel drums and a syncopated beat—buoying a giant underwater dance routine. "It rocked my world," he said. He'd play the soundtrack at home for his friends, then come to school, leap on a desk, and sing, "Under the sea!" After he found out that one of his schoolmates, Jennie, was the composer Alan Menken's niece, he begged her to get him an autograph. He bowed down before her; he pleaded; he persisted. Finally, a Post-it note arrived with an inscription from Menken: "To Lin, with lots of love. Now please stop kissing Jennie's feet!"

His classmates relished his brio. For a unit on birds, he changed the lyrics from a popular McDonald's ad in which a customer orders everything on the menu in one breath into a recitation of the name of every bird his class had studied. After singing the complete list, breathless, he pretended to faint. It was a hit. He spent hours practicing his routines in his bedroom, jumping on his He-Man sheets, dancing to the *Footloose* soundtrack, and now he'd found an appreciative audience. "I was never the brightest student at Hunter College Elementary School," he recalled, "but I was good at making up songs, and I was good at making kids laugh, which is the only currency that matters when you are surrounded by people who are much smarter than you."

At home, he was often alone. After Luis finished his term as adviser to Mayor Koch, he was appointed head of New York City Health and Hospitals. On top of that position, he founded the nonprofit Hispanic Federation to advocate and fundraise for Latino communities. Cita graduated from Stuyvesant High School and headed to Rensselaer Polytechnic Institute to study engineering, and to pay her tuition, Luz took on extra work doing forensic evaluations for the courts. Lin-Manuel hardly saw his parents except on weekends, when he joined them at the movies: action comedies with his father, psychological dramas with his mother.

He didn't feel lonely, however. His father had brought home an early VHS camcorder from the mayor's office when Lin-Manuel was seven, and since then, he'd been obsessed with making movies. He graduated from stop-motion animation with Coke bottles and G.I. Joes to live-action remakes of his favorite film sequences. He even coaxed Abuela Mundi onto the floor to reenact the 1989 medical-alarm commercial: "I've fallen, and I can't get up!" (When she saw him coming with the video camera, Mundi warned, "Nos jodimos todos ahora, aquí viene el nene con sus inventos"— meaning "Now we're all screwed, here comes the boy with his inventions!") He carried his family's two VCRs into his bedroom, hooked them up to his TV, and spent hours with his finger hovering over the record and pause buttons, editing his footage. "I fell in love," he says.

He wasn't allowed to tote the camcorder to Puerto Rico for the month he stayed with his grandparents every summer, so Abuelo Güisin borrowed a security camera from the credit union where he worked. The family ran a video store, and Lin-Manuel could watch whatever he wanted. Fueled by a mix of Looney Tunes and '80s action comedies, he told his grandfather where to point the camera as he staged ever more elaborate and gruesome sequences, putting some newly acquired blood capsules to work. The camera's audio-dubbing feature allowed him to film a fight scene and juice up the slapping and punching sounds afterward. ("I loved the musicality of action sequences," he says. "It was genuinely beautiful to watch Jackie Chan.") A later model with video-dubbing let him record a song and then superimpose his own images, a gateway to music videos and lushly scored death scenes.

One day, an elderly neighbor, Margot, looked over at the Mirandas' house and saw a body tumble off the roof. She heard a bump and started screaming, "Lin-Manuel! Lin-Manuel! Ay, dios mío!" Margot was sure Lin-Manuel had fallen to his death. It turned out that he had made a dummy out of a stuffed hoodie and pants and tossed it off the roof to complete his shot. He was experimenting, charting his own self-directed film-school course. He wasn't daunted by the limitations of being a young artist. "It was so much more interesting for me to make stuff than to think about making stuff," he says. "You couldn't exactly make a movie like you saw in the movies, but with a video camera, you could get pretty close."

At the end of sixth grade, everything came together for Lin-Manuel: music, performance, Broadway, and Puerto Rico. At Hunter, the culmination of elementary school happened to align with Lin-Manuel's interests. The entire spring term built toward it; the whole school came to see it: the sixth-grade play.

The tradition was created by a music teacher, Barbara Ames, who'd arrived at Hunter in 1985, the year Lin-Manuel began kindergarten. In her first spring, she enlisted the entire sixth grade in a production of *West Side Story*. The art teacher designed the costumes; the shop teacher helped with direction, and his wife choreographed the dances. For the second half of the year, the students researched the show, wrote the program, painted the sets, made the costumes, auditioned for parts, and rehearsed from spring break until the performance at the end of May.

The sixth-grade play directed by Ms. Ames became the highlight of the calendar. Every year she chose a show with lots of leads, and if there weren't enough singing roles to go around, she'd make up more. "Everyone wanted to have a part, and I didn't want to disappoint anyone, so I added things," she says. Five years ahead of Lin-Manuel, Bobby Lopez, the future composer of *The Book of Mormon* and *Frozen*, auditioned to play Tevye in *Fiddler on the Roof* but was cast as the Russian constable, who didn't have a song. So Ms. Ames wrote "The Constable's Song" herself and gave it to Bobby to open the second act. She did the same for girls who lacked a number in *Bye Bye Birdie*. Copyright purists might balk, but the students loved their bespoke shows. "Ms. Ames is a saint, and there should be a church in her name," one of her former students, Siobhan Lockhart, says. "What she did to support everyone's talents was astounding."

In 1992, for Lin-Manuel's sixth-grade play, Ms. Ames decided to put on a medley from each of the six previous musicals that she had staged. Lin-Manuel would get to try out for a part in every show he'd seen at Hunter! He knew what he wanted to sing for his audition. His parents had recently taken him to see *The Phantom of the Opera* on Broadway. He'd been mesmerized by Andrew Lloyd Webber's thundering synth-rock theme and the show's sympathy for an outsider songwriter. When it was his turn to audition, he sang one of the Phantom's big solos, "The Music of the Night," several octaves up.

"Lin's audition was unbelievable," Ms. Ames says. "Not that he was particularly musically distinguished, but he was adorable—such a cute kid, charming and charismatic." He got cast as a farmer in *Oklahoma!*, a son in *Fiddler*, and a backup dancer in *The Wiz*. But there was more. Ms. Ames saw star potential. He got to play three leading roles: the villainous Captain Hook in *Peter Pan*, the Sharks chief Bernardo in *West Side Story*, and the rock idol Conrad Birdie in *Bye Bye Birdie*. He was thrilled. "That was the most incredible experience I had in elementary school," he says. "It was me finding my niche."

His niche entailed more than performing. In the *West Side Story* section, part of his life at home converged with his role at Hunter. "It was the only time at school where I got to be Puerto Rican," he says. Sure, the musical's 1950s depiction of Puerto Ricans as knife-wielding gang members didn't map onto his family's experience or that of any other Puerto Ricans he knew. But in the song "America," Bernardo and Anita debate whether life is better in Manhattan or back on the island they came from, a question Lin-Manuel asked himself all the time as he shuttled between summers in Vega Alta and the rest of the year in New York. He played Bernardo by imitating his dad's accent. When Anita sang, "Life is all right in America," he shot back, "If you're all-*white* in America."

Lin-Manuel's parents could tell that Ms. Ames had given their son and his classmates something special. The nephew of a distinguished actor in Puerto Rico, Luis had won an island-wide monologue competition as a teenager; he'd given up acting to accelerate through his degrees, but he still loved musical theater. "Ms. Ames was very patient in making sure the kids were having fun," he says.

Lin-Manuel was having the time of his elementary-school life. As the Elvis-esque rocker Conrad Birdie, he strutted atop a platform in a gold-lamé jacket that Mundi had sewn specially for his short, skinny frame. All he had to do was open his mouth, and the girls in the chorus were instructed to swoon. Everyone was watching him, adoring him. He knew that his parents loved him, and they came to every performance, but they spent much of their waking hours at work. "When your parents are gone most of the time, it feels like oxygen to have all that attention focused on you," he says.

After the performance, Lin-Manuel told Ms. Ames, "This is what I want to do for the rest of my life."

2

BRICK PRISON

• •

After the thrill of the sixth-grade play, high school at Hunter felt overwhelming. It began in seventh grade, when Hunter opened its coveted spots to students from all five New York City boroughs who competed through rounds of admissions tests. There was often a sense of inferiority among rising elementary-school students, who wondered if they could keep up with the new cohort. For Lin-Manuel, that anxiety felt acute. "Seventh and eighth grade sucked for me," he says. "It was a time of real self-consciousness."

That self-consciousness came partly from recurrent math frustrations severe enough to send him to the nurse's office with headaches and stomach trouble. Lin-Manuel's body was changing, too, in ways he didn't welcome. "The way puberty expressed itself on me was my nose growing before the rest of my face," he says. "I was so sensitive about it." What his family dubbed "the Miranda nose," after his grandfather's sizable feature, made him identify less with a patriarch than with the big-beaked mascot on the Froot Loops cereal box: "I felt like fucking Toucan Sam." Some boys were starting to date girls, locked in "an arms race," as he saw it, to have their first kiss. Others were clinging to childhood, happily watching Disney after school. Lin-Manuel had crushes on girls, but he didn't know how to talk to them, and he couldn't fathom how some of his classmates had learned. "Where's the guidebook?" he wondered.

So he retreated back to the elementary-school musical-theater world where he'd been a star. High-schoolers at Hunter had to complete seventy-five hours of service credit, and Lin-Manuel logged all of his hours during seventh grade by helping his former teachers put on the sixth-grade play. It was another Ms. Ames spectacular: *A Chorus Line*. Unlike the original Broadway production, no one was cut from the chorus. Ms. Ames wrote individual backstories for each of the more than forty students; everyone got a solo turn. Bodily maturity was kept at bay; instead of "tits and ass," they sang "poise and class." Lin-Manuel was in heaven. "I couldn't really deal with the pecking order of high school, so I went back to sixth grade."

He also turned heartbreak into art, writing his own songs in a musical-theater vein. *Phantom* and *Les Misérables* were his favorites, so he composed melodramatic, anguished tunes, mostly about girls he pined for from afar. Much to his father's chagrin, Lin-Manuel had little motivation for schoolwork; it was a running joke among his friends that his grades in Spanish class weren't particularly good, even though he spoke Spanish at home. Instead, he spent his time jotting lyrics in the margins of his notebook. A characteristic ballad, "I Ran with Roses," pictured a date with a classmate as a grandiose, doomed romance:

> *I ran with roses to see you again,*
> *And it's those roses that made our love end.*
> *Out in the cold,*
> *My heart is broke with pain—*
> *You're driving me insane,*
> *Driving me insane!*

Underneath these fevered lyrics, he played a simple chord progression. He'd discovered that if he moved his right hand up the white keys on the piano in a fixed triad, the tonality would shift from major to minor (F major, G major, A minor), from optimism to heartbreak.

He'd quit piano lessons since he never wanted to practice what his teacher assigned; he just wanted to play on his own. To figure out more complex chords, he'd head after school to his friend Alex Sarlin's place on the Upper West Side. Alex had a piano and the complete *Beatles Fake Book*—all the band's songs written out with accessible piano chords. He let Lin-Manuel noodle on the keyboard while he did his homework. Alex was an artist. He drew cartoon portraits and made a weekly television show that was broadcast on a local-access channel. He could pick up any instrument and play it. Lin-Manuel couldn't. But Alex was patient as Lin-Manuel tried to plunk out a bass line, shifting the inflection of the chord in his right hand by playing different notes underneath with his left. "What chord is this?" Lin-Manuel would ask, venturing beyond a chord that matched the bass note. "That's an F over G," Alex would reply, introducing him to the world of musical suspension—dissonant, unresolved, full of possibility.

After writing songs as an escape from schoolwork, Lin-Manuel had the chance, in eighth grade, to write songs for an assignment. This was thanks to a beloved English teacher. Rembert Herbert had a commanding aura at Hunter. He was quiet, nearing fifty, with gray hair and large glasses. He wore sweater-vests and tweed jackets and rode a motorcycle. Unlike most high-school teachers, he had a doctorate. He set high standards, expecting students to revise their work until they found the perfect words, like his models James Baldwin and Ralph Ellison. His former students can still quote his maxim: "The genius must be supported by the labor."

Lin-Manuel did not earn Dr. Herbert's respect at the start of the year. For a unit on *Macbeth*, students had to pick three scenes and represent them creatively, so Lin-Manuel asked a friend to film him in front of his house in Inwood. He recited Macbeth's soliloquy in voice-over, staged a curtain-rod duel, and tagged a cheeky "Greensleeves"-scored credit sequence onto his death scene, listing the author as "Willy Shakespeare." Dr. Herbert was unimpressed. He urged Lin-Manuel to go further, to develop his ideas, to do more than slap a flimsy idea on-screen. Lin-Manuel returned to scribbling in his notebook in the back of the class.

Then Dr. Herbert assigned *The Chosen*. Lin-Manuel was captivated by Chaim Potok's novel of a Modern Orthodox boy, Reuven, who becomes friends with Danny, the brilliant son of a Hasidic rabbi. The boys meet when they face off in a fierce baseball game and Danny hits a line drive into Reuven's head, smashing his glasses. "When the chapter ended, Reuven was in the hospital, and he'd been hit in the eye with a baseball, and I was like, *What the fuck?*" Lin-Manuel says. "I was in; I was just hooked." He devoured the required chapters, then finished the rest of the book to find out what happened. It was the first time he'd sped ahead of his classmates.

Dr. Herbert put students in groups and asked each one to teach a set of chapters from the novel. Lin-Manuel leaped in. He told the students in his group that he was going to write a song for each of their chapters. He would record the vocals, too; all they had to do was lip-synch. They were relieved. Lin-Manuel set to work on his musical version of *The Chosen*. For Reuven nursing his eye injury in the hospital, he composed a Phantom-esque anthem of self-pity:

That lousy Hasidim—
I don't really need 'em.
I'd play 'em and beat 'em—
If my eye weren't in pain!

For Danny, growing up in the Hasidic rabbi's oppressively quiet home, he wrote a Jean Valjean–inspired ballad of suffering:

Now I can hear the silence, I hear it all the time.
It's a silence that no one else hears, it's a silence that's all mine.
I hear my father screaming, it's a voice that's racked with pain,
But for seventeen years, I've suffered as well.
If I tell him my plan, he'll condemn me to hell!

This one Lin-Manuel lip-synched himself. On "condemn me to hell" he slapped his desk as hard as he could, and his classmates gasped and laughed. Dr. Herbert took note.

Toward the end of that winter, the class was assigned a personal literary essay, in which students picked a book to relate to their own experience. Lin-Manuel chose the first adult novel he'd read on his own, during his miserable stay at sleepaway camp the previous summer: Stephen King's *It*. For his essay, he wrote about his fears, about the novel's creepy invasion of his nighttime imagination, about his hope that friendship would vanquish terror. When Dr. Herbert returned the paper, Lin-Manuel found an unexpected note on the back:

Lin-Manuel—This is an excellent, well-crafted essay. It confirms what I have suspected for some time—that you have been "hibernating" in the back of my class, emerging only occasionally—as

when you wrote "The Chosen" musical for class earlier this year.
It's a new semester, almost spring—join us!

This was the nudge Lin-Manuel needed, the equivalent of Harry Potter receiving a letter from Hogwarts. It was an affirmation: In the eyes of the esteemed Dr. Herbert, he had talent. "It was the first time someone who was not in my family said, 'You're a writer,'" Lin-Manuel explained. For an eighth-grader frequently overwhelmed by the strengths and brilliance of his classmates, that meant a great deal. And it was a reprimand framed as an invitation. "Dr. Herbert essentially called me out. He told me, 'That creative energy you are burning in the back of the class is what we need *in* the class. You can *use* that here.'" Dr. Herbert had taught many talented students; Lin-Manuel's prose didn't make him a standout. But he'd never had a student compose a musical for a project. He encouraged Lin-Manuel to try out for the student-written-theater club.

At Hunter, extracurricular activities abounded, especially in the arts. There were three newspapers. There were three choruses. And there were three theater groups: Hunter Theater Ensemble put on a play in the fall; Musical Repertory did a musical in the winter; and Brick Prison—winkingly named for Hunter's windowless edifice, a former armory building—produced student-written one-acts in the spring. Brick, as students called it, had been founded in the 1980s as an alternative to faculty-directed shows, though by the time Lin-Manuel arrived, all the theater productions were run by students. Cynthia Nixon was an alum. Long before *Sex and the City*, in 1984, as a senior, she performed on Broadway while also appearing in Brick Prison's *Days of Wine and Neurosis*.

A decade later, in the spring of 1994, Lin-Manuel showed up to audition for Brick. He encountered a group of upperclassmen gathered in a classroom opposite the Hunter auditorium. Although Dr. Herbert was the nominal faculty adviser, students took charge of everything: writing the plays, selecting the scripts to be produced, casting, acting, directing, designing the sets and costumes and sound and lights, making the posters and the programs, painting and sewing and building and rehearsing everything to be ready for a three-day April run. In the classroom where Lin-Manuel auditioned were two future filmmakers, a future television producer, a future theater professor, a future dancer, and a future four-time Emmy-winning comedy writer. It was heady company to join.

With six student plays picked for that year, Brick's directors had more than fifty roles to cast. For the first round, each auditioner presented a monologue. Lin-Manuel came ready. He'd memorized Edgar Allan Poe's "The Raven" in his communications class. When it was his turn, he launched into the haunted verse: "Once upon a midnight dreary, while I pondered, weak and weary . . ." He knew how to perform high-wrought anguish. He leaned into the pounding rhythm, relishing every alliteration; his eyebrows danced. After his final "Nevermore!," Rachel Axler, the future comedy writer, starred his name on the audition sheet and wrote, "Whew!"

Lin-Manuel was the only underclassman cast in two different plays. "He was this firecracker eighth-grader who came out of nowhere and was fun to be with," Siobhan Lockhart, one of the directors, says. His breakthrough role came in a dark comedy, *Swingline 457*, about a dinner party at an Upper East Side high-rise that goes awry when an obnoxious guest tosses a Swingline stapler out the window, killing someone below. Lin-Manuel and a senior played grumpy old men from the apartment across the way who popped in for comic relief, squabbling, limping, and hamming it up amid the unfolding murder investigation. "They were very, very funny," Siobhan recalls. "People loved the show."

And Lin-Manuel loved being back in a school play. "Theater felt like a magic bullet for me," he says. "This is a lane I could be good in." What's more, his talent earned him a place among older students, which alleviated the stress of the pecking order he'd felt ever since the new students arrived in seventh grade. The upperclassmen in Brick Prison didn't care who was considered cool in Lin-Manuel's class. They valued him for his good humor and the skills he showed onstage. That boosted his confidence. "When I first met him, he was a shy little boy," Adam Rauscher, a friend who also acted in *Swingline 457*, says. "Then he became the outgoing person who everyone knew."

His new friendships extended beyond rehearsal too. An older student, Chris Hayes (the future Emmy-winning MSNBC host), took the bus after school with Lin-Manuel to their distant uptown neighborhoods. They'd become friends when Lin-Manuel missed his stop; Chris noticed the younger student deep in the Bronx, on the verge of tears, and took him home so he could call his mother for directions back to Manhattan. When they were both cast in *Swingline 457*, they started riding home together after rehearsal. "We talked about everything," Chris says, "theater, music, girls." Lin-Manuel was always listening to music; he took his Walkman and headphones everywhere. He made Chris eclectic mixtapes; one might feature Black Sheep and Beck alongside the Mamas and the Papas. When it came to dating, Chris says, "we were both lovelorn and self-pitying." But when it came to creative drive, they shared a tremendous confidence. "His motor was always going. He had huge ambitions for himself."

Lin-Manuel found a model for his ambition in *Swingline 457*'s director, senior Matt Korahais. A theater devotee, he probed the script's philosophical depths, developed exercises to immerse the actors in the play's unexpected violence, and ran rehearsals late into the evening. Looking back, Matt—who now teaches theater at NYU—admits, "We took ourselves slightly more seriously than we should." But in Lin-Manuel, he found a fellow zealot, eager to listen, eager to take notes, eager to study upperclassmen for guidance. "Lin worshipped Matt Korahais," Adam says. "He wanted to be Matt." One day in the middle of the rehearsal process, Lin-Manuel showed up with a VHS tape. "These are my movies," he said to Matt. "Will you watch them and tell me what you think?" Matt took the videocassette home and played it through. Lin-Manuel had shot and edited three short movies of himself and his pals acting out comic skits in the park, playing all the parts in funny hats. Matt was impressed. "These are hilarious!" he told Lin-Manuel at the next rehearsal. This little fourteen-year-old, Matt thought, was a budding filmmaker.

At the Brick cast party at Dallas BBQ on Third Avenue, there was a virgin-daiquiri-fueled sense of generational transition, the torch being passed from the class of '94 to an upcoming cohort. Matt, feeling nostalgic, turned to Lin-Manuel. "It all goes by so fast," Matt said. "Sink your *teeth* into this school." Lin-Manuel never forgot the advice. "It was a hell of a thing for a kid to say to another kid," he reflects. "He was a talented older kid who saw me and believed in me. Maybe I've been *Talented Mr. Ripley-ing* Matt Korahais my whole life."

If he had any doubt that he was being anointed as the future of Hunter theater, one moment at Brick Prison rehearsal clarified what was expected of him. On a Saturday that spring, when he and Chris Hayes were sitting in a classroom with a bunch of the Brick officers, Dr. Herbert stopped by. Lin-Manuel often brought his video camera to school, and on this day, he was rolling. He zoomed in on his teacher, who stood in front of the blackboard wearing a pin-striped button-up shirt with a pen tucked into the breast pocket. Dr. Herbert spread his arms. "Assembled authorities on Brick Prison," he began. "Why has Brick never done a musical?"

The seniors in the room started to answer, but Lin-Manuel had already moved his camera lens to the upperclassmen who'd inspired him: Matt Korahais got a close-up, standing in a black sweatshirt and baggy jeans. So did the other officers. Lin-Manuel's camera cherished each of them in turn as though they were movie stars.

"Okay, Lin, you're on," Dr. Herbert said off camera.

"Whaaat?" he gurgled, caught off guard. He was so focused on filming the students that he hadn't been following the conversation. Matt glanced at him, concerned, then back at Dr. Herbert. Had Lin-Manuel not heard his summons to write a musical for Brick Prison? In case there was any confusion, Dr. Herbert repeated the instruction.

"You're on."

<hr />

If you had asked fourteen-year-old Lin-Manuel what he wanted to be, he wouldn't have said a musical-theater composer. He loved musicals, but that was too remote, too fancy, too inconceivable a profession. He wanted to be a filmmaker.

At Hunter, Lin-Manuel was known as "the film guy." He carried his camcorder everywhere—to class, to rehearsal, to after-school hangouts. It helped him navigate high-school dynamics. If he didn't want to pass a joint, he could stay behind the camera; if he wasn't sure how to tell a girl he liked her, he could ask her to play a part in his movie. "It was a way of short-circuiting any social hierarchies," he says. And whenever he had a creative option for a class assignment, he reached for the camera: for a third-grade book report on *The Pushcart War* that he turned into a spoof TV dispatch; for a math project on parabolic functions that he filmed as a cop procedural about a serial killer on the loose. (The detectives plot the location of each murder, discover that the points form a parabola, and catch the killer, who proclaims: "I had to kill him because he had no *function*.") Outside of school, he and his classmate James Green-Armytage filmed variety episodes they called *Lin and James's Show Spectacular*, trying to outdo *America's Funniest Home Videos* with parody skits and fight choreography. "He was always making movies," his sister says. "It's what he always wanted to do."

So when Dr. Herbert tapped him to create a musical for Brick Prison, he didn't have any plans to pen the next *Les Misérables*. His dream was to write and direct full-length movies. By 1994, when he was in eighth grade, the spate of new independent films like Quentin Tarantino's *Reservoir Dogs* and Robert Rodriguez's *El Mariachi* made it seem as though all you needed to do to make a movie was write some snappy dialogue and pick up a camera. Lin-Manuel devoured Rodriguez's memoir *Rebel Without a Crew*, which advised aspiring filmmakers to turn their fledgling scripts into low-budget films, however unsophisticated, and learn by doing. "Choosing the right heroes is everything," Lin-Manuel says. Rodriguez made him feel that "wherever you are as an artist is okay. You're not going to go from zero to *Citizen Kane*. Just get the fuck started. Make a movie with jokes with your friends."

New friends arrived at Hunter with the incoming students from the outer boroughs. One day in eighth-grade homeroom, Lin-Manuel noticed an unfamiliar boy making funny faces at him across the class, trying to get him to laugh. He made a funny face back. The boy was Andrew Gursky, who took the hour-and-a-half bus-and-subway trip to Hunter from a working-class neighborhood deep in Queens. He was obsessed with hip-hop and karate movies. "I was like, *Where have you been all my life?*" Lin-Manuel says. "He and I started forming our own crew."

Andrew introduced Lin-Manuel to the buddies he'd made the previous year: Adam Rauscher commuted even farther, from Staten Island; he wanted to make movies too. Paul Jacobs, from Queens, was quick with numbers and lacerating jokes. Aaron Leopold was more laconic; he lived in an old Greenwich Village loft with a broken door and a readily accessible roof. With Andrew vouching for Lin-Manuel, they formed an inseparable quintet.

Together, they took advantage of high-school freedom to roam the city. For teenagers at an elite school in the early '90s, New York City felt safe but still a little edgy—a playground for adventure. They played tag in Central Park. They walked around the Cloisters near Lin-Manuel's house in Inwood. They strolled past the domino players in Washington Heights, salsa blasting from the bodegas. When they had a half day at school, they'd buy tickets for a PG screening at the Eighty-Sixth Street theater and try to sneak into an R-rated film instead. They were thirteen and fourteen, on the verge of adulthood. "Andrew, Adam, Paul, and Aaron were really the first group of friends I made beyond elementary school," Lin-Manuel says. "They were the found family of my high-school experience."

Most of all, they made movies. At first, they shot action videos set to music. Lin-Manuel ripped a Genesis track off one of his sister's cassette tapes and used the video-dubbing feature on his camcorder to splice together a four-minute sequence of Adam chasing him around Inwood Hill Park. But he had larger ambitions. "I was like, 'Let's do another action video!'" Adam says. "He was like, 'I'm tired of them; James and I used to do them all the time.' That's where the idea for making *Clayton's Friends* was born. He was like, 'I want to make something bigger.'"

Clayton's Friends, Lin-Manuel's feature-directing debut, took most of ninth grade to complete. He wrote a full-length script, nearly sixty pages, and shot the script with his friends, who trekked up to Inwood for weekend sleepovers and filming sessions. There was a loose plot: After Clayton and his girlfriend break up, her brother takes revenge on Clayton and his pals, kidnapping them one by one until a final kung fu showdown vanquishes the adversary. But mostly the story provided a scaffold for comic riffs, "a weird amalgam of inside jokes and pop-culture references," Lin-Manuel says. Zany humor from *The Simpsons* and *Saturday Night Live* offered touchstones. At one point, the whole cast lip-synched an Ice-T rap; another scene used "I Feel Pretty" from *West Side Story*. Brick Prison got a shout-out: The brother wielded a powerful stick christened "Matt Korahais," after the revered *Swingline 457* director. The shot Lin-Manuel was proudest of featured Clayton's friends in suits strutting down the street to "Little Green Bag," the song Tarantino had chosen for his opening-credit sequence in *Reservoir Dogs*.

Lin-Manuel's character, unsurprisingly, had a crush. He cast the real-life object of his affection, a popular classmate of Puerto Rican descent named Amanda, as "the Girl," and constructed the script so that he would get to kiss her. (She agreed to play the part, though the affection remained one-sided.) In fact, most of his classmates assumed the entire project had been a pretext for Lin-Manuel to pursue Amanda; he even quipped that if they got married, her name would become Amanda Miranda. "But the real reason was that he wanted to build something," Aaron says. "It turned into what we did every day."

Not all the guys wanted to devote every day to Lin-Manuel's passion project. After months of shooting, Paul was ready to quit. He came from an Orthodox Jewish family and had a hard time schlepping an hour and a half from Queens to Inwood on Shabbat. That summer, Aaron decided he'd had enough too and skipped town for camp upstate. When he checked his mail, he found an irate letter from Lin-Manuel berating him for bailing before they could finish the film. Aaron thought their friendship might be over.

Then he received a second letter, apologizing for the first. Lin-Manuel confessed that his own insecurities had motivated his anger: "I had this horrible feeling that you had gone to camp to get away from me and the movie, and I started feeling really pissed at myself, and I suppose I took some of that out on you," he wrote. "If I had let this piddly shit come between us, not only would I be a bad friend, I'd be a shitty director. I got so caught up in directing that I forgot that this movie was about us, the five of us, and friendship, and please don't ever let me forget that. I mean, Jesus, the name of the movie is *Clayton's Friends*, not *Clayton's Co-workers*." He told Aaron that they could finish when he returned from camp at the end of the summer. (The letter concluded with an update: "*Amanda situation*: No pulse.")

In the dramatic language of teenage friendship, Lin-Manuel was learning to be an artistic leader, figuring out how to rally his pals around his passions. "I think I got a big dose of perspective," he reflects on his correspondence with Aaron. "I was passionate about making things then; I just didn't have leverage. And I realized that being a dick isn't good leverage. No one wants to hang out with you when you're like that." Given a second chance, he pivoted to the value their friendship continued to hold. And he led with enthusiasm—the movie was "so Goddamned good!"

Back in the city, he and Adam, who now teaches filmmaking, were hard at work editing *Clayton's Friends*. "Adam was always my ride-or-die

when it came to making movies," Lin-Manuel says. "He was as passionate about Tarantino and Rodriguez as I was." They had planned out their
shots and cuts; now they connected the Mirandas' two VCRs to the TV
and painstakingly transferred each sequence to the master version. The
movie had taken a year to make; their haircuts were different by the final
shots. "From the beginning to the end, you could see puberty," Paul, now
an accountant, says.

At last, around Halloween in tenth grade, *Clayton's Friends* was ready
to screen. Lin-Manuel invited dozens of friends over to his house for a
viewing party. "It was like the Oscars," his mother says. "They all had to
come dressed up for the opening." It took four people to haul the Mirandas' forty-inch television down the stairs to the first floor, where there
was more room to squeeze all the guests in. The house was packed. People sat on the floor, on each other's laps. With a blend of jokes, fights,
tunes, and kisses, the movie seemed perfectly crafted for the sensibilities
of fifteen-year-olds. "It played great in the room because it was puerile
humor," Lin-Manuel says. The biggest laugh came from a sequence where
Lin-Manuel did a karate fist-pump move, shouting "Yes!"; Andrew did
the fist-pump "Yes!"; then Adam did the fist-pump "Yes!" as the camera
zoomed out to reveal him sitting, pants down, on the toilet.

The jokes might have been juvenile, but the ambition of the project
felt unprecedentedly mature. *Clayton's Friends* was not, by any account, a
great film, but what was great was that Lin-Manuel had executed his goal.
"He made a feature film at fifteen!" Chris Hayes says. "He was this nuclear
reactor of creativity." Other students might mess around with a camcorder
or film a skit, but no one wrote and directed an hour-long feature.

For Lin-Manuel, the premiere was a triumph but hardly a wrap-up.
He had already begun writing his next screenplay. This time, he planned
to broaden his scope beyond his sleepover buddies. For his follow-up,
Naughtybird Curtsy, he wanted to make a movie about music set at Hunter's Battle of the Bands. "He was very growth-oriented," says Andrew,
who is now an elementary-school teacher. "He wanted to branch out.
There was no fear of failure. His attitude seemed to be: 'This is going to
work. If it doesn't work yet, that's okay; it will.'"

Lin-Manuel's most audacious choice in *Naughtybird Curtsy* was to
use original music. He asked his Jazz Chorus pals Arthur Lewis and Dan

Gonen if they could write the score. "Lin's really good at delegation," Arthur says. "He really, really appreciates other people's talents." Dan studied advanced music theory and was accomplished on four instruments; Arthur—the elementary-school *supercalifragilisticexpialidocious* whiz—had perfect pitch and could play piano by ear. The movie needed background music and a climactic song for the hero to serenade his dream girl with. They got to work composing.

Then, to their surprise, Lin turned up with the climactic song. He didn't really know how to write music, so he asked Adam to record him playing his composition, "Everything Wrong," on the keyboard in his bedroom. He was particularly proud that he'd hidden a punning reference to his longtime crush, Amanda, in the chorus:

> **A man does** *everything wrong*
> *But he sings this dumb song*
> *'Cause he loves you.*

He set the lyrics to a catchy, looping melody line. Dan and Arthur were floored. "That was the first inkling most of us had that Lin was good at writing music," Dan says. "The sense of Lin was that he was the film guy. He could play piano a little, but he kind of sucked at piano; he could sing a little, but he wasn't great. Then he wrote this song, and it was like, *Oh, he could write music!*"

The song didn't end up making it into the film. Lin-Manuel planned to shoot an actual high-school band, led by his friend Alex Sarlin, playing his song at Hunter's competition. But the guys in the band were loath to risk their performance on a number by an unknown composer. When they went onstage, they decided to play a different song instead of "Everything Wrong." Alex remembers coming offstage to find Lin-Manuel awaiting them, "super-hurt and super-betrayed."

From Lin-Manuel's adult perspective, however, the band made an understandable choice. "I was making incredibly unreasonable demands on their time," he admits. He had to learn to adjust his vision to the realities of his classmates' lives and interests. He recut his film around the song they performed, and he filed away his catchy melody line; it might come in handy for a later project.

Looking back, Alex wonders why, in a school teeming with talented artists, Lin-Manuel became the superstar. "People saw their creative output in high school as these one-offs: 'We're going to perform in the talent show,'" he explains. "But Lin really saw it as part of a larger project. He'd connect with people who had certain skills and find a way to work with them." And unlike many of his classmates, Lin-Manuel wasn't inhibited by the gap between what he could create and the work of the professional artists he admired. "A lot of us fell prey to the taste gap, feeling that we'd never play like some great band," Alex says. "A lot of us made ourselves give up. But Lin was never like that. He always saw his creative output as worthwhile. He wasn't comparing himself to his heroes. He was like: 'I'm going to make what I can right now, collaborate with anyone I can collaborate with, and learn as I go.'"

The next step was realizing what he really wanted to make.

—

Lin-Manuel had long been a hip-hop fan, but growing up, he didn't feel he had the experience or the credibility to write the kinds of rap he heard on his friends' mixtapes. In his first year of high school, though, a hip-hop album came out that would change his life. *Bizarre Ride II the Pharcyde*, the debut record from the Pharcyde, a jokey California quartet with a punning name, offered clever, self-mocking chronicles of guys who struck out with ladies. Their hit "Passin' Me By," a mournful, playful riff on unrequited love, spun like the soundtrack to Lin-Manuel's own early high-school drama. The rhymes were dense ("Now there she goes again, the dopest Ethiopian"), the digs on a rival almost Seussian ("He was a rooty-toot, a nincompoop"). He memorized the song, wore out the cassette tape, bought it again, wore it out again, bought it again. "It wasn't until this song that I realized I was allowed to write hip-hop," he explained. "It's a song about guys who can't get girls, and I said, oh, I could do that!"

At Hunter, some of Lin-Manuel's classmates liked to freestyle in the school courtyard during recess. A couple of his pals from *Clayton's Friends* could spit verses while Lin-Manuel would beatbox in the background, too scared to jump in with an improv. But writing out a verse ahead of time felt more manageable. With the Pharcyde's reedy timbre and Slinky-spring cadences in his head, he gave it a try.

Well, hello, my name is Lin,
But if you're dyslexic, call me Nil.
My rhymes are gonna kill,
So I suggest you write your will
And leave your shit to me.
I am the epitome
Of coolness, can't be rid of me
Because I will be hitting the
Mic tonight!

He wasn't an MC just yet, but he did get a dose of stardom during the winter musical of his ninth-grade year, *The Pirates of Penzance.* The student directors hadn't planned to cast a ninth-grader in any of the lead roles, let alone the Pirate King, a swashbuckling scene-stealer made famous on film by Kevin Kline. But when Lin-Manuel showed up on the Hunter auditorium stage and auditioned, it was hard to imagine anyone else in the part. He didn't seem like a typical musical-theater leading man. He could speak-sing more than croon, and he still had the physique of a scrawny fourteen-year-old. But he had spent half his childhood leaping off ledges and fighting mock duels in his home movies. He'd practiced ridiculous expressions in front of the mirror, waggling his eyebrows and undulating his stomach to imitate the Stupid Human Tricks he saw on *The Late Show with David Letterman.* He'd even played a preening pirate, a bewigged Captain Hook, in the sixth-grade play on that very stage. When he threw his body into the part, he became electrifying. He scaled the auditorium banisters and vaulted off them—fearless, rubbery, a bundle of energy. "Lin just had that crazy thing, that spark," Rachel Axler, the production's vocal director, recalls. He was absolutely the closest thing a ninth-grader could have been to Kevin Kline."

He took inspiration from a senior in the cast, Loren Hammonds, who had already appeared on *Star Search* and performed with a hip-hop group called Dujeous that was starting to get radio play. Lin-Manuel got up the courage to show Loren one of his raps. Loren took the ninth-grader seriously. They started talking about the groups they both loved: the Pharcyde, De La Soul, A Tribe Called Quest. The Notorious B.I.G.'s first album, *Ready to Die,* had dropped that fall and impressed them with its storytelling flow. They knew that Hunter had a bit of a hip-hop pedigree; the rapper Young MC, of "Bust a Move" fame, was an alum. Gilbert and Sullivan's patter songs felt like proto-rap, in a way, with their internal rhymes and rapid syllables, and Lin-Manuel paid close attention to the Major-General's famous song: "I Am the Very Model of a Modern Major General." Maybe hip-hop offered an artistic path ahead.

Lin-Manuel also took note of a girl in the female chorus. Most of the Major-General's daughters fluttered like pretty flowers, choosing names for their characters like Lily and Rose. One girl, however, stuck her brown hair in pigtails, donned giant glasses, and called herself Petunia. She hunched over, lurching around the stage and shoving her glasses up the bridge of her nose. When a suitor approached her, she crouched down, grinned, and let out a snort that left the audience—and much of the cast—in stitches.

She was a tenth-grader named Meredith Summerville. Her parents were ministers at a Methodist church in Bay Ridge, Brooklyn, an hour-and-a-half subway ride south of Hunter. She sang beautifully, she thought deeply, and as the hilariously nerdy Petunia, she began to come out of her shell. Lin-Manuel was so impressed that he had to reach for an unusual superlative when he signed her closing-night poster: "ON stage, you are funnier than an entire boot full of drunken Peruvian midget clams. OFF stage you are a great and dear friend." Meredith saw beyond Lin-Manuel's stage bravado; she could tell he was thoughtful and kind, optimistic and hardworking. At the *Pirates* cast sleepover, in their pajamas, they laughed together all night.

In May, Meredith was tapped to become the assistant director of the following year's Musical Rep production: *Godspell*, Stephen Schwartz's 1971 folk-pop retelling of the Gospel According to Matthew. Coming off his triumph as the Pirate King, Lin-Manuel hoped he could play Jesus, but he was cast as Judas instead. He still got a crowd-pleasing number; in the vaudevillian "All for the Best," Jesus offered upbeat bromides about suffering on earth leading to rewards in heaven, while Lin-Manuel cavorted around him, twirling a cane to a soft-shoe shuffle as he motored through a cynical patter about inequality. ("LIN ENUNCIATE—SLOWER," Meredith wrote in her rehearsal notebook.) At the end of the song, he dropped into a shimmy half-split, his go-to dance move. But he also had a chance to explore a less showy side as the ensemble's goofy antics deepened into tragedy.

For Meredith, growing up in her parents' church, *Godspell* offered rich material. During the February break, students weren't allowed to rehearse at school, so they convened at the Summervilles' church basement, where Meredith had long talks with Lin-Manuel about his character's shifting relationships. When Jesus told Judas to turn the other cheek, he delivered the lesson with an unexpected slap. As Judas, Lin-Manuel was stung, confused. "Since he saw the world in a different way, it was impossible for them to connect, and their relationship broke down," Meredith says. "It wasn't about sin and redemption; it was about what happens when you don't believe in your friends, and you betray them." Through his filmmaking exploits, Lin-Manuel had learned to understand that dynamic on both sides. He knew what it felt like to become the charismatic leader who goes too far, who expects too much. And he delivered a much more emotional performance than anticipated by many of his classmates, who remembered his Pirate King hijinks. "At the end of the show, I was blown away by Lin's serious acting," says his castmate Lona Kaplan-Werner, who'd also been in *Pirates*. "I'd never seen that before; it felt very deep and meaningful."

Initially, Meredith regarded Lin-Manuel as a friend. Then they began flirting, sometimes even in the pages of her rehearsal notebook. For her birthday, he made her one of his bespoke specialties: a two-cassette mixtape. Between tracks from Pearl Jam, P. M. Dawn, and *Les Misérables*, he slipped in "Hold Me, Thrill Me, Kiss Me" and "I Only Have Eyes for You."

In spring came the junior semiformal dance. As a sophomore, Lin-Manuel couldn't invite anyone. Meredith, however, was a junior. She asked Lin-Manuel to be her date. To her surprise, he hesitated. "I don't know," he said. "Can I think about it?" Then he ran away. A few moments later, he returned with his reply: "Yes!" He had to take a beat to decide, he told her later; he couldn't say yes immediately because it was too big of a deal. In the romantic melodrama of high-school courtship, it felt like a defining moment of his life.

Meredith was responsible for another moment that proved, in Lin-Manuel's life, perhaps even more defining. Over the next year, they became nearly inseparable, hanging out together whenever they could. "It seemed as good as a high-school relationship can be: loving, equal, both into the same things," their friend Chris Hayes remembers. Lin-Manuel valued the sense of warmth he found at the Summervilles' church, which struck him as more inviting than the strict Catholic services that he had to attend when he stayed with Luz's mother in New Jersey. The Mirandas, in turn, impressed Meredith with their loving frankness. Mundi made off-color jokes in Spanish while she cooked and cleaned. After work, Luis relaxed with his son and debated feminist ideas with Meredith. When Luz wasn't seeing patients in her downstairs office, she would talk about adolescent psychology or watch videos, laughing to herself. On the TV in his room, Lin-Manuel showed Meredith his favorite movies: *Fiddler on the Roof*, *The Little Mermaid*, and his dad's gospel of self-making, *The Unsinkable Molly Brown*.

Although Lin-Manuel loved musicals, he had not yet written one, even years after Dr. Herbert summoned him to the task. It was a daunting call; the musicals he knew were about French history or haunted opera houses or pirates or Jesus—fun to act out but far from his reality. The 1980s and early 1990s on Broadway were dominated by mega-musicals, spectacular British imports with giant sets and pop-opera scores—the opposite of the indie film scene's DIY aesthetic that had inspired him to create *Clayton's Friends*. He liked writing songs, but movies seemed like the form in which he could tell the stories that excited him.

Then, for her boyfriend's seventeenth birthday in 1997, Meredith planned a surprise. She took him to the Empire State Building, then to dinner, then guided him through Times Square to the Nederlander theater. She produced two tickets. It was January 16, eight p.m., eastern standard time. They were going to see *Rent*.

Meredith had seen it already, and she knew she had to take Lin-Manuel. "He was floored," she says. Even from the back row of the mezzanine, he felt as though *Rent* were speaking directly to him. Here, for the first time on a Broadway stage, he saw actors who looked like people he encountered in New York City every day: Black, white, Latino, Jewish, Christian, gay, straight. And in Jonathan Larson's score, these East Village bohemians—aspiring artists, friends, and lovers, forming a community of care in the face of government and corporate indifference—were singing pop-rock numbers that sounded like the music he would put on a '90s mixtape. "*Rent* rocked my conception of what musical theater could be," Lin-Manuel said. "It felt like, 'Oh, this guy wrote this downtown, and some of these songs only have three chords, and he's writing about being an artist and being afraid of selling out, and being afraid of dying, and I'm scared of all those things.'"

As he watched the musical, he identified with the narrator, Mark, a filmmaker who obsessively chronicles his friends' hopes and heartbreaks. "Mark lives for his work, and Mark's in love with his work," his roommate Roger sang. Lin-Manuel approved. But then Roger continued, accusing Mark of hiding in his work. Lin-Manuel got nervous. Hiding from what? Roger explained: Mark was afraid to confront his fear of isolation. Lin-Manuel felt personally called out. "You pretend to create and observe, when you really detach from feeling alive," Roger sang. That's what Lin-Manuel's friends said when he held up his camera instead of horsing around with them, when he asked a girl to be in his movie instead of telling her how he felt. "That's when Jonathan Larson reached out and punched me straight in the heart," he said. He hadn't realized that a musical could send him a personal message—a warning, even—naming the feelings he was almost afraid to admit. "No one had ever told me you can write about the things you know in a musical. They don't have to come from some far-off place." *Rent* gave him permission to summon his own fears and fantasies onstage.

Over February break, Lin-Manuel wrote his first musical. He began, he says, with "this one chord progression I couldn't get out of my head," a spiraling figure in the right hand over a staggered bass line that changed the figure's tonality, sometimes major, sometimes minor. It sounded unresolved, obsessive, a fantasia of anxiety.

He had an idea for a story to match that music: "If I write a dream, anything is possible." His central character would fall asleep and encounter everything that terrified him. When Lin-Manuel visited his grandfather's video store in Vega Alta, the cover of *Nightmare on Elm Street 2: Freddy's Revenge* frightened him so much that he had to run past it, only sneaking a peak at the hideous, clawed monster who killed victims in their dreams. He decided to call his musical *Nightmare in D Major*.

For the monster that haunted the dreams of Lin-Manuel's hero, Hunter provided inspiration. He'd recently comforted Meredith in the hallway after she had to dissect a fetal pig in AP Biology. He imagined a scenario both terrifying and ludicrous: The fetal pig could come back to life and threaten revenge for being cut up. "I knew kids would like it, because half of them had taken AP Bio too," he says.

He found, to his surprise, that the writing process led him to deeper fears. A melody that he'd been playing with for a while acquired words in the voice of a little girl—someone like Allie, his preschool friend who'd drowned. That painful memory could surface when triggered. In seventh grade, he briefly dated a girl from Staten Island. She was headstrong, zesty, popular. One day, he learned she'd been hit by a car. She didn't die, but it took her a long time to recover. He journeyed out to Staten Island to visit her—a train to a boat to another train to the hospital. She was seriously injured. "That scared the shit out of me," he says. He developed an uncontrollable fear that anyone he loved was going to get hurt or die.

When he and Meredith began dating, the specter of his earlier girlfriends haunted their relationship. "I started having all these morbid fantasies," he says, "like she's getting on the train to her house and I never see her again."

Luz had a pair of mantras for her son when he experienced anxiety. She helped him breathe deeply, sang to him, and reminded him that every experience, however painful, was transitory: "This too shall pass." And she told him that even a stressful episode might prove useful. "You want to be a writer? Remember this feeling. It's all grist for the mill." When he got a summer job at McDonald's and his math phobia flared up so severely at having to speed-calculate the orders that he dreamed the pencil behind his ear had impaled his skull, she said, "Honey, you never know how this job might inform your work somewhere in the future. It's all grist for the mill." Lin-Manuel calls his mom "the nurturer and caretaker of my artistic side," adding, "There's nothing like unconditional belief from someone who loves you." Her refrains offered the coping mechanisms he needed: Instead of shying away from negative emotions, he could turn them into art.

By his junior year, his fears had magnified. "My very vivid sense that I'm going to die or someone I love is going to die really kicked into overload with adolescence," he says. He became obsessed with artists whose promising lives were cut short. In his bedroom, he put up a poster of the martial arts actor Brandon Lee, who died in 1993 while making his first big film, *The Crow*, when a gun misfired on set. *Rent* turned him on to another doomed artist: Jonathan Larson, who died of an undiagnosed heart condition the night before his musical opened. "Those stories scared me and fascinated me," he says, "because I felt like I had that promise, and I felt like I could be that story."

His relationship with Meredith both accentuated his anxieties and helped him navigate them. "We talked a lot about that early trauma and how it manifested in me calling her all the time," he says. Meredith, who went on to become a child psychologist, understood. Although he usually projected an upbeat persona with his friends, he let her see his darker side. "He was the kind of kid who would go into the sad parts of things and not run away from them," she says. "I was too."

And so, as he wrote his musical, he listened to the character of a little girl who sang a high, clear, childlike melody:

> *You probably do not remember me,*
> *But in fourth grade you were in love with me.*
> *You don't know my name,*
> *But you know my face.*
> *Sometimes I get just a bit sad*
> *When I think that you have forgotten me,*
> *But I'll always be*
> *In your dreams,*
> *In your dreams . . .*

He built the musical around her—Suzy, he called her. The hero, Dylan, wakes up from a nightmare and is comforted by his girlfriend, Marie. But just as she goes to get him a cup of tea, he falls back asleep and meets the fetal pig he dissected in AP Biology. It's wielding a knife, vowing revenge. Then Suzy appears, and as soon as Dylan recognizes her, he learns that she had died, and that he couldn't save her. The pig comes back, this time with its knife pointed at Marie. Can Dylan rescue his current girlfriend from Suzy's fate? At the moment the pig is about to strike, Dylan wakes up. Marie has returned with the cup of tea, just in time to save him. "It was a one-to-one manifestation of what I was going through," Lin-Manuel says. "The main character was DyLIN. Meredith was Marie." It was all grist for the mill.

For each character, he came up with a different musical motif. Dylan had a swinging rock style. Suzy sounded sweet and innocent, a little like the young Cosette in *Les Misérables*. The fetal pig sang with an insistent menace, made comical by the fact that the ghost of a porcine fetus was singing at all:

Pig, I am just a fetal pig,
I am not very big,
So why did you cut me up in Bio class?
Is getting a good grade
Worth me getting slayed?

"The fetal pig was scary but also funny," Meredith remembers. "That was effective. The show didn't seem maudlin in a way that would turn off other kids." A lighter note also came from a Jamaican dance-hall character, DJ Bony, who tries, unsuccessfully, to shoot the pig. There was even a Slick Rick–style MC to guide the audience through Dylan's "historical and hysterical" unconscious.

To tie together this dream mélange of family, school, and pop-culture references, Lin-Manuel turned to one of his favorite musical-theater techniques. "Even though at the time I only have four chords and limited musicality, I can use themes and reprises." He loved when a phrase returned with a new meaning. "The first musical I learned did that: *Les Misérables.*" Just as Fantine's deathbed refrain in the first act is echoed at the end of the musical when Jean Valjean dies, the melody of Dylan's opening song with Marie comes back around in their concluding duet. Lin-Manuel returned to his spiraling initial chord progression when he wrote Dylan's standoff with the fetal pig. What was in one sense a limitation—he didn't know very many chords—became a strength: the sung-through musical sounded like a unified composition. He played the songs into his four-track recorder and submitted the cassette to Brick Prison.

It wasn't a guarantee that his submission would be chosen. The first time he sent in a script to Brick, as a ninth-grader coming off his triumph in *Pirates*, it was rejected. (His play was called *Bathroom Humor*; it more or less lived up to its title.) The next year, he wrote another silly script called *Green Eggs and Sam*—a mixture of dark comedy and violence that he calls "Tarantino-esque"—which made it onstage.

By junior year, he was ready to tap more profound material. When the Brick officers received the cassette for *Nightmare in D Major*, they were amazed. A Hunter student had written an original musical. And it was good. More than good. "Upon first listen, I was totally blown away," Chris Hayes, who lobbied to direct the musical, says. "It was so recognizably *him*: fully formed, addictively singable."

Chris brought on a music director who arranged the score for a student band. ("It was very Larson-rock-band-y: guitar, bass, drums," Lin-Manuel says.) As they rehearsed with the cast in the chorus room on the second floor, Lin-Manuel occasionally popped in. The first time they ran through Suzy's song, he had to leave the room crying.

Even though he didn't tell them about all of his experiences, it never occurred to him to keep his art private. "I knew it wasn't complete until there was an audience," he says. It was a lesson he'd drawn from Chaim Potok, the author of *The Chosen*. After that novel captivated him in Dr. Herbert's eighth-grade English class, he went on to read Potok's portrait of an artist, *My Name Is Asher Lev*. Asher is a painter, but his masterpiece—a portrait of his mother on a cross, her son and her husband looking on—horrifies his Orthodox Jewish community. As Lin-Manuel remembers the novel: "He could have destroyed the painting, but art needs an audience. The completion of the loop is to share it, whatever slings and arrows may come. If you're not going to share yourself, you're not an artist."

Not many slings and arrows awaited him that May when *Nightmare in D Major* concluded the Brick Prison program. From the moment the band kicked into *Nightmare*'s spiraling overture, the audience applauded. Chris's production featured eerie blue and red lighting shifts for the dream sequences, pop-and-lock choreography for the dance-hall number, and a snout mask for the fetal pig. Lin-Manuel's instincts had been right; the fetal pig delighted his classmates. Many of them can sing "Pig, I am just a fetal pig / I am not very big" to this day. That was another upside of his limited piano technique: Since he couldn't play complex, nuanced music, any tune that made it through his fingers would easily lodge in a listener's ear. "It was catchy as hell," recalls Arthur Lewis, who played Dylan and arranged to record a cast album. "It blew everyone's minds. No one at Hunter had ever done a student-written musical before."

Lin-Manuel hadn't told his mother, who was in the audience, that writing this musical had allowed him to process his grief. But he didn't have to. Luz knew. "It came out in art form," she says. Watching her son work through his fears, using his demons to fuel his creativity, she could discern another aftershock from his childhood trauma. "He had a new sense of time," she says. "He knew not to waste it, because it's too precious."

3

DREAM SHOW

••

For her senior show, Meredith chose to direct *A Chorus Line*, the 1975 hit drawn from the real-life stories of dancers trying out for a Broadway ensemble. She enticed Lin-Manuel to be her assistant director with the promise that he'd get to choose the musical the following year. "Lin was unclear whether he wanted to have that executive role or just be onstage doing what he was comfortable with," Meredith says. "He was like, 'I'm just an actor.' I was like, 'No, you have something to say. You can pick your show and do it your way.'" That persuaded him. "I liked the applause; I liked being a ham onstage," he says. "I wanted that Conrad Birdie feeling. But Meredith said: 'You've got more to offer. It's not the dopamine hit of being onstage, but it's incredibly satisfying in other ways. You're going to learn a lot.'"

They started researching the musical a year in advance, and they interviewed student choreographers, music directors, and designers to build their team. Come November, more than eighty students crowded outside the chorus room to await their turn to audition. The parallels between their aspirations and the premise of *A Chorus Line* didn't have to be spelled out.

When the directors met with their new company, they stressed the time commitment: Musical Rep required four after-school rehearsals per week, plus full-day sessions on weekends and over vacations. "Rep will be your *life*," Meredith told the group. "It's mine." She continued, "We're going to have fun, but you have to know when to be serious about your work. We have a show to put on. Every one of you will be onstage for the *whole show*. That should probably freak you out. But you can handle it. It'll be so rewarding."

Meredith's combination of high expectations and positive motivation offered a model for Lin-Manuel. He could get frustrated with the actors she'd delegated him to coach. A younger student in the cast drove Lin-Manuel crazy by coasting on cuteness instead of probing below his character's surface, even more infuriating because Lin-Manuel knew that's what he himself would have done as a ninth-grader, before his *Godspell* breakthrough. He and Meredith both valued emotional truth over technical polish. "We were always looking for how to make it *real*," Meredith says. "We believed together that the thrust of this work had to be the story."

But how to get the actors to reach that deeper level? When one actor skipped rehearsals over February break to go on vacation, Meredith didn't flip out as Lin-Manuel had done when his pal Aaron chose summer camp over finishing *Clayton's Friends*. Instead of getting angry, Meredith sat down with the truant actor to figure out how to catch her up. "Meredith is a wonderful artist and a fundamentally decent person, and she led that way," Lin-Manuel says. "I learned so much from her."

For some students, the musical's drama mirrored their experiences at school. "Hunter's a frickin' pressure cooker," says Chris Hayes, who played a lead in the show. Students had to take multiple tests to get in, and once they did, they found themselves in an even more competitive pool—trying out for clubs, vying for leadership positions, preparing for college applications. "The life of constantly auditioning was something we had from the age of twelve," Michael Frazer, an older student, says. "We felt like we were in *A Chorus Line* every day."

Not all Hunterites felt that way. Some remember a collaborative atmosphere where students supported each other, gaining the confidence and freedom to thrive in their areas of strength. For Lin-Manuel, the pressure varied across activities. He didn't flourish academically, seldom getting As unless he could do a creative project, so he had no interest in competing for grades. With artistic leadership, though, he threw himself in. "There were departments where I really wanted the ball," he says. "Lose spring break to go rehearse in a church basement? Fuck yeah! But show you my grade on the lab report? Fuck you!"

Now that he was writing and directing musicals, he didn't have time to make full-length movies. But whenever he could submit a film for a class assignment, he would. For an American history unit in social studies, he decided to make a movie of the 1804 duel between Alexander Hamilton and Aaron Burr. His neighborhood offered all the locations he'd need to shoot. Outside his window, Inwood Hill Park preserved the city's last natural forest, still looking much as it would have in 1804. The houses where Hamilton and Burr had lived were nearby, too, in Washington Heights. He and Meredith walked around Inwood, taking turns toting his camcorder, as he figured out the shots. "The Burr-Hamilton duel always interested him," she says. "He'd say: 'That's my neighborhood!' But then he dramatized it. He would look for depth in these relationships."

In Burr and Hamilton's rivalry, he found another variation on the curdled friendship that Meredith had helped him to explore in *Godspell* with Jesus and Judas. And in Hamilton's untimely death, he could hear an echo of his own fascination with talented figures whose lives were cut short: Brandon Lee, Jonathan Larson. He was also struck by learning that Hamilton's son had died in a duel, defending his father's honor on the same location where Hamilton would face Burr. "I remember there was some serious psychological stuff happening," he says.

In Lin-Manuel's shooting script, when Hamilton's conflict with Burr escalates, Hamilton tells his wife, Elizabeth, that he's been thinking about their son's death. As Lin-Manuel imagined the scene, Elizabeth asks her husband not to dwell on the subject: "Dueling is a sin, Alexander." That warning determines Hamilton's choice: When he goes to meet Burr, he will not fire his shot. Still grieving his son's death, he is nearly suicidal; he risks his own life rather than taking another's. In the script, he writes a letter to his wife on the morning of the duel, narrating in voice-over the historical Hamilton's own words: "Adieu, best of wives and best of women."

Lin-Manuel never got to shoot the script. As he and Meredith walked back from the Dyckman Farmhouse, a man grabbed the video camera out of Meredith's hands, jumped into a waiting car, and sped away. They'd been mugged. Without his camera, he couldn't make the movie, so he submitted his script instead. Lin-Manuel remembers his teacher's disappointment: The script turned history into personal drama, a complex chronicle into amateur psychology. "He thought that 'Hamilton's son died, so he was suicidal' was a very facile explanation," Lin-Manuel says. "And it was a lit-tle cliché. His son died in a duel, so he decided to die in a duel. It was that simple. I got a B-minus."

Surprisingly, Lin-Manuel fared better on a math project. He took Billy Joel's doo-wop standard "For the Longest Time" and rewrote the lyrics to fit a trigonometry unit, giving it the title "For the Law of Sines." To back him up on the song, he enlisted four guys from Jazz Chorus: Arthur, Dan, Mark Roaquin, and David Davidson. It was the only time Lin-Manuel ever got above a C in math. The doo-wop quintet had fun performing together, so they formed an a cappella group. Their repertoire wasn't extensive, mostly "For the Longest Time" and "Goodnight Sweetheart" to start. But they carved out practice time between Jazz Chorus rehearsals and met up at breaks in the courtyard. Riffing on an inside joke, they decided to call themselves Fat Joe and the Boys.

Like the actors in *Clayton's Friends*, Fat Joe and the Boys became what Lin-Manuel calls a "found family"—a cohort of friends who joined him on artistic adventures. They sang at school assemblies; they busked in subway stations; they performed at concerts for the Jazz Chorus, which, thanks to its charismatic, enterprising director, Campbelle Austin, toured to New York Knicks games, nearby colleges, and, one spring break, even to Senegal. As a choral singer, Lin-Manuel was irrepressible. He'd burst into the rehearsal room belting a song, often one from Disney's new movie *Mulan*: "'Let's get down to business to defeat the Huns'!" ("I could always hear him before I could see him," one of his teachers says.) Straining to reach a note above his range, he'd leap on top of a table. He led vocal warm-ups that roused the group's spirits; "Lin, do your thing," Mr. Austin would tell him before the Knicks games. "He didn't have the best voice," Mr. Austin says, "but his enthusiasm, his energy, the light in his eyes—all that made the music come alive."

He needed all of his energy for the major endeavor of his senior year: directing the winter musical. Meredith had graduated and gone off to Yale, though they remained a couple. (After one visit to New Haven, he came back proudly sporting a T-shirt that said YALE GRANDMA.) It was his turn to pick the show.

His dream was to direct *West Side Story*. Ever since Ms. Ames had cast him as Bernardo in Hunter's sixth-grade production and his mom had rented the movie for him to watch, he had been captivated by the musical, which, with Stephen Sondheim's witty lyrics, staged the question of where Puerto Ricans belonged. "It was the only show where I got to bring my identity to school," he says. "Doing *West Side Story* in sixth grade and then directing it as a senior felt very full circle."

The challenge of putting on a *Romeo and Juliet*–style musical tragedy about white and Puerto Rican gangs at Hunter was that the school didn't have many Latino students. So, like the 1961 film, Hunter's production ended up with mostly non–Puerto Rican actors playing the Sharks. The movie used brownface makeup and exaggerated accents, but Lin-Manuel worked to make his version culturally authentic. He had a secret weapon: the boundless energy of Luis A. Miranda Jr. That winter, his father often left the office early so he could show Hunter's white, Asian-American, and Black students how to act Puerto Rican. "My job was to teach them how to pronounce the Spanish phrases with a Puerto Rican intonation," Luis says. Lin-Manuel made him a worksheet of all the Spanish in the show, and they also brainstormed a list of Puerto Rican expressions the Sharks could shout during the song "America." Under Luis's tutelage, the actors practiced saying "Wepa!" and "Muévete!" Luis was glad to support his son's effort to represent their family's culture. "It was important to Lin-Manuel that they sound Puerto Rican," he says, "even though they were gringos saying these lines."

Meredith had shown Lin-Manuel that truthful storytelling was more important than perfect artistry and that supportive leadership could bring out the best in a company. "I felt like *A Chorus Line* prepared me," he says. "I felt qualified to direct." In the areas where he didn't feel qualified, he trusted his collaborators. "Meredith was always a great teacher in that regard," he says. "You have to delegate. The choreographers and designers are going to come up with something I didn't see in my head."

Student leaders were essentially ordering around their friends, and for some, it could be difficult to maintain authority. Lin-Manuel did it with enthusiasm. He started every rehearsal with improv games, nonsense rhymes, and rhythm patterns he'd picked up at after-school sessions with the Creative Arts Team youth program. When the cast had to learn tricky steps for the "Dance at the Gym," he declared it National Mambo Week and brought in food and mambo-themed warm-up activities to keep everyone excited. (With hips that seemed to dance on their own, he nicknamed himself "Butt Brain.") He roped the directing team into filming a parody video at his house to screen at the cast party; he called it *Shmest Side Shmory*. His natural exuberance became a motivational strategy. "There were diehards like me—I know I'm going to be doing it as long as possible—and there were folks for whom Rep is an extracurricular, so how do I make it fun?" he says. "When you're truly doing something for the love of it, and you can't hire or fire anyone, it's really about a shared vision. It's about how we can make something bigger together than we can on our own."

The biggest inspiration came one day at lunchtime in room 210. The cast and crew of *West Side Story* crammed into the windowless classroom. A few students dashed up from a Jazz Chorus performance in the auditorium, and when they arrived at the doorway, they froze. There, sitting in a chair, wearing a brown sweater, his gray beard trimmed and his hooded eyes aglint, was Stephen Sondheim.

As it happened, Sondheim's writing partner on *Pacific Overtures* and *Assassins*, the playwright John Weidman, had a daughter at Hunter who was two grades below Lin-Manuel. She'd come home and told her dad that the senior who was directing *West Side Story* wanted to invite Sondheim to speak to the drama club. "Steve loved kids," Weidman says, "and he had a real interest in teaching. I thought it might be something he'd enjoy." He called Sondheim, who said that if Weidman accompanied him, he'd do it.

On the appointed day, Weidman met Sondheim at Hunter, and they walked into the packed classroom. As the director, Lin-Manuel was expected to ask the first question. Everyone looked to him. "All I could come up with," he says, "was 'What was it *like*?'"

Sondheim looked confused. "What was it like?"

"Yeah," Lin-Manuel said. "What was it like making *West Side Story*?"

"Oh, I see," Sondheim replied. For the rest of the lunch period, he told them. But rather than present the origin story of his triumphs, he gave the students a glimpse of his missteps. He shared lyrics that had been jettisoned, songs that were reordered, verses he wished he'd improved. He revealed that he'd written lyrics for the show's famous dance prologue, but the choreographer, Jerome Robbins, decided he could convey the rivalry better through movement, so the words were cut. Sondheim explained

that Riff, the leader of the Jets, got his name because he carried around a trumpet—or he did until the book writer, Arthur Laurents, asked him, "When was the last time you saw a gang member carrying a fucking bugle?" No more trumpet.

Masterpieces, the students learned, didn't emerge fully formed from a single creator's head. They were the product of collaboration, negotiation, and constant revision. Sondheim had taken the students inside the artistic process. "What he taught me was that the process was messy. It didn't have to be perfect," Lin-Manuel said. "That's the first thing that pulled back the curtain on how to make a show."

When the lunch period ended, Sondheim stood by the door shaking each student's hand as they left. The Musical Rep crew felt validated: Sondheim had told them that he preferred the Broadway order of the Jets' songs—first "Cool," then "Gee, Officer Krupke"—rather than the film's, and that was the choice Lin-Manuel had made for their production. Somehow, the deity had blessed their show.

After the opening-night performance, after the applause and cheers and curtain call, Una LaMarche, who played one of the Shark girls, spotted Lin-Manuel weeping in his mother's arms. "The show was over, she went up to hug him, and his shoulders were heaving," Una says. "Seeing a teenage boy in a public place crying out of joy and happiness just stayed with me. It showed how much it meant to him."

To this day, Lin-Manuel says that his goal as a writer and composer is to re-create his Musical Rep experience. "I was a kid who figured out who I was in the context of the drama clubs at my school. I think a part of my brain is always just trying to make the best school play."

—

While Lin-Manuel was rehearsing *West Side Story*, he heard about a ne' musical heading to Broadway, *The Capeman*, that also featured Puer' Rican characters. The subject, admittedly, seemed like a dubious choic the true story of Salvador Agron, a Puerto Rican–born gang meml known for his black cape who went to prison for stabbing two white b in a 1959 Hell's Kitchen fight. *West Side Story* had already covered Pu Rican gangsters with artistic verve; did Broadway need more La'

brandishing knives? But *The Capeman* boasted songs by Paul Simon, whose "Bridge over Troubled Water" had moved Lin-Manuel to tears when he was a boy. What's more, the young Agron would be played by one of Lin-Manuel's favorite singers, the Nuyorican crossover star Marc Anthony, and the older Agron by a Miranda family hero, the Panama-born singer and activist Rubén Blades. "No one was ever more excited for a show than I was for *The Capeman*," he says.

He loved the album that Paul Simon recorded of the musical's songs, and he took the whole Hunter *West Side Story* team to the Marquis Theatre so they could experience the show. He explained to his friends who these Latino stars were: "Marc Anthony is our Frank Sinatra! Rubén Blades is our Bob Dylan!" His enthusiasm proved infectious; the team was convinced it was going to be "the best musical ever!" But more than two hours later, they sat in a daze, disappointed. *The Capeman* didn't work onstage. It was long and boring and confusing. The *New York Times* review compared seeing the musical to "watching a mortally wounded animal." *The Capeman* closed after only sixty-eight performances, losing its eleven-million-dollar investment—one of the biggest flops in Broadway history. To Lin-Manuel, it felt like a wake-up call. "You better get your shit together," Lin-Manuel remembers thinking. "No one's going to write your dream show for you."

At eighteen, he wasn't ready to write his own show with a Latin score. But after the success of *Nightmare in D Major* the year before, he did want to compose another show for Brick Prison. With graduation approaching, he thought back to the start of high school, those anguished, unmoored months when the rush of excitement about new students entering Hunter mingled with the anxieties and possibilities of starting to notice girls and hoping they noticed him. "All my spin-the-bottle traumas were still fresh," he says. "So I just wrote about my first co-ed party."

He called it *7 Minutes in Heaven*, after a spin-the-bottle variant that puts a couple in a closet for seven minutes. Instead of the stream-of-consciousness dream structure of *Nightmare*, he plotted out a romantic comedy set in the recognizable realm of Hunter social life. From the vantage point of a senior, he imagined a seventh-grader not unlike himself, a character named Justin Gomez, looking forward to an unchaperoned birthday party. Over bright ascending arpeggios, Justin sang with a mix of fear and hope alone in a spotlight:

Well, I'm only just thirteen,
There's a lot I haven't seen,
But I know that I'll see a lot tonight.
And you know, the girls are all twice my height . . .
I can hardly wait!

Lin-Manuel matched Justin with a seventh-grade heroine, Beverly, whose name he remembered from Stephen King's *It*. His Beverly doesn't have to confront a horror-movie monster, but she does face a subtler fear: a body that's becoming unrecognizable. Thinking back to the year his nose grew faster than the rest of his face, he gave Beverly a solo sung facing a mirror—less the upbeat delight of Maria's "I Feel Pretty" than the uncertain introspection of a *Chorus Line* confessional. Over moody piano chords, she sang:

Staring at my own eyes,
I can see how much my face has grown.
Is this what I'll look like when I'm old?
'Cause it's kinda strange, about to change . . .
There is a party tonight.
Amy hired a band to come and play,
And I've been feeling sick inside all day.
I wish Amy's parents hadn't gone away,
'Cause everyone's acting crazy.

Lin-Manuel worked on Beverly's song in his bedroom with his filmmaking partner Adam Rauscher. It was a space in between childhood and adolescence: Garfield sheets on the bed, a Cindy Crawford poster on the wall. Adam held the camera on Lin-Manuel as he plucked out the notes on his keyboard. They remembered their early-high-school frustration when the social rules seemed to morph without explanation. For a bridge to the song, Lin-Manuel portrayed that disorientation through Beverly's eyes:

In sixth grade everything was very clear.
"You guys go play, we're fine right over here."
But suddenly we're interested in what they have to say?
They're JUST as stupid as they were last year!

Lin-Manuel also remembered the anxious thrill of his first seventh-grade crush, when he would sit in the back of the classroom pining for a girl. For the final verse, he imagined how it would have felt to be on the receiving end of a Lin-Manuel look.

Last week in Mr. Haag's class,
Justin Gomez turned and smiled at me.
I just froze and smiled back sheepishly,
Turning CRIMSON RED,
The blood rushing to my head,
I thought to myself,
"Oh God, my stomach feels strange,
And my palms are all sweaty and gross."
And my reflection is changing,
And I wonder if I look this scared up close.
Because I am afraid.
I don't know what to make of seventh grade.

At the end of the song, Beverly picks up a tube of lip gloss and turns back toward the mirror. In two dozen lines, she'd gone through confusion at her own reflection, nausea at anticipating the party, annoyance at new social expectations, an anxious metamorphosis at Justin's smile, and the decision to put on makeup. Beverly's song had a beginning, a middle, and an end, taking her to a different place than where she'd started.

It felt like a different place for Lin-Manuel too. "It's the first time I wrote a real song where a character goes on a journey," he says. "Everything in *Nightmare* was song fragments, snapshots of where the characters were. But just through the osmosis of mounting shows and seeing shows, the writing was getting more interesting." What's more, Beverly's journey felt true to his voice, no longer an imitation of *Rent* or *Les Misérables*. The voice was vulnerable, funny, self-reflective, honest. "It's the first song I wrote that sounds like me."

Part of his newfound sophistication came from having done more shows; another part came from working with a musical arranger. Mark Roaquin, a senior who accompanied Jazz Chorus and conducted the band for *West Side Story*, helped Lin-Manuel notate the instrumental parts for *7 Minutes*. "Lin would pluck out notes on the piano and I would write them down," Mark says. He might suggest doubling a note in the left hand to amplify the bass sound or adding a missing part of a chord to fill in the harmony. Mark noticed that Lin-Manuel tended not to follow standard chord progressions; he would move to an unexpected chord, though not so far afield that a listener would get lost. "I loved pointing out to Lin: 'This is cool, because you'd expect to go *here*, but you're doing *that* instead,'" Mark says.

Earlier in high school, when Lin-Manuel visited Alex Sarlin's apartment to work on his lovelorn songs, Alex had relayed a lesson from his own piano teacher: You could jump from any major chord to another major chord or between any two minor chords, even if they weren't in the same key, and it wouldn't sound jarring. "You don't have to know eight chord progressions or complex theory or what Sondheim did," Alex explains. "You can just go with your gut."

That lesson freed Lin-Manuel. He didn't know eight chord progressions, but he could hear when a chord matched a character's feelings. And now he could let the chords follow the dramatic swerves of a character's journey, like Beverly's shifting emotions, rather than hewing to a traditional pattern. As an arranger, Mark picked up on those surprise chords and drew out their colors to make them even more interesting—adding tension with an unresolved seventh chord, supplying power with a reinforced fifth note. Scoring for violin and flute heightened Beverly's anxious reflections. A pulsing drum represented her heartbeat. As Mark says, Lin-Manuel "was excited to collaborate, to spout something creative and to have me formalize it."

The other surprise in Lin-Manuel's composition came from his choice of characters. Seniors expected to star in the shows, but Lin-Manuel had written all the lead roles for thirteen-year-olds. He had thought back to the seniors who took a chance on him when he auditioned for Brick as an eighth-grader, with Dr. Herbert's encouragement. "I wished there were more parts for younger kids," he says. "After directing *West Side Story*, I knew there were talented kids in earlier grades." His fellow seniors noted the unusual casting—some with resentment, but most with admiration.

"To be a twelfth-grade boy and to be like, 'There's a talent pool of eighth-grade girls who deserve to have their light shine'—it was so thoughtful," his classmate Emily Pinkowitz says. "He was figuring out how to lift everyone up."

In the show, Lin-Manuel flanked Beverly and Justin with a pair of friends each, one sexually confident and adventurous, the other goofily immature, creating male and female triptychs of the varied paths he'd experienced into adolescence. He studded their dialogue with pop-culture markers his Hunter audience would recognize: early-'90s references to television shows like *Saved by the Bell* and the reggae hit "Informer." Then, at the party, the spin-the-bottle game sends Beverly and Justin to the closet together. "Go, Justin! Go, Justin!" the rest of the kids shout outside the closet door. But instead of a scene of macho conquest, Lin-Manuel envisioned tender insecurity. "I have to say . . . I'm—new at this. And I'm afraid," Justin stammers to Beverly.

"Hey, it's okay," she reassures him, "me too."

As the partygoers count the time remaining ("Three minutes left!"), Beverly takes Justin's trembling hand.

"Hold me steady," he sings.

"Are you ready?" she asks.

Just as they lean in to kiss, the host's parents arrive home, and everyone flees.

Over its four performances, the twenty-minute-long *7 Minutes* gave its audiences approximately eighty minutes in heaven. Justin's endearing awkwardness drew laughs. Beverly's mirror solo earned a big mid-show ovation. After they fumble their first kiss, the show ends with Justin's sung confession: "This isn't how a first kiss ought to be! I'm sorry, but it's true . . . / But I want my second kiss to be with you." The auditorium sighed and applauded.

"I was proud of the ending more than anything," Lin-Manuel says. "It wasn't like the John Hughes stuff my sister was watching. It was sad but still romantic, still hopeful. It was the beginning of a little complexity." Since high school at Hunter had only one entry point, all the students in the audience had been seventh-graders there, and everyone remembered the awkward excitement of embarking on young adulthood. The show's director, Lona Kaplan-Werner, a skilled singer who'd helped Lin-Manuel record the demos for *Nightmare*, was impressed with his growth as a composer since his junior year. "*Nightmare* was a series of vignettes strung together. In *7 Minutes*, the characters were deeper; the storylines flowed; there were relationships between the characters. It had a higher level of sophistication even from one year to the next." The show felt more conceptually developed for Lin-Manuel too. "It was my first show with a theme," he says. "When Amy's mom sings, 'They grow up too fast . . . what's the hurry?' I remember going, 'Oh, that's some real shit I just wrote!'"

As the end of senior year neared, Lin-Manuel looked for a college where he could double major in theater and film, preferably one close to Meredith. Given his C average across his math classes, Yale was out of the question. He'd heard about musicals that Chris Hayes was putting on at Brown, but he didn't get in. He was accepted, however, at Wesleyan, a liberal arts college in Middletown, Connecticut, which was only half an hour's drive from Meredith in New Haven. That April, he took the bus to Middletown for Wesleyan's admitted-student day.

Wesleyan's film program had been founded by a legendary professor, Jeanine Basinger, whose seminar on Alfred Hitchcock was open only to a select group of advanced film majors. But a friend from Hunter arranged to sneak Lin-Manuel into the classroom. At one point, he mustered the courage to raise his hand and volunteer an interpretation. An older student, who happened to be Martin Scorsese's daughter, shot back a counterargument. Professor Basinger let the discussion run for two and a half hours, long past the scheduled end. Lin-Manuel had to sprint down the hill to catch his bus back to New York City.

"I remember being like, *I want to go to school where class runs over because everyone's so excited about what they're discussing*," Lin-Manuel says. "Gone will be the days when I'm begging everyone to come to my house to make a movie." When he moved into his dorm room at the end of August, he hung a Puerto Rican flag out his window and blasted Marc Anthony. He was going to find his people.

4

LA CASA

● ●

*L*in-Manuel arrived at Wesleyan like a hurricane. As soon as he moved into his dorm, he asked the other freshmen if they wanted to see a musical he'd written in high school. Five new friends from down the hall filed into his room, expecting to watch a grainy VHS tape. To their surprise, Lin-Manuel performed the entirety of *7 Minutes in Heaven* himself, a cappella, acting and singing all the parts as they sat on the bed facing him, gobsmacked. To indicate which character he was playing, he'd rotate his Kangol cap. "I'd never seen anything like it," one of the freshmen, Jake Cohen, says. The one-man dorm-room show was almost too much, he says, but "Lin was so impressive that you couldn't help but be swept up in it. I think everyone in that room was like, 'I'd be surprised if this guy doesn't get famous someday.'"

Part of Lin-Manuel's confidence in sharing his work came from his Hunter successes. Over the past four years, he'd starred in, directed, and written his own musicals, made two feature films, and been lauded for all of it. Part came from his lifelong love of applause. And part came from dating Meredith. When he'd started high school, he felt adrift and insecure. When he entered college, he had a steady, long-term relationship to anchor him, both a romantic pairing and an artistic partnership. In his sister's old Saturn wagon that his parents gave him after he passed his driver's test the day before he left for Wesleyan, he often popped down to New Haven for the weekend, rapping to Big Pun and OutKast on the way, and stayed in Meredith's dorm, no parents in sight. He and Meredith wowed her roommates with karaoke duets from *Les Misérables*. Back on the Wesleyan campus, Lin-Manuel got the part of an alluring cowboy in *Molly's Dream*, a surreal comedy by María Irene Fornés. Before winter break, he was cast as Jesus in a senior's main-stage production of *Jesus Christ Superstar*.

Lin-Manuel's timing was lucky. Musicals weren't often performed at Wesleyan; the productions tended toward the politically engaged avant-garde. The theater department faculty favored works of European modernism—Chekhov, Strindberg, Brecht—and students put on weighty twentieth-century plays like *Equus* and *Waiting for Godot*.

But one risk-taking senior came up with an unconventional approach. Dani Snyder (now Dani Snyder-Young, a theater professor) was studying Prague's political theater, exploring Jewish resistance movements during the Nazi occupation. She'd learned about the tension between the Jewish elders who wanted to accommodate the occupiers to protect their people from reprisals and the more radical elements who wanted to resist. Suddenly, Judas's lyrics from *Jesus Christ Superstar* popped into her head: "We are occupied! Have you forgotten how put down we are? / . . . They'll crush us if we go too far." She decided to stage *Jesus Christ Superstar* and set it in Prague's Jewish Quarter in 1941.

With her concept in place, Dani needed a superstar. Lin-Manuel auditioned, and when the cast list appeared, he ran back to his dorm room to tell his friends: "I'm Jesus!" He'd been itching to play Jesus ever since *Godspell* in tenth grade. The Jesus-Judas dynamic fascinated him as a case study in not only fraught friendship but leadership. In composer Andrew Lloyd Webber and lyricist Tim Rice's retelling of the Gospels, both Judas and Jesus want to help their people, but they disagree on tactics. Judas favors caution, fearful of riling up the Romans, whereas Jesus is a revolutionary, the head of an unruly mob that eventually turns on him. Backed by the department's resources, Dani developed a dramatic staging with Jesus's opponents gradually revealing their Nazi armbands. "The fun thing about doing a show that big was learning what I didn't know in high school," Lin-Manuel says. "I thought I knew everything, but it was a different level of professionalism than I was used to."

Many Wesleyan students' first glimpse of Lin-Manuel came as he stood on the stage of the Center for the Arts in a white suit, a yellow star affixed to his vest, a barbed-wire crown on his head. It was also their introduction to the Miranda family; his parents brought a busload of friends and relatives up to Middletown for the Saturday-night show, and when the bus got caught in a snowstorm, the performance was delayed for a few minutes until the Miranda delegation arrived.

When it was time for Jesus's big solo, the audience saw something unexpected. Usually, Jesus was portrayed as a rock god. His anthem came on "Gethsemane (I Only Want to Say)," a tortured meditation on mortality the night before his crucifixion that climaxed on a wailing "Why?" several octaves into the stratosphere. On the Wesleyan stage, Lin-Manuel couldn't reach falsetto heaven, but he brought something else—less virtuosic, more vulnerable. He spoke-sang the words, his brown eyes swelling, his mouth agape, his eyebrows arched in agony, as he pleaded: "Why should I *die*?" His voice wasn't pretty, but it sounded genuine, like a nineteen-year-old Latino New Yorker grappling with his lifelong fear of dying young.

The audience sat in silence, stunned. Then they started to applaud. "He was incredible," says Meredith, who came up for the performance. "He was exploring a desperate situation; it felt like an important shift in the depth and intensity of what he was willing to do onstage." This *Superstar* unnerved the audience. Luz was so distraught at seeing her son crucified that she prayed her rosary every night for a month afterward.

Emboldened by what he'd learned from Dani about staging an ambitious show, he decided to remount *7 Minutes in Heaven*, his senior musical, with college students instead of thirteen-year-olds. He applied to stage it in the basement of his dorm, an erstwhile café that had become a multipurpose space for improv-comedy shows and poetry slams. The WestCo Café didn't have a lighting grid, so every night, his design team borrowed lights from a senior who was putting on a play in the campus gym. "I was like, 'Who is this freshman, and why are we taking down the lights?'" the senior, whose name was Thomas Kail, said he asked his lighting crew. "I was told, 'It's this kid, his name is Lin-Manuel Miranda, he wrote a musical, and he's staged it in his dorm.' I was like, 'Well, he sounds like a disaster, and he's stealing our stuff.'"

This was Lin-Manuel's first year of college-level classes, and he found it stressful to spend every free moment at rehearsals. He started to have trouble falling asleep. As a child, when he felt school-related anxieties, his mother would soothe him at bedtime by singing him lullabies. Now, as a college freshman, he turned to his mother again. "He called me and said, 'Mom, I'm having a hard time sleeping. Would you record some of the songs you used to sing to help me go to sleep?'" Luz says. "I said, 'Sure, honey.'" She sang "April Showers" and "California, Here I Come" into a cassette tape and sent it to her son. She could tell he was feeling more comfortable when he turned the greeting on his dorm-room phone line into a song.

Soon, everyone's phone at Wesleyan had a Lin-Manuel original jingle. In the landline era, students had to dial a designated extension to hear their voice messages, and the college advertised upcoming events on an announcement service, the Bulletin Broadcast Review, that played automatically before the messages. The official announcements tended to be rote recordings, but Lin-Manuel found out that he could record his own announcements to advertise his shows. He composed goofy ditties on his keyboard and sang them into the announcement line: "Bulletin Broadcast Review / I wrote this song for you!" It was his first experiment in mass media, a way to perform for thousands of students at once. Even students who'd never met him knew of him from his jingles, a publicity gambit that also functioned as a creative outlet. "I just wanted to make stuff and have people react to it," he says.

To Lin-Manuel's disappointment, Wesleyan's film program didn't offer as many opportunities to make stuff as he had hoped. The class on film production was reserved for juniors who had been accepted into the major, and only then did they gain access to the department's equipment. To reach that inner circle, freshmen and sophomores had to earn top grades in gateway classes focused on film history and theory. Although Lin-Manuel enjoyed discussing classic MGM musicals, he wasn't as excited in his classes as he had been at Hunter when he was shooting his own movies. "It felt like a long distance from theory to making," he says.

Meanwhile, theater at Wesleyan was "much more DIY, hands-on." He was starring in shows, directing his own musical, helping backstage on his friends' plays. The theater department's introductory requirement was the opposite of the film program's; in Basic Production Technique, students put in hundreds of hours on actual productions. What's more, Wesleyan's theater department offered a fund to support students' projects, whereas film majors had to cover much of the cost of their senior theses themselves. "People were like, 'This guy's rich, so his film looks great,'" Lin-Manuel says. "I'm fucked!" His parents were already working multiple jobs to pay his tuition. He decided to declare his theater major. "It became about the future you can see versus the future you can't."

At the end of his freshman year, Lin-Manuel applied to live in the Latino program house, La Casa de Albizu Campos. It took its name from a Puerto Rican independence leader, Pedro Albizu Campos, who was jailed after nationalist uprisings against US control of the island. (Lin-Manuel's great-uncle Gilberto Concepción de Gracia, the founding president of the Puerto Rican Independence Party, represented Albizu Campos in his legal appeal.) The students chosen to live in La Casa for their sophomore year planned events for the whole campus, and Lin-Manuel offered to contribute in the performing arts. That fall, he joined seven other sophomores in the two-story wood-frame house half a mile from the main campus, set back from the street by a row of trees, facing the Malcolm X House. On the mantelpiece in the living room, he placed a photo of his parents and an album by Menudo, the Puerto Rican boy band where Ricky Martin got his start. For the first time in his life, he was living with Latinos beyond his own family.

Most of his friends at Hunter and even at Wesleyan had been white. Now he had friends right outside his door who were Puerto Rican, Guatemalan, El Salvadoran. They came from different backgrounds—one's parents worked at a bodega, another's had graduated from Wesleyan, another's hadn't attended college. But most of their parents, like Lin-Manuel's, had immigrated to New York, and most of them, like him, grew up straddling multiple geographies, languages, pronunciations of their names. At a predominantly white institution like Wesleyan, La Casa felt like their own island, a place where they could fry plátanos in the kitchen and blast salsa and merengue at their Thursday-night house parties. They also put on talent shows with Caliente, the Latin dance troupe; Lin-Manuel played a piragua guy selling shaved ice from a cart in a sketch about summertime pleasures in the city set to Gran Combo's "Un Verano en Nueva York."

Their acts of cultural translation echoed Latin artists beyond Wesleyan. The year Lin-Manuel's cohort moved into La Casa, 1999, coincided with the so-called Latin Explosion in pop music. Ricky Martin topped the charts with "Livin' la Vida Loca," a Spanglish title engineered to bring Latin sounds to non-Spanish-speaking audiences. Enrique Iglesias followed with his hit "Bailamos." Jennifer Lopez launched her music career, and Marc Anthony released his first English-language album. Lin-Manuel and his housemates were tickled to see the artists they'd grown up listening to in Spanish gaining national recognition. When Marc Anthony's concert at Madison Square Garden played on HBO, they watched it together, mocking his histrionics and loving them too. Their bicultural identities had started to map onto American pop culture.

Lin-Manuel developed a new ambition: to write a full-length musical that reflected all of his identity. His twenty-minute Brick Prison shows had tapped into his hopes and nightmares, but their songs still sounded like secondhand *Rent*: pop-rock numbers with guitar, bass, and drums. Jonathan Larson's lesson wasn't that you should write a '90s rock musical. It was that you should tell an urgent story from your life with the music that you love. Lin-Manuel loved the salsa and bachata that he'd grown up dancing to with his parents. He loved the hip-hop on mixtapes he traded with his high-school friends. He loved his parents' cast albums, too, and his sister's 1980s pop cassettes, and Disney scores, and action-movie soundtracks, and the 1990s slow jams he put on special mixtapes for Meredith. But he'd never brought all those parts of himself into one score. And aside from asking his dad to teach the Hunter *West Side Story* cast how to sound Puerto Rican, he hadn't made a show that felt like home, in all its overlapping complexities. La Casa opened the door for him to try his own story. "Between the Latin-pop crossover that was happening and *my* Latin crossover that was happening at the same time," he says, "it was like I had permission to draw on this music I'd been listening to all my life."

He started with two songs. "I was intimidated by Latin music, by polyrhythmic complexity," he says. So he took a familiar setup that he could score to a salsa tune. He opened on a pair of guys, one a romantic monogamist, the other a cynical playboy—a variation on the friend contrasts from *7 Minutes*. He constructed a first name out of his own for the romantic, a sensitive songwriter—*Lin*coln. For the cynic, he borrowed the first name of a smooth young gangster in the movie *Carlito's Way*, "Benny Blanco from the Bronx." The guys were in their twenties, ribbing one another as they waited for the A Train to take them home to Washington Heights. Over a jaunty piano polyrhythm, they pop into adjacent phone booths, where Lincoln croons his love to his "baby doll" while Benny boasts of a night with a "superfreak" he met last week.

Lin-Manuel was working through newfound emotions, as his long-term commitment to Meredith came up against his college friends' attractions and hookups. "Our college time was less optimal than our high-school time," Meredith remembers. "I felt like I kind of limited my social relationships in college because of how close I was to him." They still enjoyed wonderful visits, goofing around and supporting each other's pursuits. Lin-Manuel went to Yale to see Meredith perform a leading role in *As You Like It*, and when she was feeling homesick, he surprised her by turning up in a tuxedo for a black-tie party in her dorm. But he, too, started to wonder if he was limiting himself. He had crushes on classmates and castmates. If he stayed with Meredith, would he end up missing out or getting hurt? For the second song in his new musical, he wrote a tender ballad that Benny's mom sings to him in a flashback after his father walks out on the family. "Never give your heart away," she warns on a rueful descending melody, hoping to protect him from heartbreak. "Save it for yourself."

Equipped with his two songs, Lin-Manuel mustered the courage to approach a senior who had started the Playwright's Attic, a program for student writers to develop original work—a kind of Brick Prison at Wesleyan. Usually, the Playwright's Attic hosted readings of plays, but Lin-Manuel asked if he could workshop a musical instead. "There was a snobbish sense at Wesleyan that musical theater wasn't serious theater," M. Graham Smith, the senior (who went by Matt at the time), says. "Lin really wanted to change that." Impressed by this new student's ambition, Matt agreed to direct a reading of the opening scene. Lin-Manuel was thrilled. He couldn't believe that the senior theater star wanted to stage his nascent show. Matt, in turn, admired the sophomore's willingness to probe vulnerable feelings at a college that favored sardonic, intellectual approaches to art. "It's rare to meet someone who feels so comfortable and confident in the size of his emotions," says Matt, now a professional director. "There's a real joy to his generosity and creativity."

Under Matt's guidance, the Playwright's Attic reading went well. Matt told Lin-Manuel to keep writing; perhaps they could put on a full production in the spring. In the notebook for his astronomy class, Lin-Manuel sketched a subway train below the title he had in mind: "In the Heights."

Then Matt asked Lin-Manuel to meet him in the campus center. He had bad news. Given the demands of his own senior project, he didn't have time to direct the full show. Lin-Manuel's face fell. "I had a day of heartbreak," he says, "but I was too pregnant with it not to do it. If Matt wasn't going to direct it, I had to do it myself." With Matt's support, he applied to Second Stage, the student-run theater group, for a spring slot. He got it.

With a production deadline looming, he sped ahead. Over winter break, back in his parents' home, he composed a dozen songs. "Lin would sing new songs into my voicemail," Matt says. "There would be a song that got cut off after the two-minute limit, and then he'd keep singing on a return call." He wrote a salsa fantasy song for the heroine, Nina Rosario, who comes home from Yale wondering if she'll still find the Washington Heights of her dreams. He wrote a spoof Britney Spears pop number for Nina's best friend, Vanessa, who attracts boys at a nightclub. He wrote a pointed freestyle introduction for Benny, questioning the violence pinned to Latinos on Broadway from *West Side Story* through *The Capeman*. He wrote a Pharcyde-style rap for Benny's bodega buddy Usnavi, misnamed by his Dominican immigrant parents for the US Navy vessel that brought them over. ("I'm Usnavi, the kid sippin' Mondavi, with business sovvy / Or is it savvy? Either way, you're glad to have me.") He wrote a merengue chorus, a pop bolero, and an R&B ballad. "Something was bubbling up inside him," his mother says.

He drew inspiration from both his newfound sense of Latino community in La Casa and his changing relationship with Meredith. During winter break, she'd left for a semester in the Dominican Republic. "I needed space," she says. "We were so intertwined that I felt I wasn't able to develop." He worried about what would happen to them. His mother could sense his roiling emotions. "He was going through angst," Luz says. "He came home and went into a room, and it all came out." He cried as he imagined each of his characters' frustrated passions. Lincoln leaves endless messages for a woman who never returns his calls. Lincoln's sister, Nina, pines for his best friend, Benny, but after Nina and Benny spend the night together, Lincoln finds them in bed and, furious, reveals that

Benny's also been hooking up with Nina's friend Vanessa. Then comes the big twist: To get revenge on Lincoln, Nina tells Benny that Lincoln's girlfriend is imaginary. From reading his song notebook, she knows that the person Lincoln really loves is Benny. "Now everybody's spoken! / And everybody's broken, cracked wide open!" she sings in the show's climax.

The story of a man in love with his male best friend had been playing in Lin-Manuel's imagination for a while. The summer before he left for college, his own best friend from elementary school shared that he was gay and had started dating a man. "I felt the awesome responsibility of being trusted with that," Lin-Manuel says. "I couldn't imagine holding that in—not just one person I have a crush on, but an entire gender. That 'What if?' went into the creation of *In the Heights*." At spin-the-bottle parties in college, among sexually fluid theater majors, Lin-Manuel kissed boys as well as girls. (A joke at the time described Wesleyan as "50 percent gay, 25 percent bi, 25 percent freshmen.") In his sophomore year, he became enamored with Matt, the senior director, and "between my talent crush on him and my crush on him," he says, "I didn't know which way was up. He was a gorgeous boy making beautiful art. It wasn't a far leap to put those feelings into Lincoln."

But what about Lin-Manuel's feelings for Meredith? While she studied in the Dominican Republic, they talked nearly every night. "I dragged the phone into my room," she says. "I almost got kicked out of my homestay." She helped Lin-Manuel work through his ideas for *In the Heights* and shared his sense of discovery when he figured out Lincoln's love for Benny. He even visited her on the island. But when he returned to Connecticut, he felt bereft. He couldn't be with her, but because she was his girlfriend, he couldn't be with anyone else either. His housemates often found him in the living room at La Casa under a blanket, curled up in a ball. They heard him writing at all hours in his bedroom, tinkering on his keyboard. "I sublimated my emotional life into working on the show," he says. "I don't think it's a coincidence that no one has a happy ending in that draft of *In the Heights*. There are unrequited crushes everywhere. Everyone's in love, and no one can have it."

Lin-Manuel sent Meredith a copy of the script, inscribed to her: "My salty tears and greatest joys fill this manuscript, and every page is for you.

Without you, there would be no *In the Heights*. Your love and existence inspire me to no end. You know that I am yours, and your life is my own." She could tell, though, that the musical's uncertain storylines reflected his confusion about their future. "He was kind of wrestling with our relationship through those characters," Meredith says.

With the script in place, he started rallying his team. His friend Sara Elisa Lesin (now Miller), a dancer born in Venezuela, choreographed *Jesus Christ Superstar*; he sent her a cassette with *In the Heights* song demos labeled *Get to work!* The props designer from *Superstar* scoured New England for spare phone booths. A Musical Rep friend who was a year ahead of him at Wesleyan agreed to be the vocal director. As in high school, he was eager to collaborate with classmates who could compensate for the skills he lacked. (Matt would be credited in the program as "consigliere.")

Lin-Manuel posted an audition notice headlined "¡WEPA!" to solicit "as diverse a cast as humanly possible" for songs that "range from pop to Salsa to Hip-Hop and back." As at Hunter, Wesleyan's theater program didn't have many student actors of color, but now Lin-Manuel could recruit his friends from groups across campus who weren't the standard theater kids. Neighbors from La Casa filled in the community parts. All that was missing was an actress who could play Nina. She had to dance, fall in love, and carry the show's title song, "En Washington Heights."

Aileen Payumo had just transferred to Wesleyan as a sophomore. The daughter of a statesman in the Philippines, she hadn't yet found her people on campus, but when she said she loved musical theater, an older student told her to try out for *In the Heights*. When she arrived at the designated time, however, she saw that her name was crossed out; she'd been cast in a different show. Lin-Manuel was leaving the room. "Hi! I'm Aileen. Can I please audition?" she begged. He agreed. She sang "On My Own," the heartbreak ballad from *Les Misérables*. She had silky black hair, a radiant smile, and a gorgeous voice, strong and sweet. She got the part.

The newly formed ensemble started to cohere under Lin-Manuel's direction. "It felt like we were bringing elements of our hood to the story," Julio Pabón, a dancer who played Usnavi, says. Born in the Bronx, he was the son of a Puerto Rican civil rights leader who became the city's director of Hispanic affairs. Julio had done plays in high school, but *In the Heights* tapped a different side of him, even a different walk. "I'd never acted out anything where I had to bop to a hip-hop beat," he says. "You do that with your boys; you do that at a party. You don't do that in front of an audience. It felt like we were partying on stage."

But soon Lin-Manuel ran into another problem. *In the Heights* was scheduled to begin its three-day run on the same April 2000 weekend as the campus millennium concert, in which all the best musicians were performing. "I was like, 'Oh, shit, I won't have a band!'" He worked out a solution: He could use the Wesleyan theater fund to rent a recording studio in Middletown a few weeks before the performances. (His dad chipped in too.) His coveted musicians came in to lay down the tracks—trumpet, drums, bass—that would play during the show, and he joined them on keyboard. Then he brought in the cast to record the songs, even though they hadn't finished rehearsing. He figured that if the show was a hit, they could sell a cast album and make back the cost of the studio rental. To attract audiences, he recorded a special jingle for the Bulletin Broadcast Review.

On opening night, the cast sensed something happening. The audience loved the salsa dancing in the club. They laughed at the story of Usnavi's name. They swooned for Aileen's singing voice. They perked up for Usnavi's and Benny's raps. They gasped at the revelation that Lincoln was in love with Benny. At the end, they gave the cast a standing ovation. The next night, the line for tickets ran around the block. "People were camping out, trying to get in off the cancellation line," Owen Panettieri, the house manager, says. "It was very unusual for somebody to be doing an original musical, and people were interested in seeing the show." Since the cast came from so many varied parts of campus life, a sizable portion of the student population had a connection to the performance. "The diversity of the show meant a bigger audience," Lin-Manuel notes. Luis and Luz brought the Miranda caravan, too, a bus full of neighbors eager to see Washington Heights re-created in a theater. Everyone from La Casa turned out as well. Leana Amáez, who lived upstairs from Lin-Manuel, was born in East Harlem and had seen *West Side Story* and *The Capeman*. This was a new vision. "My housemates were performing this genuinely joyful representation of Latinidad that I had never seen on a stage," she recalls. "It's not just Lin's voice that's in that show. It's hip-hop, it's the story of immigrants, it's all the people who influenced him."

Word got out that this original musical by a sophomore was worth seeing. A couple of popular seniors in the theater program, Neil Patrick Stewart and John Buffalo Mailer, hadn't reserved tickets but showed up anyway, expecting to be admitted. No luck. They ended up watching the show perched in the rafters above the lighting booth, impressed by the sophomore's audacity and creativity. They were graduating shortly and planned to found a theater company in New York. Neil bought a CD of the cast recording, hoping the new company could put it on.

In the Heights was a triumph. After a weekend of sold-out performances, Aileen and the other actors felt like rock stars, hailed across campus. Lin-Manuel had made his dream show.

When he returned home to New York at the end of the spring semester, though, he didn't feel settled. Meredith was coming back from the Dominican Republic, and neither of them knew what to do. Like many high-school relationships, theirs might not have had a future, but it still felt painful to face cracking the bond that had been so meaningful for both of them. "We were worried about needing to break up but not wanting to admit it," Meredith says. Their worlds were so enmeshed that, for her, the prospect of ending their relationship felt like blowing up her life. She'd become so close to the Mirandas that Mundi kept a picture of Meredith in her bedroom. Luis adored her as well; he thought her care and insightfulness made her a wonderful influence on his son. But she and Lin-Manuel felt stuck. "We genuinely loved each other," he says. "We didn't want to be in the relationship, but we didn't know how to get out of it."

He developed a nervous tic, incessantly cracking his neck until the pain became unbearable. Luz took him to a specialist who said there was nothing wrong with him physically but that nervous tics were caused by stress. "What's going on?" the doctor asked. Lin-Manuel burst into tears. He confessed that he wanted to end his relationship, but he didn't want to hurt his girlfriend.

Instead of offering medicine or physical therapy, the doctor told him a story. He said that another aspiring artist, the composer Giuseppe Verdi, didn't write his first masterpiece until after the untimely death of his wife and children. "You're trying to avoid going through pain or causing pain," the doctor said. "I'm here to tell you that you'll have to survive it to be any kind of artist."

It was a striking lesson. The next day, after a walk through New York City and a heartfelt talk, Lin-Manuel and Meredith broke up.

When he heard the news, Luis shouted at Luz: "What the fuck kind of doctor did you take him to?"

5

BASKET CASE

• •

*A*fter a summer in therapy, where he talked through his feelings about ending his relationship with Meredith, Lin-Manuel returned to Wesleyan for his junior year, uncoupled for the first time since tenth grade. Having finished his stint in La Casa, he and Sara, the choreographer for *Superstar* and *Heights*, moved into an apartment together. Sara had a boyfriend, and Lin-Manuel started testing out the opportunities of single life in college. Now he could act on all the crushes he'd harbored while Meredith was far away. He soon learned that *West Side Story* didn't work as a seduction movie. "Once 'Gee, Officer Krupke' came on, I had to turn it off. You can't make out to that!"

He was also finding the freedom to perform with groups across campus. Even though Wesleyan identified itself as a multicultural university, many students found its campus somewhat self-segregated. Black and Latino students had separate program houses and often sat at separate tables in the cafeteria. The improv-comedy diehards didn't always mix with the a cappella singers; the dancers might avoid the theater kids. But Lin-Manuel was a cultural omnivore. He soloed with Ebony Singers, the gospel choir. He recorded an album with the Mazel Tones, the Jewish a cappella group. He danced with Caliente, the Latin crew. He toted his keyboard to play improv music games with Desperate Measures, a comedy troupe. "Lin was at the center of the Venn diagram," Alex Horwitz, a filmmaker and one of the improv guys, says. "He moved effortlessly between groups. He just loved it all equally."

Out of these disparate influences, he got an idea for his next project. As he drove around Middletown in his old Saturn wagon, he played mixtapes of songs from the 1990s, his formative high-school listening era. "I was making mixes for myself in the car, and slowly the mixes were turning into a narrative in my head," he says. If he figured out the right songs, he could bring together all the school cliques—the punks and the jocks, the clowns and the stoners, the hip-hop heads and the grunge headbangers— on a wave of '90s pop-culture nostalgia. He'd always been drawn to songs that told a story, like Pearl Jam's "Jeremy," an anguished grunge hit about a teenage loner who fantasizes about ruling his world but, neglected by his parents and bullied by classmates, finally shoots himself at school. What if Jeremy were the protagonist of a '90s outsider musical?

The show could open with Pearl Jam's song, establishing the story, then flash back to show Jeremy's path to ending his life. His defining number could be "Basket Case," by Green Day, the alt-rock cry of a neurotic begging for someone to heed his anxieties. He could be taunted by the alpha boys who rapped insults from the Pharcyde's "Ya Mama." And what if Jeremy fell in love with the enraged heroine of Alanis Morissette's breakup anthem "You Oughta Know"? "I was unlocking the one-act play inside these pop songs," Lin-Manuel says. "I was trying to prove Jonathan Larson's thesis that pop music and theater music could be friends again and that there are good stories in both."

Back in his apartment, he mentioned to his friend Alex Horwitz that he had an idea for a jukebox musical—a story about a high-school shooter told through '90s pop songs. "He told me the contours of the story, and it worked so well," Alex says. "The cleverness of it couldn't be denied. All the puzzle pieces fit together." Granted, the premise was dark, and the high-school shootings at Columbine two years earlier were a recent memory, if not yet a horrifyingly common one. But for college theater kids, the more angsty and intense the narrative, the better. ("At Wesleyan, it wasn't enough to crucify Jesus Christ," M. Graham Smith says, remembering the Nazi setting of the *Superstar* production. "You also had to put him in a concentration camp.") Lin-Manuel decided to name his musical after the Green Day song, with a slangy spelling: *Basketcase: A Luv Story.* Alex, who'd drawn the poster for *In the Heights* the year before—an uptown apartment building morphing into the A Train—sketched an illustration for the new show: a stick figure with angry eyebrows brandishing a gun.

Lin-Manuel had a more personal impulse behind the show as well. *Basketcase*'s tormented protagonist, Jeremy, was another of Lin-Manuel's heroes who, like Jonathan Larson and Alexander Hamilton, had his promising life cut short by an early death. Breaking up with Meredith had also revived Lin-Manuel's fear that anyone he loved would come to harm. In *Basketcase*, the fate that *Nightmare in D Major* had narrowly avoided—a girlfriend killed amid high-school terrors—comes true. Jeremy's girlfriend dies, thanks to a minor character who gives her too many hallucinogens at a party. That minor character was the role Lin-Manuel chose to play—a boy who admits, in the chorus of a self-lacerating Eminem rap, that the girl's suffering is "My Fault."

Lin-Manuel had begun dating Aileen Payumo, the dark-haired, strong-voiced star of *In the Heights*. Everyone seemed to cherish Aileen; classmates remember her as "effervescent," "sweetly honest," "adorable." An in-demand performer from the moment she arrived at Wesleyan from the Philippines, her roommate says, "She and Lin matched in that way: outsiders able to shine in the Wesleyan theater community." Once Aileen got to know the Mirandas, she saw Lin-Manuel's theater ventures as emblematic of their influence. "His father gave him that drive," she says, "but his mother gave him his heart. He feels so deeply, and he is able to translate that into art. I really fell in love with his heart." To impress Aileen, Lin-Manuel taught himself a bit of her first language, making flash cards with Tagalog and English phrases: "*Mahal kita*, I love you."

As he approached the end of college, Lin-Manuel tried to figure out his path forward. Knowing he'd need to spend most of his senior year working on his thesis, he auditioned actors for *Basketcase* in the spring of his junior year, planning to put on the show when they returned to campus in September. Aileen agreed to serve as vocal coach. And thanks to her, he met another key partner. That junior year, Aileen produced the musical *Once on This Island*, and Lin-Manuel thought that the orchestra for the show sounded terrific. After the show, he introduced himself to the music director, a fellow junior and saxophone virtuoso named Bill Sherman. "He came up to me," Bill says, "and said, 'I'm Aileen's boyfriend. I don't know you, and you don't know me, but I think we should work together for a really long time.'" Bill suggested they start with a drink.

They hit it off. A big, goofy guy from Long Island who'd dropped out of a frat, Bill had serious music chops. He'd studied jazz; he'd traveled to Ghana to learn West African rhythms; and he fronted Wesleyan's highlife band, Professor Neon. In Bill, Lin-Manuel recognized a versatile artist who was fun to hang with and could make his musical ideas fly. He asked Bill to direct the music for *Basketcase*. Bill was happy to team up with an ambitious kid who seemed like "a sponge of everything." Even though everyone knew the recorded versions of the '90s songs, Lin-Manuel wanted the music to be played live with the actors doing the vocals. He'd had a hard time writing down the instrumental parts for *In the Heights*, but Bill could write out a score easily, and he knew how to communicate with musicians. "Bill orchestrated Eminem and Destiny's Child," Lin-Manuel says. "And he got me a really rocking band."

Basketcase was set to open in the student-run theater on Thursday, September 13, 2001. That Tuesday, the company had a tech rehearsal scheduled for the evening. Lin-Manuel planned to drive into New York City to vote in Tuesday's primary election and return for rehearsal. Before leaving Middletown that morning, he stopped by a record store to pick up Bob Dylan's new CD so he could listen to it in his car on the day it was released: September 11. When he got to the register, the clerk, who looked like a stoner, mentioned that someone had just tried to blow up the World Trade Center. Lin-Manuel knew that a failed bombing had happened in the '90s. *This guy's out of his mind*, he thought. He bought the CD, got back in his car, and turned on the radio. Then he heard the news: The Twin Towers had fallen.

The rest of the day was a dizzying swirl. He stayed in Middletown and kept trying to call his parents, but the telephone lines were jammed. Friends wandered by, checking the news, seeking solace. Updates trickled in. His parents turned out to be safe on the opposite end of Manhattan. That evening, he convened the *Basketcase* company. Opening night was in two days. One of the actors had a brother who'd worked in the Towers. It was Lin-Manuel's first experience having the world outside the theater upstage the show. "We've made this thing; the world has changed; now what do we do?" he wondered. He decided to take his cue from the cast. It would be a group decision. "We don't have to do the show," he told them. "We can cancel or postpone." But the cast shared a sense that they wanted to be doing something—even, or perhaps especially, a show that dealt with violence and death and grief. That night, they ran through the show together. People cried. "Everyone was grateful to work on something that was angsty and fucked up but not geopolitical," Lin-Manuel says. "It felt healthy and therapeutic instead of sitting at home."

On Thursday, he took a step that was unusual for the time: He came onstage at the theater to give the audience a content warning before the performance. He acknowledged that it had been a terrible week and that the show included heavy material. He explained that the cast had decided to proceed, for some as an escape from the attacks, for others as a way of processing them. He also inserted a note in the program:

> This is, in many ways, a fun rock show. But it is also a musical tragedy, with some violent, disturbing images and a sad ending. If you've seen too many of those in the past few days, please use your discretion on whether you are too upset to see this show tonight. Thank you for coming regardless.

His friend Alex, who'd designed the poster and the program, was in the house as a representative of the student theater company. "My memory of it is that the audience needed it and loved it," he says. "Just like Lin, the music was so omnivorous that there was something in there for all of us. He was able to empathize with different characters: the jocks and the nerds and the weirdos each have their moment. It was a nineties outsider's howl in musical form." For some observers, it felt more fully realized than *In the Heights*, more seamless and coherent in its integration of character, story, and song. In 2001, the jukebox-musical genre seemed like an innovation. ABBA had attracted audiences by fitting its back catalog to a romance plot in *Mamma Mia!*, and the movie *Moulin Rouge* had set a love story to familiar pop songs, but *Basketcase* felt both fresh and inviting to college students who'd just come out of the '90s themselves.

The show accomplished what Lin-Manuel had hoped: It demonstrated that pop music could tell a powerful story onstage. It also established him as the leading stage writer at Wesleyan. After *7 Minutes in Heaven, In the*

Heights, and *Basketcase,* the name Lin-Manuel Miranda had become so synonymous with theatrical premieres that a sophomore jokingly advertised a one-act festival that October with an email that began:

Come see . . .
absolutely nothing
by LIN-MANUEL MIRANDA!!!

None of these stage successes, however, translated into course credits. All the shows Lin-Manuel wrote at Wesleyan were, like his productions at Hunter, extracurricular activities put on through student-run theater organizations that allowed him to experiment and collaborate with little faculty intervention. But to earn his degree, he needed to complete a senior thesis in his major. What hadn't he done yet? He thought back on the shows he'd composed so far. *Nightmare in D Major* and *7 Minutes in Heaven* had been twenty-minute one-acts. *In the Heights* and *Basketcase* were eighty-minute shows without an intermission. For his theater thesis, he set out to write an original, full-length, two-act musical.

As a senior at Wesleyan with another transition on the horizon, he reflected on the start of college. As a freshman, he had been in a long-distance relationship with his high-school girlfriend. And then that relationship ended. He still felt bad about the breakup—his sense of growing apart while Meredith studied abroad, not knowing how to talk with her about wanting freedom, then abruptly ending it all after the conversation with his doctor. "I wish I'd handled the breakup with Meredith better," he says. "If there was a future version of me that could go back in time and do it over, that would be great."

But what if there were? What if he wrote a future version of himself? His mom liked to show him intense psychological dramas, like *Last Tango in Paris,* where an older man has a torrid, violent affair with a younger woman. What if, somehow, his older self traveled back in time to make things right with Meredith? He wanted to write a strong role for Aileen; as a theater major, she needed a big part to satisfy departmental requirements. So he decided to switch the genders in his and Meredith's situation. He'd write about a girl who goes to college while her high-school boyfriend studies abroad. The older version of the boyfriend could travel back in time to warn her not to wait around for his younger self. "And then I took the further leap: What if he had an affair with Meredith?" He envisioned it as "*Last Tango* meets *Back to the Future.*"

He ran the idea past Alex Horwitz, who'd been so enthusiastic about *Basketcase.* The new story, however, didn't make sense to him. "It was a head-scratcher," Alex says. "I was skeptical of the conceit." How did the older version of the boyfriend travel back in time? "I remember saying to Lin: 'Was it God? Is there a sci-fi element? Did lightning strike? Was it a hoax because the older guy was kind of a creep?' Lin said: 'It doesn't matter.'" He didn't think it was important to explain the time travel; he just wanted to explore whether his relationship with Meredith would have ended better if he'd been more mature.

Lin-Manuel's ambitions extended beyond college romance. He also wanted to explore a theory of lyric writing in musical theater. That October, he played a few of his songs for his friend Alex's father, Murray Horwitz, who'd won a Tony Award for creating the musical *Ain't Misbehavin'.* Murray was the first musical-theater professional that Lin-Manuel had gotten to know personally, and he valued the veteran's advice. Murray had his eye on Lin-Manuel too; after Alex's mom talked with Lin-Manuel at one of Alex's improv-comedy shows, she said to Murray, "I don't know what 'it' is, but that kid's got it!"

Murray sat on Lin-Manuel's bed as he ran through the numbers on his keyboard. Then Murray stopped him. "That's sloppy, Lin," he said, shaking his head. "The whole section is really sloppy, man." What concerned Murray were the rhymes. "You can have loose, lazy rhymes in rock, pop, do whatever you want," he explained. "But this is musical theater. Your lyrics must be airtight." He asked if Lin-Manuel owned a rhyming dictionary; when the reply was negative, Murray popped over to the campus bookstore and got him one. And he recommended that the aspiring lyricist consult Ira Gershwin's *Lyrics on Several Occasions.* "Gershwin is a *motherfucker,*" he said approvingly.

For the written version of his thesis, Lin-Manuel decided to preface his script with a twenty-page essay addressing the question Murray had raised for him: "What makes a lyric work?" In addition to Gershwin, he examined two other renowned lyricists, Oscar Hammerstein II and Alan Jay Lerner. But rather than focusing on their perfect rhyming couplets,

Lin-Manuel looked for moments when they stretched language, using slang, coining new words, or eschewing rhyme altogether. He was testing the purist philosophy that Murray had expressed. In *Porgy and Bess*, he noted, Gershwin took two words that probably wouldn't appear together in a rhyming dictionary—*children* and *villain*—and coupled them through their colloquial pronunciation in Black vernacular: "Dey tell all you chillun / De debble's a villun." In *Show Boat*, Hammerstein linked an untutored dockworker's ideas through repeated vowel sounds instead of showy pure rhyme: Ol' Man River "mus' know sumpin' / But don't say nuthin'." In *My Fair Lady*, Lerner drew on the Cockney dialect practice of inserting expletives in the middle of other words to give Eliza Doolittle her "oh so loverly" fantasy of "sittin' abso-bloomin'-lutely still." None of these lyrics struck Lin-Manuel as loose or lazy, though; instead, he saw the lyricists refreshing musical-theater form by drawing on the popular language of their respective eras, choosing the kinds of expressions their characters would use—notably Black and working-class characters.

Having discovered antecedents for the kind of lyrics he wanted to try, Lin-Manuel turned in the second half of his essay to a discussion of the lyrics in his thesis. He drew on influences as varied as Washington Heights lingo, the speech patterns of his relatives in Vega Alta, and the verses of Method Man to justify slangy rhyme pairs like *relationship* and *great and shit*.

The elders he had to satisfy in his thesis, however, were not Murray Horwitz and Ira Gershwin. To get his thesis approved, he needed the ratification of the theater faculty, and in 2001, the Wesleyan theater department was the domain of Professor Bill Francisco. An imposing man in his late sixties, Bill—as he was widely known—charmed, frustrated, dazzled, and terrified his students. Sometimes Bill seemed on board with the project. But rehearsals could be challenging. The central premise of the show remained elusive. When Annie, the heroine played by Aileen, asks the older version of her high-school boyfriend how he's appeared in her college dorm, he sings, "This is the part of the story I can't explain"; the joke around the production went "This is the part of the story Lin can't explain." At one point, Bill abruptly got up and shouted at Lin-Manuel, "Does this whole thing exist because you can't get laid?"

Still, he was driven to complete the project. That fall, Aileen took him to the West Village to see an autobiographical musical by Jonathan Larson, posthumously produced, called *Tick, Tick . . . Boom!*. It was their first time downtown since the World Trade Center attacks. A sense of precariousness—their own uncertainty about graduation, their memories of 9/11, their knowledge of Larson's early death—hovered over the evening. Seeing *Rent* with Meredith on his seventeenth birthday had made Lin-Manuel want to write musicals. But *Tick, Tick . . . Boom!* wasn't the origin story of *Rent*. It was the story of failure. Larson was singing on the eve of his thirtieth birthday, having spent the past decade working on a sci-fi rock musical that no one would produce. He heard the clock of mortality tick-ticking away while his friends left the city or moved into higher-paying fields. "It was a sneak preview of what my 20s would be," Lin-Manuel wrote. He'd thought that he was going to follow Larson to musical-theater stardom. Was he more likely to follow him to failure? Would he have the courage to keep creating even if he never lived to see professional success? After the show, Aileen had been planning to take him out for a night on the town. But when they left the theater, she saw something was off. "He was stunned," she says. "He looked like he'd been punched in the gut." He mumbled apologetically, "I have to go," then disappeared into the night.

He made it back to Middletown and raced to finish his show. However much time he had left in his life to write, he didn't have much time remaining at Wesleyan. He called his musical *On Borrowed Time*. Alex made the poster, superimposing a clock dial over an abstract photo of Aileen.

On Borrowed Time went up at the main-stage theater at the Center for the Arts the weekend after Valentine's Day. In the program, Lin-Manuel made sure to add a note calling the musical a "work-in-progress." ("Chances are, the author is backstage right now, writing more dialogue for these poor actors to memorize for tonight's show.") He thanked his advisers, perhaps flatteringly, "for their endless patience, guidance and wisdom," along with Murray Horwitz ("You are a rhyme Nazi. For this, I thank you"). He concluded, a bit cryptically for those who didn't know Meredith Summerville, "This play is for M.S. Thank you for everything."

Even as a work in progress, the show was enormously ambitious. "I was trying to push in directions I hadn't pushed before," Lin-Manuel says. With Bill Sherman arranging his score, he'd attempted a cappella harmonies, organ and cello themes, and a Gran Combo–style *montuno*. He even wrote a hip-hop party song about getting high with a refrain, "Time to Get Blizzy," that one of his roommates dared him to include. "Most people in their senior thesis try to do one thing," Matthew Lerner, the assistant stage manager, says. "Lin was trying to do six things at the same time. He was trying to work out his own psychodrama about his relationship and also make a Broadway-caliber play that was fun and also play with themes of sexuality and also make the story feel like it has delivered for you."

It didn't work. The songs were entertaining, but as Alex had warned Lin-Manuel, the audience never connected with its time-travel conceit. Bill says he didn't get it either: "I remember standing in the pit conducting and being like, *I have no idea what this is about!*" Lin-Manuel knew he had failed at the defining moment when Annie's high-school boyfriend, Michael, reveals his older self. He'd hoped that would make for a moving surprise, like the moment in *In the Heights* when the audience learned that Lincoln was secretly in love with his best friend, Benny, and everyone gasped. But when it came time for the old man lurking under a baseball cap in Annie's dorm to reveal his identity, there wasn't a gasp. The crew had tried to age the actor, who started off playing younger Michael, by graying his hair with talcum powder. As he sang, "Annie, don't you recognize my face?" he took off his cap and sat down, and the powder flew up from his hair in a cloud: *poof!* It was supposed to be a moment of heartbreak. Instead, the audience laughed. "I'll never forget that laugh," Lin-Manuel says. "My stomach feels sick at it still. There was no spell that's going to be cast. It was my fault in fifty different ways."

College, however, offered a space to fail in safety. "I think *On Borrowed Time* was basically all the best mistakes he's ever made," Aileen says. "That's where he learned a lot of his lessons." He'd rushed the process. He'd forced his ideas. He'd ignored collaborative input. But the audience had given him its own feedback. At old Michael's line "This is the part of the story I can't explain," there were more laughs. "People kept pressing me on how the time-travel worked, and I'm like, 'I don't care!'" Lin-Manuel says. "That was to the detriment of the work. The audience cares. I did not have anywhere near the craft to get anyone to buy into the premise." As his current girlfriend playing a version of his previous girlfriend, Aileen felt that there were emotional concerns underlying the craft lessons. "He was not willing to kill his baby," she says. "He really wanted this guy going back in time to fuck his young ex-girlfriend, and he wouldn't get rid of that." His mom, who didn't think the thesis was very good, wondered if all the tortured psychodramas she'd shown him had clouded his judgment.

Still, it wasn't a disaster. He'd tried new musical styles, new story structures, new lyrical forms. "I am learning," he wrote at the end of his thesis essay. "With every song I write, I am learning."

What was a learning experience for him, however, felt different for the person who, in some ways, *On Borrowed Time* was about. Meredith had graduated from Yale, found a new boyfriend, and moved to New Orleans to start Teach for America when she received the script and the cast recording in the mail from Lin-Manuel. They hadn't talked much since their breakup. She knew that he'd drawn on their relationship when he wrote *In the Heights*, and she remembered that he'd often put his anxieties about her onstage, even going back to the hero's girlfriend in *Nightmare in D Major*. But she didn't know that he'd written an entire main-stage show at Wesleyan that, she felt, made their private life uncomfortably public. As she read the script, she felt she was seeing not only their intimate history revealed but also an imagined version of her younger self having sex with a strange older man. "It was hard for me to process," she says. "He was working through big emotions, and that was his right, but I felt embarrassed at being put on display like that. It wasn't just his art; it was also my life." She wished that he had shared his feelings about their relationship with her directly before presenting them in a campus musical.

Lin-Manuel admits now that "there's a certain amount of selfishness involved" in taking the view that everything he experienced was grist for the mill. The lesson he had drawn from *My Name Is Asher Lev*—that an artist expresses what he truly feels and makes that perspective public, even if it hurts the people closest to him—did not come without consequences.

That was, however, how he'd learned to make art. Then, as graduation approached in 2002, he saw the other thesis from a senior who'd been awarded a main-stage production that year. Bajir Cannon was, in many ways, Lin-Manuel's counterpart in Wesleyan theater. Both were seniors, both advisees of Bill Francisco, both highly lauded for innovative work. But while Lin-Manuel wrote catchy musical-theater numbers, Bajir ventured into a visually adventurous mode of experimental drama based in ritual movement and symbolic design. For his thesis, Bajir adapted Antoine de Saint-Exupéry's *The Little Prince* into an exploration of love and creation. He ringed the Center for the Arts with candles and ushered the audience onstage, where they sat surrounded by black curtains. Then, at each point in the Little Prince's journey, a curtain vanished to reveal another facet of the imaginary world. A character appeared from the ceiling, spotlighted from above; the set cracked open; there was music and wonder. At the end, the Little Prince and his author, Saint-Exupéry, walked off the stage and out of the theater together, and the audience followed them, guided by lanterns that hung like floating stars. Lin-Manuel calls it "the greatest piece of theater I've ever seen."

On the drive home afterward, Aileen saw Lin-Manuel looking the same way he had after *Tick, Tick . . . Boom!*—gut-punched. "It was frustration and envy," he says. "Bajir had done everything I wanted to do. And he did it better." In the car with Aileen that night, he burst into tears. "I was crying because it was a genuinely moving piece of theater," he says. "But intermingled with that was the feeling that I *had* the school's resources and I fucking *wasted* them." All the confidence he'd built up went *poof*, like the powder in Michael's hair. He felt like a seventh-grader again, overwhelmed by his brilliant classmates. "I was right back at Hunter, and Bajir was the more talented kid."

No one knew what lay ahead. Late into the night, Wesleyan students often speculated about who would make it beyond the supportive cocoon of college theater. Sure, you might put on a show that sold out the student-run theater for three or four performances. Maybe that even earned you the esteem of your professors or older alumni. But would that translate into professional success? "We all had different people we would have thrown money into the hat for," Matthew Lerner says. "Lin was in that top echelon of people. But there was always this question: So these are the best musical-theater kids at Wesleyan, and we think they're great, but do we have any context? Is there a Lin at Vassar too?"

They were about to find out.

6

THE DRAMA BOOK SHOP

• •

As Lin-Manuel walked down the stairs to the dim basement of the Drama Book Shop in Midtown Manhattan a few weeks after graduating in May 2002, he wasn't sure what to expect. He was meeting a group of Wesleyan grads who called themselves Back House Productions. On the plus side, they'd told him that they wanted to work on *In the Heights*, the musical he'd written his sophomore year. On the minus side, they'd announced on their website that they were going to produce *In the Heights* without asking him first. Who were these guys anyway?

Three of the four he vaguely knew from college. Neil Patrick Stewart and John Buffalo Mailer, Wesleyan theater majors, had caught a sold-out performance of *In the Heights* when they were seniors, perched above the lighting booth. Anthony Veneziale, a film major and improv-comedy buff, had been the TA for a film class Lin-Manuel visited as a high-school senior, and though he graduated before Lin-Manuel arrived, he'd kept an eye on the enthusiastic student. However, the fourth guy, who had the trim build of a soccer midfielder and a mop of curly black hair, was a mystery. He was a director named Tommy Kail.

Lin-Manuel had met Tommy once before, and it hadn't gone well. The Back House crew had come up to Wesleyan in February to see their prospect's thesis production, *On Borrowed Time*. The show befuddled them. A time-travel musical? With a man on his deathbed trying to reunite with his high-school girlfriend? "I didn't care for the show," Tommy says. It was

Lin-Manuel's earlier show, the one about his neighborhood in Manhattan, that Back House wanted to develop.

He and Tommy remember that afternoon the same way—as a time-lapse movie. First there were five guys chatting in the basement, then four, then three, and finally, as evening fell, just the two of them, still talking about what *In the Heights* could be. They grabbed a bite to eat down the block, and Tommy says, "The conversation never stopped." Tommy was bursting with ideas to share. He wasn't trying to fix the show, he says; "I was just trying to actualize the thing Lin wanted to build." For instance, the Wesleyan version opened with the pals Benny and Lincoln leaving *Rent*-esque messages from separate phone booths, but Tommy thought the show should open with its third song, "En Washington Heights," so the audience could be introduced to the characters' world. He also thought that Benny and Lincoln's rapping sidekick, Usnavi, should become the show's narrator; since Usnavi ran the bodega, he knew everyone's business, so he could serve as the audience's guide to the neighborhood.

Lin-Manuel was bowled over. At Hunter and Wesleyan, his directors had seen their job as taking what he'd written and putting it onstage. He'd never had a director like Tommy, a collaborator who examined the structure of his musical so that it could connect more fully with an audience. "Two thoughts occur to me," he later recalled. "The first is: 'This guy is smarter and understands the show better than anyone I've ever met.' The second is, 'Crap. I have to completely rewrite this show.'"

What he didn't know was that Tommy had spent the past two years listening to the Wesleyan cast recording of *In the Heights*. Tommy grew up near Washington, DC, and had entered Wesleyan as a quick-witted American history major with an interest in coaching sports. The first time he directed a show, Tommy realized it was like coaching. He loved it. After graduation, he went to work at a theater in New Jersey as an assistant stage manager. By the end of the year, he'd started directing there. Soon after, he took a job as Audra McDonald's personal assistant.

Tommy had only a vague sense of the *In the Heights* composer, Lin-Manuel Miranda; he remembered him as that annoying freshman who'd nabbed the lights from Tommy's senior play for his production of *7 Minutes in Heaven*. But Neil told him to listen to the recording of *In the Heights*, so Tommy put on his headphones. What he heard surprised him. "It felt like someone was talking to me," he says. He heard young people living in New York, joking about movies, confessing crushes, rapping and singing about their dreams. "It felt like if my friends and I musicalized our life, this is what it would be," he says. "I hadn't imagined musical theater could sound like that."

Tommy listened to the *Heights* recording over and over again, waiting for Lin-Manuel to graduate so that they could start working on the show together. "I wore that CD out," he says. "It was fun; it was witty; it was alive." As he learned more about musical theater, he started envisioning ways to strengthen Lin-Manuel's composition. "Listening to that CD was his grad school," Neil says.

The Back House crew enjoyed a unique advantage over all the other college grads who started tiny theater companies in New York every year. In a city with impossibly expensive real estate, they had space. Alan Hubby, the owner of the venerable Drama Book Shop, happened to see an evening of comic one-acts they'd staged, and he liked their youthful energy. Hubby offered them the use of the shop's basement at its new location on Fortieth Street if they would do the work to convert it into a black-box theater, hauling out the junk and repainting it. ("The joke was that Back House was a moving company," Anthony says.) They didn't mind the labor, and they welcomed the chance to become the resident theater company at a hub for dramatic literature. "It occurred to us that since our lobby would be the greatest theater bookstore in the world, we should focus on playwrights and developing new work," Neil says. "So here's Lin, this playwright with a new work."

Tommy came up with a plan to develop *Heights*. They'd tackle the opening twenty minutes of the show first, then the next twenty, and so on. He gave Lin-Manuel deadlines: Every Friday, he had to bring in a new version of the song they were working on. Tommy was acting like a coach, and Lin-Manuel responded. "He's someone who moves the ball down the field every time," Tommy says. "When he brings in a rewrite, it's always a little bit closer to what we're chasing." For the updated opening number, now called "In the Heights," Lin-Manuel worked on a rap for Usnavi that set up his role as the welcoming narrator. Another of Tommy's ideas was that, for the moment, Lin-Manuel should play Usnavi. That part was changing faster than the others, and it would be easier for Lin-Manuel to perform the new raps than to teach them to someone else.

The start of the show offered a good example. After a few Pharcyde-inspired rhymes about romantic ineptitude, Lin-Manuel landed on an introduction:

I am Usnavi, and you prob'ly never heard my name.
Reports of my fame are greatly exaggerated,
Exacerbated by the fact that my syntax
Is highly complicated 'cause I emigrated
From the single greatest little place in the Caribbean:
Dominican Republic. We love it.
Now back to the subject.
It don't matter if you're white, Black, Asian, or Latin,
I'm reportin' to you live from the top of Manhattan.

Like his favorite Nuyorican rapper, Big Pun, Lin-Manuel laced these lines with complex internal rhymes: *exaggerated* and *exacerbated*, *complicated* and *emigrated*. By coupling *Latin* and *Manhattan*, he planted a flag for his uptown immigrant neighborhood, now mostly Dominican, as the island's hip-hop hub. And under the guise of humility ("you prob'ly never heard my name"), he landed a brag on behalf of his verses and the Caribbean lineage of the MCs who preceded him. He and Tommy both revered Big Pun; in fact, one of the moments that connected them at their first meeting came when they jointly recited Pun's notorious tongue-twister "Dead in the middle of Little Italy little did we know that we riddled two middlemen who didn't do diddly." But lest the audience be put off by inside references, they designed what they called on-ramps, points of entry for people who hadn't grown up in Inwood memorizing Pun and Pharcyde. Anticipating audience members adrift, Usnavi predicts:

Now some of y'all are thinking:
"Whoa, I'm up shit's creek,
I've never been north of 96th Street!"

For an on-ramp, he reminds them of a musical predecessor on that uptown ride:

Tonight you'll hear a story that is mad compelling, son,
But first you gotta make like my man Duke Ellington:
You must "Take the A Train"
Even farther than Harlem to Northern Manhattan and maintain
While I explain the drama from the past few nights—
Relax, sit tight, you're in Washington Heights!

A jazzy piano riff accompanied the line "Take the A Train" as Lin-Manuel sang in Duke Ellington's cadence, performing a kind of hip-hop sample from an earlier master. As Tommy explains the choice: "Usnavi comes out and says: 'You may not have come from here, but here are folks who have taken the journey. You rode with them; will you come with me?'"

Word started to get out that the journey was worth taking. Back House held auditions for the other roles, though Tommy and Lin-Manuel both looked so young that they asked an older friend, Andy Gale, to sit in to lend an air of legitimacy to the process. The first actor who showed up was a powerful singer named Doreen Montalvo who'd already starred in *La Lupe*, an off-Broadway musical about a Cuban salsa diva. Tommy could hardly believe it: "Doreen was a grown-up, and she was auditioning for our show!" As Lin-Manuel says, "She sang our *hair* back." With her mature voice, she was perfect for Benny's mother, the character who delivered the cautionary ballad "Never Give Your Heart Away." Now they needed a Benny.

Christopher Jackson didn't expect much when he walked into the Drama Book Shop. Following a four-year run in *The Lion King* on Broadway, he'd had a series of knee surgeries and grown disillusioned with the business. But a friend suggested that he meet a team of creators who were working on a new show. Chris knocked on the basement door, and a curly-haired white guy who, according to Chris, "looked like he was fifteen" welcomed him in. He entered an unremarkable black-box theater and saw "this skinny Puerto Rican kid sitting behind the piano" and not playing particularly well. Chris—tall, muscular, Black, with the stature of a church-trained singer who'd considered going into the ministry—was dubious. "I was twenty-seven," he says. "I thought anyone who was a serious musical-theater creator had to look like Stephen Sondheim." He'd planned to sing his standard audition number, but the skinny kid handed him a sheet of lyrics with no music. ("Another red flag," Chris says.) Then the kid started to rap those lyrics.

Chris perked up. "It was *so* well written," he recalls. He joined in on his part. In that scene, Benny and Lincoln were playing handball at an uptown park, trading boasts and roasts. "It positioned us as homeboys," Chris says. "It set the stage for the kind of relationship we would have." Lin-Manuel dropped a bunch of hip-hop references; Chris picked them up. When Chris mentioned that he couldn't rouse himself out of bed each day without listening to Talib Kweli's new hit "Get By," Lin-Manuel shouted: "Me too!" On the spot, the Back House team told Chris he was cast.

The basement of the Drama Book Shop became another artistic community for Lin-Manuel. The Back House guys loved their new protégé's poise and zest. "Lin's energy is infectious," Anthony says. "He percolates in the room." As the cast continued to expand, Tommy and Lin-Manuel worked to develop the eighty-minute Wesleyan one-act version of *Heights* into a two-act show, ending the first act with a blackout that shuts the salsa club down. (It was a dramatic beat borrowed from *Rent* but also inspired by memories of summertime power outages that left Washington Heights in the dark while air conditioners continued to hum in whiter Midtown neighborhoods.) Though Usnavi took on the narrator's role, the basic plot remained the same love triangle: Lincoln Rosario, a closeted songwriter, pines in secret for his best friend, Benny, the barrio lothario, who's starting to notice Lincoln's younger sister, Nina, who's back in Washington Heights after a year in college and who is hopelessly besotted with Benny.

Lin-Manuel also found himself back uptown after college. To get home from the Drama Book Shop, he'd take the A Train on Duke Ellington's route from Fortieth Street to 212th Street, north of Washington Heights, where his dad had found an apartment for him and a rotating cast of roommates from Wesleyan. The apartment at 5000 Broadway was a sagging prewar suite with a long hallway and three bedrooms—one for Lin-Manuel; one for Sara, who'd choreographed his college shows (and now directs his family's philanthropy); and one for Bill, his college music director. They skateboarded down the hall, played Grand Theft Auto, watched *The Little Mermaid*, and subsisted on pizza bagels and baked beans. On Sunday nights, they walked twelve blocks down Broadway to Luz and Luis's house, where they got a home-cooked meal and, thanks to the Mirandas' cable subscription, caught the latest episode of *The Sopranos*. "We were starving bozo artists," Bill recalls happily.

Lin-Manuel began to enjoy a new relationship with his sister, who managed finances for their dad in the basement of 5000 Broadway, a few floors below his apartment. The six-year age difference between Cita and her brother no longer seemed as significant as it had when she was a senior in high school and he was in elementary school. "Once he came back to New York, we could share friends and do things together," Cita says. They'd see movies or just hang out at the apartment. They'd chill with Tommy and the Back House crew and with other Wesleyan friends, like Sara and Bill. Lin-Manuel's worlds were coming together.

Though Bill hadn't met Lin-Manuel until after the Wesleyan production of *In the Heights*, he jumped on board as the arranger for Back House's workshops. "The walls in our apartment were really thin," Bill recalls, "so Lin would be working on a song in his room, and I'd shout out, 'Change that!'" On the wall in his bedroom, Lin-Manuel hung a framed poster of *On Borrowed Time* with Aileen's blurred face underneath the outline of a clock. It might have been there to remind him that his next musical would turn out better if he listened to his collaborators' advice. In the bathroom between two of their bedrooms, they kept a CD player and a wall rack of albums. One side held hip-hop—the Notorious B.I.G., Eminem, Big Pun. The other side had Latin music—Gilberto Santa Rosa, Juan Luis Guerra. In the middle were musicals by Stephen Sondheim and Jonathan Larson. "You would take a CD down from the wall and play it in the bathroom," Bill says. "The whole texture of *In the Heights* was painted from that wall."

As the show developed, the Back House crew scraped together money to put on readings in the Drama Book Shop basement, hoping to attract well-connected producers to fund a full production. "I had a very *Muppets Take Manhattan* view of how this would turn out," Lin-Manuel admits. "I was sure a producer would find us." The Muppets template, however, did not materialize. "It was frustrating," Neil says. "Every time we did a reading, people would say, 'Hey, this is amazing! Good luck with it!' And then they'd leave. What were we supposed to do next?"

Lin-Manuel felt a particular source of urgency to get his show funded because Bajir Cannon, the other big theater star at Wesleyan during Lin-Manuel's time there, had already found a production company to mount his thesis show. Tommy, however, was patient. The first play he'd directed in New York had been trashed by the *Times*, and he felt it was more important to get *Heights* right than to produce it quickly. "I was so chomping at the bit to get my show up in New York," Lin-Manuel says. "Tommy's like, 'We just have to make the best thing we can make, and the rest will take care of itself.' I'm like, 'But Bajir already has producers!'"

Finally, a veteran producer came to see one of their Drama Book Shop readings. He liked the show. He wanted a meeting. This was the chance they'd been hungering for. At the meeting, however, the producer expressed a concern. Whether or not Nina would go back to college didn't seem like high-enough stakes for the story. "What if she's pregnant?" he suggested. "What if she had a boyfriend who beat her? What if she got caught with drugs?" Raise the stakes, and he might produce the show.

"Tommy could see my face fall," Lin-Manuel says. Tommy knew how desperately Lin-Manuel wanted a production, but he also knew that drugs and violence weren't the way to help *In the Heights* succeed. They were trying to escape the shadow of *West Side Story* and *The Capeman*, not extend it. After the producer left, Tommy turned to Lin-Manuel. "We don't need him," Tommy said. "That's not the show you want to make. We'll just keep working."

Tommy's confidence inspired Lin-Manuel to continue. He felt he'd made the right choice when he learned that Bajir had had to compromise on his own show. Bajir couldn't get the rights for his source material and had to rewrite the script, and the downtown theater company that produced it didn't have the resources to re-create all the ingenious stage effects from Wesleyan. "It was still beautiful," Lin-Manuel says, "because Bajir just makes beautiful things, but it wasn't the masterpiece we'd seen in college." After a few more years struggling to create shows in New York, Bajir grew disillusioned with the theater industry and shifted to making videos in Japan.

That disillusionment was the standard trajectory for college graduates who came to New York hoping to replicate their artistic success on campus. The stars of Wesleyan theater and film imagined being interviewed on NPR, lauded in the *New York Times*, backed by well-funded producers, honored on Broadway. For most of them, it didn't happen. It wasn't for lack of promise. It was that they didn't meet collaborators who could improve their work; they didn't find the producers who could fund their vision; they didn't get the opportunities to reach a larger audience. As Lin-Manuel's college girlfriend Aileen put it: "We are all Bajir."

In 2002, Lin-Manuel hadn't made a career in the arts yet. He still had to pay the rent, and he wasn't earning anything from developing *In the Heights*. His current paycheck came courtesy of an old connection. Toward the end of his senior year at Wesleyan, he'd called his eighth-grade English teacher, Dr. Herbert. "I'm graduating from college, and I'm moving back to New York to be a writer," he said. "I don't have a job or a clue of what I'm going to do to make money. Can I come substitute at Hunter?" He got an interview at Hunter's English department, and by the end of the summer, he had a job as a part-time teacher for two sections of seventh-grade English.

Lin-Manuel liked teaching. He wore a button-down shirt and a tie and revisited the titles that had engaged him as a student: *Of Mice and Men*, *The House on Mango Street*, *A Midsummer Night's Dream*. He helped advise Brick Prison. "I did my best Rembert Herbert impression," he says. Dr. Herbert gave him suggestions when he had trouble connecting with a student. He'd gone into the classroom expecting to be an entertainer, tapping his stage training, but quickly learned that his job was to elicit his students' best ideas. "It was another lesson in collaboration," he said. He began each class with a free-write to help the students settle in and get their creativity flowing, the same strategy he used riding the subway when he felt stuck on a song. Being a teacher felt like a comfortable, meaningful role, particularly in the very building that had nourished his own development.

After school, he often visited Aileen, who'd also moved to New York to chase her theater dreams. She'd found an apartment a few blocks from Hunter on the Upper East Side, a convenient location for a part-time Hunter teacher and aspiring writer to pop by. For a few of the Drama Book Shop readings, she reprised her Wesleyan role as Nina, but Tommy wanted to keep Lin-Manuel's professional life separate from his romantic life. As with many college relationships, theirs had trouble transitioning to the working world. Lin-Manuel devoted most of his free time to making *In the Heights*, while Aileen was trying to get acting jobs. "It was emotionally difficult to be in the same professional field as him," she says. One evening in 2003, they went to a new Jason Robert Brown musical, *The Last Five Years*, about a writer whose career takes off while his relationship with his wife, a struggling actor, falls apart. "I was bawling," Aileen says. Neither of them wanted their next five years to play out like the story they'd watched onstage. When Aileen landed a part in a European tour of *Hair*, they decided that they'd remain friends but they would start seeing other people.

The final choice Lin-Manuel had to make in that first year out of college was, perhaps, the most consequential. His stint as a part-time teacher went well—so well that Hunter offered him a full-time job for the following year. That would give him something he'd never had before—a real salary, health care, security. And it wasn't just the offer of a stable life that appealed to him. "I really enjoyed teaching, especially at Hunter," he says. "It was very tempting to have a full-time job in the place that nurtured me." On the one hand, if he took the job, he'd be teaching on weekdays plus grading papers and planning lessons in the evenings and on weekends, so he wouldn't have time to work on his musical. On the other hand, if he turned down the job, he'd be gambling his financial well-being on a musical that had yet to earn a single cent.

He decided to ask for guidance from a source he didn't often consult for career recommendations: his father.

Whenever young Lin-Manuel said he wanted a life in the arts, Luis's advice had been "Be a lawyer!" One of Luis's uncles was a professional actor in Puerto Rico, and Luis had seen how hard it was for him to make a living. It didn't seem like a safe career path, especially if you wanted to support a family.

Luz disagreed about their son's trajectory. "From the get-go, Luis kept saying, 'He should be a lawyer!'" she recalls. "And I said: 'Lawyers love to fight. He's not a fighter. He's a collaborator.'" That clash over Lin-Manuel's direction persisted in high school. Luis was frustrated that his son applied himself only in classes that allowed creative projects. He hired Lin-Manuel to work for his political consulting company over the summer a few times, but the stints always ended in misery. "For better or worse," Lin-Manuel said, "I cannot get myself to care about things I don't care about."

He wrote this conflict into early numbers for Lincoln, his songwriting alter ego. "I'll never live up to your expectations," Lincoln sings about his father. "I love you but you'll never see me the way I see myself / When

I'm alone / With a notebook and a microphone." Now the Hunter English department had offered Lin-Manuel a way out of the lonely, precarious composer's life. He had never seen law school as a viable option, but a full-time teaching job would provide the economic security Luis had always wanted for him. He emailed his father, asking for direction.

His father emailed him back the same evening. Lin-Manuel was surprised at what Luis had written. "Dear baby," his father began tenderly. To help his son make this decision, he'd have to share two turning points in his own life. The first: At nineteen, Luis had been accepted to law school; he had an apartment and a job and could see a comfortable future in Puerto Rico. "But for some weird reason, that until this day I cannot explain, I took the most difficult road," Luis wrote. He left everything on the island behind and accepted an offer to study psychology at NYU. "I guess my parents thought I was crazy," he admitted, "but they only encouraged me to do what I wanted to do."

The second crossroads came when he was twenty-four, after he'd finished his graduate work. He planned to return to Puerto Rico; he'd even found an apartment and shipped his furniture back from New York. But then he met Luz and decided to stay in New York, marry her, and adopt her daughter. "Again, my parents must have thought that I was crazy but again, they supported my decision," he told Lin-Manuel. "In both instances I followed my heart."

Both decisions were, objectively, "the wrong decisions," and yet without those gutsy, irrational choices, Luis wouldn't have the wonderful life he and Luz had built together. And so, he concluded, he wished he could tell his son to take the safe option but recognized that "if I were to tell you that, I would be glazing over my own life." He encouraged Lin-Manuel to listen to his own heart, work hard, "and learn from anyone who is willing to help you be a better professional and person." Luis was eager to help, too, if his son would permit it. Whatever happened, Luis assured him, "I will always be there—*en las buenas y en las malas*. That's what being a dad is all about."

Lin-Manuel couldn't quite believe that his dad had given him permission to reject the stable route. If he decided to bet on himself, even if that meant making a living by cobbling together odd jobs—substitute teaching at Hunter part-time, writing campaign-ad background music for his dad's political candidates, dancing for hire at bar mitzvahs—and never knowing where the rent was coming from, his dad would support him. So he chose to follow his heart. Together with Tommy and the Back House guys, he would make *In the Heights* a reality.

But how? They'd said no to the only producer who'd made them an offer. Lin-Manuel had just turned down a steady job. He was ending his relationship with his girlfriend. The future was not clear.

Then Jill Furman walked into the basement of the Drama Book Shop.

7

VOLTRON

• •

Jill Furman hadn't planned to become a Broadway producer. She wanted to produce films. Her first movie didn't take off, but an actor from the movie told her that she had to see a new musical called *In the Heights* in the basement of the Drama Book Shop. "It's like a Latino *Rent*!" he raved.

Jill was skeptical. "I thought, *Oh, everything's a something* Rent." But in February 2003, Jill went to a *Heights* workshop. "I wasn't looking to be in theater," she recalls. "But then this guy playing Usnavi came out onstage. He started rapping about his day and his bodega and his community. He was charming and infectious and so full of verve. And I was like, *Oh my God, who is he?*" She sat forward in her seat. She felt a frisson of excitement. "I thought, *I need to help more people see this kid.*"

After the show, Jill introduced herself to Tommy and said that she wanted to produce *In the Heights*. Partnering with Jill made sense to the Back House crew—she believed in the show that Lin-Manuel wanted to make.

Since Jill was relatively new to the business, she wanted to connect them with other producers as well. Finding the right partners for *In the Heights* wasn't easy, particularly if, like the producer that Tommy and Lin-Manuel turned down, their views of Latino communities came from the nightly news and *West Side Story*. (Jill remembers one producer asking, "Where are the prostitutes?") In an era when big Broadway hits increasingly started out as movies, like *The Lion King* and *The Producers*, it was risky to invest in an original story, especially one by an unknown writer, let alone a show without any stars involved. Not many producers were interested in gambling on a first-time composer coming up with the next *Rent*. Except, perhaps, the people who had produced *Rent*.

Kevin McCollum, a producer who'd won a Best Musical Tony for *Rent* and was about to win another for *Avenue Q*, got word that there was a new show he ought to see. In June 2003, the *In the Heights* team did a reading at Repertorio Español, a theater where Luis had a connection. Kevin showed up. "I kind of understood the story, I didn't care a ton, and I thought the music was fine," he says. "But every time the character Usnavi spoke, I wanted to hear more from that guy." Over pizza afterward, Jill and Kevin talked, and Jill was impressed with Kevin's instincts about the material: He wanted to make Washington Heights a character, like the New York neighborhoods in *Rent* and *Avenue Q*. They agreed to coproduce the musical. After dinner, Kevin called his producing partner, Jeffrey Seller, and told him that he'd found their next show.

For Lin-Manuel, walking into Kevin and Jeffrey's office felt like the manifestation of all his dreams. "I had the moonshot," he says—producers who had experience bringing new work to Broadway. And not just any new work but the work of the author who'd made Lin-Manuel want to write musicals in the first place. Jonathan Larson had been his hero since he saw *Rent* on his seventeenth birthday. He knew from the autobiographical *Tick, Tick . . . Boom!* that Larson had struggled for years to get his show produced, and it wasn't until he was almost thirty and met Jeffrey Seller, an energetic producer fresh out of the University of Michigan hungry for new voices, that he found a path forward. Lin-Manuel was only twenty-three. *I'm already getting there faster*, he recalls thinking. "It felt *so close*." The next song he wrote, in which Nina's friend Vanessa fantasizes about leaving Washington Heights to pursue her dreams, was called "It Won't Be Long Now."

From Kevin's perspective, they weren't quite there yet. He told Jeffrey not to see the show until they developed it further. "Kevin was always more enthusiastic about more things than I was," Jeffrey says. "He'd bring home all the stray pets and I'd tell him to throw them out of the house. He wanted to ensure I didn't do that this time." Before *In the Heights* would be ready for viewing, the team needed to figure out what story they were telling. A New York City love triangle hinging on Lincoln, the songwriter, felt less exciting to Kevin than what Lin-Manuel had told him about his own family's history: his father leaving Puerto Rico to get his education, his parents working around the clock so he could afford to go to college, a feeling of not quite belonging in either Puerto Rico or elite stateside schools. "Rather than trying to write *Rent*, maybe write closer to what you've experienced," Kevin advised. The generational struggle intrigued him—an immigrant father's aspirations, children with their own direction. "We kind of need a *Fiddler on the Roof* for the Hispanic community," he suggested. "And Usnavi could be our Tevye."

Tommy had been thinking along similar lines. When he pitched Lin-Manuel on turning Usnavi into the musical's narrator, he had in mind Tevye's relationship with the audience—the genial, funny interlocutor who could interpret a culturally specific world for the newcomers in the seats who might not know its language, rhythms, and customs. "*Fiddler* was a huge archetype for us," Tommy says. As they got to work revising *Heights*, a revival of *Fiddler* opened on Broadway. Tommy saw it four times.

Fiddler set a family's story amid a larger community in transition—changing marriage traditions, the threat of Cossack pogroms—and perhaps their musical could show the pressures that were starting to affect Washington Heights. Lin-Manuel sometimes boosted his income by writing freelance culture stories for a bilingual newspaper covering northern Manhattan that his father had founded, and he'd noticed changes in his childhood neighborhood; for instance, a Starbucks on a corner where there used to be a locally owned shop. That "beacon of gentrification," as he put it, turned into a new lyric: "A Starbucks on 181st Street, who will be the next one to go? / This isn't the same little neighborhood I used to know."

At the same time they were figuring out what *In the Heights* could become, they were learning what it should avoid. A key lesson came when Kevin and Jeffrey sent Lin-Manuel and Tommy to see *Avenue Q*, the cheeky new puppet musical they'd produced. Lin-Manuel was particularly excited because the composer, Bobby Lopez, had gone to Hunter, too, five years ahead of him. As a kindergartner, Lin-Manuel had seen a sixth-grade Bobby play the Russian constable in *Fiddler*, singing a special number that Ms. Ames wrote for him. And now, in the summer of 2003, Bobby's own musical, with lyrics by Jeff Marx and a book by Jeff Whitty, was opening on Broadway. Lin-Manuel could see his own future unfolding.

When he went to the show, however, he saw more than his future. He saw his plot. At Wesleyan, he'd been excited to figure out the twist that his central character, Lincoln, was secretly gay and had a crush on his best friend that he couldn't admit. It felt like a revelatory story.

But *Avenue Q* was a step ahead of him. One of its lead puppet characters, Rod, was also closeted and in love with his best friend, but the story was played as a tender joke—everyone else on the block knew Rod was gay and just wanted to support him. There was even a sweetly comic song, "If You Were Gay," in which Rod's roommate assures him that he'd still be loved if he came out. At the end of the show, when he finally announced that he was gay, it was a laugh line, surprising no one. "It was funnier and truer than what I'd written," Lin-Manuel recalls.

He decided to scrap the closeted love story and focus instead on Lincoln's relationship with his father. The pressure of being a hardworking immigrant's son was, he felt, something he could address from his own perspective, as Kevin had encouraged him to do. "I wrote many father-son songs that were probably my own therapy," he admits.

Pressure also came from being the sole creator of an entire show. Most musicals have a composer, a lyricist, and a book writer (the person who comes up with the story and writes any non-sung dialogue). Sometimes one person does both the book and the lyrics or the lyrics and the music, but only very rarely does a single person take on all three jobs. Lin-Manuel had been doing it all—rewriting the story, coming up with new lyrics, blending salsa and hip-hop musical lines. "He was trying to bite off more than he could chew," Jill Furman says.

Kevin knew it would take a long time for Lin-Manuel to finish the show if he wrote it alone, even with Tommy's direction and Bill's arrangements. Jonathan Larson had done it for *Rent*, but it had taken him six years to complete. As Lin-Manuel remembers it, Kevin started envisioning different possibilities. Was Lin-Manuel perhaps more of a book-and-lyrics guy than a composer? Would it be helpful to bring on someone else? Kevin never said Lin-Manuel couldn't write the music; everyone had agreed that was Lin-Manuel's call. Kevin doesn't even remember suggesting that they needed another composer. But the conversation disoriented Lin-Manuel.

He hadn't imagined a world in which he wasn't the composer. "It sent me reeling," he says.

He didn't write anything for the next six months. Tommy tried to get him back on weekly deadlines; it didn't work. "The room was tilted when we were with the producers," Tommy says. "It knocked Lin off the keyboard." He wasn't a trained musician or composer, and the notes in his head didn't come out easily on the piano the way they did for some of his gifted Hunter pals. Writing out a bass line or a piano part was arduous, and he still felt daunted by Latin polyrhythms. Maybe he did need someone else to write the music.

Lin-Manuel went as far as getting names of other Latino composers. But when it came to calling them, he felt his stomach seize up. "It forced a moment of clarity," he recalls. He'd grown up in the show's neighborhood and had heard its music all his life. *If I don't know how to write this score, I don't know anything*, he remembers thinking. He was the composer. But he wouldn't mind help with the book. Every time someone mentioned a problem with the story, he tried to solve it by writing a song. The dialogue wasn't his strong suit. "I realized I'd be happy to work with a playwright to make the story stronger," he says.

Jill set out to find one. A mutual friend recommended a new writer, then finishing her MFA in playwrighting at Brown, who also had a degree in music composition from Yale. Lin-Manuel was a little intimidated. "You should meet her," Jill told him. So over dinner at the Market Café, a few blocks from the Drama Book Shop, he met Quiara Alegría Hudes. By the end of the night, he felt like he was at a family gathering.

Quiara's childhood in Philadelphia rhymed with Lin-Manuel's in New York: She was born on the mainland into a family that came from Puerto Rico, grew up in an urban neighborhood speaking mostly English, nurtured by a beloved abuela, with parents involved in community activism, then left the community to go to school. Her path mirrored the character of Nina's as well. She was the first in her family to attend college, and when she left Philly and arrived at Yale, she felt out of place in a Eurocentric music department that prized Chopin over *montunos*. Just as Lin-Manuel found his community by moving into La Casa and composing *In the Heights*, Quiara re-created a North Philly barrio at Yale by writing musicals that drew on her mother's Afro-Caribbean heritage. Her MFA thesis at Brown, a Latina coming-of-age fantasy called *The Adventures of Barrio Grrrl!*, was even more sexually imaginative than Lin-Manuel's college thesis. And they both grooved to Juan Luis Guerra. "I was so artistically smitten," Lin-Manuel says. "I realized we came from the same place."

After dinner, they hugged, and Lin-Manuel ducked into the Forty-Second Street subway station. He couldn't wait, though, until he arrived at 207th Street to get cell service, so he popped back out on the other side of the station, called Tommy, and told him: "She's the one."

The summer of 2004, they started, as Lin-Manuel puts it, "reconfiguring the show from the ground up." Quiara could see promising elements in the draft script, but she wanted to adjust their importance. "To me the story was about the community and not who loved who," she says. She took stock of the current inhabitants of their fictional Washington Heights. As Lin-Manuel had revised his college version, bringing out Usnavi's narrator role, he'd started to add supporting characters: ladies who worked at the neighborhood salon; an Abuela Claudia based on his own Abuela Mundi. Much of the narrative real estate, though, still went to the male-friendship trio of Usnavi, Benny, and Lincoln.

That didn't match Quiara's sense of Latino community. "When I read the script, I saw a lot of female characters but zero female leads," she said. "That's really not my experience. I wanted to make these women badasses." They should have their own professional aspirations, emotional complexity, grounded physicality, and community ties. Thinking about the people whom her mother, a community organizer, and her stepfather, a contractor, served in North Philly, she wanted to draw out the economic landscape of the neighborhood. The script included three businesses on a block in Washington Heights: the bodega, the salon, and the Rosario family's car service. Rather than simply furnishing the setting, those businesses could fuel the story. "What does it mean to maintain a business in a gentrifying neighborhood where profit is razor-thin?" she wondered. "That was in Lin's script; I just had to point to it."

Tommy could tell that Quiara's sensibility provided what Lin-Manuel needed. "Lin and I went, 'She's so much smarter than we are!'" he recalls. "And she has an immediate warmth, a deep soul that's accessible. I think Lin felt unburdened and liberated to have a collaborator who was open-hearted and openhanded." Both describe their collaboration as a sibling bond that mapped onto their real family roles, with Quiara the responsible older sister, a little more prone to take on the weight of the world, and Lin-Manuel the ebullient younger brother, eager to captivate an audience. Freed of the burden of writing the book, Lin-Manuel could devote his time to the part of the project he loved: writing songs. Quiara came into the Drama Book Shop with pages for a scene in the salon, fleshing out the dynamics among the women who worked there, and he turned the scene into a sparkling, clever Spanglish number about the news in the barrio, "No Me Diga."

Working on the arrangements, Bill felt a difference with Quiara's elevated dialogue. Her words could match the effervescence of Lin-Manuel's lyrics, making the transition from speech to song—always a challenge in a musical—much more believable. In the new script, when Vanessa asked if Usnavi could dance, his cousin responded, "Like a drunk Chita Rivera." To coin a term of endearment, Quiara adapted a Spanish idiom for "sweetheart"—*corazón de melon*, literally "heart of watermelon"—into a novel expression for Abuela Claudia to welcome Nina: "the watermelon of my heart." (Lin-Manuel calls Quiara "the high priestess of the unexpected but apt metaphor.") Plus, she was better positioned to shape a storyline for Nina's struggles with college, romance, and family expectations. "We were a bunch of dudes trying to write about a girl," Bill says. "It wasn't really very arc-y. Quiara gave it an arc."

Lin-Manuel still faced the challenge of translating the music he heard in his mind into musical notation so the actors could learn the songs. He created demos on a tape recorder, which meant his score was limited by what he could play. His fingers just didn't move as fast on the keyboard as the rhythms did in his head. "I was shooting for something more ambitious than what I could make," he says. The actor Janet Dacal, who was playing one of the salon ladies, recognized that "Lin needed someone to voice his musical mind."

Fortunately, Janet knew just the musician. She remembered a pianist who used to accompany her vocal competitions in Miami. His name was Alex Lacamoire—Lac for short. His parents came from Cuba. And even though he had a hearing impairment, he could re-create any music by ear and sight-read any written score. He'd already done the arrangements for a rock musical, *Bat Boy*, and was currently the associate music director for Broadway's *Wicked*. He even looked like a cross between Tommy and Lin-Manuel, with the former's curly black hair and the latter's goatee. "He had the musical background and the Latin background," Janet says. "He was perfect."

Lac remembers getting a cassette tape with demos from *In the Heights*. "I pop in the cassette, I press play, and the first thing I hear is the sound of a hip-hop beat played on buckets, like on a street corner. Then I hear this Puerto Rican dude rapping over the buckets, and I'm hearing these over-the-bar-line rhymes, and I'm like, *This is amazing!*" He saw song titles in Spanish. He heard lyrics in Spanglish. He could recognize himself in the show. "It felt like, *Oh my God, I need to be involved!*"

When he met Lin-Manuel, Lac understood his role. Unlike most musical-theater composers, Lin-Manuel didn't write full piano accompaniments, and he hadn't yet learned to use a music-software program like Garage Band. "Lin was typing out lyrics with chord changes," Lac says. "He needed some kind of instrument to translate the songs in his head out into the world." Lac could provide that instrument.

Lin-Manuel would start at the piano, describe the feel of a song, and play it as best he could. Then he'd step aside and say, "Lac, you play it." Lac knew what to do. In his hands, the song would explode in Technicolor, like Dorothy opening the door into Oz. "I could hear everything fully formed in my head off of Lin's demonstration," he says. Tommy calls Lac "the Force Multiplier."

Lin-Manuel did most of the composing on the piano in the basement of the Drama Book Shop, which was on the way from his apartment in Inwood out to Queens, where he now taught in an arts program for at-risk youth. Bill, who was working in the MTV mailroom, joined him there on his lunch break, and Lac—the only Broadway professional in their crew—would pop over from the Gershwin, where he was conducting *Wicked*. "Paciencia y Fe," a song imagining Abuela Claudia's fraught journey from Cuba to Washington Heights, was farther from Lin-Manuel's own experience than anything else he'd written, and he was proud of it. The song took an immigrant housecleaner, someone often overlooked, and made her a hero, holding center stage as she told her life story on an epic scale. But it was way too long, double the length of the typical two-and-a-half-page song. Bill and Lac played it through from Lin-Manuel's lyrics and chord symbols and told him to cut it down. A week later, he brought back a more concise version. Tommy suggested they record a demo for Doreen Montalvo, who would play Abuela Claudia in the next workshop.

Lin-Manuel sang Claudia's vocal line while Lac improvised the piano part. "Lin knew what he wanted it to sound like, but he couldn't play it," Bill says. With a feel for Cuban rhythms and a grasp of the composer's intent, Lac figured it out. "As the song progressed, I knew what the breaks needed to be, what the rhythmic motifs could be," Lac says. Something magical started to happen. Lin-Manuel delivered a phrase; Lac made up a response on the keyboard. "We were on a high, going back and forth," Lac recalls. "I saw opportunities for pianistic answers to the vocal lines. I saw the spaces Lin was leaving me as an arranger to communicate."

It felt like they were creating the song together in real time. When Lin-Manuel swelled for the powerful refrain *¡Paciencia y fe!*, Lac crescendoed the chords, and when the song needed a whisper, they intuited the hush together. "We just fed off each other," Lac remembers. "We had entered an amazing space that you couldn't have planned. After it was over, we were both like, 'Oh my God, what the fuck just happened?'" They delivered the demo to Doreen.

"That was the light-bulb moment," Bill says. "That's when we found the sound of the show."

Two years after graduating from Wesleyan and walking into the Drama Book Shop, Lin-Manuel finally had the team he needed to bring *In the Heights* to professional life. He had created the musical world. Quiara took charge of the story. Bill figured out the big-picture arrangements. Lac worked on the musical details. Tommy kept them all moving in the same direction, building an environment where everyone's talents could flourish and the best idea won, no matter who proposed it. To describe this squad, Lin-Manuel thought back to a cartoon he used to watch in elementary school called *Voltron*, about five robots that join forces to form a super-robot, wielding powers none of the individuals alone possessed. "The summer of 2004," he says, "is when Lac, Quiara, Bill, Tommy, and I become Voltron."

With an actual Voltron robot toy on hand, they filled in Kevin and Jill on their progress. Now that they had a new book, new songs, and a new creative team, Kevin thought they were ready at last to bring in Jeffrey, his producing partner. At a reading at the Manhattan Theatre Club that December, Jeffrey experienced the show for the first time. When he'd heard Jonathan Larson perform the show that became *Tick, Tick...Boom!* more than a decade earlier, the thrill of it had made the hair on his arms stand up. When Lin-Manuel came onstage as Usnavi, rapping a welcome to his neighborhood, and then the community entered behind him singing "In the Heights" in salsa-tuned harmony, Jeffrey felt the same thrill. "I fell in love with the community going to work, fighting with each other, loving each other, surviving blackouts with each other, learning how to make their way," he says. "I knew I was hearing something I'd never heard before."

One song particularly impressed him: "Paciencia y Fe." "I thought it was one of the most moving soliloquies and arias I'd ever heard," he recalls. "It moved me to tears. I'm thinking: *How the fuck did this twenty-four-year-old write a song about an elderly Cuban woman making her journey to the Upper East Side?*"

Quiara, who'd observed Lin-Manuel writing when they got together, sometimes at the Drama Book Shop, sometimes at one of their apartments, had a guess. "It's got to be his empathy and openness," she says. That sensitivity he felt as a child, crying when he saw perils on the news or heard "Bridge over Troubled Water," had become a special ability, nourished by his mother's reassurance that it was all right to feel deeply. As a four-year-old, he'd broken down in tears at the scene in *Mary Poppins* where the elderly lady feeds the birds. Now he'd imagined a version of his Abuela Mundi as that older woman, taking the birds as a metaphor for her flight from Havana to New York. ("Research and empathy" are his best composing tools, he says.) Quiara had seen him chuckle to himself when he was working on a comic number and go through a full box of tissues when he composed a sad song. "He doesn't have a lot of armor," she muses. "It's his own specific superpower: He'll crack his heart open, and his heart will go out and find the song's truth on the wind."

Lin-Manuel had also developed the confidence that the truth he found was worth sharing. In 2003, writing an application for a funding grant administered by the Jonathan Larson Performing Arts Foundation, he wasn't shy about expressing his ambition to take his place alongside his composer hero. "I want to change the landscape of American Musical Theatre," he wrote. Like Larson before him, he wanted to use the music of his own generation—hip-hop especially—to put new voices and stories onstage.

He hadn't gotten the grant. Nor had he been accepted to the premier incubator for new musicals, the O'Neill National Music Theater Conference, where *Avenue Q* was developed. (It had been a long shot anyway; every year, only two or three musicals were chosen out of over three hundred applications.) But those rejections had come before Voltron. After Quiara and Lac joined the team, Lin-Manuel applied to the O'Neill again, and this time, *In the Heights* was accepted.

For two weeks in July 2005, the cast and the creative team stayed at the O'Neill Theater Center, a waterfront estate in Connecticut, and worked on the show. At the end of those two weeks, they gave performances to present what they'd accomplished.

After the final O'Neill performance, the producers called Voltron together. The creators expected to hear the good news that they were ready for a full production. Instead, Jill delivered a disappointing verdict. In the eyes of the producers, the show had taken a step backward. The changes Voltron had made at the conference didn't work. "The show was a mess," Jeffrey says.

Lin-Manuel was stunned by the producers' judgment. It wasn't clear how *In the Heights* would continue. "At the O'Neill, things came crashing down," Jill remembers. "It was make-or-break."

8

THE O'NEILL

••

Two weeks earlier, the O'Neill conference had started off strong, with a flurry of new songs and the arrival of new cast members. They flew through revisions and rehearsals, and at the end of the first week, most of the company headed back to New York for a day off, but Lin-Manuel stayed at the estate to keep writing. He toted his laptop and his Casio keyboard around the grounds, hardly sleeping. Lac, who'd been teaching vocal arrangements to the cast, noticed that instead of the old tape-recording process for making demos, Lin-Manuel had started to use the computer to layer his voice onto recorded tracks and add in harmonies. "Once he figured out how to use that, his brain opened up," Lac says. Now the "Blackout" section at the end of act 1 could become a complex fugue, weaving together different characters' melody lines, like the choral act-closers Lin-Manuel loved: "One Day More" from *Les Misérables* and "A Weekend in the Country" from Stephen Sondheim's *A Little Night Music*.

When Lac and the rest returned to Connecticut on Sunday night, they found Lin-Manuel sobbing in the barn, his eyes puffy and red. He was all right, he assured them. He'd just been working on a song. This one was for Lincoln and Nina's parents, Kevin and Camila. Over a lilting bachata beat, he'd composed a memory triptych called "On My Shoulders": Kevin hoisting five-year-old Lincoln on his shoulders at the Puerto Rican Day parade so he could watch the procession and wave the flag; Camila filming Nina's high-school graduation, a camera on her shoulder, as her daughter accepts her diploma; then both parents hoping that their children will surpass them, promising: "We're always here to catch you if you fall." The final line echoed the assurance Luis Miranda had conveyed in his letter to his son: "I will always be there—*en las buenas y en las malas.*"

While Lin-Manuel tapped into his well of family emotions, Tommy steered the company forward. During that sweltering July in Connecticut, he kept the mood light. Unlike directors who took over the rehearsal room and delivered their criticisms to individual actors in front of the whole company, Tommy gave actors space to explore, then had private conversations with each of them to see how they felt, answer any questions, and offer other ways in. And in contrast to directors who created from a position of conflict, Tommy wanted to show that great art could emerge from a friendly, supportive environment. In his flip-phone contact list, Kevin McCollum stored Tommy's number under the name "The Future."

At the conclusion of their stay, the *Heights* company put on a series of evening presentations in the O'Neill barn. The conference stipulated that Lin-Manuel could write only, not perform, but he happened to have a double on hand. When Javier Muñoz was cast as Lincoln for the Manhattan Theatre Club workshop, he discovered that he and Lin-Manuel mirrored each other. They listened to the same music; they ate the same snacks; they'd liked the same He-Man and ThunderCats cartoons growing up. "It was like I found my twin buddy," Javier recalls. Lin-Manuel joked: "I don't know where I end and you begin."

Javier loved playing Lincoln. The conflict between a father who wanted his son to take over the family's car service and a gay son who wanted to become a songwriter resonated with Javier, a gay Latino actor. "It's a common thing in Latin families," he says, "the machismo, traditional father, and the son who needs to break through." He relished Lincoln's solo numbers, lyrical arias that explored the clash between the character's desires, personal and artistic, and the expectations placed on him. And he valued the range of complex Latino characters that *In the Heights* put onstage, a contrast to the types of minor roles he was usually called on to play. "We're not just Gang Member Number Two or Drug Dealer Number Three," he explains. "Lin-Manuel helped to break the idea of what a leading man can look like."

At the O'Neill, however, salsa pop star Huey Dunbar took over the part of Lincoln. Tommy asked Javier if he'd play Usnavi instead, freeing up Lin-Manuel to compose and respond to the show from the audience. That meant Javier had to internalize all the hip-hop cadences Lin-Manuel had channeled into Usnavi. "I spent a month living in Lin's brain," he says. Lin-Manuel called it Rap School. The curriculum was a CD that Lin-Manuel burned for Javier featuring all the artists that influenced Usnavi's bars: Big Pun, Jay-Z, Eminem, Biggie, the Pharcyde. As the other actors strolled across the O'Neill estate's grassy lawn in front of the Long Island Sound, they'd see Javier facing a tree, practicing his raps.

For the final shows, held in the barn, the actors stood at rehearsal stands with scripts in hand, Lac accompanying them on piano. Huey Dunbar soared as Lincoln. Javier drove the story as Usnavi, his raps buoyant and inviting. Lin-Manuel felt good about what they'd achieved. And the audience—a mix of industry folks, friends, and members of the two other companies in residence—responded. "It was enthusiastic, alive, electric in that barn," Tommy recalls. Voltron had accomplished what they'd set out to do.

Then the producers—Jill, Kevin, and Jeffrey—asked them to sit down around a picnic table. It was a difficult conversation—heartbreaking, from Lin-Manuel's perspective. "We thought we'd done great work at the O'Neill," he recalls. "They said: 'You don't have it. This isn't ready for a production.'" What he'd seen as progress—developing Lincoln's relationship with his father, enhancing Nina's role, fleshing out the neighborhood characters—they saw as muddying the show with too many storylines, all of them superficial.

"In a musical," Jeffrey says, "you can have an A story and a B story. If you're really lucky, you can have a C story. *Heights* had Lincoln and the car shop, Nina coming home from school, Benny being interested in Nina and working with the parents. You throw Abuela on top of that, the neighborhood salon ladies on top of *that*, and a brother who's a closeted gay songwriter on top of *that*, and you've got too many dishes in the kitchen sink."

So what should they do? "They had to lose the story that's least interesting," Jeffrey says. "You need real estate for what's best."

At the end of the meeting, the producers told Voltron to figure out the next step on their own. Then they left.

"It was a gut punch for them," Jill recalls. "They were wondering if they weren't good enough, if they weren't going to get there. They were really disheartened."

Lin-Manuel, Tommy, and the team knew this was a decisive moment. If they didn't make the right choice, the producers might lose interest; plenty of musicals never made it to a professional production, even with the O'Neill's support. The show's fate was in their hands.

They got up from the picnic table. They looked at each other. And to a person, Lin-Manuel says, each one had the same idea: "We gotta kill Lincoln."

Since the first Wesleyan readings, Lincoln had been the show's pivotal character. He was Lin-Manuel's dramatic surrogate, the songwriter with the composer's own nickname nested in his. The revelation of his desire had provided the original plot, and even when the show no longer hinged on a love triangle, it was his need to break from his family's business and become an artist that anchored the story. But in a way, he'd become a vestige of an earlier version of the show, holding it back. The narrative no longer wanted to revolve around Lin-Manuel's adolescent issues—crushes and career choices. It had become the story of a community, evolving under economic and racial forces, and it was about education, about the legacy parents pass on. Everyone agreed: Lincoln had to go.

"Murder your darlings" is common writing advice, but it's hard to execute. In college, Lin-Manuel was so attached to his plot for *On Borrowed Time* that he refused to change it even when his collaborators told him it didn't make sense. Now he was willing to let go of Lincoln. Once Voltron made that decision, he says, "suddenly there was space. Suddenly Nina could have complex issues with her parents. We could make her three-D. We could tell more community stories." The producers were relieved too. "It was hard for him to kill his baby," Jill says, "but he could do it because he understood that it was making the show stronger."

Still, after the intensity of the O'Neill, everyone needed a break. Bill and Lin-Manuel had started the conference by hopping in a car with Chris Jackson and driving to Connecticut. They ended it by hopping on a plane with Chris and Tommy and flying to Scotland. They were going to freestyle.

—

It had started as a lark three years earlier, just after Lin-Manuel graduated from college and moved to New York. Anthony Veneziale, the improv-comedy whiz from Wesleyan who was managing the Drama Book Shop theater for Back House, would pop into the basement during *Heights* rehearsal breaks because he'd heard that Lin-Manuel was up for impromptu rap sessions. They'd make up bars about whatever had happened that day until Tommy told them to get back to work.

In high school and even during most of college, Lin-Manuel hadn't felt comfortable freestyling in front of his friends; he preferred to compose a verse in his head beforehand. But on a spring-break road trip to Vegas his senior year with a couple of housemates, he drew the graveyard shift and had to keep himself awake for four hours driving a rickety Volvo across the Kansas flatlands. Fueled by nothing but Red Bull and a bunch of mixtapes, he began improvising raps over whoever's songs played on the car stereo—NSYNC, Fat Joe—while his friends slumbered. "You get past the point of sense and start making connections," he says. "After that part of the trip, I was freestyling all the time, because I'd done it as a survival technique."

Anthony wanted to try their freestyle sessions in front of an audience, and his improv group needed an extra hour to fill out their set. So Lin-Manuel joined him onstage for improvised raps over recorded beats. Instead of standard rap-battle takedowns, they'd end with a love battle, serenading people in the audience. For a concert the day after a blackout in 2003, they didn't have their electronic beats, so Lin-Manuel's longtime Hunter friend Arthur Lewis hopped onstage and played accompaniment on the piano. Bill Sherman joined in on sax. With a nod to John Coltrane's "A Love Supreme" and their own love battles, they decided to call themselves Freestyle Love Supreme.

After their group expanded a little more—Chris Jackson provided his soulful vocals; a skilled beatboxer named Chris "Shockwave" Sullivan added sound effects and improv rhythms that could adjust to the rappers' flow—Anthony invited Tommy to a show. Tommy started envisioning a structure: A series of improv games drawing on suggestions from the audience would generate material for the raps and provide an entertaining evening. Anthony, a genial host, would guide the audience through the show, introducing each game and soliciting input from the crowd. For people who couldn't believe that they were coming up with raps on the spot, they added an opening segment—"Foundations of Freestyle"—where audience members wrote words on slips of paper and put them in a hat, and then Chris read them to Lin-Manuel, who improvised a verse about each word over Shockwave's beats.

In one game, called "What Y'all Know?," audience members shouted out topics, and Anthony, Lin-Manuel, and Chris picked one each to unpack in their freestyle. "Maya Angelou!" someone yelled one night. Lin-Manuel claimed her. Maya Angelou had been his favorite author in ninth grade; he'd read her memoirs, her poems, everything he could find. He ransacked his memory for material while Shockwave introduced a beat and Bill and Arthur laid down a groove behind him. Then he started making up rhyming couplets, working toward the title he knew:

Yo, she grew up rough and wild,
Saw things no one should see as a child,
Abused, she saw horrible things,
And so she wrote about it: I Know Why the Caged Bird Sings*!*

When he first started improvising raps, he led with the recognizable phrase. Now he knew to hold it in reserve, setting up a rhyme for a more satisfying payoff. Gaining confidence, he leaned toward the audience, his finger in the air as he remembered another data point and plugged it into a rhyme:

Aw, overcame it all, yes,
In the first touring company of Porgy and Bess*!*
Yeah, traveled Europe with bravery,
She said, "They don't have the same legacy of slavery."

His momentum gathering, his hands waving, his flow accelerated:

A poet, oh my gosh, that's not the end of the story yet.

And then the music dropped out for him to land the climactic line:

The first U.S. Black female poet laureate!

The audience cheered and the guys onstage whooped as the music came back in for Lin-Manuel's victory refrain:

So what *y'all know about Maya Angelou?*

Jill Furman told Tommy that she wanted to produce Freestyle Love Supreme too. "I needed more people to see it," she says. "It was virtuosic. The fact that they could do this off the top of their domes, at the speed of light, working together and engaging the audience, was incredible." They pitched themselves as an improv/hip-hop mash-up: *Whose Line Is It Anyway?* meets the Wu-Tang Clan. In 2004, Freestyle Love Supreme (aka FLS) landed an eight-week residency at Ars Nova, a performance space for new work in Midtown—the first professional run Lin-Manuel had ever experienced. He got stomachaches before every show.

But he also got an agent: John Buzzetti, a talented and tenacious young negotiator who'd just scored his first big hit with *Avenue Q.* Buzzetti had caught a reading of *In the Heights* in the Drama Book Shop basement and admired the guy who played Usnavi, not knowing that he'd also written the show. When Buzzetti saw Lin-Manuel freestyling onstage with FLS at Ars Nova, he was amazed. This was the artist, he thought, who could bring nonbelievers into musical theater. At the end of their first meeting, Buzzetti told Lin-Manuel, with his characteristic directness, "We're going to make you so much money!"

The FLS run at Ars Nova led to a spot at the Aspen Comedy Festival in Colorado and then, in August 2005, just after the O'Neill conference concluded, at the Edinburgh Festival Fringe. In Scotland, Tommy and Lin-Manuel were eager to get some distance from their heartbreak at the O'Neill. They busked on street corners and slapped FLS stickers on lampposts, unburdened for a little while. The *Telegraph* hailed them as "a bunch of fresh-faced, quick-witted New York kids who improvise rap tunes to audience suggestions." They were having fun. "To be across the ocean was liberating for us," Tommy recalls. "In Edinburgh, no one cared about *Heights*. And with FLS, there was a lack of preciousness when you're making up a show every night."

When the Edinburgh sojourn ended and he returned to revising *Heights*, Lin-Manuel found that improv rapping had strengthened his verses for the musical. He calls freestyle "the opposing muscle group" of composing a musical—one requires spontaneity and speed as you invent something that will vanish the moment it's spoken; the other takes planning, patience, revision. Each enhances the other. "My writing on *Heights* got faster and stronger because I was freestyling with Anthony," he says. The hip-hop sections in *Heights* became more conversational, the transitions from speech to song more seamless. "From freestyle, I have firsthand data about what it feels like to break into song, which is what it should feel like in musical theater," he says.

For dozens of FLS performances, he'd listened to Chris Jackson's cadences as he rapped, so when he wrote Benny's verse to kick off "96,000," a song fantasizing about winning a $96,000 lottery payout, he tried to follow the easy confidence of Chris's natural flow:

> *Yo. If I won the lotto tomorrow*
> *Well I know I wouldn't bother goin' on no spending spree.*
> *I'd pick a business school and pay the entrance fee!*
> *Then maybe if you're lucky, you'll stay friends with me!*

Lin-Manuel and Quiara had already revised the script to make Benny's character more closely resemble Chris—now he was Black instead of Latino, and he focused on his career instead of chasing women. The next step was to make Benny sound like Chris too. It was a strategy Lin-Manuel had learned from watching Ms. Ames write new verses for every sixth-grader who wanted to sing: Tailor the part to the person playing it. As Tommy puts it, "Lin likes making suits for people."

Lin-Manuel realized that he could change a character's cadence to indicate how they were feeling. For Usnavi's verse in "96,000," he started off with a methodical, measured flow, stressing every fourth syllable, as Usnavi brings Benny's fantasy down to earth:

> *It's silly when we get into these crazy hypotheticals.*
> *You really want some bread? Then go ahead, create a set of goals*

And cross them off the list as you pursue 'em,
And with those ninety-six I know exactly what I'm doin'.

Then Vanessa enters, knocking a crushed-out Usnavi off course. As his heart skips a beat, so does his flow, skittering into a syncopated fluster:

I take that back, well if it isn't Little Miss Exquisite . . .
I'd sell my lottery ticket to get your digits.

Lin-Manuel himself was about to experience a romantic jolt from a real-life Vanessa. A few months before the O'Neill conference and the Scotland trip, during the Ars Nova run, he'd joined a new social media website called TheFacebook.com, hoping to reconnect with classmates whom he could invite to an FLS show. As he searched for Hunter alumni, he spotted a cute profile picture for a woman who looked familiar.

Her name was Vanessa Nadal. She was stylish, smart, with dark hair, dark eyes, and a winning smile, a blend of her Austrian mother and her Dominican father. Though she'd been two years behind Lin-Manuel in school, he remembered her, one of only a handful of Latinas at Hunter. One afternoon in his senior year while he was blasting Marc Anthony from his boombox in the courtyard, she'd come up to him, a pretty tenth-grader exuding confidence, and asked him to dance. They salsaed together for a song. Then she left. Now, he saw on her profile, she'd graduated from MIT with a major in chemical engineering and was working nearby in New Jersey as a scientist at Johnson and Johnson. Among her interests, she listed salsa and hip-hop.

He messaged her an invitation to an FLS show.

She showed up. She was impressed. Afterward, the group went to a nearby bar, then Lin-Manuel invited her to join him at a speakeasy. They hit it off, talking about Marc Anthony and Jay-Z—just as friends, she assumed. Over the next few months, they kept in touch. At the O'Neill, he texted her for scientific advice. He'd written a verse for Nina: "The guys think I'm foxy / Discussing de-oxy- / ribo-nucleic acid." Was it pronounced "*dee*-oxy" or "*die*-oxy," he asked. She texted back.

Then, after FLS returned from Edinburgh, in the fall of 2005, she brought a big group to one of their shows. "I knew my friends would like it," Vanessa says. "And when Lin was onstage, I was like, 'Oh, that guy's really smart. I like him.'"

After the show, she invited him to join her group for ice cream. Then they decamped to a beer garden with some of her Brooklyn roommates. Around midnight, the roommates announced they were heading home. Vanessa told them she'd stay with Lin-Manuel.

It was a misty night, and as the two of them wondered what to do next, a car skidded on the street in front of them. Vanessa, who'd been playing a lot of video games, exclaimed, "Whoa, that was like Grand Theft Auto!"

Lin-Manuel's heart leaped.

They went up to 5000 Broadway. They played Grand Theft Auto. They listened to Marc Anthony. They salsaed in the living room. The night turned into morning.

The next day, Lin-Manuel phoned his sister, Cita, who was now married with a newborn son, to tell her about the date. "He hadn't ever called me to tell me about a first date before," Cita says. "He was so excited. He was like, 'She went to MIT, she's smart, she's beautiful, and she plays video games!'"

For another date, they explored the neighborhood where, it turned out, they'd both grown up. They started at Lin-Manuel's apartment in Inwood and walked down to Vanessa's parents' apartment in Washington Heights, stopping to show each other their favorite places. Like Lin-Manuel's father, Vanessa's mother grew up in a small town and flew to New York at nineteen, eager to see more of the world. Their lives felt intertwined already, knit together by family parallels, a shared school, the same barrio, common friends, mutual interests, a reciprocated spark.

Lin-Manuel couldn't wait to tell Tommy that he'd met the most amazing woman. On the phone, he recounted their Washington Heights date until Tommy cut him off: "Stop talking to me and write the *Benny and Nina love song right fucking now.*"

It poured out in a giddy duet, intermingling his and Vanessa's perspectives, the rhythms tumbling forward. At the beginning of the song, he gave Nina the sentiment he felt as a child riding the A Train with Mundi: "I used to think we lived at the top of the world / When the world was just a subway map." Rediscovering Washington Heights with Vanessa, seeing it through her eyes, made him feel that sense of possibility again, expansive and familiar.

Even on their first date, it was clear that Vanessa was a much better video-game player than Lin-Manuel. In Grand Theft Auto: San Andreas, which he'd started playing on his PlayStation 2 a year before, you had to complete missions for your avatar to gain assets and enter new parts of the game. Lin-Manuel hadn't completed any missions; he just stole bikes and got shot. As a result, his avatar was spindly and unimpressive. "You have to do the missions!" Vanessa told him. Her burly avatar had a mansion, two cars, and two girlfriends. To him, that felt like a metaphor for their relative professional positions. He was still substitute-teaching and living in a messy bedroom while she had an impressive job as a scientist and drove to work in her own car.

"I was like, *I gotta quit fucking around,*" he says. "*This woman has her shit together. If I'm going to be worthy of her, I gotta do the missions.*"

In real life, that meant finishing his show.

9

OFF BROADWAY

● ●

*L*in-Manuel got to work. He was pleased to find himself unembarrassed writing in front of Vanessa, even if she could hear him "caterwauling," he says. Vanessa, for her part, couldn't work alongside him while he was composing. "He's so loud!" she says. Her office was an hour away in New Jersey; he made her mix CDs with hip-hop and salsa to enliven the commute, and she made him mixes as well, favoring Dominican bachata and merengue alongside Nas and Fiona Apple. Given her own mixed ethnicity, she valued a boyfriend whose taste spanned genres. "I've always taken being mixed as a superpower," she says. "If I'm Austrian and Dominican, I can wear a dirndl and listen to merengue. I liked that Lin appreciated those crossings."

As he worked on the songs in *Heights*, he'd often pop over to Quiara's apartment on the Upper West Side, a block from the McDonald's where he'd worked in high school. "Quiara gives me discipline," he says. "I just need to be in the room with someone working harder." He'd bring coffee; she'd write new monologues for Usnavi; he'd see if he could turn them into songs. "I love the look on Quiara's face when she's writing," he says, "because she's like me: She acts the characters out." When he was ready to share a section with her, he'd perch on the sofa, buzzing, not quite sitting down. Quiara calls it "excited kneeling."

They had a goal. The producers had agreed to fund a four-week workshop in March 2006 for potential investors, called a "backers' audition." Kevin and Jeffrey had finished construction on 37 Arts, a new performance space on West Thirty-Seventh Street near the Hudson River that could host the presentation. Once Lin-Manuel decided to cut Lincoln, the producers could tell that he was serious about getting the show to the finish line.

With Lincoln out of the way, Lin-Manuel delved into Nina's relationship with her father. Lin-Manuel didn't want to make Kevin Rosario a villain, so he needed a song explaining Kevin's perspective. But imagining himself in a father's position—maybe even a version of his own father's position—was tough. At first, he avoided it. Although his father had become an enthusiastic champion of his work on *Heights*, Lin-Manuel still had more than twenty years of their relationship to process. He wasn't ready to dig that deeply into his daddy issues, so he procrastinated by composing an upbeat salsa ditty for a side character, the Piragua Guy, who sells shaved ice topped with flavored syrups in the neighborhood. (He's another emblem of resistance to gentrification, facing a corporate threat from a Mister Softee ice cream truck.) Happy with that one, he shared "Piragua" with Tommy. "Lin, go write the dad song," Tommy told him.

Back at it, Lin-Manuel had a breakthrough. What if Kevin wasn't the blocking figure that he'd been for Lincoln, frustrating his son's dreams of becoming a songwriter by forcing him into the family business? What if instead Kevin was an overzealous supporter, working around the clock so that the next generation could surpass him, as Luis had done for Lin-Manuel? He invented a backstory: Kevin's father had cut sugarcane in Puerto Rico, but Kevin wanted a bigger life. "I didn't have to look farther than my own father to find that drive," Lin-Manuel says. When Kevin told his father that he was getting on a plane to leave the island and change the world, his father slapped his face, looking at him as though he were *inútil*—useless. When Nina drops out of college because of economic pressure, Kevin feels useless again. He resolves to sell the taxi business to pay for Nina's tuition—or else, he sings in a final crescendo, "all my work, all my life / Everything I've sacrificed will have been useless." With a life history of ambition undercut by self-doubt, he wanted to ensure that his daughter could go farther than he had. "'Inútil' is the song I'm proudest of," Lin-Manuel says, looking back. "Little baby Lin took a big leap to get inside Kevin."

A parallel between Nina's and Usnavi's stories started to come into focus. Nina had left the barrio for college but was returning, unsure of where she fit in. Usnavi was anchored to the barrio, running the neighborhood bodega with his cousin Sonny but pining to fly back to the Dominican Republic where he'd been born. At the end of the show, each would decide whether to stay or go. That was a compelling storyline. But in a musical, as the producer Kevin McCollum often reminded them, "plot is less important than stakes." They had to show why the story mattered, why the characters felt emotions so urgently that they'd burst into song. They all knew one of the legends of *Fiddler on the Roof*: When its writers were stuck on the opening number, the director, Jerome Robbins, pressed them to articulate what the show was about. "It's about a dairyman trying to marry off his daughters," they said. "No," Robbins said, "what's the show *really* about?" They pondered the question. "Well," they replied, "it's about . . . tradition." "*That's* your opening number," Robbins told them. They'd found the stakes. Kevin pushed Lin-Manuel and Quiara to do the same.

Then, at Lac's apartment on Eighty-Sixth Street, they cracked it. "We were spinning our wheels," Lin-Manuel says, "until we got to the concept of *home*. This is an immigrant neighborhood where everyone is from somewhere else, so what the fuck does *home* even mean?" That had been an open question in his life ever since he'd started leaving Washington Heights for Hunter during the school year and for Vega Alta in the summers. The question of home resonated for Quiara, too, having bounced between her divorced parents' households and journeyed back and forth from Philly to Yale and Puerto Rico. "Now that we know what the theme is, we can always be having a conversation about what Nina's relationship is to it and what Usnavi's relationship is," Quiara says. Usnavi had to figure out whether his home was in the Dominican Republic or with his cousin in Washington Heights. Nina had to decide if her sense of home with her family was secure enough that she could venture into a less hospitable space for an education.

Kevin loved it. Home felt like a question both specific to Washington Heights and universal for anyone in the audience. "Wherever you're from, you have to decide where your home is," he says. The search for home was a quintessentially New York story, where so many immigrant groups had forged new communities. And it offered stakes that could drive the trajectory Kevin always sought in a musical: begin on earth and end in the heavens. *In the Heights* started with a neighborhood facing earthly problems: rents going up, college tuition rising, the summer heat bearing down. The solutions appear earthly as well: Kevin Rosario sells the taxi business to pay Nina's college tuition; Abuela Claudia wins the $96,000 lottery payout and gives a third to Usnavi so that he can fly back to the DR and open a beachside bar. (That plotline was Lin-Manuel's wish for his Abuela Mundi, who always played the slot machines at their neighborhood bodega but never won big.)

Ultimately, though, the show leaves the earthly realm. In the unrelieved swelter of the blackout, Abuela Claudia passes away. After mourning her, Usnavi plans to depart, but Sonny surprises him: Using his third of the lottery payout, Sonny commissioned the neighborhood graffiti artist to make a mural for the bodega grate. When they pull the grate down, Usnavi sees a portrait of his beloved Abuela Claudia above her motto, *Paciencia y Fe*. He realizes that he belongs in Washington Heights, where he can honor Claudia's legacy by telling her stories. His island isn't in the Caribbean; it's in New York. "You hear that music in the air?" he raps in the finale. "Take the train to the top of the world and I'm there." In the show's final words, above a swelling chorus and an ebullient trumpet, he declares: "I'm home!"

For the cast, *In the Heights* had become a home as well. According to Andréa Burns, who played Daniela, the salon owner, "The most beautiful experience was being in a company with actors who came from all different Latin American countries and realizing how much we have in common." Dialects, cuisines, and musical cadences might vary with national origins, but everyone could recognize a loving abuela, an overprotective father, the neighborhood gossip who cuts hair, and the uniting importance of family, culture, tradition. When Javier Muñoz joined the company, he organized a potluck and invited the actors to contribute specialties from their upbringing. He brought Puerto Rican ceviche; Andréa brought Venezuelan empanadas; Mandy Gonzalez, who played Nina, brought Mexican enchiladas. "You can't help but create community through food," Javier says. On the rooftop at 37 Arts, they continued the festivities, eating and dancing together into the night. Janet Dacal, who played Carla, the other salon lady, called it "party *con* pay"—they were getting paid to have fun with their friends. "We became a family," Andréa says.

That sense of uniting a chosen family across differences animated the musical's second-act showstopper: "Carnaval del Barrio." To counter the feeling of abjection brought on by the blackout, the residents of the neighborhood rally themselves for a block party modeled on the communal *parrandas* of Puerto Rican towns. As the party escalates, neighbors raise flags celebrating each of the places that they've come from: the Dominican Republic, Puerto Rico, Mexico, Cuba. The song conjures a spirit of community resilience through Latinidad, recognizing a common purpose across many points of origin. In a way, it was the musical counterpart to Luis's work with the Hispanic Federation, which brought distinct cultures together as one political force. Although the presentation at 37 Arts was essentially a staged reading—a performance without costumes or props—the company waved actual flags during "Carnaval." "As Latin actors, we had never felt so seen," Andréa says. "We were all rooting for the show so hard. The question was: Will audience members accept this as truth? Or will they prefer the stereotypical violent images?"

Among the invited audience members at 37 Arts was a filmmaker, Andrew Fried, who'd been impressed by Freestyle Love Supreme and had begun shooting a documentary about the group during its trip to Edinburgh. He'd heard about *In the Heights* when Tommy and Lin-Manuel discussed it but assumed that it was a side project, something Lin-Manuel had tried in college and would soon let go of. At the presentation, however, Andrew was astonished. "When they took out the flags during 'Carnaval del Barrio,' it was this magical thing," he recalls. He ended up producing a documentary about *In the Heights* too.

The message for Kevin and the producing team was clear: *We've got to put this in front of an audience.* They knew they couldn't open on Broadway yet, but they thought they could raise three million dollars for an off-Broadway run at 37 Arts. Three years after Jill saw a reading, six years after the Wesleyan version, Kevin told the team: "Let's just produce the fucker!"

For the fully staged production at 37 Arts, *Heights* needed a choreographer. The producers brought in Andy Blankenbuehler, a Broadway dance veteran a few years older than the rest of Voltron. He didn't get their *West*

Wing references, but he got their music. Andy says that before *Heights*, he was "a B-minus choreographer." When he heard a score on the piano, the way most composers wrote it, without the full orchestration, he found it hard to discern enough specificity to work out precise movements. But because Lin-Manuel wasn't a pianist, he had started making song demos on Garage Band, the music-software program that came installed on Apple computers, complete with bass, drums, horns, and vocal layers. "No one had ever sent me a demo," Andy says. "My career completely changed with Lin." The first time Andy heard a *Heights* demo, he was riding in a car after a dental procedure, his mouth numb. Listening to "96,000," he started bawling. It was so unexpectedly precise that it opened every possibility for him. "We talk about seeing the numbers, like in *The Matrix*," Andy says. "When I heard that music, I saw the numbers. I knew exactly how I would choreograph it."

Instead of choreographing steps, Andy choreographed ideas. He'd tell the dancers why they were moving and give them an image to embody. He took inspiration from breakdancing, from salsa and merengue, from Justin Timberlake and Bob Fosse, even from his morning walk to Starbucks. Looking down at Times Square from his dance studio on Forty-Third Street, he saw people constrained by their individual agendas, walking in straight lines. "That's what I'm going to choreograph in the opening number," he decided, "because people feel they don't have choices. But then when they're in community, they realize they have options, and they move in a circle." It was his own homage to Jerome Robbins's choreography for *Fiddler on the Roof*: the circle of community.

As the off-Broadway production moved ahead, Lin-Manuel ran into Bobby Lopez, his fellow Hunter alum and the Tony-winning composer of *Avenue Q*. He invited Bobby to lunch, and over matzo ball soup at Cafe Edison, he pumped the more experienced writer for information. What was it like to work with Kevin and Jeffrey as producers? What was it like to develop a show, take it to off Broadway, and finally get it to Broadway?

Bobby confessed that it had been a horrible experience. "I told him that I started drinking," Bobby says. "I was banging my head against the wall. You're always dealing with what doesn't work. It's so stressful, you feel vulnerable, and finally you get through it and find your way. But my lesson was that it's impossible to enjoy the process."

To Bobby's surprise, whenever he encountered Lin-Manuel after that, the younger composer did not appear to be banging his head against the wall. "He seemed to be having a fucking ball at every stage of the process!" Bobby says. "He's so annoyingly well adjusted." Quiara noticed the same phenomenon. "He loved being the leader of the ensemble, and they could feel it, and they loved being led by Lin," she says. The cast called him "the Touchstone." "It was stressful," Quiara grants, "but he found a way to enjoy it that was remarkable."

For Lin-Manuel, that positive approach was simply how Meredith had taught him to lead at Hunter. If it was your show, you were responsible for setting the tone; if you needed your cast to learn to dance, you declared it National Mambo Week. "It was a real by-product of doing student theater," he says. "All I can do is make it a fun enough experience that people want to come back." He remembered losing cast members to summer camp, to sports, to other projects. "This has to be the most fun option," he felt. And beyond a recruitment strategy, he believed that enjoying the process would lead to better work.

He also had his new relationship with Vanessa to buoy him. He arranged dates where she could get to know his friends and family, then told her after a month, "Okay, you've met all the important people in my life." That impressed her. "I was like, 'Oh, that's really cool that you took the time to set up meetings with the people who really matter to you, because that must mean I really matter to you too,'" she recalls.

His emotional expressiveness also endeared him to her. He was an artist, deeply connected to his feelings; she was a rational scientist. "I thought he was a good counterpart to me," she says. "I'm very logical, not super-emotional, direct in my speech and my actions. In my teens and twenties, there was still a trope that women were too emotional to be in business. Naturally, I internalized that a logical, unemotional mindset would help me succeed. I always thought of calm rationality as a strength, but many seemed to think that was odd for a woman." She recalls that Lin-Manuel "was one of the few people who didn't make me feel like that was a weakness." He admired her logical mind. He didn't need her to emote; when they went to the movies, he'd be the one crying. "I had never met a man who was both secure about his masculinity and so unapologetic about his emotional vulnerability," she continues. "It shifted my mindset about what emotional strength could be. Emotions didn't have to cripple me or make people see me as unfit. Being nice didn't have to mean I was placating or submissive. I knew that I would learn from him."

Everything seemed to be falling into place, but nothing was guaranteed. Lin-Manuel dreamed that with *Heights*, he might follow Bobby Lopez's *Avenue Q* trajectory to Broadway and Tony victories. Another one of Kevin and Jeffrey's productions, however, offered a reminder that no one could predict what would happen in show business. Two months before *Heights* was scheduled to start its off-Broadway performances, *High Fidelity*, a ten-million-dollar musical adapted from the popular rom-com of the same name, opened on Broadway. It was a known property with an established Broadway director and well-respected writers. Kevin and Jeffrey had invested; Lac had even helped with the orchestrations. "It was our big-brother show," Lin-Manuel says. "That was the show that was supposed to pay for *Heights*." But *High Fidelity* received middling reviews, and ticket sales never took off. When it closed ten days after it opened, Lin-Manuel recalls, "It put the fear of God into us."

Lin-Manuel's longstanding fear of premature death flared up again as opening night approached. What if he never lived to see his work in the world? Anything could happen. After all, Jonathan Larson had died of an aortic aneurysm the night before *Rent*'s first performance. Lin-Manuel's stomach started acting up. He was scared to cross the street.

One day at 37 Arts, Karen Olivo, who played Vanessa (and who now goes by K O and uses the pronouns *they/them*), popped by his dressing room on the way to a costume change after hearing he was sick. He sat at his desk, his head in his hands. "Bro, what's up?" K O asked. When he raised his head, K O says, "He was gray. It was the only time I've seen him not his exuberant self." He was worried that he'd let people down if he couldn't perform that day. K O told him that the choice had been made for him: He was sitting this one out. His understudy could take over. "It was one of those moments when you realize that our fearless leader, our touchstone, is not impervious," K O says. "After that, we tried to take care of him." They brought him Luna Bars to make sure he got enough calories; Olga Merediz, a Broadway veteran who'd taken over the role of Abuela Claudia, went to Chinatown for herbs to soothe Lin-Manuel's stomach. "I felt motherly toward him," Olga says. "He had a lot on his shoulders, and he feels it in his body."

Quiara felt the anxiety too. "If one of us tripped on a sidewalk crack," she says, "we would joke: 'Well, that's it!'" (Her aunt, a professional musician, would tell her: "Don't die like Jonathan Larson!") She was also eight months pregnant; she and her husband were expecting their first child a few weeks after opening night. She and Lin-Manuel both channeled their nerves into last-minute revisions. He was proud of a triple-time couplet he wrote for Carla in "Carnaval del Barrio" that he felt encapsulated the whole show's hyphenated sense of home:

> My mom is Dominican-Cuban, my dad is from Chile and P.R., which
>   means:
> I'm Chile-Domini-Curican, but I always say I'm from Queens!

Quiara kept tweaking a faltering scene with Nina and Benny all the way through the final tech rehearsal, when the actors synched up with the lighting and sound cues. After tech ended, the show had to freeze—meaning that no more changes were allowed. "I was trying to put in a laugh line so the audience wouldn't notice that the scene didn't work," Quiara recalls. "I was literally throwing paper at Mandy and Chris, saying, 'Try these lines!'" The stage manager announced that they had to stop. There was nothing more Quiara could do to fix the scene. She walked around the corner to meet her husband for dinner, returned afterward to the theater alone, and realized her water had broken.

It was an hour to curtain. The baby was coming three weeks early. Tommy rushed her home in a cab, and her husband took her to the hospital, where she delivered by emergency C-section. Her daughter and her show arrived on the same night.

Back in Theater A at 37 Arts, *In the Heights* began its first performance for a paying New York audience. It was February 2007. The set looked like Lin-Manuel's childhood view of his neighborhood when his Abuela Mundi took him to piano lessons: Downstage, the A Train subway station entrance at 181st Street; upstage, looming above the bodega, the outline of the George Washington Bridge. Signs for a German-Jewish bakery and an Irish car service hearkened back to earlier waves of immigrants in the neighborhood.

Then the beat dropped: a son clave rhythm, five syncopated clacks—the foundation of salsa, the same beat that Leonard Bernstein borrowed for the start of "America" in *West Side Story*. *Clack, clack, clack. Clack-clack.* Over the beat, a graffiti artist appeared, breakdancing and spinning his paint cans; he was about to tag the bodega when Usnavi entered and chased him away. Sporting a Kangol cap, a red guayabera, a white tank top, and baggy jeans, Lin-Manuel began the show:

> *Lights up on Washington Heights, up at the break of day.*
> *I wake up, and I got this little punk I gotta chase away.*
> *Pop the grate at the crack of dawn, sing*
> *While I wipe down the awning.*

Glimpsing the audience, he welcomed them with a Biggie-style slant rhyme:

> *Hey, y'all, good* mawn-*ing.*

A Puerto Rican beat, a hip-hop couplet, a musical-theater narrator—the show's synthesis of forms taught the audience how to listen from the opening verse. Like Tevye denominating the shtetl's papas and mamas, Usnavi introduced the audience to each of his neighbors as they entered. And when the opening number ended, everyone chorused together: "En Washington Heights!"

That final five-note phrase was all that remained from the Wesleyan version written seven years earlier. Every song, every scene, every line of dialogue, every musical part had been reworked along the way.

Friends from Wesleyan who came to see the off-Broadway production marveled at how much it had changed. The eighty-minute college one-act tracking youthful relationships that all ended in heartbreak had become a full-fledged two-act about a Latino neighborhood facing the threat of economic displacement. For Owen Panettieri, who'd managed the Wesleyan box office, an undergrad production had grown into a professional musical. The first version was, he says, "a very entertaining college show, put together with no budget, no sleep, and Lin trying to write and finish and direct it." Now Owen could tell that Lin-Manuel had expanded his dramatic focus beyond his own relationships, and he'd developed a greater facility with language after freestyling for years. Aileen Payumo, the original Nina, credited Lin-Manuel with taking feedback that improved the show, even if it meant getting rid of its central character. "In killing Lincoln, he killed what the original *In the Heights* was about," she says. "And in doing that, he created an *In the Heights* that was so much better, about the whole community."

Was it good enough to become a hit? On opening night, February 8, 2007, the critic for the *New York Times* wasn't sure. Charles Isherwood's review praised the exuberant cast, the lively hip-hop and Latin score, and the joyous choreography. But Isherwood felt the story was undermined by "sentimental simplicity." As the company had feared, a Latino neighborhood that didn't look like *West Side Story* or images on the news proved a tough sell. "Mr. Miranda and Ms. Hudes's panorama of barrio life is untagged by any graffiti suggesting authentic despair, serious hardship or violence," Isherwood lamented, calling the book "unfortunately underspiced."

David Rooney's review for *Variety* struck a similar note, finding the performances charming, the music fresh, and the dancing delightful, even if the plotlines seemed "pedestrian," leaning toward "sentimental cliché." He, too, doubted the portrayal of Washington Heights. "There may be financial woes," Rooney granted, "but there's little evidence of drugs, crime, violence or machismo in this idealized fairy-tale world." Only Jeremy McCarter, writing for *New York* magazine, heralded the show as a breakthrough—"a musical that owes more to Big Pun than to Bernstein"—noting that, in its contemporary idiom and its complex treatment of the effects of gentrification, it "could only have been written right here and now."

The producers took stock. "It got mixed to good reviews, but they weren't *money* reviews," Jill says. Though the show ran through July, it wasn't selling out its small, off-Broadway house. Still, Kevin felt they'd learned that *Heights* was a New York show, and it could attract a New York audience for a Broadway run, at least for a few months. "We could lose our money, but it was worth it," he says.

But *Heights* had no name actors, no recognizable source material, no rave reviews, and no record of box office success. If the show couldn't pack a three-hundred-seat theater off Broadway, how would it fill a thirteen-hundred-seat house on Broadway? In 2007, according to the Broadway League, Hispanic audiences made up less than 6 percent of Broadway ticket buyers. Most Broadway audiences were white, often out-of-town tourists eager to see a familiar name or title. A Broadway show cost about ten million dollars to mount, and conventional wisdom held that four out of five Broadway shows failed to earn back their investment. To become one of the rare successes, a show needed something special. *Heights* did not seem likely to earn that distinction.

As Jill recalls, "So many people in the industry thought we were nuts!" Yet the team had confidence, she says. "We knew the work we had to do."

10

BROADWAY

• •

*J*effrey Seller had a plan. For *In the Heights* to get ready for Broadway, it needed showstoppers—musical numbers that soared until the audience exploded with applause. That would not only allow ticket buyers to feel that they'd had an ecstatic experience but also address the critics' concern that the musical didn't feel momentous enough, that it didn't have high enough stakes. If the creative team could show that the barrio characters' dreams of education, economic security, and finding home felt epic and urgent to them, perhaps audiences would feel it too.

Jeffrey turned to their reliable model: *Fiddler on the Roof.* He'd read a book, *The Making of a Musical,* by Jerome Robbins's assistant director, that described the development of *Fiddler's* big first-act number, "To Life." The song started with a single voice—Tevye toasting the occasion of his daughter's engagement—then swelled into a communal celebration, a lively dance, a dream of prosperity, a rousing affirmation of life. Jeffrey thought that was a lesson for the big first-act number in *Heights,* "96,000," when each character imagined what they'd do if they won the lottery. "When we did '96,000' off Broadway, it was a great number, but it never got over the rafters," he recalls. Instead of building to an emphatic climax, the song faded away like a fleeting dream. Jeffrey handed each of the six creatives—Lin-Manuel, Tommy, Quiara, Bill, Lac, and Andy—a copy of *The Making of a Musical* and told them, "You must turn '96,000' into 'To Life.'"

Part of the problem was that the song lacked a button—a musical bounce that signaled the song's satisfying end and cued the audience applause. "Lin's songs are great, but he doesn't often write endings," Bill notes. For the off-Broadway production, Lin-Manuel's agent, John Buzzetti, kept pressing the point. "It was one of my obsessions," he says. "They never wanted to button any number. I was begging them: *You have to button it!*" As an opening-night gag gift at 37 Arts, Tommy gave Lin-Manuel a bagful of little buttons.

To tackle "96,000," Voltron convened in Andy's dance studio, where he developed choreography in front of a giant mirror. The film crew that was making a documentary about *In the Heights* captured what happened next.

As the creative team sat around a table, scores open, Tommy set the agenda: "This needs to be that moment in the show when someone's watching the big number, and it needs to go to a place that no one expects."

Lac elaborated on the problem they'd been facing. As arrangers, he and Bill had been tinkering with the ending, taking bits of Lin-Manuel's lyrics and attempting to splice them into a dramatic finale. "I'm trying to think about why so many of our numbers don't have that button that feels like it resolves, like *Ah, we're here,*" Lac said.

In the final lines of "96,000," the ensemble sang:

No tiptoein'
We'll get the dough 'n'
Once we get goin'
We're never gonna stop!

Lac wondered if they were getting to that *stop* too quickly; they should be building to it gradually, ratcheting up tension toward the final exclamation point.

Lin-Manuel jumped in with a possibility. What if they repeated the line "No tiptoein' / We'll get the dough 'n'" in an unexpected way?

Lac started playing the piano and singing the vocal line from the end of the number. Andy leaped in front of the mirror and improvised steps to the music.

Then Andy came back to the piano. "I felt like it needed to repeat," he said.

"Like real quiet," Lin-Manuel told Lac.

Lac played it again and Andy and Lin-Manuel tried it in front of the mirror. Tommy and Quiara conferred in the corner.

Andy went back to the piano with another idea for the build. "I want to do this totally stop-time thing." He tilted his torso backward in slow motion as though he were dodging a bullet in *The Matrix*. It looked cool. "But have we earned it yet?" Andy asked.

Lac offered a solution. "What if that movement happens when he wants to go soft?" he suggested, imitating the slow-motion tilt as he pointed at Lin-Manuel.

Andy and Lin-Manuel danced it. They froze their bodies and repeated "No tiptoein'" in a whisper as the piano cut out. Then they started to crescendo with the piano on "We'll get the dough 'n'," building through "Once we get goin'," and rushing toward the mirror on "We're never gonna—"

But instead of resolving, they held off the ending. They added one more repetition to build up the tension even more until the final time at full volume: "We're never gonna stop!"

Lac cascaded chords down the keyboard as Andy skittered to a halt, laughing. Lac pounded one final chord—the button that said, *Ah, we're here!*

Lin-Manuel nodded. Quiara grinned. Lac tilted his head back and guffawed. Andy slapped the top of the piano.

"There we go," Bill said. "That's a song."

The collaboration worked. Tommy set the task; Lin-Manuel generated an idea; Bill, Lac, and Andy made it better. As Lin-Manuel put it, "Now that thing has a button, a zipper, and Velcro on it."

To make room for new material, Lin-Manuel had to cut Chris Jackson's second-act solo, which shared information the audience already knew. "He cut some *amazing* songs," Quiara says, "songs that are musically stunning, that would be a lot of people's A-material." But if they didn't serve the story, they had to go. When Stephen Sondheim visited Hunter, back when Lin-Manuel was a senior, the master had talked about cutting the lyrics to an entire song he'd written to open the show because Jerome Robbins wanted to introduce the world through dance instead. Lin-Manuel took the lesson from his role model: "Sometimes you throw out good stuff so you can get to the best stuff, and it's about the best idea in the room winning."

As *Heights* evolved, he cut dozens of songs, including "Never Give Your Heart Away" and "On My Shoulders"—forty songs or more, all told. Vanessa appreciated his discipline. It appealed to her logical side. "One of Lin's super-strengths is being able to edit his work," she says. "His goal is to get the story told. If he has to cut a song, he figures he'll find another time to use it." Writing *Heights*, in fact, confirmed that nothing was truly lost. For the opening notes of "96,000," Lin-Manuel repurposed the theme from the song he'd written for his high-school film *Naughtybird Curtsy* but hadn't used because the band didn't want to perform it. It wasn't the last time he'd return to high-school castoffs for a musical motif. He collected all the discarded material; he called it his "Junk in the Trunk."

All these revisions were necessary to make *Heights* Broadway-ready. "Nobody's first show goes to Broadway," Bobby Lopez, the composer of *Avenue Q* and *The Book of Mormon*, points out. "You can't have learned enough. There's no chance that you have the skill and craft and the relationships to collaborators and producers and the connection to what you need to say and what people need to hear. College kids don't have that. It was only possible for Lin because *Heights* was completely rewritten as a wholly different thing."

No song went through more iterations, more scrapped versions, than Nina's solo "Breathe." It came right after the opening number and had to define her journey. "If you ask any composer," Bill says, "they'd say the second song, the 'I Want' song, is the hardest. 'Breathe' was like forty-five different songs before it became 'Breathe.'" At Wesleyan, when Nina was defined by her crush on Benny, her solo was a slow torch song, "I Fell in Love on a Saturday." At the early workshops in the Drama Book Shop, that song became a number called "Nina's Diary." At the O'Neill, when Nina's character started to wrestle with cultural expectations, the solo was an upbeat salsa number about Latina stereotypes called "Sizzling Hot." As her character navigated the conflict with college and family, the song morphed into "Almost Home." Then a composer friend of Jeffrey's who saw the O'Neill presentation pointed out that all the songs were in a standard 4/4 meter and that the show's rhythm could use more variety, so Lin-Manuel decided to differentiate Nina from her community by writing a song for her in a lilting 3/4 meter instead.

By the off-Broadway run at 37 Arts, Lin-Manuel had found the refrain Nina would sing as she carried the weight of her family's expectations: "Just breathe." Coming back home after dropping out of college, she
worried about disappointing everyone who'd believed in her. "I was painfully aware of how hard my parents worked so I could do what I wanted,"
Lin-Manuel said. "My parents didn't kill themselves so I could just *think*
about writing a play and continue substitute-teaching for the rest of my
life."

For Broadway, the song needed a bridge—a middle section that
would travel to a different register and return, transformed, for the final
verse. Lin-Manuel sought an image for Nina's uncertainty as she returned
to her neighborhood, singing with her "eyes on the horizon." That was
it—the horizon viewed from Washington Heights when you looked out
over the Hudson River. Lin-Manuel had seen it looming all his life: the
George Washington Bridge—or, as the locals called it, the GWB. There,
he realized, he could find the ending for the musical bridge, its question
contained in the letters *GWB*: "Just me and the GWB asking, 'Gee, Nina,
what'll you be?'"

Lin-Manuel sent a demo to Mandy Gonzalez, a powerhouse vocalist
who'd turned down an offer to play Elphaba in *Wicked* to stay available in
case *Heights* made it to Broadway. As the daughter of Mexican and Jewish
parents, she says, "I knew Nina. Being the person who wanted to make her
family proud, feeling like she's letting people down—I get that." As a present for Broadway, Lin-Manuel made Mandy a CD mixtape that included
every previous version of "Breathe."

There were always more revisions to make—a sharper punch line, a
snappier rhyme, a simpler phrase—and to procrastinate, Lin-Manuel took
on side projects. In August 2007, as he readied *Heights* for Broadway, Disney released *High School Musical 2*, a follow-up to its popular TV film starring Zac Efron as a basketball star torn between playing for his team and
performing in the school musical. In the sequel, Efron sang an anguished
solo called "Bet on It" in which he expressed his inner conflict by scamper-
ing around a golf course and leaping into a sand trap. One of Lin-Manuel's
costars, K O, happened to see the video and sent a clip to Lin-Manuel with
the comment "Bro, isn't this insane?"

Immediately, he shot a message back: "I'm remaking this."

Perhaps K O shouldn't have been surprised by the reaction. "Bet on It" hit several Lin-Manuel teenage sweet spots: an emotionally overwrought high-school star, a kinetic music video, and the opportunity to jump off things. Lin-Manuel rewrote the lyrics ("Will I be in the Heights? You know you can / Bet on it, bet on it!") and enlisted a Hunter student to film him.

What Lin-Manuel had in mind, beyond a parodic homage to *High School Musical 2*, was a promotional video for the Broadway transfer. He cavorted across Central Park, and then the camera zoomed in on him as he sang a reworked "Bet on It" bridge, now a marketing rap:

Hi, my name is Lin Miranda.
I know you don't know who I am but I
Wore these pants and I'm willin' to dance
Like an idiot if ya just gimme the chance
To just plug my show and reach the people,
Bust my flow cuz the flow is lethal.
It's called In the Heights *and life is sweet, yo!*

Lin-Manuel uploaded the video to a website that by 2007 had become one of the most-trafficked places on the internet: YouTube.com. Back at Wesleyan, when he'd wanted to promote his shows with a custom rap, he had only the scope of the campus message service, the Bulletin Broadcast Review, to reach an audience. Now he could share "Heights Cool Musical Too . . . Bet on It!" on a platform that the whole digital world could see. He'd started posting videos to YouTube the previous year, but "Bet on It" was his first complete music video. It would eventually get more than a million views.

In the fall of 2007, seeking higher production values, he asked the documentary film crew that was following *In the Heights* to Broadway if they'd be willing to shoot another music video parody for him. Rihanna had the song of the year, singing, "You can stand under my um-buh-rella," as she danced in black leather beneath falling raindrops. For his version of "Umbrella," Lin-Manuel coaxed Olga Merediz into a housedress and black leather gloves to sing, "You can come home to your a-bu-ela!" Shot with black-clad backup dancers, hip-hop choreography, and the occasional tossed bottle of water for aquatic effects, "In the Heights . . . Abuela" went up on YouTube too.

It wasn't uncommon for a Broadway-bound show to release an official advertising video through traditional media. The producers for *In the Heights* even commissioned a thirty-second TV commercial, taking the extra step to film the cast performing sections of the opening number, "96,000," and the finale in an actual Washington Heights neighborhood. But for the show's creator to make his own promotional videos as pop-culture spoofs and release them himself through social media was unprecedented.

One night in January 2008, Lin-Manuel and Tommy walked through Times Square, wearing backpacks over their jackets, the documentary crew trailing them.

"What I love is the people who look and see how unfamous we are," Tommy said.

Lin-Manuel laughed.

"There's a good chance no one will ever know who you are," Tommy mused.

"Right."

Then they turned the corner onto Forty-Sixth Street and saw a sign for their show gleaming above the Richard Rodgers Theatre. The street-level marquee still advertised the previous production that had played there, a revival of *Cyrano de Bergerac* starring Kevin Kline, whose glorious performance as the Pirate King in *The Pirates of Penzance* had spurred a ninth-grade Lin-Manuel to bound onto the Hunter auditorium stage. On top of the building, in blue and red capital letters, a billboard spelled out IN THE HEIGHTS.

"I guess we gotta do it now," Tommy said, grinning, as they stared at the sign. They were standing across the street from the billboard in front of a theater where the stage version of *The Little Mermaid* was opening.

"Yeah, we have to finish the show," Lin-Manuel deadpanned. A twenty-foot-high image of him as Usnavi loomed on the side of the Richard Rodgers Theatre.

As opening night approached, everyone stepped up their game. Jeffrey pressed the company to do better each day. Andy, the choreographer, made a list jokingly titled "People Who Can Still Fuck It Up." After the orchestra rehearsal with the cast, he crossed off the names of Lac, Bill, and Lin-Manuel. Only his and Tommy's names remained. Andy taught the cast the final freeze move for the button of "96,000." Then it was Sunday, March 9, 2008.

"I thank you for everything," Tommy told the company before the performance. "They'll let us do it again on Tuesday, so let's have a great opening."

Each of the producers gave a pre-curtain speech. "I feel like it's commencement," Jeffrey said, "because Lin, Tommy, Quiara—you're done writing *In the Heights*. Now we give *In the Heights* to the world."

Lin-Manuel had spent the day making personalized mixtapes for each member of the cast. "The whole thing is to keep your head down and stay focused," he told the documentary crew following him. "Cast gifts are great. It's good to spend your day thinking about other people, because otherwise you're doomed." He now lived in an apartment closer to the theater district on a desolate stretch of West End Avenue between Hell's Kitchen and the Upper West Side that he'd dubbed "Upper West Hell." Near the front door, he put up framed posters of *The Capeman* (the musical that made him realize no one was going to write his dream show for him) and *Basketcase* (the musical in which he'd proven that he could tell a story through the pop genres he loved). On the wall above his keyboard hung signed posters from Brick Prison, a reminder of the first musicals he'd ever written and of the collaborative energy it took to bring them to life. In ten years, he'd gone from being the high-school composer of *7 Minutes in Heaven* to the Broadway creator and star of *In the Heights*. A week earlier, during the show's previews, *Time* magazine had hailed *In the Heights*, with its representation of hope and change, as "the first musical of the Barack Obama era." Lin-Manuel admitted to the film crew, "I feel like I've pulled a cloud out of the sky and get to sit in it."

Before Lin-Manuel left for the Richard Rodgers, Vanessa gave him a good-luck kiss. He brought his preferred preshow meal—a chicken breast sandwich and matzo ball soup from Cafe Edison across the street from the theater—to his dressing room, which was a little home away from home: He had a cupboard and a fridge stocked with snacks, a loft bed above his mirror for quick naps, and a TV connected to his PlayStation. On the wall, he put up his gift from Janet Dacal and Andréa Burns, the salon ladies: a poster with all the silly notes he'd passed them during the off-Broadway run, written on the backs of lottery tickets from the bodega. He swung by the other dressing rooms for jokes and hugs. K O, clad in a bathrobe, always shouted, "Dreams come true, bitches!" Tommy popped by the dressing rooms too. "Don't embarrass me," he told the cast. The mood was festive but anxious. "It's like prom night—with career ramifications," Lin-Manuel said.

Back in Lin-Manuel's dressing room, his family crowded in to wish him well. A few minutes before curtain, everyone filed out—except his sister. When she'd seen *Heights* off Broadway, Cita was blown away. "I got a little anxiety attack," she recalls. "I was like, *Oh my God, he did it! This could be amazing for him, and it could bring the Latino experience to Broadway.* I was so full of emotion and anxiety that I felt sick." Now, as her younger brother's show was about to open on Broadway, she thought back to their childhood. Little Lin-Manuel often asked her to listen to the songs he made up on the piano outside her room. At the time, she found his requests annoying; she had schoolwork to do. But here he was, a twenty-eight-year-old moments away from taking the stage in a musical he'd composed himself. She wanted him to know that she wished she'd listened more.

"Lin, I'm so sorry," she began. "When you played songs as a boy and I wouldn't listen, I should have—"

He cut her off. "Cita, I can't do this right now!" he exclaimed. He was grateful and moved, but he needed to conserve his emotions for the performance.

Backstage, all the actors joined up and held hands. Chris Jackson, whom the cast called "our pastor in residence," led a prayer circle. ("Theater is church to me," he says.) He told everyone to stay safe and to lead with love. "Ultimately," he wished, "may we all be better when we leave than when we came in." After their "Amen," Lin-Manuel screamed, "Eat 'em up!" He drank a cup of water and chewed an Altoid. Then he hugged Olga Merediz, took a deep breath, and made his entrance.

The applause started as soon as he stepped onstage. It hardly stopped until the end of the night. "Breathe" soared. The button on the end of "96,000" landed with an explosion. "Carnaval del Barrio" lifted the roof of the Richard Rodgers. At the end of the finale, when Usnavi declared, "I'm home," thirteen hundred audience members rose in a standing ovation.

After the cast's final bow, Lin-Manuel let out an exultant "Wepa!" Someone in the orchestra pit handed him a microphone. He held it up to his mouth to speak, then crossed his arms and took in the ovation. He blinked away tears. Chris, standing next to him, squeezed his shoulders. Lin-Manuel tried the microphone again. "Forgive me for speaking slowly," he told the audience. "I don't ever want to forget this moment as long as I live." Each of his collaborators joined him onstage. He wrapped Tommy in a fierce hug. Then he turned back to the audience one more time and quoted Abuela Claudia's question at the end of "Paciencia y Fe": "Ay, mama, what do you do when your dreams come true?"

On their way to the opening-night party, the producers looked for the review from the *New York Times*, which could determine their fortunes. An opening-night audience nearly always responds enthusiastically, as it's mostly composed of friends, family, and invited guests. The press was another matter. When he reviewed *Heights* off Broadway, the critic Charles Isherwood was measured in his enthusiasm, enumerating the musical's "not inconsiderable flaws," even as he praised its exuberance. The show needed a more resounding rave to draw audiences for an extended run. A pan could close them in a week—the fate of the producers' previous Broadway show, *High Fidelity*. Kevin called their public relations rep for an update. He was promised the review within the hour.

Kevin, Jeffrey, and Jill arrived at the party, and the PR rep drew them aside. He had the review on his phone. As the producers huddled in anticipation, the rep read it to them aloud.

"It has been lamented in certain circles that they don't make Broadway musical stars the way they used to," Charles Isherwood began. But "the theater has not gone out of the star-making business entirely. If you stroll down to the Richard Rodgers Theater, where the spirited musical 'In the Heights' opened on Sunday night, you'll discover a singular new sensation, Lin-Manuel Miranda, commanding the spotlight as if he were born in the wings."

Kevin started to laugh in relief and exultation. Jeffrey joined in, nodding. Jill held her hands to her mouth. "Oh my God," she said. Their belief in the young man Jill spotted in the basement of the Drama Book Shop had been validated by the paper of record in laudatory terms that could blaze from the marquee.

The rep read the rest of the review. Isherwood still faulted the story—"basically a salsa-flavored soap opera"—but granted that "when this musical erupts in one of its expressions of collective joy, the energy it gives off could light up the George Washington Bridge for a year or two." Jeffrey beamed. The buttons had worked. "After all," the review concluded, "this scrappy little musical about chasing your dreams and finding your true home is Mr. Miranda's own dream come true. He couldn't look more at home."

At that moment, however, Lin-Manuel did not feel at home. His father was behaving oddly. Though Lin-Manuel had hoped to read the review in private, Luis pressed him to read it aloud at the party. "I don't want to," Lin-Manuel said, but his dad snapped that he had to. Something was off.

The next day, his mother told him. Luis's own father, Lin-Manuel's Abuelo Güisin, was dying in Vega Alta. The family had kept his illness from Lin-Manuel because they wanted him to focus on the show. Now that *Heights* had opened successfully, they could tell him the truth.

Lin-Manuel felt bereft. He considered his grandfather one of his best friends. Although he was a quiet, traditional man, he adored the sensitive, creative boy whom he'd escort from New York to Puerto Rico on the plane, joking that Lin-Manuel, a vegetarian at the time, should order the chicken entrée so that his grandfather could eat it. "I remember thinking he was the funniest person," Lin-Manuel says. "I never felt anything but unconditional love from him."

One of the *In the Heights* investors loaned the Mirandas a private plane so they could fly together to Puerto Rico, where Luis's sister, Yamilla, met them. Abuelo Güisin lay intubated in the hospital. He held Lin-Manuel's hand as his grandson said goodbye. Three hours later, while the Mirandas were flying back home, Luis A. Miranda Sr. passed away. "I had to wait until they landed in New York to say my father died," Yamilla recalls, in tears. "It's like he was waiting for Lin-Manuel to come."

When he returned to the show, Lin-Manuel found a process of grieving built into the performance. In the second act, after "Carnaval del Barrio," the neighborhood learns that Abuela Claudia has passed away in the punishing summer heat. Usnavi delivers her eulogy:

Abuela Claudia had simple pleasures.
She sang the praises of things we ignore:

Glass Coke bottles, bread crumbs, a sky full of stars,
She cherished these things, she'd say "Alabanza."
"Alabanza" means to raise this thing to God's face
And to sing, quite literally, "Praise to this."
When she was here, the path was clear.
And she was just here, she was just here . . .

In the performances the week after Abuelo Güisin's funeral, Cita could tell that Lin-Manuel was singing about their grandfather. As he puts it, "My mourning became the second act of the show."

Even though Luis was grieving, too, he was never one to wallow. He was a relentless political operative. He made things happen for the people and causes he cared about. By 2008, he'd helped get Chuck Schumer and Hillary Clinton elected senators from New York. He knew how to turn out the Latino vote. And now he saw it as his job to turn out Latino audiences for his son's show.

That meant tapping his connections in public relations to spread the message in uptown communities that didn't always see Broadway as accessible or relevant. "Luis was extremely helpful to us in cultivating the Latino market," Jill says. "He was doing on-the-ground work for us as a very supportive cheerleading father." Off Broadway, when the show didn't have any marketing buzz, Luis reached out to Latino groups and sold batches of tickets. "My dad was filling the seats from the beginning," Cita says. "He got the word out: This is about you guys!" (In the year after *In the Heights* opened at the Richard Rodgers, Hispanic attendance on Broadway increased by 50 percent.) As part of his community outreach, Luis asked Lin-Manuel to do events at the Northern Manhattan Arts Alliance, which the Hispanic Federation supported. As Quiara recalls, "Luis insisted that you can't come from the community and tell its stories and not acknowledge that community is full of artists too."

Once *Heights* opened on Broadway, its producers turned their eyes to the Tony Awards that June. Even with quotable reviews, performances weren't selling out; the show's ticket sales were reaching only half the box office potential. Winning the coveted Best Musical award was the best marketing possible—free advertising on a nationally televised broadcast that could extend the run of a show by months or even years. But *Heights*

faced fierce competition. According to the *New York Times*, the most energetic support for Best Musical in the 2008 season came for *Passing Strange*,
the rocker Stew's autobiographical show about a young Black man coming
of age as an artist. With the feel of a club concert, the show received rave
reviews when it transferred from the Public Theater to Broadway, and its
galvanizing score—a witty mix of punk, funk, and blues—earned it fer-
vent partisans. Lin-Manuel and Stew each admired the other's work, and
their companies cheered each other on. They didn't want the narrative to
become "the brown folks versus the Black folks," as Eisa Davis, a *Passing
Strange* actor, put it. But producers counted on Tonys to boost their sales,
so the competition began.

Kevin and Jeffrey had run victorious Tony campaigns before, none
more dramatic than in 2004 when their underdog puppet show *Avenue Q*
beat the juggernaut *Wicked* for Best Musical behind the slogan "Vote with
your heart!" Lin-Manuel knew the producers would shift the voting criteria to their advantage by raising doubts about whether *Passing Strange*,
however phenomenal, was really a musical. "Their strategy was: *Passing
Strange* is an iconoclastic thing that breaks the borders of what a musical
does, and *In the Heights* is an innovative musical from a guy who's going to
write ten more."

Would their strategy work? In the days before the ceremony at Radio
City Music Hall, the *Times* put *Passing Strange* in the lead. The two shows
split early awards: Stew won for Best Book of a Musical, while Andy Blankenbuehler won for Best Choreography and Alex Lacamoire and Bill Sherman won for Best Orchestrations. Then came the award for Best Original
Score. Lin-Manuel was facing not only Stew but also his childhood hero
Alan Menken, who was nominated for the stage adaptation of *The Little
Mermaid*. In a black suit and black tie, Lin-Manuel sat in the orchestra section on the aisle next to Vanessa, Luz, Luis, and Cita. Up in the mezzanine,
his aunt Yamilla from Vega Alta sat with the rest of his family. Luis had told
her: "We have to be in *white mode*." That meant applauding quietly, no
screaming allowed.

The previous year's winner for Best Original Score, *Spring Awakening*
composer Duncan Sheik, came onstage and announced the nominees. He
smiled as he read the winner's name. "And the Tony Award for Best Score
goes to . . . *In the Heights*! Music and lyrics by Lin-Manuel Miranda."

Lin-Manuel stood up, fist-bumped Vanessa, and made a beeline for the stage, eyes focused. He hugged Duncan Sheik, took the statuette, and gazed at the cheering audience, mouth agape. He didn't have a speech in hand; he'd watched a documentary about the 2004 season where a producer for *Wicked* brought a speech but didn't win, so out of superstition, he'd decided not to write anything down. But he had mapped out some rhyming couplets in his head. He launched into a rap:

> *I used to dream about this moment, now I'm in it.*
> *Tell the conductor to hold the baton a minute!*
> *I'll start with Alex Lacamoire and Bill Sherman,*
> *Kevin McCollum, Jeffrey Seller, and Jill Furman,*
> *Quiara for keeping the pages turning,*
> *Tommy Kail for keeping the engine burning,*
> *For being so discerning through every all-nighter,*
> *Dr. Herbert for telling me: "You're a writer."*
> *I have to thank Andy Blank for every spank.*
> *Matter of fact, thank John Buzzetti for every drink.*
> *Thank the cast and crew for having each other's back, son.*
> *I don't know about God, but I believe in Chris Jackson!*

At the paean to Chris, the *Heights* section erupted. They were so unexpectedly exuberant that Lin-Manuel lost the thread of the rap and forgot all the other couplets he'd prepared. His mind went blank.

For the past five years, however, he had performed with Freestyle Love Supreme, improvising raps based on whatever the audience threw at him. He had some practice finding words on the spot. From here on, he was truly freestyling.

"I don't know what else I got, I'm off the dome," he began. He thought of his musical's theme, which could give him another rhyming line: "I know I wrote a little show about home."

His hero Stephen Sondheim had just been given a lifetime achievement award, so perhaps he could riff on a line from one of Sondheim's songs about making art, "Finishing the Hat," from *Sunday in the Park with George*, which was nominated for Best Revival of a Musical that year. He tried it: "Mr. Sondheim, look, I made a hat / Where there never was a hat!" Seussian inspiration struck: "It's a Latin hat at that!"

Lac jumped up and clapped in the aisle. Bill pumped his fist.

Then Lin-Manuel looked to his family in the audience. "Mom, Dad, and Cita, I wrote a play. / Y'all came to every play. / Thanks for being here today."

Next to his family sat his girlfriend. "Vanessa, who still leaves me breathless, / Thanks for loving me when I was broke, and making breakfast." The audience laughed.

He knew how he would wrap up: "And with that I want to thank all my Latino people. / This is for Abuelo Güisin and Puerto Rico!" Out of his suit pocket, he pulled a Puerto Rican flag and waved it high.

The *Heights* section leaped to its feet, applauding. The Tony Awards had turned into "Carnaval del Barrio."

For the final award of the night, Whoopi Goldberg came out to present Best Musical. As a child, Lin-Manuel had watched on television when she won the Best Supporting Actress Oscar for *Ghost*. "I'll never forget," he recalled, "at the top of her acceptance speech she said, 'Ever since I was a little kid, I wanted this.'" Sitting at home with his mother, he felt inspired. "For me, it was like she was saying, 'If you want this, you can get it, too. I'm proof that you can.' It was as if she reached through the screen to talk to me." Even Luz registered the power of the speech. She'd remind her son, "Remember what Whoopi said."

Now Whoopi was onstage in front of him. "And the winner, the 2008 Tony Award goes to . . ." She opened the envelope. "*In the Heights*."

The entire *Heights* company swarmed the stage. Lin-Manuel and Whoopi did a few salsa steps.

Jeffrey steered Jill to the microphone. "*In the Heights* is a show about family and chasing your dreams," she said. "Thank you to our Broadway family for helping to make our dreams come true."

Kevin and Jeffrey hoisted Lin-Manuel on their shoulders. "We love Broadway!" they shouted. Everyone pumped their fists in the air. Luis could hear Yamilla screaming from the mezzanine.

There would be parties, photo shoots, interviews, fan requests. Eight more performances the next week. And the week after. In the month after

In the Heights won Best Musical, it started selling out shows and grossing over one million dollars per week. This was Lin-Manuel's new career. At twenty-eight, Lin-Manuel was the youngest composer ever to win a Tony.

He'd worked nearly nonstop on *Heights* since he'd graduated from college in 2002. He needed a vacation. That summer, he and Vanessa flew to an all-inclusive resort in Mexico. (His understudy could play Usnavi for a few performances.) In Playa del Carmen, they drank margaritas and watched *Mad Men*. They had their own rooftop pool. "If I marry V," he messaged Tommy, "I don't know how I can top this place."

Above the sparkling waters of the Caribbean, Lin-Manuel reclined in a hammock, a book in his hand. He'd brought one hefty volume to read on the trip: a biography of Alexander Hamilton.

11

THE WHITE HOUSE

●●

*I*t seemed obvious. So obvious, in fact, that he googled it to check that no one had done it already. Surely someone had turned Alexander Hamilton's life into a musical. Lin-Manuel felt genuinely surprised when nothing turned up.

The idea had struck him by the second chapter of Ron Chernow's Hamilton biography. Looking for a big book to sustain him through the Mexico trip, he'd picked up the eight-hundred-page tome at the Borders bookstore in Columbus Circle, near his apartment. He liked reading about famous people's lives; his favorite book as a child had been *Chuck Amuck*, Looney Tunes animator Chuck Jones's memoir. And he'd harbored a fascination with Hamilton since high school, when he'd done his American history project on the Burr-Hamilton duel. Like Jonathan Larson, Hamilton exemplified the life of genius cut short—plus Hamilton's own son died in a duel on the very grounds where his father would face Burr a few years later. Chernow's 2004 book featured enthusiastic blurbs on the cover, so he'd bought it.

He started reading even before he and Vanessa left for vacation. The beginning of the biography turned out to be astonishingly dramatic. By the time Hamilton turned fourteen, his Scottish father had abandoned him, his unmarried mother had died in bed next to him, the cousin who took him in had killed himself, and he was left a penniless orphan on the Caribbean island of St. Croix at the windy outskirts of the British Empire.

How could such an unfortunate youth grow up to become an architect of the new American Republic as its first treasury secretary? Lin-Manuel was hooked.

In the second chapter, in 1772, a hurricane struck St. Croix. Hamilton wrote a letter describing the devastation so poetically that the local newspaper published it. As Chernow explained, "Hamilton did not know it, but he had just written his way out of poverty." A collection was taken up to give this promising author an education in the mainland colonies. Soon he arrived on a boat in New York City, ready to make himself into a new man.

For Lin-Manuel, that moment provided a key. *I know this guy*, he thought. The precocious kid from the Caribbean who got a scholarship to study in New York—that was his father's story. Even before Luis graduated from the University of Puerto Rico at nineteen and took a spot in a graduate program at NYU, he had started his own business; he was selling wholesale records at age ten. Hamilton, also a hustler, had started clerking for an export business at fourteen. The immigrant striver, always a little insecure, always working twice as hard to earn his place—that wasn't the image of the Founding Father, stately and impassive, that Lin-Manuel had seen on the ten-dollar bill. But he recognized such an insatiable drive from his own father and, as he learned from Chernow, Hamilton proved equally relentless. Over drinks before the trip, he told Jeremy McCarter, the *New York* magazine critic who'd championed the innovation of *In the Heights*, that he'd found his next project.

His idea wasn't just to retell the origins of America as a Caribbean-immigrant story, which would have been audacious enough. It was something even more audacious: to tell the story using the language of hip-hop. Hamilton didn't remind Lin-Manuel of his father only. The story of an impoverished child who'd earned renown through the power of his words also echoed the trajectory of Lin-Manuel's favorite rappers: the Notorious B.I.G., who went from public housing to the pinnacle of hip-hop, and Jay-Z, a teenage drug dealer turned music mogul.

As Lin-Manuel continued reading Chernow's biography in the hammock in Playa del Carmen, he found more and more examples of Hamilton's transformative words. Hamilton became a prolific pamphleteer during the revolution. He wrote under a pseudonym, rapper-style, to eviscerate his opponents. He became General George Washington's secretary, writing letters to Congress for supplies, then a vociferous supporter of the new Constitution, writing dozens of the *Federalist Papers* to secure its ratification. "Chernow kept proving me right," Lin-Manuel says. "Hamilton's a writer. He's an MC."

And then, like many a notorious MC, Hamilton wrote his way into feuds. He faced off with Thomas Jefferson, his rival in Washington's cabinet, and, fatally, with Aaron Burr, who challenged him to a duel after Hamilton refused to apologize for attacking his reputation. Like Biggie, like Tupac, Hamilton was gunned down in his prime. His life was a hip-hop narrative.

Over the next few years, Lin-Manuel would encounter plenty of people who thought the parallel that struck him as obvious sounded ridiculous. But when he shared his idea with Vanessa that summer in 2008, she didn't balk. "He sees connections," she says. As a rap fan herself, she knew the genre could tell complex stories.

From the resort, he messaged Tommy over Google Chat. Tommy had no qualms about the idea. "Go where the juice is," Tommy encouraged him. Lin-Manuel also called his agent, John Buzzetti, who loved the approach. "All he had to say to me," Buzzetti recalls, "was: 'Think about hip-hop artists who had to write themselves out of their situation and think about my dad and his drive.' I was sold." Emboldened by the faith of his confidants, he started to write.

At the outset, he did not conceive of the project as a stage musical. He thought of it as a concept album—a series of songs unified around a single story. *Jesus Christ Superstar*—another brazen retelling of an iconic narrative through a popular music form—had begun as a rock-opera concept album in 1970. The format felt liberating. Throughout the development of *In the Heights*, he'd been told that he had to welcome the audience and make sure every line could be readily understood on first hearing. That wasn't the way he experienced hip-hop albums, though; he had to listen to Big Pun and Nas over and over to grasp their verses' meanings, let alone their allusions and wordplay. "I wanted to give myself the right to write music and lyrics that bear repeat listening," he says. "Thinking of it as an album set me free."

Taking *Jesus Christ Superstar* as a template also offered him a point of view on the story. Andrew Lloyd Webber and Tim Rice had drawn their inspiration from a Bob Dylan song: What if Judas was the tragic hero of the narrative? What if the audience saw Jesus through the eyes of his friend and former ally who'd ended up betraying him and became history's unredeemable villain? When Lin-Manuel played Jesus his freshman year at Wesleyan, he experienced that dynamic onstage; Judas sang the opening number, inviting the audience to look back on the unknown man from Nazareth as he'd been before the populace deified him. "Okay," Lin-Manuel says. "Hamilton is my Jesus, so Burr is my Judas."

Burr would open the show. But how to begin? Lin-Manuel's previous musicals had dramatized short time frames: one night for *7 Minutes in Heaven*, three days for *In the Heights*, a college year for *On Borrowed Time*. Now he wanted to present an entire biography that also encompassed the birth of a nation. "I had an instinct," he says. "I'm going to have to learn how to compress more than I've ever compressed." From memorizing hip-hop verses, he knew that rap could pack in more words per minute than any other song form. He would need all of his lyrical dexterity to handle the weight of exposition he had taken on. And perhaps that challenge could become the drama of the opening line itself: a sentence that went on and on, accumulating clauses, straining to contain the span of Hamilton's life. By the end of the first sentence, he hoped, a listener would be convinced that Hamilton was extraordinary and that Burr—jealous, curious, skeptical, furious—was the person to narrate his story.

In Playa del Carmen, Lin-Manuel began that sentence. It didn't need to be a declaration, he realized. He could project his own incredulity at Hamilton's trajectory onto Burr. The opening song could start with Burr's question:

> *How does a bastard, orphan, son of a whore and a*
> *Scotsman, dropped in the middle of a forgotten*
> *Spot in the Caribbean by providence, impoverished, in squalor*
> *Grow up to be a hero and a scholar?*

It was a thirty-seven-word sentence, its subject (*a bastard*) separated from the main verb (*grow up*) by a chain of descriptions, obstacles, internal rhymes, assonances, alliterations—vulgar and lofty, dense and suspenseful. He had found the voice of the project, elevated enough to accommodate Hamilton's own writing, accessible enough that a contemporary audience could get it, layered and textured enough to reward repeat listening. It was an eighteenth-century story in a late-twentieth-century form. He could string the songs into an auditory narrative, changing tempo and style to shape an experience the way he did on the mixes he'd been making for his friends and family since childhood. He decided to call it *The Hamilton Mixtape*.

He had one sentence done.

Returning from Mexico, he couldn't wait to share his idea. Back at the Richard Rodgers, performing *In the Heights*, he found a moment with Chris Jackson during the salon ladies' number when they were standing together, mics off, at the bodega upstage.

"I think I've got my next thing," he told Chris.

"That's awesome!" Chris said. "What's it about?"

"It's a hip-hop thing about the treasury secretary."

The treasury secretary? Chris wondered. But before he could ask anything else, they had to come downstage for "96,000."

The next day, Tommy walked by Chris backstage.

"What's up, G-Dubs?" Tommy said.

"G-Dubs?"

"G-Dubs—George Washington," Tommy explained. "Lin didn't mention it? He's writing this thing about Alexander Hamilton, and he wants you to play George Washington."

That night, Chris went to the Borders at Penn Station and looked for books on the first president.

Lin-Manuel had already begun dream-casting *The Hamilton Mixtape* in his imagination. Washington occupied the authoritative, paternal place among the Founders that Chris held in the *Heights* company: a man of stature, a natural leader with a richly expressive voice. For another role, he reached into his hip-hop pantheon. When he read in Chernow's biography that Hamilton's first friend in New York was an apprentice tailor with the incredible name of Hercules Mulligan, he immediately thought that such a swaggering sobriquet could only fit Busta Rhymes.

Next, he needed to consult with Ron Chernow himself. When Lin-Manuel told his friends about his project that fall, he learned of an unexpected connection. A classmate at Hunter and Wesleyan, Una La-Marche, happened to know Ron; her dad had moved into the Chernows' old apartment. Although Una thought the idea of a series of raps about

Alexander Hamilton sounded a little weird, she offered to reach out on Lin-Manuel's behalf. In October, she emailed her father:

Hiya Daddy!

Two questions:

1. *Would it be OK to come to your apt with a few friends tomorrow to watch America's Next Top Model?*
2. *I hung out with Lin last night and—top-secret news—he is working on a hip-hop album based on the life of Alexander Hamilton. It turns out he was inspired by Ron Chernow's biography. Would you help me set the two of them up?*

Love,
Una

Her dad responded to the questions in the order they'd been asked: It was fine for Una and her friends to watch *America's Next Top Model* at his apartment. And though a hip-hop album about Alexander Hamilton sounded like a joke, he was happy to help.

With an introduction secured, Lin-Manuel invited Ron to a Sunday matinee of *In the Heights*. After the show, he asked Ron on the spot to become the historical adviser for *The Hamilton Mixtape*. Ron was surprised. "I gather my book made an impact on you," he said. Lin-Manuel replied that when he'd read the biography on vacation, hip-hop songs started rising off the page.

Ron had never heard that reaction before. Was it a parody? If Lin-Manuel was envisioning a satirical put-down of a historical figure, he didn't want to be involved. But Lin-Manuel assured him that he was utterly sincere. He said he saw Hamilton's story as a classic hip-hop narrative of writing one's way out of poverty.

"I didn't quite know what he was talking about," Ron admits.

Ron, nearing sixty at the time, was a Yale- and Cambridge-educated historian, the author of several bestselling biographies, and the winner of a National Book Award. Hip-hop fell outside his area of expertise. Curious but skeptical, he asked Lin-Manuel, "Can hip-hop be the vehicle for telling such a complex story about a complex man?"

"Ron, I'm going to educate you about hip-hop," Lin-Manuel told him. He explained that hip-hop featured wordplay, assonance, end rhymes, internal rhymes—a host of lyrical techniques to convey complexity. Ron was astonished. As he later reflected, "For my generation, hip-hop was cold, violent, and misogynistic, whereas in Lin's hands, it was like Cole Porter!" He agreed to serve as historical adviser.

A few weeks later, Lin showed up at Ron's apartment in Brooklyn. He had the first song ready to share. Between *Heights* performances, he'd been working on the lyrics, trying to turn the opening sections of the biography into an introductory number. Chernow began his portrait not with Hamilton himself but with Hamilton's widow, Eliza, who outlived him by half a century and devoted those years to preserving his legacy. At first, Lin-Manuel tried a hook for Eliza to eulogize her husband: "There are no monuments for you, my love." But then he learned that wasn't true; there were plenty of monuments commemorating Hamilton. So he stuck with Burr's question: "How does a bastard . . . grow up to be a hero and a scholar?" Between the beginning and the end of that sentence, Lin-Manuel had a lot of narrative to fill in. Compression became his goal. Chernow described the childhood hardships that Hamilton survived in the first chapter and concluded his second chapter with Hamilton setting sail for New York to get an education. "I set a dare for myself," Lin-Manuel recalls. "At the end of the opening song, can Hamilton be on the boat?"

Lin-Manuel sang Ron the opening number, playing Burr and snapping his fingers to keep the beat. Burr recounted Hamilton's amazing rise from a Caribbean orphan to a New Yorker on the make. When Lin-Manuel finished, he asked Ron, a little nervously, for his opinion.

"It's the most amazing thing I've ever heard!" Ron told him. "You've taken the first thirty or forty pages of my book and condensed it into a three-minute song!"

Ron, who had been an English major at Yale, particularly admired the linguistic style Lin-Manuel had figured out, a fusion of heightened phrases (*impoverished, in squalor*) and colloquial expressions (*the ten-dollar Founding Father without a father*). Lin-Manuel had converted him to *The Hamilton Mixtape* "because of his verbal resources," Ron says.

"He'd established the style, applying hip-hop to something it's never been applied to before."

Lin-Manuel soon found a larger audience for the opening number. In early 2009, his father got a call from David Axelrod, a political consultant who'd worked with Luis on New York mayoral campaigns. As a college student, Lin-Manuel wrote background music for one campaign's ads— menacing chords for the negative portion attacking a rival, then upbeat salsa to promote the candidate, Fernando Ferrer, who was running to become the city's first Hispanic mayor. (Axelrod remembered Luis telling him that his son was very talented but would never be able to make a living.) After Ferrer lost the mayoral race, Axelrod joined the presidential campaign for a freshman senator from Illinois, and in 2008, when that senator won, he named Axelrod his senior adviser. One of the first events that Barack and Michelle Obama planned to host at the White House was a poetry jam—a fittingly fresh approach to American culture for a couple who had danced to Beyoncé at the inaugural ball. *In the Heights* had won the 2008 Tony for Best Musical, and in 2009, it picked up a Grammy for Best Musical Theater Album and was a finalist for the Pulitzer Prize in Drama. Axelrod asked Luis if Lin-Manuel would perform a solo number from his award-winning show for "An Evening of Music, Poetry, and the Spoken Word" at the White House that May.

Lin-Manuel thought about what number to sing. None of Usnavi's numbers in *Heights* really worked as solos. They all relied on trading verses with his friends or singing along with a chorus from the community. He had an idea, though—risky, but potentially rewarding—for a song he'd never performed in public. If there was ever an audience that would be interested in a rap about the first treasury secretary, he thought, it would be at the White House. President Obama had recently announced his first cabinet nominee, Timothy Geithner for secretary of the treasury. For an evening designed to showcase the power of words, the story of Hamilton rising on the strength of his pen, delivered in hip-hop form, might fit the bill. He passed along the lyrics for the one song he'd written. The White House decided to have him close the program.

With the song approved, Lin-Manuel went to Alex Lacamoire. He'd been writing to a beat that he created on a music software program, but for the White House, he wanted the accompaniment to be live. He'd learned from early Freestyle Love Supreme concerts that prerecorded beats had problems—if his timing shifted in performance or the audience responded unexpectedly, it was hard to get back on track. "It's the fucking president!" Lin-Manuel says. "I don't want to sing to a beat." He hoped that Lac could adapt the electronic sounds into a piano part.

He brought Lac a lyric sheet with chords and a demo he'd recorded in Logic, the music software program. His demo began with seven staccato F-sharps, like an eighteenth-century military fanfare: *DUM da-da-da DUM DUM DUM*. Lac could play that on the piano easily. To bridge past and present, Lin-Manuel wanted to use a hip-hop sample—the sound of a door slam to reinforce the downbeat before he began to rap. He'd found a sound effect in Logic called Door Squeak 3, a whiny hinge that inched up in pitch and fell back down. Could Lac transcribe the sound of the door squeak? No problem. Lac worked out a four-note phrase—*dee-dee-DEE-dee*—that mimicked the sound effect's melody. With a few more piano figures to heighten the drama in each verse, Lac had his arrangement ready.

On May 12, 2009, Lac and Lin-Manuel went to Washington, DC. They shared a van with James Earl Jones, who was going to perform a speech from *Othello*. The performance was held in the East Room of the White House—a lofty state room designed for public audiences by George Washington himself. President Obama and the First Lady sat at the front table with Joe and Jill Biden next to them. It was an intimidating affair.

After James Earl Jones recited Shakespeare, the bassist Esperanza Spalding performed a Lauryn Hill song, and several slam-poetry champions held the audience rapt, Lin-Manuel took the stage. Lac sat at a mahogany Steinway grand piano with gilded eagles for legs. Gilbert Stuart's portrait of George Washington gazed down on them from the wall. In a slim black suit and a white shirt unbuttoned at the collar under a black tie, Lin-Manuel looked out, as nervous as he'd been since his first piano recital as a child.

"Um, I'm, I'm thrilled, uh, the White House called me, uh, tonight," he stammered. As he took in the room, he made the mistake of locking eyes with President Obama. "That's too scary," he later remembered thinking. He shifted his gaze to the First Lady. That didn't help. But then he saw Michelle Obama's mother, Marian Robinson. She gave him a smile. "I was like, 'Okay, I can look at First Abuela.'"

He gained a little confidence. "I'm actually working on a hip-hop album," he announced. "It's a concept album about the life of someone I think embodies hip-hop: Treasury Secretary Alexander Hamilton."

He gulped. There were chuckles in the audience. The First Lady smiled. The president looked up thoughtfully, his chin resting on his hand.

"You laugh, but it's true!" Lin-Manuel insisted, gathering steam. "He was born a penniless orphan in St. Croix of illegitimate birth, became George Washington's right-hand man, became treasury secretary, caught beef with every other Founding Father, and all on the strength of his writing." Gesturing with one hand while holding the microphone in the other, he summed up: "I think he embodies the word's ability to make a difference. So I'm going to be doing the first song from that tonight."

He introduced Alex Lacamoire at the piano and explained that with Lac's accompaniment, he'd be playing Vice President Aaron Burr.

"Uh, and snap along if you like."

He spun in a little circle, raised his eyebrows to cue Lac, and practiced a few rapid words under his breath, his head down. Then he stood erect, eyes forward, right hand behind his back, left hand with the mic raised to his mouth, as Lac played the fanfare and the door squeak: *DUM da-da-da DUM DUM DUM, dee-dee-DEE-dee.*

He began: "How does a bastard, orphan, son of a whore and a Scotsman . . ." He snapped on the backbeat, and the audience picked up the rhythm. That settled him in.

He loosened up, crouching down on "forgotten spot in the Caribbean." Soon he was smiling. As Lac launched into an eighth-note-filled hip-hop motif, Lin-Manuel started rocking his shoulders and waving his hand, his eyebrows dancing:

Well, the word got around, they said, "This kid is insane, man,"
Took up a collection just to send him to the mainland.
"Get your education, don't forget from whence you came, and
The world's gonna know your name. What's your name, man?"

Lac crescendoed and then suddenly cut back to a bare chord. Lin-Manuel, as Burr, looked dead center:

Alexander Hamilton.
His name is Alexander Hamilton.
And there's a million things he hasn't done,
But just you wait, just you wait . . .

The audience laughed again, but this time there was applause too. The First Lady clasped her hands and nodded. President Obama was grinning.

Lin-Manuel continued, energized, through the verses that chronicled the death of Hamilton's mother and cousin, his determination to fend for himself, his reading and working and clerking, and his passage on a ship to New York. He ended with Burr's confession: "Yeah, I'm the damn genius that shot him."

As Lac rumbled a final chord, Lin-Manuel dropped his head and raised his left hand in the shape of a pistol—thumb out, index finger pointed up, the other fingers curled. President Obama rose to his feet applauding, his smile wide. The rest of the audience rose with him.

After the performance, the political commentator George Stephanopoulos came up to Lin-Manuel and told him the president was talking about his song. As Lin-Manuel remembered it, Stephanopoulos said the president had called for his own treasury secretary: "Where is Timothy Geithner? We need him to hear the Hamilton rap!"

To Lin-Manuel, it felt like a dream come true.

HBO was filming the evening, and a few months later, the White House released a high-quality video of each performer. Lin-Manuel contacted Ron Chernow. "Remember that song I did for you?" he said. "I performed it at the White House!" He told Ron to go on YouTube and check it out.

Ron watched the video in awe. "I thought: *He only had one song, and he's already performed it to a standing ovation from the president. Where does he go from here?*"

12

WORKING

• •

*T*he invitation from the White House was far from the only request that Lin-Manuel fielded in the wake of *Heights'* success. The offers were starting to arrive even as *Heights* headed to Broadway. Like Whoopi Goldberg appearing as if by magic from his childhood television screen to award Lin-Manuel's first professional musical a Tony, an array of heroes opened their doors and invited him in. He leaped at the chance to learn from them directly.

The first summons came from Stephen Schwartz, the composer and lyricist of the pop-inflected scores of *Wicked*, *Pippin*, and, most notably for Lin-Manuel, *Godspell*, which had given him his first taste of Judas as a theatrical rival to Jesus. In the 1970s, Schwartz created an anthology show called *Working* based on Studs Terkel's interviews with ordinary Americans in different jobs: a trucker, a millworker, a waitress, a cleaning woman. The show was a series of musical monologues, and Schwartz invited a range of pop and theater artists—among them James Taylor, Micki Grant, Mary Rodgers, and Craig Carnelia—to contribute songs. Over the years, he'd updated the show, and for a planned 2008 revival, he wanted to kick off the show with a new song about someone's first job. Alex Lacamoire, who'd done many of the arrangements for *Wicked*, had told him about an impressive new songwriter, Lin-Manuel Miranda, and so Schwartz went to see *In the Heights* off Broadway. He loved it.

When Lin-Manuel learned from his agent that Stephen Schwartz was going to call, he waited by his phone. "I had real postpartum feelings after

Heights opened," he recalls. "I was grateful when Stephen Schwartz came along." Lin-Manuel knew exactly what he would write about for a first-job number: the summer in high school that he worked at McDonald's. He'd hated it—the drudgery of the register, the pressure of turning out an order in the allotted time, the anxiety of having to do arithmetic, all of it reprieved only by the joy of an occasional delivery run—but his mother had told him to remember the experience. "Honey, you never know how this job may inform your work somewhere in the future," Luz counseled. Now he could turn that workplace torment into musical material.

Schwartz was delighted when he heard the demo for "Delivery," the new song. "The thing with Lin is more than just blazing talent as a songwriter," he says. "Lin is such an erudite student of musical theater. He knows about show structure, which is something many other talented songwriters don't share. He knew we were looking for the first solo song in the show, so he imbued it with the energy and catchiness and rhythmic irresistibility that would fit that spot." After six years of rewriting Nina's "I Want" song for *Heights*, Lin-Manuel had learned how to compose an initial solo number with drive and verve. His mother was delighted too. The McDonald's job had paid dividends. "See," she told him, "it's all grist for the mill!"

Schwartz had discussed adding a song from the perspective of undocumented workers, who came under frequent political attack in 2008. While polishing his own show about immigration, Lin-Manuel agreed. "We talked about how every immigrant group gets their foothold in America by doing the jobs no one else is willing to do," he recalled. He thought of his own Abuela Mundi taking care of him while his parents worked late and of all the immigrant nannies who'd cared for his friends at Hunter. That gave him an idea for a duet: two undocumented workers taking care of people at opposite ends of their lives, one a Filipina nanny for a young girl, the other a Latino caretaker for an elderly man. For the nanny's Tagalog refrain, he worked in an expression of love—"Mahal kita minamahal kita"—that he'd learned from his college girlfriend Aileen.

Schwartz felt prescient for inviting the young composer to join the *Working* team. "Lin wrote a truly great song about undocumented workers," he says, "one of the best songs in the show." He introduced Lin-Manuel to Craig Carnelia, Micki Grant, and the other songwriters. It felt like a glorious initiation. "There's a joy in working with other people who do the same thing we do that I learned from Stephen," Lin-Manuel says. "By letting me write those songs, he welcomed me into a larger community in a very tangible way."

That community kept getting larger. Lin-Manuel relished joining the musical-theater world in Midtown Manhattan, and he made sure to pay tribute to his forebears. For an AIDS benefit in 2007, he rewrote "Tradition," the opening number from *Fiddler on the Roof*, as a hip-hop jam, "Tradizzle," trading a fiddle for a turntable. The *Heights* company came out in prayer shawls as the shtetl ensemble, then stripped down to tank tops and breakdanced. Lin-Manuel, wearing a yarmulke on top of his Kangol cap, played Tevye to the beat of Big Pun: "Yo, dead in the middle of little Anatizzle, I got a riddle: / How do we keep fiddlin' instead of fizzlin'?" (After Joseph Stein, the book writer for *Fiddler*, saw *In the Heights*, he went backstage to tell the cast how much he liked it. Lin-Manuel replied, "You should, because we stole it from you!")

Broadway performers in other shows found skits like "Tradizzle" so endearing that they agreed to join Lin-Manuel's subsequent hijinks. In the summer of 2008, *Legally Blonde: The Musical* had run a reality-show competition on MTV to find a replacement for its star. Lin-Manuel had loved the show, *The Search for the Next Elle Woods*, so after *In the Heights* won the Tony, he and a Wesleyan theater friend, Owen Panettieri, came up with their own spoof version: *Legally Brown: The Search for the Next Piragua Guy*. On the fictional premise that their beloved Piragua Guy, Eliseo Roman, had to be replaced, they convinced Broadway headliners from that season—Allison Janney, Norm Lewis, Matthew Morrison, Cheyenne Jackson—to pretend to try out for the part.

In the 37 Arts Theater, the actors improvised reality-style digs at each other as they competed in mock challenges: Doing sit-ups while holding bottles of flavored syrup; flipping a towel and shouting ¡*Wepa!* (One contestant revealed "a surprising medical condition": an inability to speak Spanish.) Lin-Manuel enlisted Andrew Fried, the filmmaker who'd helmed the documentaries on Freestyle Love Supreme and *Heights*, to produce *Legally Brown* as a six-part web series on YouTube. "It was all Lin wanted to talk about," Fried says. "He's very playful and childlike. He won all these awards, and he wanted to spend all his capital on getting people to audition for *The Search for the Next Piragua Guy.*"

In a way, Lin-Manuel was getting to live out his high-school fantasies on a professional scale—making spoof movies, mashing up Broadway and hip-hop. Later that summer, when he returned from his vacation with Vanessa in Mexico, he accepted an invitation that he could hardly have fathomed when he was in high school. He went to a stately five-story town house in Turtle Bay Gardens on East Forty-Ninth Street and rang the doorbell.

Stephen Sondheim let him in.

It was a business call. A *West Side Story* revival was in the works, and Lin-Manuel had been hired to translate the Sharks' lyrics into Spanish. Kevin McCollum and Jeffrey Seller, who were producing, had connected Lin-Manuel with Arthur Laurents, the original book writer, who, at age ninety-one, was directing the revival. Laurents's late partner had seen a Spanish-language production of *West Side Story* in Colombia and had been struck that the Sharks seemed less villainized when they spoke the same language as the audience. Laurents thought that if the Sharks could sing in their own language on Broadway, it might put them on more even footing with the Jets, who got more stage time. He'd pieced together a bilingual version of the script with extant Spanish translations, and he asked Lin-Manuel to write new versions of the lyrics.

West Side Story had been the show closest to Lin-Manuel's heart since he'd played Bernardo in sixth grade. He wrote *In the Heights* in part to give voice to the Puerto Rican community he knew in Manhattan. Here was an invitation to continue that project by joining the surviving members of a legendary creative team: Laurents, Jerome Robbins, Leonard Bernstein, and Stephen Sondheim. He was happy to help.

The next step was to meet with Sondheim, the original lyricist, to decide which songs to translate. "Let me know if you need help with Steve," Arthur Laurents, a notoriously cantankerous collaborator himself, told Lin-Manuel. "He can be . . . a lot."

However, in Turtle Bay, the conversation flowed easily. Sondheim, at seventy-eight, remembered visiting Hunter's *West Side Story* cast ten years earlier, and though he didn't recall Lin-Manuel specifically, he did remember sharing the lyrics that Jerome Robbins had cut. Lin-Manuel said that he would like to translate the lyrics for "I Feel Pretty," Maria and the Shark girls' comic number. "Boy, you'll be doing me a favor," Sondheim replied; he'd never liked those lyrics in English. "Just make sure it rhymes in the same places, because that's what my ear will detect."

Lin-Manuel also proposed translating "A Boy Like That / I Have a Love," Anita and Maria's second-act duet. He suggested starting it in Spanish, with Anita furious that her boyfriend, Maria's brother, had been killed by an American, and ending it in English, with Maria professing her love for that American boy. Sondheim approved, but he dissuaded Lin-Manuel from trying his hand at translating the song "America." "That meter's really hard," Sondheim told him. "Don't bite off more than you can chew."

Then Sondheim asked what else the twenty-eight-year-old was working on. When Lin-Manuel shared his new idea for a hip-hop album about Alexander Hamilton, Sondheim threw his head back and guffawed. "That is *fantastic*!" he exclaimed. "No one will expect that from you." After an hour of drinks and playing with Sondheim's dogs, Lin-Manuel had to go. "Keep me posted," Sondheim told him. "Don't be shy! And by the way," he added, "let me know if you need help with Arthur. He can be . . . a lot."

Lin-Manuel got to work on what he called "the hardest bilingual crossword puzzle I've ever done." For help, he relied on his father, who'd loved *West Side Story* ever since he saw it as a ten-year-old; he'd been moved to tears by Maria's story. The goal for the revival was for the Puerto Rican characters to sound like they'd grown up speaking Puerto Rican Spanish, which Luis knew firsthand. "I was the Google Translate," he says. He liked going to sleep with a challenge and waking up with solutions, so before he went to bed, he'd try to figure out Spanish options for the rhyming words in "I Feel Pretty." He never thought that his son's work was particularly difficult—it wasn't solving intractable political problems; it was just writing songs! Now Lin-Manuel was gratified to get a call from his mother saying that his father finally appreciated the craft of what he did. "You've got your dad mumbling at all hours," Luz reported. Lin-Manuel sent some of his father's suggestions back for revision: "No, Dad, it needs to have nine syllables." Trying to keep the rhythm and the internal rhymes consistent, per Sondheim's request, Luis realized, "That's difficult to do!"

"I Feel Pretty" turned out as sparkly and musical in Spanish as it was in English. Lin-Manuel upheld Sondheim's rhyme scheme even as he tweaked the imagery:

I feel pretty, oh so pretty,	*Hoy me siento tan hermosa*
I feel pretty, and witty, and bright	*Tan graciosa que puedo volar*
And I pity	*Y no hay diosa*
Any girl who isn't me tonight.	*En el mundo que me va alcanzar.*

The *pretty/witty/pity* triple rhyme became *hermosa/graciosa/diosa*, still conveying Maria's sense of playful supremacy but now with the metaphor that she could fly (*volar*) and that no goddess (*diosa*) in the world could reach her (*alcanzar*).

The trickier translations came in "A Boy Like That," which Lin-Manuel called "Un Hombre Asi." He wanted Anita's rage at Tony to come through more powerfully than the word *boy* conveyed, so he made the case to substitute a Spanish curse word, *cabrón*—a fighting insult that was closer to "bastard" or "asshole." And instead of rhyming *brother* with *another*, he paired *hermano* with *americano*, a more potent term for Anita, who feels rejected by the country she'd previously praised in "America." Urging Maria to forget Tony, Anita sings:

A boy like that who'd kill your brother	*Ese cabrón mató a tu hermano*
Forget that boy and find another	*Olvida a ese americano*

Soon he heard these words in the singing voice of Karen Olivo. With Lin-Manuel's reluctant approval, Kevin and Jeffrey agreed to let Arthur Laurents poach K O, who'd been playing Vanessa in *Heights*, for the role of Anita in the revival. K O could give *cabrón* a wallop. "Anita's using her words as weapons," K O says. "Lin's translations hit so much harder than the lyrics in English."

In performance, however, English-dominant audiences in the United States didn't respond quite as sympathetically to the Spanish lyrics as the audience in Colombia had. For an out-of-town run in Washington, DC, in December 2008, the production tried displaying English supertitles during the Spanish songs, but some audience members found those distracting. Laurents heard complaints that the Spanish was hard to follow, and he worried that for audiences that didn't speak Spanish, "Un Hombre Asi" wouldn't set up the ensuing scene, when Anita agrees to deliver a message from Maria to Tony but is violently assaulted by the Jets. A few months into the 2009 Broadway run, Laurents and the producers decided to change the lyrics back to English. K O regretted the choice. "I really wish audiences hadn't been so xenophobic," they say.

Still, K O valued the collaboration with Lin-Manuel. Even though K O was a powerhouse singer with a fierce, funny stage presence, they felt nervous joining a new company in the role that had made Chita Rivera and Rita Moreno icons. K O asked Lin-Manuel if he could come to the first day of rehearsal; he said that of course he would, and he checked in to make sure they felt good as the day progressed. When K O worried about doing press interviews for the role, Lin-Manuel offered tips. "He said, 'You know what they're going to ask you, so think of what's authentic, then memorize it, and then give it to them when they want it.' I was like, 'That's brilliant!'"

As performances continued, however, K O found that enduring the Jets' assault night after night wore them down. "I'm a survivor of rape," K O says, "so the scene was getting me depressed. There's a lot of trauma to work through, and as an actor, your body doesn't know the difference. I told Lin that it was hard for me to do the show. He made me a CD called 'Karen's Booty Shaking Mix' and said, 'When you get off that stage, put this on.'" The beats helped K O shake off the triggering scene, and they stuck with the show. In June 2009, they won a Tony Award for their performance as Anita.

By then, Lin-Manuel had premiered *The Hamilton Mixtape* at the White House, but he was tempted by yet another project. Buzzetti told him that the *Heights* choreographer, Andy Blankenbuehler, wanted to meet with him about a musical that he was directing. "I was interested in anything Andy wanted to do," Lin-Manuel says. "I thought he did brilliant work."

Andy delivered his pitch: *Bring It On: The Musical.* Lin-Manuel wasn't sold. He'd enjoyed the campy 2000 movie about rival cheerleading squads, but he didn't want to adapt a film for the stage. It felt derivative, and audiences, he thought, wouldn't want innovation; they'd just be waiting for their favorite lines. But Andy explained that they wouldn't be adapting the movie or any of its sequels; they'd be creating an original story within the general world of *Bring It On*. That intrigued Lin-Manuel. Andy said that the musical's book would be by Jeff Whitty, who'd written the clever, Tony-winning script for *Avenue Q*. Lin-Manuel's interest rose. Jeff Whitty's take, Andy said, was a backstage drama: "*All About Eve*, with cheerleaders."

Lin-Manuel liked the idea. But he didn't think he had time to write an entire score while also working on the Hamilton project. "I don't want you to write the whole score," Andy told him. In Whitty's concept, a popular white cheerleader from Truman High School is transferred to Jackson High, a school that's mostly Black and Latino, and when her rival takes over her old Truman squad, she has to ally with her Jackson classmates to form a new team and get revenge. Andy wanted Lin-Manuel to write the Black and Latino songs for Jackson. He had another composer for Truman: Tom Kitt, who'd written the score for *Next to Normal*, a searing rock musical about mental illness that had won a Pulitzer Prize. "I'd known Tom Kitt for a long time," Lin-Manuel says, "and I thought he was brilliant." The lure of collaboration was powerful.

He started imagining the possibilities. Writing beats for Andy's cheerleading-stunt choreography could be amazing. Crafting jokes with Jeff Whitty would sharpen his comedy. Composing alongside Tom Kitt would be a master class. Lin-Manuel loved working with other artists and expanding his tool kit by learning from them. Still, he had his own idea for a hip-hop album about a Caribbean immigrant that he was burning to finish.

To make his decision, he thought of a story he'd heard about Stephen Sondheim. At around Lin-Manuel's age, Sondheim wanted to get his own original musical on Broadway. But then he was asked to audition as a lyricist for a new adaptation of *Romeo and Juliet* with choreography by Jerome Robbins, a book by Arthur Laurents, and music by Leonard Bernstein. Sondheim wasn't sure whether to pursue the gig until he discussed it with his mentor, the great lyricist Oscar Hammerstein II. "It was he who persuaded me that if I was offered the job, I should leap at it," Sondheim recalled. "The show had an interesting idea, he said, and here was a chance to work with three of the most gifted and experienced men in music and theater; my desire to compose could be satisfied at any time." After the success of *West Side Story*, Sondheim went on to compose original Broadway shows for decades.

Lin-Manuel reflected on the parallel. He'd poured everything he knew into *Heights*. Maybe he needed to learn some more before he could write the Hamilton album. "I became my own Oscar Hammerstein," he says. "Part of my brain was going, *Write your own thing*. And part was going, *Jerome Robbins! Leonard Bernstein!*"

He told Andy he was in.

13

BRING IT ON

• •

In the fall of 2009, Lin-Manuel moved to Spain. While *Heights* was transferring to Broadway, Vanessa had left her research lab to earn a degree at Fordham Law School, near Lin-Manuel's apartment on the Upper West Side, and after two years studying in Manhattan, she decided to take the fall term of her final year abroad in Madrid. ("Law was a good fit for me," she says, "because I don't back down from an argument, and I like to get to the truth.") Lin-Manuel hadn't been able to study abroad in college between all his stage productions, so he leaped at the chance to live with her there. They'd been together for four years.

Vanessa was pleased but not surprised by her boyfriend's success. Theater as a field held little interest for her; she hadn't seen any of Lin-Manuel's shows at Hunter, even though she had friends in his productions. An award-winning Broadway hit seemed like the expected next step in his career. "I knew so little about the theater world that I didn't realize anything beyond Broadway existed," she says. "I thought it was inevitable that he'd get the Tony, because who else had woven together Spanish and hip-hop? I probably was less impressed than I should have been." She respected his work, and he respected hers, and although they supported each other—he liked to bring her food while she studied for final exams—neither was enmeshed in the other's professional world. For Lin-Manuel, it felt refreshing to have a partner who wasn't a musical-theater fan. Vanessa kept him grounded. She was funny and caring, and she loved music, but she didn't flip out when he had a visit with Stephen Sondheim. She had an imperturbable sense of self. His former girlfriend Aileen could see the difference between their college romance and his more mature relationship with Vanessa. "She was the rock and he was the kite," Aileen says. "He could fly far because he had that rock."

Before the law-school term began, they took a few weeks to backpack across Europe. They started in Austria, where he met her family on her mother's side, then continued to Venice, Rome, Florence, Athens, and the Greek island of Mykonos. It was a romantic trip. Vanessa felt valued by Lin-Manuel, and she cherished his humor and smarts, his diligence and kindness, his confidence and generosity. She came to a realization: "I think I'm going to marry this guy." Maybe he'd propose on the trip, she thought; after all, they were visiting one gorgeous site after another.

Lin-Manuel had the same realization, but not until later, when he was on a plane back to New York for a *Bring It On* workshop. "I was like, *Wow, we had the best time everywhere, and I can't wait to get back to her—we should really get married.*" His own parents loved Vanessa. "She's amazing," Luz says. "She's so solid and secure in herself." In Washington Heights, he took Vanessa's parents to dinner and asked for their blessing. Then he went to the diamond district in Midtown Manhattan with Luis and got an engagement ring. He'd told Vanessa's father, Frank Nadal, that he was going to hire a mariachi band when he returned to Madrid and make the proposal a special event. "No you're not." Frank laughed. "You're going to propose the moment you see her."

When Lin-Manuel rejoined Vanessa in Madrid, the day before Halloween, she assumed the moment had passed. She'd started classes, and she'd have to study for the bar the following summer; she wouldn't have time to plan a wedding. *There's no way he would propose now*, she thought. *That would be clueless. I'll propose to him after the bar.*

But Lin-Manuel had the ring in his pocket. "It was going ba-*bum*, ba-*bum*, ba-*bum*, like 'The Tell-Tale Heart'!" he recalls. He put it in his bag. On the day he arrived, Vanessa showed him her favorite sights around the city. They passed violinists in a plaza. *This would be a good place to propose*, Lin-Manuel thought. But the ring was in his bag back at their apartment. They went home, then headed out to a late dinner. He asked to go back to the plaza they'd visited. Now there were little kids playing soccer—less romantic than violinists. He suggested they stroll to a nearby church. It was closed; she didn't understand why he insisted on going there. But he wanted to get away from the soccer game. "Come with me," he said. In front of the church, he pulled out the ring.

Vanessa said yes.

They had two more months together in Madrid. During the day, Vanessa went to law-school classes, and Lin-Manuel worked on his musical projects. He had the opening song for *The Hamilton Mixtape* that covered the title character's childhood until he came to New York, and he'd started writing two more, a rap that would demonstrate Hamilton's verbal genius and a song to introduce George Washington, Hamilton's mentor. He played around with a beat for Washington's number, then walked through the streets of Madrid listening to it on his headphones, coming up with lyrics.

Since Washington was the commander in chief of the Continental Army, he thought of another general who'd introduced himself in song: the modern major-general in *The Pirates of Penzance*. He thought he could improve Gilbert's rhyme at the start of the number, "I am the very model of a modern major-general, / I've information vegetable, animal, and mineral." Rhyming *general* and *mineral* wasn't bad, but after years of improvising with Freestyle Love Supreme, he'd learned how to break down a word's syllables to come up with something more surprising. For General Washington, he framed the *Pirates* line with a new display of assonance and alliteration, bumping to his own heavy bass beat:

> *The model of a modern major general,*
> *The venerated Virginian veteran whose men are all*
> *Linin' up to put him up on a pedestal . . .*

Initially, as he scribbled lyrics in his notebook, he imagined Burr rapping these lines, taking the Revolutionary War commander down a peg. Then he decided it would be more powerful to have the general address the audience himself—"Can I be real a second? For just a millisecond? / Let down my guard and tell the people how I feel a second?"—showing the vulnerable man who looked at being venerated with a skeptical eye.

But solving a syllabic problem was easier than determining the structure of the mixtape. The quantity of historical material felt overwhelming.

He couldn't possibly squeeze all eight hundred pages of Chernow's biography into a single album, so he'd have to figure out a way to focus the story. He wasn't sure how to do it. Should he start by mapping out the key episodes in Hamilton's life, research those, and then write the songs? Or should he keep writing the songs that excited him and reverse-engineer a story from the moments he'd chosen to musicalize? For *In the Heights*, he had to figure out the story himself until Quiara came on board, but for that show, he wasn't beholden to historical accuracy. For *Bring It On*, he didn't have to worry about the structure; Jeff Whitty's script told him what the songs needed to cover. The mixtape posed a new challenge. He felt stuck.

Then he remembered Stephen Sondheim's parting remarks when they'd met the previous year: "Keep me posted. Don't be shy!" He decided to take him at his word.

In November, he sent an email to Sondheim. He knew that the veteran composer had written two big musicals drawn from history: *Pacific Overtures*, which dramatized Japan's first encounter with the US military, and *Assassins*, an anthology show about the curdled dreamers who had tried to assassinate US presidents over the centuries. Both were collaborations with the book writer John Weidman, whose daughter, one of Vanessa's best friends, had gone to Hunter and who'd helped Lin-Manuel invite Sondheim to visit Musical Rep.

Lin-Manuel's email stated the problem: "I have three songs written, and I'm at a crossroads. My questions are these: Did you begin with music or research? In working with John, did you write songs as you went along, or did John sketch out historical parameters and did you consider your research and writing from there?" He included a link to the YouTube video of his White House performance.

To his delight, Sondheim replied. "Dear Lin," he wrote, "first of all, let me tell you how terrific your song from the Hamilton project is." That was a thrill to hear. Lin-Manuel still remembered Sondheim throwing his head back when he first heard about *The Hamilton Mixtape* and shouting, "That is *fantastic*!" Enthusiasm from Sondheim could fuel him for years.

Sondheim offered advice as well as praise. He wasn't prescriptive. The contours of the story could take their own shape; a collection of stand-alone numbers could work just as well as a sung-through drama. Content dictates form—Sondheim's favorite maxim. "The answers to your questions really revolve around the structure you've chosen for your show," he explained. "Will it be a continuous narrative or a collage like *Assassins*? It needs discussion, which I would be happy to have with you when you're back in New York." But the risk of a rap album, Sondheim felt, was rhythmic monotony. The ear could tire from a relentless verbal barrage. "If there's anything I'd caution you on," he wrote, "I'd say keep a look out for variety."

Lin-Manuel felt both validated and daunted. He could create the mixtape however he chose. But that meant he had to choose. And maybe a hip-hop album required not only lyrical complexity but musical nuance and surprise as well.

Fortunately, he had another mentor who had let him know that when he felt overwhelmed, he wasn't alone. That November in Madrid, he received a visit from the legendary composer John Kander, who'd written the scores for *Cabaret*, *Chicago*, and dozens of other shows. Kander had gone to see *In the Heights* off Broadway because he knew Andy Blankenbuehler, the choreographer. Though he wasn't much of a hip-hop fan, the eighty-year-old found himself drawn to the twenty-seven-year-old rapping onstage: "I had to lean forward to understand every word he said because he was so fucking brilliant!" Afterward, Kander invited the show's writer to lunch. It was an exciting and somewhat intimidating offer; Kander was a famously brilliant pianist who could compose a song between dinner and dessert. But when he and Lin-Manuel sat down together, the first thing Kander said was a confession of self-doubt: "Do you ever stare at the piano and feel like you don't know what you're doing?"

They started having regular lunches near Kander's apartment on the Upper West Side. "He immediately leveled the playing field," Lin-Manuel says. "He was so curious. He wanted to know how I wrote *Heights*. He wanted to talk craft. He was an amazing sounding board." A plainspoken, self-deprecating Midwesterner from Kansas City, Kander says he always left their lunches feeling invigorated, eager to write more. "It's terrible to say writing is fun, because you're supposed to suffer," Kander says. "But I think we share the possibility that it could be fun." He also loved Lin-Manuel's appreciation for the artists who preceded him. "We are all a kind of synthesis of the past," Kander says. "The reason Lin is *so* good is because he acknowledges that he can use anything that he wants from his past." ("I just want to be Rubén Blades, Juan Luis Guerra, Big Pun, and John Kander combined when I grow up," Lin-Manuel once admitted, only half joking.) When they emailed each other, Kander addressed Lin-Manuel as "Boy Genius," or "BG" for short. Lin-Manuel called him "S.," for the "Source."

When *In the Heights* opened on Broadway, Lin-Manuel kept a note from Kander taped to his dressing-room mirror for inspiration. He brought Kander to meet a group of Hunter students who were putting on *Cabaret* and was delighted when his new mentor told him: "Whoa! Those kids are smart!" Kander loved the songs about the fast-food delivery boy and the immigrant caretakers that Lin-Manuel wrote for *Working*. He loved the "Tradizzle" homage to *Fiddler on the Roof* too. And as Lin-Manuel started to research *The Hamilton Mixtape*, Kander noted the "Santa Claus pack of books" that he'd tote to their meetings. One day, Lin-Manuel arrived at lunch without any books. "What happened?" Kander asked. "Oh," Lin-Manuel replied, "my mom bought me a Kindle." Kander got one too.

Just before Thanksgiving in 2009, a Spanish production of *Chicago* opened in Madrid, and Kander and his husband went to see it. Lin-Manuel's friend Bill Sherman happened to be visiting too and could hardly believe that they were palling around Spain with the guy who'd composed "Cell Block Tango" and "All That Jazz." ("This is the most surreal shit!" Bill marveled.) For Lin-Manuel, newly engaged, a mentor like Kander offered a marital guide along with musical inspiration. "I've had good models," he says. "John Kander has been married for many years. John Weidman raised a family and wrote *Assassins*. Those people destroyed the myth that you have to be fucked up to make great art." You could write about crazed characters who shot their way to fame, then leave that neurosis onstage and go home as a good husband and father.

When Vanessa's semester concluded, she and Lin-Manuel returned to New York. The view over the George Washington Bridge after months away made him weep. They'd found an apartment together even farther uptown, on 218th Street, about as far north as Manhattan went. In the spring, she finished law school at Fordham, and while she prepped for the bar exam that summer, he got out of her hair, flying to Los Angeles for five weeks to play Usnavi in the national tour of *In the Heights* at the Pantages Theatre. Universal Pictures had acquired the rights for a film version of *Heights*, to be directed by *High School Musical*'s Kenny Ortega, with Lin-Manuel reprising Usnavi on-screen. Jumping into the tour felt like a great way to prepare. When he arrived at Universal Studios, a three-hundred-person flash mob surprised him by launching into "96,000." His erstwhile college show had become a national sensation.

During his stay in LA, he got a drink with Hugh Laurie, with whom he'd acted on a few episodes of *House* the previous summer. (The show's producer, a fan of *In the Heights*, had sent her writing staff a video of Lin-Manuel rapping his Tony acceptance speech and instructed them to create a character for him.) Lin-Manuel mentioned that he was working on an album about Alexander Hamilton and wanted to write a breakup number for King George III to sing to the American colonies. Laurie waggled a finger. "Awwww, you'll be back," he ad-libbed. Laughing, Lin-Manuel committed the line to memory.

He got home three days before the bar exam, in time to help Vanessa practice questions on her index cards. While she studied, he planned the music for their wedding. Family friends ran a bed-and-breakfast at the historic Belvedere Mansion in upstate New York and reserved it for the couple that Labor Day weekend in 2010. Feeling flush with weekly checks from *In the Heights*, he mapped out what he calls "essentially a three-day music festival." He booked the great salsa bandleader Gilberto Santa Rosa and a full Latin orchestra for the reception. He tasked Lac, his arranger and orchestrator, with directing a choir and a chamber ensemble for the ceremony itself. He even recruited his hero Rubén Blades to perform. "I didn't tell Vanessa how much we were spending," he confesses.

At the ceremony on the mansion's lawn, after the vows, the chorus Lac had assembled—many of them actors from the original Broadway cast of *Heights*—sang Stevie Wonder's "Happier Than the Morning Sun." As they reached the final lines, the sun broke through the clouds and shone down on the married couple like a blessing. Lin-Manuel pointed at the sky incredulously while he held hands with Vanessa, who was beaming and crying.

Then, at the reception, Vanessa's father, Frank, turned his toast into a rendition of *Fiddler on the Roof*'s celebration song "To Life." As the band kicked in, his new son-in-law met him at the microphone. "'Here's to the father I tried to be,'" Frank sang. "'Here's to my bride-to-be,'" Lin-Manuel responded. The entire wedding party joined them for their own surprise flash mob on the dance floor—Broadway stars, childhood friends, and college pals all spinning and sidling in sync.

Vanessa gasped in delight and covered her face with her hands.

The *New York Times* covered the wedding for its Vows column and reported that "the bride looked like a young Elizabeth Taylor in an Oscar de la Renta strapless gown with a low-cut bodice and a wildly frilly skirt that appeared to be made of feathers, clouds, whipped cream and youth." Vanessa told the reporter why she wanted to spend her life with Lin-Manuel: "He gets me in a way that no one else does. I'm a scientist at heart. I try very hard not to let my emotions cloud my judgments and he'll see through that and see what I'm really feeling." Lin-Manuel offered the reporter his appraisal of Vanessa: "She knows she's dope. She's beautiful but not vain. She's smart but not arrogant. It's like, all killer, no filler."

After the wedding, they left for their honeymoon in the South Pacific. Vacations with Vanessa often became part relaxation, part writing retreat, and she worked as well. On the island of Bora Bora, Lin-Manuel took up Hugh Laurie's suggestion for King George's breakup song. Since the king represented the old guard that the revolutionaries were fighting against, he'd sing in an earlier generation's pop style. Why not a 1960s British Invasion sound for the ruler who'd sent the redcoats to quash the colonists' rebellion? Lin-Manuel didn't have a piano nearby, so he imagined a simple, catchy chorus: "You'll be back, / Soon you'll see, / You'll remember you belong to me." He kept it in his head until he could figure out the chords back in the United States.

They returned to unexpected news from Jeffrey Seller: *In the Heights* was closing. After a healthy two-year run on Broadway, sales had tapered off, and the show was bringing in only half its potential gross. Fortunately, Vanessa had passed the bar and would start as a law firm associate while Lin-Manuel went from gig to gig. No one was paying him to write *The Hamilton Mixtape*, but he'd been hired to write half the score for *Bring It On*, the cheerleader musical. It would open for an out-of-town tryout in Atlanta in January 2011. "I knew *Hamilton* would be a long time aborning, and this seemed like less work," he says. "It's never less work; this was just as hard. But there's no *Hamilton* without *Bring It On*."

He knew the show had to sound different from the scores he'd written before. There would be hip-hop and R&B elements, but the soundscape of cheerleading competitions drew heavily on electronic genres. "If it doesn't sound like processed dance music," he says, "you're losing what the competitions are about." So instead of turning to the piano, he dove into the possibilities of music software.

On his laptop, he had the sophisticated program Logic Pro. He decided to learn how to use the program more fully. "I took a quantum leap in technology on *Bring It On*," he says. "When you're writing dance music, you have to get the fanciest woo-woo sounds." Andy Blankenbuehler had given him images to show the heroine's transition from her privileged white school to the urban world of Jackson High: metal detectors going off, lockers slamming shut. Lin-Manuel accepted the challenge. In Logic Pro, he found a sound effect for the locker slam called Metal Door 3 and set it to a syncopated beat. Insistent sirens evoked the metal detectors, and an electronic pulse flickered between pitches to propel the song forward. For another song set at the cheerleading competition, he went full techno, with an electronic drumbeat, distorted vocals, and throbbing effects. He even recorded Vanessa saying "Deduction" and then processed her voice so that it sounded like a robot announcer. "I was playing with all the bells and whistles," he says. "It was so much fun to build. It's the closest I've come to writing songs the way a pop producer would."

When Andy received Lin-Manuel's initial demo in an email, he felt inspired. "It was the first thing that proved that the show existed," he says. "We were talking about characters and ideas, but there was nothing you could touch. Then suddenly we had a demo that was so good. I could listen to it a thousand times on the treadmill; I could play it for producers. That's when the show started to take shape." The book writer, Jeff Whitty, loved the demo too. "I'd never worked with music that felt that effortlessly contemporary," he says. "It was almost futuristic."

Lin-Manuel joined forces with the other side of the *Bring It On* composing team. Tom Kitt, the composer, had partnered with lyricist Amanda Green; they'd collaborated on the short-lived *High Fidelity* musical and welcomed another chance to work together. ("What is *Bring It On* that it needs two lyricists and two composers?" Stephen Sondheim wrote to Lin-Manuel drily.) Initially, each team stuck to its own school and sound, rather like the demarcation in the show between Truman and Jackson High: Broadway pop at Truman for Tom and Amanda, hip-hop and electronic dance music at Jackson for Lin-Manuel. But just as students from the two schools eventually combined to form a new squad, the writing teams started to blend too. "The funny thing about the show was that its metaphor became our process," Lin-Manuel says. "We thought, *I'll write the urban school, and you'll write the white school.* And then we wrote everything together."

Their first melded effort came on a song called "Friday Night, Jackson." It was a party number. As Jeff Whitty outlined in the script, Jackson's fierce dance crew would show off their moves and haze Campbell, the new student, by making her wear the leprechaun costume of the school mascot. But her commitment to the role would win the crowd over, and a Jackson boy would start to fall in love with the Truman girl. Amanda says, "We wanted to make it like the dance at the gym in *West Side Story*," where Tony spots Maria across the floor.

They convened at Amanda's apartment. Lin-Manuel started at the piano. He'd come in with a simple but unexpected chord progression, D to F-sharp: "Something that's a little scary and a little exciting that we can both mess around with," he said. For the dance section, he "tried to Rihanna the hell out of the beat," giving it a bouncy syncopation as the Jackson guys shout "Hey! Hey! Hey! Hey!" on the offbeats. "Yo, hip-hop is the national pastime, / Tick-tock, now it's 'shakin' that ass' time," the basketball captain raps, watching his girlfriend lead the dance crew.

When it was time for the Jackson boy to spot Campbell going all out in the leprechaun suit, Tom Kitt slid onto the piano bench next to Lin-Manuel. "I knew that we had to drop into this romantic, stylized moment," Tom explained, "so I wanted to keep Lin's chord progression and just start playing around." He broke up the D and F-sharp chords into lilting arpeggios, as though time were slowing down. Amanda came up with a lyric for the mesmerized onlooker: "Look at her dancing with skill and with joy / Even dressed like a strange and deranged Irish boy." As the moment passed, the beat sped up again, going back to Lin-Manuel's opening hip-hop cadence. Tom was excited. "That was an early score for us to get in the room and feed off each other."

They found that they enjoyed each other's energy. Tom was a piano whiz, enamored of Kander and Sondheim, but also a rock fan who'd arranged *American Idiot*, the Green Day jukebox musical. (Lin-Manuel was delighted that someone had made a show like he'd imagined when he took another Green Day title for *Basketcase*, his jukebox musical a decade earlier.) Amanda Green shared Lin-Manuel's taste for hammy antics and brought her own sense of raunchy playfulness to their lyrics. (During the leprechaun-dance sequence, she was proud to contribute a mock-Irish chant for the guys in the background: "Erin go bra-less, Erin go shake, / Break me off a piece of that chocolate cake!") Lin-Manuel nicknamed Amanda "Greensauce," which she loved. She regaled him with stories of her colorful father, Adolph Green, who'd written songs for *Singin' in the Rain* and *On the Town*. Lin-Manuel still thought of himself as a newcomer to the musical scene; Sondheim and Laurents called him "the little *pisher*." He was astonished when the actor cast as Campbell said that it was so nice to meet him because she'd studied him in college. "I was like, 'What?'" he recalls. "*Heights* was only a few years ago. How are you studying me? How did I become the elder statesman?"

Within the company, however, Andy Blankenbuehler held sway. "He had the whole show in his head," Lin-Manuel says. "We had to translate his directorial brain." Since Andy could hear the rhythm for the cheer routines he was choreographing, Lin-Manuel would ask him to sing the tempo aloud: *koo-kada-KAH-kada-koo-KAH-koo-KAH*. "I'd literally Shazam the beats-per-minute," he says. Sometimes Andy would tell the composers that an actor couldn't sing a note they'd written. When they asked why, Andy would explain that on that particular beat, the actor would be upside down, flipping twenty feet in the air.

For the ensemble, Andy cast actual cheerleaders to pull off the aerial stunts. Since most were new to musical theater, they needed big signs in the rehearsal room that read UPSTAGE and DOWNSTAGE to help them get their bearings. But when they started working, their craft and athleticism wowed the company. "All of us were floored by what a sport it is, and what an art form it is," Jeff Whitty says. Lin-Manuel added a verse in the opening number for Campbell to rebut the cynics at her school:

You never met me face-to-face
If you think cheerleaders are a waste of space.

We work and we fight and we train and hustle,
We get mani-pedis, but we're made of muscle.

Athletic stunts, however, carried risks. On the day of the first performance in Atlanta, one of the cheerleaders twisted her ankle. They didn't have enough time to rehearse her replacement, so they had to cancel the show that night. Then the first actor cast as Campbell broke her foot and had to leave the company. "We were asked to do some nutso things," Adrienne Warren, who played Danielle, the head Jackson dancer, says. "Lin was the biggest cheer mom. You could see him get tense during a tumble run and then relax when the stunt was landed, just like a parent."

The writers also saw Lin-Manuel as their cheerleader. "He's a keep-the-ball-in-the-air kind of guy," Amanda says. Once, when she got stuck on a lyric, she called him, exhausted and frustrated. "Let me take the baton," he told her; he knew she'd come through later. Another time, after a series of long days in Andy's studio, Jeff started to sour. Lin-Manuel pulled him aside. "We've got to get through this together," Lin-Manuel told him gently. "We can't bring the room down." It was what Jeff needed to hear. "I was like, *Oh my God, he's absolutely right. I've got to be the cheerleader too.* It's what Lin does so well—there's an ineffable bounce when you're creating through joy."

That bounce became audible in the finale, which Tom and Amanda wrote with Lin-Manuel. "I remember the three of us goofing together at Amanda's house, feeling playful and energized," Tom says. Jeff had written a scene for Campbell and her Jackson teammates after nationals; they'd lost the competition, but in the mode of a high-school sports story, they'd found a greater reward in their new friendship. "I may not have a trophy, but I've got you," the script said. That line struck Amanda. "'I've Got You'—that's the song," she decided. She played her collaborators a number called "I've Got Love" from the musical *Purlie* as an example of the joyful vibe they were chasing. Tom translated that feeling into a jaunty groove at the piano. Amanda recorded it on her iPhone and worked on a lyric to match: "Hey, girl! We killed it and we know it / Don't need the gold to show it when you know it inside." For the bridge, Lin-Manuel hooked the title phrase to a rap list of famous pop-culture duos: "I got you / Like Sam and Frodo / Like Dorothy and Toto / Notre Dame and Quasimodo!" The list continued: "Like Lucy and Ricky / Like Justin and Selena"—and then the mic-drop rhyme—"Word, we be holdin' court like Venus and Serena!"

They tried it in performance, and it earned a huge ovation. But Andy felt the finale should be less chipper, more moving. Late one night at the end of technical rehearsals, Andy turned to Lin-Manuel and Tom and asked them to rewrite the number. "They went into a janitor's closet," Andy recalls, "and they came back at midnight with a new song they'd written on a paper plate." It wove reprises of all the prior songs into a tear-jerking finale, a testament to the characters' growth. The next day, the cast performed the number at the end of the show. In Lin-Manuel's words, "It ate shit." *Bring It On*, they'd learned, didn't want a moving, reflective finale. It needed an upbeat crowd-pleaser. When Andy went to bed after that performance, he told his wife, "I don't know anything about show business." The following day, "I Got You" went back in the show. Andy kept the paper plate in his office as a reminder.

Bring It On ran for a month in Atlanta, began a national tour in Los Angeles in November 2011, and opened on Broadway in August 2012. Each iteration of *Bring It On* required revisions; Amanda called the Broadway incarnation "Version 5.67." The challenge for the songwriters, as with so many musicals, was to figure out the lead character's "I Want" number. "Campbell's a pretty blond cheerleader," Amanda says. "She's already perfect. So what does she want? We racked our brains."

From an earlier attempt, Tom had a melody, urgent and introspective, and Amanda had written introductory verses. Then Lin-Manuel came up with the key metaphor. He only had to remember his own high-school self. "Me as perfectionist, taking extracurriculars really seriously—that was my way into Campbell," he says. "These kids rehearse and rehearse for a four-minute routine. I took working on *A Chorus Line* with Meredith that seriously. Cheer felt like what I loved in theater taken to extremis. It's all for that one perfect moment when you get in front of an audience." That became the title of the song: What Campbell wanted was "One Perfect Moment."

To write the lyrics from the perspective of a high-schooler, Lin-Manuel took a unique step. He went to his parents' house and spent the night in his childhood bedroom. He had Tom's melody, a series of descending triplets, looping on his iPod. In the room where he'd edited *Clayton's Friends* on his camcorder, the images started to come, like shots in a home movie.

> *Fade in on Campbell: An average teenager, almost grown.*
> *Close up on average grades from the average life she's known.*
> *Now zoom in the lens on the rest of her friends as she stays alone*
> *Doing the work, getting it right.*

He stayed up all night working on the song. "I was really proud of the camera metaphors," he says. "And the fun was getting to play in Tom Kitt–melody land." He enjoyed slipping a love letter to theater collaborations into a show about cheerleaders. The whole team had noticed that their song titles were mirroring their process: "It's All Happening," "I Got You." As previews began on Broadway, they wrote one more number together, this one for Campbell and Danielle, called, fittingly, "We're Not Done."

The show marked the Broadway debut of a whopping thirty actors, including Taylor Louderman (Campbell), who would later be nominated for a Tony for *Mean Girls*; Adrienne Warren (Danielle), who went on to win a Tony for *Tina: The Tina Turner Musical*; and Ariana DeBose (Danielle's fellow dancer Nautica), who would win an Oscar for *West Side Story*. *Bring It On* itself received Tony nominations for Best Musical and for Andy Blankenbuehler's choreography. It also featured one of the first transgender characters on Broadway: Jackson High's self-empowerment diva, La Cienega.

Reviews lauded the acrobatic dance numbers and the fresh musical sounds, though the high-school sports-and-friendship arc felt familiar in the wake of TV productions like *High School Musical* and *Glee*. Ticket sales, however, never took off. "I chalk it up to the timing," Lin-Manuel's agent, John Buzzetti, says. "I think audiences saw a cheerleading skirt in an ad and were like, 'I want nothing to do with it; I'm over that high-school shit.'" Lin-Manuel thought the problem lay in calibrating expectations for a film adaptation. "People who were fans of the movie were like, 'This isn't the movie,'" he says. *Bring It On* closed after only six months.

Even if it didn't reach the success of *In the Heights*, it felt like a valuable stage in Lin-Manuel's education. "We write musicals, and one out of five shows that reaches Broadway makes its money back," he explained. "That's a four-out-of-five failure rate in terms of seeing a return on your investment. So what is the lesson you take away from that? You cannot do something because you think it will make money. You have to do it because you love it or because you believe you will learn from it."

He didn't need a trophy; he'd wanted a chance to pick up new skills from his collaborators. Thanks to the drumbeat in Andy's head, he'd gotten to play with an electronic tool kit, building songs like a pop producer. Thanks to Tom and Amanda, he'd gotten to see how other songwriters approached their work, playing with the possibilities that their melodies and lyrics opened up. Thanks to Jeff's script, he got to practice mapping his musical intuitions onto material that didn't come from his own experience, writing songs that centered female ambition and friendship. "All of that," he says, "became trial and error for *Hamilton*."

14

AMERICAN SONGBOOK

••

*I*n Tommy Kail's philosophy of directing, *when* you make a request matters as much as what you're asking for. When Lin-Manuel showed him the initial songs for *The Hamilton Mixtape*, "to have imposed structure on the thing would have killed the thing," he says. "That wasn't an appropriate way to try to harness what was happening. So I just said to him, 'Go where the juice is. Write what you feel. Who cares about a timeline?'"

Tommy recognized a different moment, however, on June 20, 2011, just over two years after the White House poetry jam. He'd directed another Broadway show, *Lombardi*, in the interim, drawing on his sports background to helm a play about the legendary football coach, but even as he and Lin-Manuel worked on separate projects, they kept up their collaboration through the *Heights* tour and Freestyle Love Supreme shows.

This particular June evening was a benefit for Ars Nova, the experimental theater that had given FLS its first professional gig seven years earlier. As a break from their usual improv sets, each member of the group picked a number they'd already written to perform. Lin-Manuel thought about debuting a new song he'd been working on for the Hamilton project, but it felt a little risky. This wasn't the White House; no cabinet members would seed the audience with a built-in appetite for tales of the first treasury secretary. The style might prove challenging to comprehend at first hearing too. FLS gigs featured clever wordplay, but their freestyle rhythms kept the bars from getting too dense; you could make up only so many internal rhymes on the spot. Lin-Manuel's goal for the new song was to showcase Hamilton's revolutionary brilliance. He'd spent a year working on these lyrics, packing every line full of puns, references, and rhymes. "I was trying to prove my thesis that Hamilton's intellect is what propels him through the narrative," he explained. "He's Big Pun times Eminem times Jay-Z in terms of how much I'm trying to make it rhyme. I'm calling on all the ancestors of this flow to say that Hamilton is the future."

The first time he shared the song with his friend Bill Sherman, Bill was more boggled than impressed. "He sang it to me over the phone," Bill recalls, "and it was really long, so I was like, 'It's really long!'" Stephen Sondheim had a similar response when Lin-Manuel sent him a draft, though he understood the motivation behind the style. "We all suffer from verbosity in our first drafts, and verbosity is part of the style of what you're doing," Sondheim acknowledged. "Nevertheless . . ."

But Lin-Manuel was undeterred. He had latched onto Hamilton because of his verbosity, his graphomania, his linguistic excess. This was a man who could produce an eighty-page pamphlet rebutting a British loyalist without a second thought. His "I Want" song had to feel like a verbal onslaught—almost too much to take in at once. Ars Nova audiences didn't mind a risk. He decided to give it a try.

At the benefit on the evening of June 20, he launched into Hamilton's declaration of purpose as an ambitious scholarship kid newly arrived in New York:

> *I am not throwing away my shot!*
> *I am not throwing away my shot!*
> *Hey yo, I'm just like my country,*
> *I'm young, scrappy, and hungry*
> *And I'm not throwing away my shot!*

The central metaphor came to him by intuition. He knew a duel would arrive at the end of the story, so he thought something about a shot would accrue resonance: a gunshot, an opportunity. The chorus to Eminem's "Lose Yourself" on the *8 Mile* soundtrack provided inspiration: "You only get one shot, do not miss your chance to blow / This opportunity comes once in a lifetime, yo." If Hamilton was, as Lin-Manuel later described him, "Eminem meets Sweeney Todd," a blend of verbal belligerence and almost maniacal relentlessness, he wouldn't miss his shot to prove it. The slant rhyme of *country* and *hungry* might irk musical-theater purists, but it could draw in hip-hop connoisseurs craving an unexpected couplet, and it made the sonic case that Hamilton's ambition, like that of the nascent American Republic, lunged past conventional bounds.

Then Lin-Manuel began the verse. He knew his goal: "I wanted Hamilton's first verse to feel off-the-cuff and make you think: *How could he possibly freestyle that eloquently*?" He started with a direct statement, then gained complexity as the internal rhymes piled up:

I've just got a scholarship to King's College.
I prob'ly shouldn't brag, but dag, I amaze and astonish.
The problem is I've got a lot of brains but no polish.
I gotta holler just to be heard. With every word, I drop knowledge.
I'm a diamond in the rough, a shiny piece of coal
Tryin' to reach my goal, my power of speech: unimpeachable.
Seventeen years old, but my mind is older.
These New York City streets get colder, I shoulder
Ev'ry burden, ev'ry disadvantage I have learned to manage,
I ain't got a gun to brandish, I walk these streets famished.
The plan is to fan this spark into a flame,
But damn, it's gettin' dark, so let me spell out the name.

He tripped up. The polysyllabic patter proved too intricate for him to motor through, even though he'd written every line in his notebook and gone over it multiple times. The performance stopped. Shockwave, who was beatboxing behind him, had to halt.

Lin-Manuel gathered himself and started over. This time, though, the audience was with him. The hip-hop fans in the theater could hear shout-outs to the greatest MCs: Tupac's "holla if ya hear me"; Big Pun's "I'm a diamond in the rough." The Notorious B.I.G.'s famous spelling of his name ("It's the N-O, T-O, R-I, O / U-S, you just lay down, slow") echoed in Alexander Hamilton's cadence:

It's the A-L, E-X, A-N, D
E-R. We are meant to be

A colony that runs independently.
Meanwhile Britain keeps shittin' on us endlessly.

By presenting Hamilton as an astoundingly dexterous freestyler, Lin-Manuel wasn't only proving his thesis that the Founding Father's brilliance drove his life story. He was also establishing hip-hop as the language of American Revolution, youthful and brash, muscular and literate, urgent and self-aware, capacious enough to fit eighteenth-century rhetoric alongside twenty-first-century street slang.

In the song's bridge, he continued to span the centuries. He shouted, "Whoa, whoa, whoa!" on a leaping octave interval that he based on the '90s AOL startup dial sound. ("I wanted it to feel like his words are reverberating out into the world, and I associate that with the first time I signed into the Internet," he explained.) He expanded Hamilton's reach with a line lifted directly from Busta Rhymes's "Pass the Courvoisier": "Don't this shit make my people wanna rise up!" And then, in the final verse, Hamilton's lyrics became suddenly confessional with what Lin-Manuel called the most autobiographical line he'd written: "I imagine death so much it feels more like a memory." Both he and Hamilton had loved ones die in their childhood; both wondered why they were the ones to survive; both took the threat of mortality as a spur to speed ahead.

As he raced to his conclusion, Lin-Manuel ratcheted up the intensity even higher. "I'm trying to make it the densest couplets I can write," he said, "so you could kick the tire on any part of the line and it's un-fuck-with-able." He channeled Big Pun's most pugilistic bars into a pyrotechnic finale:

I'm past patiently waitin'. I'm passionately smashin'
Ev'ry expectation, ev'ry action's an act of creation.
I'm laughin' in the face of casualties and sorrow,
For the first time, I'm thinkin' past tomorrow,
And I am not throwing away my shot!

The audience was riveted. Tommy Kail, watching the performance in Ars Nova's ninety-nine-seat theater, "felt the room lean all the way forward." He'd heard Lin-Manuel's demos, and he'd seen the video from the

White House. But sensing the kinetic response from a group of electrified listeners was a different experience. "You could feel the hair on the backs of everyone's necks was standing up—it really felt like something amazing was happening," Kail said. This wasn't just a mixtape. "It was a thunderclap moment because I realized there was a version of this that could be done live. I didn't know what it looked like, I didn't know what it was going to be, but I knew Lin had to keep writing."

At the reception after the show, admirers crowded around Lin-Manuel. Tommy recognized an opportunity. "When we were upstairs afterwards, and everyone was patting him on the back, I saw my moment." He went up to the evening's star.

"That went well," Lin-Manuel said.

"Yeah," Tommy agreed. "That was good." Then he made his pitch. "So, you've written two songs in two and a half years. We're gonna be very old by the time this is actually complete. So why don't we expedite it a little bit?" He suggested picking a date six months from then and seeing what happened if they aimed for two songs a month.

The next day, still on a high from the performance, Lin-Manuel called Tommy. Lincoln Center had offered him a slot to open its American Songbook concert series in six months, on January 11, 2012. January 11 also happened to be Hamilton's birthday. It felt like kismet. If he wrote a song or two each month, then with the four songs he'd started already—the opening number, Washington's song, King George's song, and "My Shot"—they'd have a set for the concert.

Tommy didn't know if the concert would end up yielding an album or a stage show. But he knew that a structure would allow Lin-Manuel to move forward. "Tommy's good at setting deadlines," Lin-Manuel says. "When I don't have deadlines, it doesn't happen." His father could never understand why he waited until the last minute to do his work. Luz was the same way; in graduate school, Luis would complete his course assignments far in advance, whereas Luz wouldn't finish hers until the night before they were due. "It almost gave me pause in continuing to date her," Luis admits. "Who waits until the night before for assignments you fucking got on the first day of class?" But Luz always turned her assignments in on time, and so did her son. He just needed a deadline. Or, as his sister puts it, "Lin always needs a Tommy in his life."

Tommy made a proposal for approaching the next six months. Before they influenced the other's thinking about the project, they would each go through Chernow's biography and write a list of the scenes they thought should be included: "What's interesting to you? What's a song? Who's a character? What's a moment?" Then they would compare lists and see where they overlapped.

Lin-Manuel liked the idea. When he'd gotten mired in research during his semester in Spain, he'd emailed John Weidman, the book writer for *Pacific Overtures* and *Assassins* and the father of his Hunter classmate, for advice about finding his way through a mass of historical information. "Do you recommend writing about the sections of Hamilton's life that are most attractive personally," he asked, "and writing the connective tissue later, if I find that there are large, Buick-sized holes in the storytelling?" Weidman replied, "Absolutely." Especially if Lin-Manuel was envisioning an album first, Weidman encouraged him to "let your imagination go to the places where it naturally wants to go." If there were holes, he could go back and fill them in, but he'd be building a narrative out of enthusiasm, not chronological duty. Now Tommy was offering a concrete way to take an inventory of his enthusiasm. They made their lists.

One of the moments they both chose was the scene where Hamilton met the woman he would marry: Elizabeth Schuyler, the wealthy daughter of a prominent New Yorker and an advantageous match for a penniless, immigrant orphan. This scene offered a chance to heed Sondheim's advice and introduce variety to the score. After so much revolutionary hip-hop, Eliza could sing in a different genre. Their courtship took place at a winter ball where soldiers in the Continental Army mingled with society ladies. Picturing them together, Lin-Manuel started to hear the kind of slow dance that he and a date would sway to at the Hunter prom, a classic doo-wop love song like "Earth Angel" by the Penguins. He could write a song like that.

Using Logic, he picked out a simple triple rhythm, a relaxed waltz beat with a little pop fillip, and imagined what Eliza would say. Chernow's account described her as less outgoing and flirtatious than her sisters Angelica and Peggy, though she never wavered in her love for Alexander. This gave Lin-Manuel an opening. "I have never been the pretty one, / Or the funny one, or the witty one," he sang on his demo, the inverse of Maria's pretty and witty self-portrait that he'd translated for *West Side Story*.

"I stayed on the side, watched my sister shine / Took it all in stride, 'til that night." When Eliza spots Alexander, however, she is transformed: "I grabbed my sister and whispered / 'Oh no! This one's mine.'"

Lin-Manuel and Vanessa were staying in Montauk, on the eastern tip of Long Island, where his parents had a vacation condo. He played her the demo of "This One's Mine," expecting her to fall for the love song too. She wasn't impressed. "This doesn't feel like your final draft," she told him.

Frustrated, he stomped out to a gazebo on the property. He knew she was right. "I just threw out everything I had, took the best lines, and went back to work," he says. "I tried a totally different tack." Instead of singing like a '50s doo-wop crooner, Eliza would sing like Beyoncé.

That summer, Beyoncé had released her fourth album, which included a raucous romantic number called "Countdown" that Lin-Manuel considered a perfect song. "Grrrrind up on it, girl, show him how you ride it," Beyoncé advised with an alluring growl. Eliza needed a little of that edge. "Grind to the rhythm as we wine and dine," Lin-Manuel had her sing in his new version of the courtship ball. "Grab my sister and whisper, 'Yo, this one's mine.'" As her previous "Oh no" turned into a confident "Yo," Eliza moved to a bouncy groove, with the guys chiming in a playful "Hey" on the offbeats, like Lin-Manuel had used for the dance party in *Bring It On*. No longer reticent, she became jubilant.

Beyoncé also played with stressing syllables, emphasizing the beat just before the end of the line—"lip *lock*in'" and "keep *flock*in'," in one couplet. Lin-Manuel adapted that cadence for Eliza's anxious heartbeat after her first encounter with Hamilton:

Two weeks later, in the livin' room stress*in',*
My father's stone-faced while you're askin' for his bless*in'.*

For the chorus, Eliza let loose on an exultant riff, infatuated and playful:

Boy, you got me helpless!
Look into your eyes and the sky's the limit.

Though it might seem disempowering for Eliza to describe herself as giddily *helpless* at the start of her relationship with Hamilton, Lin-Manuel wanted to set her up for an arc to the end of her story, when she would become the one taking action to secure Hamilton's legacy after his death. He also thought that *helpless* might prove a useful term to reprise later on, like *my shot*. In Chernow's account, Hamilton's heart was drawn to women he perceived as helpless—first his mother, abandoned and dying beside him, and later on a mistreated woman named Maria Reynolds, with whom he had a notorious affair. "A woman in distress would evoke his mother," Lin-Manuel says, "rousing not only his lust but his empathy in a way that short-circuits reason. So to have Eliza sing 'Helpless' I thought would be helpful for a line that could come back."

For the final verse, Lin-Manuel had Hamilton woo Eliza with a rap, an homage to the hip-hop/R&B duets from the 1990s that he loved.

In three verses, Lin-Manuel had covered three weeks and gone from first encounter to courtship to marriage. Best of all, he'd drafted it in a week and revised it in a day. Tommy's deadlines were starting to work.

Vanessa noticed that Lin-Manuel got his best writing done when they were out of town. He'd started Aaron Burr's opening number in Mexico, George Washington's rap in Spain, King George's song in Bora Bora, and Eliza's number in Montauk. When he wrote a song in New York, as he did with "My Shot," it took him a year. "In New York, he was constantly getting sidetracked by other gigs and getting to know the people in his industry," she says. "He's happier when he writes, and I saw that. At the time, I was the stable breadwinner at a law firm. There were a lot of times when I was like, 'We're going on vacation so he can work.'" On a beach in the Caribbean, they'd take kite-surfing lessons together in the morning, then she'd leave him in the hotel to write in the afternoon. "For me, writing is a real mix of intense focus and intense drift," he says. "You have to be able to daydream a bit to let stuff in, but also you have to have the time to do that."

That Thanksgiving, Lin-Manuel, Vanessa, and Vanessa's family visited a beach town in the Dominican Republic called Cabarete. Its nominal echo of Kander and Ebb's *Cabaret* put Lin-Manuel in a musical mood. "Wilkommen, Bienvenue, Welcome: Oh Cabarete, Oh Cabarete, Oh Cabarete," he mused. It was a time of mingled emotions. One of Vanessa's aunts passed away during their trip, but there was also new life: One day on the beach, a little stray puppy ambled up and nipped Vanessa on her ankle.

They resolved that if the puppy returned the next day, they'd adopt her. She did. They named her Tobillo—Spanish for "ankle."

On that trip, feeling a sense of loss and renewal, Lin-Manuel continued working on another scene he'd circled in the Chernow biography: A moment just after the carnage of the Revolutionary War when Aaron Burr and Alexander Hamilton each welcomed his first child. Burr had a daughter named Theodosia, after her mother; Hamilton had a son named Philip, after Eliza's father. Lin-Manuel and Tommy agreed that they didn't want to make Hamilton the hero and Burr the villain; they wanted to show both men as striving and flawed humans whose lives paralleled each other's until their final, fatal encounter. "We were always much more compelled by the idea of two best friends, one of whom ends up killing the other, rather than two enemies who end up pointing guns at each other," Tommy said. Showing the two new fathers side by side could help to establish that bond.

In Cabarete, Lin-Manuel completed a duet for Burr and Hamilton to greet their newborns. He wanted it to feel simple, emotional, understated—a sonic respite from the military drums and bass. Instead, it would be a gentle folk song with a high, floating melody. Burr sang first:

Dear Theodosia, what to say to you?
You have my eyes. You have your mother's name.
When you came into the world, you cried
And it broke my heart.

Hamilton serenaded his baby, too, in parallel terms to Burr. And then together, Burr and Hamilton imagined a future for their children in a new country:

You will come of age with our young nation.
We'll bleed and fight for you,
We'll make it right for you.
If we lay a strong enough foundation
We'll pass it on to you,
We'll give the world to you,
And you'll blow us all away
Someday, someday.

Vanessa couldn't believe that her husband had transported himself into the position of a new father merely by staring at their adopted puppy. "It's amazing that he's able to feel things that haven't happened to him," she says. Lin-Manuel says it wasn't that simple; he'd already begun writing the song before Tobillo appeared. For Lin-Manuel's mother, hearing "Dear Theodosia" prompted one thought about her son and daughter-in-law. "They'd been married already for a year," Luz says, "and we hadn't said anything about having kids. After that song, I turned to Vanessa and I went, 'You gotta give him a baby!'" Vanessa was aghast; she didn't think the decision was hers alone to make. When Luz learned that her son had finished the song after finding a puppy, she burst out laughing.

In January 2012, when it was time for the Lincoln Center concert, Lin-Manuel had eleven songs. He'd sent each one to Ron Chernow to check for historical accuracy. "I can't think of a single time that I didn't say, 'Great, keep going!'" Ron says. "I was just amazed at the variety and versatility of the music." Later on, Lin-Manuel invited Ron to come to a rehearsal with the cast. Chernow arrived at a studio in the garment district, opened the door, and saw the actors who would be playing the Founding Fathers. "I was flabbergasted," Ron recalls. He hadn't expected to see a room full of people of color.

Tommy had populated the cast with a mix of Freestyle Love Supreme and *In the Heights* veterans. (Chris Jackson, as Lin-Manuel had dreamed, was George Washington.) The goal, Tommy said, was to "eliminate distance between then and now, to make the world onstage reflect the world that we live in." Lin-Manuel saw the casting as a question of skill—"the people who can pull off hip-hop the best"—and of national identity. "This is an American story," he said, "and we're all Americans and we have a right to play these parts." As soon as the actors in the rehearsal room started to sing, Chernow was converted. "They not only had beautiful voices, but they had a special feel for the material," he says. "And of course, Chris Jackson is just incomparable."

To accompany the actors, Lac put together a band. From arranging *Bring It On*, he'd figured out that too much electronic percussion could oversaturate the sound. "You don't want machines to overpower humans," he says. "I learned by doing it the wrong way in *Bring It On*." For this concert, they'd need some prerecorded samples: an explosion, a horse whinny. But for the most part, the sounds would come from live musicians. Shockwave, the FLS beatboxer, would provide specialty effects alongside a drummer and a percussionist, plus a guitar, a bass, and Lac on keys.

The Allen Room at Lincoln Center could accommodate about four hundred people—the largest audience yet for *The Hamilton Mixtape*. Ron Chernow was there. John Kander was there. Stephen Sondheim was there. Jill Furman, Kevin McCollum, and Jeffrey Seller, the *Heights* producers, were there, eager to see their protégé's next project. A critic from the *New York Times* was there, too, ready to report on the buzzy song cycle whose premiere at the White House had become a viral YouTube hit.

Lin-Manuel bounded onstage in white sneakers and his customary black suit, white shirt, and black tie loose at the collar. Behind him, a giant window looked east over the twinkling nightscape of Central Park and the city beyond. He was about to turn thirty-two, the age at which Sondheim had his first solo-composed show on Broadway.

"New York City! How y'all doin'?" Lin-Manuel shouted, taking a seat on a stool and grabbing a bottle of water. "You coulda been anywhere in the world," he continued, riffing on a classic Jay-Z intro, "and you're here tonight, at the opening of the American Songbook series." For an overture, he and Lac had remixed Jay-Z and Alicia Keys's "Empire State of Mind" with other New York anthems by Kander and Ebb, Billy Joel, and Sondheim. "This is a dream come true," Lin-Manuel said, jumping up again. He promised to share the new *Hamilton* songs he'd been writing. "But first," he announced, "I want to play you some songs that formed the DNA of my brain."

Those songs were the hip-hop he'd imbibed in high school and college. He invited his FLS buddies to join him for a tour through his own personal mixtape: the Pharcyde, the Notorious B.I.G., Big Pun, Eminem, Talib Kweli. It was a brazen opening to a Lincoln Center concert. The American Songbook series had, in recent years, expanded beyond Broadway classics to include folk, pop, and rock, but it had never hosted a rap medley. The thesis presented in the Allen Room was clear: Hip-hop formed the new American songbook.

With Lin-Manuel's musical origins established, he segued to the nascent *Hamilton Mixtape*. "The video at the White House was like Beyoncé announcing the baby bump—I'm pregnant!" he joked. "Tonight you're going to see some very detailed ultrasounds." He kicked off this portion with "My Shot," the rap he'd performed at Ars Nova, now arranged by Lac for band and chorus. Then Lin-Manuel said, "It's time you met the father of our country. He doesn't look the way he does on the dollar bill." Chris Jackson came out to rap "Right Hand Man," Washington's plea for assistance in the face of a British invasion, over a thundering bass beat. The invasion itself was personified by King George—Broadway leading man Gavin Creel in a Burger King crown—who sang his Beatles-esque piano ballad "You'll Be Back" with a condescending sneer. Hamilton's saga continued through romance ("Helpless"), warfare (a grim rap at the revolution's nadir called "Valley Forge"), and, after the war, the promise of a new generation ("Dear Theodosia").

The dramatic high point came at the dawn of the republic as President Washington's newly appointed secretaries of state and treasury, Jefferson and Hamilton, clashed over the nature of America's fledgling government. Lin-Manuel envisioned these cabinet debates as actual rap battles in the mode of the freestyle face-offs in Eminem's *8 Mile*—but instead of simply trying to dis an opponent, Hamilton and Jefferson vied over the future of their country. Should it become an energetic modern economy with a national bank, as the New Yorker Hamilton proposed, or a haven for slave-owning states free from federal intervention, as the Virginian Jefferson argued?

Dis they did as they fought over Hamilton's plan for the federal government to take over debts accrued by the states. Chris Jackson, as President Washington, emceed while Shockwave laid down a beat. It was a version of American history the audience had never heard before. Jefferson shot down Hamilton's claim that his financial plan wasn't in his own self-interest: "Oooh, if the shoe fits, wear it. / If New York's in debt, why should Virginia bear it?"

When the president gave Hamilton his chance to respond, he took aim at both Jefferson and his Virginian ally James Madison, firing a barrage of internal rhymes to demolish his opponents:

Thomas Jefferson, always hesitant with the President,
Reticent, there isn't a plan he doesn't jettison.
Madison, you fat ass, venison isn't medicine.

Damn, you in worse shape than the national debt is in!
Sittin' there useless as two shits—
Secretary Jefferson, bend over, I'll show you where my shoe fits!

The Allen Room erupted in laughter and applause as President Washington told everyone to settle down. Hamilton and Jefferson squared off for one more rap battle, this time over whether America should support the French Revolution. Madison, Jefferson's hype man, landed a punch line adapted from Biggie's "Juicy"—"And if you don't know, now you know, Mr. President"—but the president declared Hamilton, who counseled neutrality, the winner.

But why, Lin-Manuel asked the room, "is Hamilton on our money but he was never our president?" The answer he offered was that Hamilton's many firsts included not only creating Wall Street but also prompting the nation's first sex scandal. "When he was accused of using Treasury funds to cover up this affair, he blew up his own spot. He released a pamphlet graphically detailing the affair, and it basically ended his career." In what Lin-Manuel called "a musical version of that pamphlet," Mandy Gonzalez took the mic as a soulful Maria Reynolds, the woman with whom Hamilton slept, for a sultry slow jam called "Say No to This" (with a brief, haunting reprise of "Helpless" tucked in).

Lin-Manuel ended the concert by describing two duels—first the duel in which Hamilton's son was killed defending his father's honor, then the duel when Burr, tired of being slighted by his longtime rival, shot Hamilton, who "threw away his shot into the air." For the finale, the entire company sang "Alexander Hamilton," no longer the monologue from the White House but a full choral and band arrangement. On the final downbeat, Lin-Manuel thrust his hand in the shape of a pistol into the air. The audience rose to their feet.

Lin-Manuel took in the ovation. He acknowledged Lac and the band. He smiled. He crossed his arms. He dropped his mouth open in disbelief. He was a six-year-old kid again at his first piano recital, basking in the applause. He stepped back to the microphone. Almost apologetically, he said, "We know another one."

His sister, sitting in the audience, couldn't believe it. After the encore

(Chris and Mandy singing "When You're Home" from *In the Heights*), when the crowd finally dispersed, Cita accosted Lin-Manuel. "It was just like our first piano recital," she said, "when you yelled, 'I know ANOTHER one!' and played three more songs!"

But her brother wasn't looking backward. That evening secured his project's future. The *Times* review raved about the Lincoln Center performance. It didn't matter whether *The Hamilton Mixtape* was a concept album or a future Broadway musical, the critic Stephen Holden wrote. "What it is, is hot. Its language is a seamless marriage of hip-hop argot and raw American history made startlingly alive; the music arranged for a sextet by Lacamoire is flexible, undigitized hip-hop rock fusion. Mr. Miranda, the musical-theater force behind 'In the Heights,' has outdone himself in a project that is an obvious game changer."

The performance changed the game for Lin-Manuel too. Tommy's instinct had been right: The audience response made it clear that *The Hamilton Mixtape* should become a live show.

The next day, Jeffrey Seller called Lin-Manuel and Tommy. "This is a musical," he told them. "And if you want me to produce it, I would love to." Kevin McCollum wanted to produce it too. The problem was, Kevin and Jeffrey had split up the week before the concert. They were no longer a producing team. Lin-Manuel and Tommy would have to choose one or the other.

Lin-Manuel told his agent, John Buzzetti, that whatever they decided, they had to make sure that Jill Furman also got to be a producer; she'd supported *Heights* and FLS from the start. It wasn't easy to make the final call. Buzzetti knew he would have to notify either Kevin or Jeffrey that he hadn't been chosen.

Lin-Manuel thought back to his experience working with the producers on *In the Heights*. "Everyone's notes were valuable," he says. "Jill's the keeper of the flame. She had a long-view perspective, since she'd seen *Heights* from its Drama Book Shop basement days. Kevin is a font of ideas; he pitches a lot of things at you, some outlandish, some really good. Jeffrey's good at synthesizing: 'Do this and this.'"

It was a tough decision. Jeffrey sent Tommy and Lin-Manuel an email to make his case:

Though I've expressed to each of you separately my enthusiasm for Hamilton, I thought it good to tell you both today that, if I become your producer, I will be a passionate advocate, cheerleader, sounding board, constructive critic, and barker.

I have a new company name, Adventureland. It's the name of a play I wrote in the 4th grade about my two best friends and I journeying through a land filled with fun, danger, and plenty of adventure. It was where I wanted to be in the 4th grade and it's where I want to be now. It's where you guys often toil, and, no doubt, it's where Alexander Hamilton travelled for much of his life.

I look forward to getting back in a room with both of you to start talking about a new musical.

I'm ready.

That sounded good to Lin-Manuel. Jeffrey was the synthesizer; he put their ideas into action. Lin-Manuel wanted to skip straight to that step.

He sent Buzzetti and Tommy a one-word message: "Adventureland!"

Buzzetti wrote back: "Today's the day, bitches. Jesus take the wheel!"

15

NON-STOP

• •

If *The Hamilton Mixtape* was to become a musical, it required a book writer. Lin-Manuel had to focus on the songs, so he needed someone to take responsibility for telling the story and crafting the non-musical scenes, as Quiara Alegría Hudes had done for the book of *In the Heights*. At the Lincoln Center performance, he talked the audience through the transitions between musical numbers, relating the general contours of Hamilton's life story from his Caribbean origins and the Revolutionary War through his feuds on Washington's cabinet, his sex scandal, and his duel with Burr. Lin-Manuel's amusing narration could smooth over what he'd called the "Buick-sized holes in the storytelling" the same way he'd patched the plot gaps as Usnavi in the early *Heights* days. But now he could use a real playwright to assume narrative duties. "I wanted to work with a book writer," he says, and he had one in mind—a playwright who shared his love of hip-hop and had a feel for kinetic New York stories.

For much of 2012, he and the playwright (whose name remains confidential) met for brainstorming conversations and work sessions. They shared lunch; they traded '90s rap references; they motivated each other to write. Tommy supported them. In January 2013, they did a private reading with actors just for Tommy and Jeffrey to see their progress.

The dialogue scenes didn't work. "Every time they stopped to talk, the show lost energy," Jeffrey says. "It was like a balloon that kept running out of helium." At the end of the reading, they all walked away deflated. It felt like the end of the O'Neill National Music Theater Conference when they'd learned that *In the Heights* had taken a step backward. "It was a big disappointment," Jeffrey says.

The next day, Tommy called Jeffrey to check in. "We have to lose the book," Jeffrey told him. "We can't stop to talk. The talking is killing it."

That meant Lin-Manuel would have to write the whole show by himself.

Fortunately, he agreed with Jeffrey. He thought the playwright's scenes were great, but he realized that "*Hamilton* starts too fast to slow down." And though it was daunting to contemplate writing the entire show without a collaborator on the book, it seemed like the best option. He could convey the story through the songs. The show's pace had become his own propulsion. He was bursting to finish it.

To test the new material, Jeffrey booked a one-week reading that summer at New York Stage and Film, a popular incubator for new work upstate at Vassar College. The goal was to have a complete first act to perform. On top of composing the songs, Lin-Manuel now had the book writer's responsibility of keeping the narrative clear and moving the story along between numbers without losing the show's rhythmic drive.

As an inspiration, he thought of the conversational interludes on Jay-Z's album *Reasonable Doubt*. A short track like "Friend or Foe" advanced a plot—Jay-Z dispatches a couple of thugs who challenge his supremacy—while keeping its rap pulse palpable. "You're twitchin', don' do that, you makin' me nervous," Jay-Z tells the challengers. "My crew, well, they do pack, them dudes is murderers." That casual tone with more than a hint of menace, a chatty rhythm fraught with import, was what Lin-Manuel wanted. "It sounds like a dude talking, and it happens to rhyme in three places," he explained. (*Crew/do/dudes*, plus the slant rhyme of *nervous/murderers*.)

He'd experimented before with this kind of rhythmic rhyming dialogue—a sort of rap recitative—in *Bring It On*. For the number where Campbell was transferred to Jackson High, he imagined her misreading the new school's social cues, mistaking a mixtape swap for a drug deal. As Campbell looked on, two Jackson students traded a memory stick with chopped-and-screwed rap remixes, speaking in the beats and assonance of the hip-hop they're swapping:

RANDALL: What's up, man?

CAMERON: Yo, what it do, kid? You got the stuff?

RANDALL: Chopped and screwed it.

CAMERON: Damn, I can't wait to use it.

RANDALL: I'm telling you, it's crack, so don't lose it.

CAMERON: Check it out, it's that cute Campbell Soup kid.

CAMPBELL: Campbell.

RANDALL: I'm sorry, who's this?

CAMPBELL: Are you guys selling crack?

RANDALL: Don't be stupid. Dude, it's a memory stick full of music.

It sounded like two dudes and a girl talking, and it happened to rhyme, loosely, in nine places (*do, kid / screwed it / use it / lose it / Soup kid / who's this / stupid / Dude it's / music*).

For the Vassar reading, Lin-Manuel aimed for that conversational pulse. In particular, he needed dialogue to get from Burr's opening number to Hamilton's "I Want" song, "My Shot." What kind of spoken scene would bridge those songs? Chernow's biography didn't specify when Hamilton and Burr first met, so perhaps Lin-Manuel could imagine an encounter that would set them on their converging course.

To start, he made a list of every word he could think of that rhymed with *Burr*. In his notebook, he scrawled down possibilities, some simple, some less expected: *sir, sure, pure, demure, curiouser*. He could also put two words together for an internal rhyme: *Burr, sir*. That sounded like it could appear in an exchange like Jay-Z's or Randall and Cameron's. Its rhythm also summoned his childhood memories of Dr. Seuss, who piled up rhyming syllables in picture books like *Fox in Socks*: "I get all those ticks and clocks, sir, / mixed up with the chicks and tocks, sir. / I can't do it, Mr. Fox, sir." He liked the feel of rhyming on the penultimate syllable—a little comic, a little off-kilter, a touch of old-fashioned formality from the additional *sir*. If he was playing with more than one syllable, then other possibilities opened up: *service, sir; nervous, sir*.

He decided to try it. He'd learned from Chernow that Burr was a prodigy, admitted to Princeton at age thirteen and graduating at sixteen. Hamilton, eager to outrace death at every turn, would surely have envied

Burr's accelerated pace and sought to emulate it. A Princeton administrator, however, rejected Hamilton's request to graduate "with as much rapidity as his exertions would enable him to do." That could provide fodder for his first encounter with Burr. List of rhymes in hand, Lin-Manuel put them in play.

HAMILTON: Pardon me, are you Aaron Burr, sir?

BURR: That depends. Who's asking?

HAMILTON: Oh, well, sure, sir.
I'm Alexander Hamilton. I'm at your service, sir.
I have been looking for you.

BURR: I'm getting nervous.

HAMILTON: Sir . . .
I heard your name at Princeton.
I was seeking an accelerated course of study
When I got sort of out of sorts with a buddy
Of yours. I may have punched him. It's a blur, sir.
He handles the financials?

BURR: You punched the bursar.

When Ron heard this exchange in rehearsal, he balked. Why would Hamilton hit the bursar, the head of Princeton's finances? "That never happened," he told Lin-Manuel. "It seems very out of character. Hamilton wanted to go to Princeton; the last thing he would have done was punch the bursar." But Lin-Manuel wouldn't budge. It wasn't until Ron saw the line in performance that he got it: *bursar* was a pun on *Burr, sir*. "The rhyme was too good to pass up," Lin-Manuel admitted.

Sondheim got it the first time. He'd had the experience as a young songwriter of surprising his hero Cole Porter with an unexpected rhyme when he'd sung his lyrics to a number from *Gypsy*: "Wherever I go, I know he goes. / Wherever I go, I know she goes. / No fits, no fights, no feuds and no egos— / Amigos, / Together!" At *Amigos*, the quadruple rhyme, Sondheim heard a gasp. Porter hadn't anticipated it and was delighted. "Surprising a pro is one of the greatest joys a writer can experience," Sondheim later reflected; that gasp "may well be the high point of my lyric-writing life." More than half a century later, the writer whom Lin-Manuel calls "the God MC Sondheezy" was in the audience for "Aaron Burr, Sir." At "punched the bursar," Lin-Manuel heard him let out a cackle. Surprising Sondheim was a high point of his lyric-writing life. "I wish I could bottle that laugh," he wrote that night.

Lin-Manuel's imagination seemed so fertile that his friends thought he was surprising even himself. Quiara got to hear early demos as he wrote them; once, he opened his laptop as he was hopping out of a taxi so that he could play her a new song. "He was *buzzing*," she says. Her own career had continued to rise, too; in 2012, she won the Pulitzer Prize for a play that mined her family's history, and she was awarded a distinguished chair in playwriting at Wesleyan. (She'd bring in Lin-Manuel and Tommy, golden alumni, to visit her classes.) Looking back, she considers *In the Heights* a less mature work. "I love it, but it's that youthful inspiration piece born before you have the tools," she says. She could see Lin-Manuel's development since then. "With *Bring It On*, he's already a more facile writer, a more technical writer. It's a lot of fun, but it's not really using his full capability, his own point of view. When he started working on *Hamilton*, something new was happening for him. He was going to create the world the way he saw it."

That meant connecting his skill to subject matter that matched his ambition. He wasn't writing about high-schoolers preparing for a competition. He was trying to retell the origin story of a country. "He was finding ideas that were as rich as his technical capabilities," Quiara says.

That sense of ideas sizzling out of him emerged in a song Lin-Manuel wrote for the Vassar reading to showcase Hamilton's virtuosity—which Hamilton used not only for his own glory but in service of the revolutionary cause. Chernow's biography described the young collegian rebutting a loyalist to the British crown, Samuel Seabury, who wrote a set of anti-revolutionary pamphlets under the name "A Westchester Farmer." In only a few weeks, Hamilton produced an eighty-page response, "The Farmer Refuted," to demolish Seabury's arguments. Lin-Manuel wrote his version even faster. Seabury would sing in an eighteenth-century style, a throwback to the old guard, with inverted clauses over tinkling harpsichord triplets: "Heed not the rabble who scream revolution, / They have not your interests at heart." Hamilton, in a musical embodiment of the future, would rap his retort.

What's more, he'd build his hip-hop takedown from Seabury's own words. Lin-Manuel cherished a tribute to Big Pun from another Puerto Rican rapper, Joell Ortiz, that rhymed on the same syllables that Pun had used. For "Farmer Refuted," he tried out the technique. When Seabury attempted to repeat his warning, Hamilton stole his thunder.

SEABURY:	HAMILTON:
Heed not the **rabble**	**He'd** have you all un**ravel**
Who **scream**	At the sound of **screams** but the
Revolution,	**Revolution** is comin'.
They **have not** your interests at **Heart.**	The **have-nots** are gonna win this, it's **Hard** to listen to you with a straight face.

Hamilton's glee at unraveling Seabury's rhetoric seemed a mirror for the songwriter's brio, though Lin-Manuel said he had just as much fun writing the loyalist's music—"getting my Bach on," as he put it. Bach and Big Pun, Jay-Z and Dr. Seuss—whatever inspiration served the story became fair game. "Lin has a magpie mind," Chernow says. "He picks up things in the atmosphere and synthesizes them so that it all sounds of a piece."

—

As he worked on his mixtape musical, he generated so much material that he needed an outlet beyond the score itself. To his benefit (and occasional peril), social media came to the rescue. He joined Twitter in 2009 just after he premiered the first song from *The Hamilton Mixtape*. At first, he'd simply tweet updates about FLS gigs, *Heights*, and *Bring It On* with birthday wishes for friends and praise for colleagues' shows mixed in. Then, as his following grew, he started to envision Twitter as its own virtual community. He christened it "Twitterico." Part alternate stage, part fantasy island, it provided an audience that could welcome every part of him—home videos of his childhood performances, photos of his dog, musical-theater jokes, deep rap cuts, puns galore ("Add homonyms ad hominem," he tweeted), Power Rangers references and Spanglish tongue-twisters and TV recaps and cross-cultural mash-ups.

He began greeting his followers with a "Gmorning Twitterico" each day and bidding them "Gnight" when he signed off, with a playful message apt for the occasion. (One Christmas Eve: "Feliz Usnavidad!") He kept his tone upbeat, a refuge from the rancor that defined other corners of Twitter. In a series of tweets the week before the Lincoln Center concert in 2012, as the number of his followers neared 14,000, he offered a mock definition of the "Sovereign State of Twitterico": "Population: 13,862. Ethnicity: Twittericans. National Motto: 'Wepa!' Major Exports: Limericks, Shenanigans, Youtubes. Natural Resources: musical theater/hip-hop references. National languages: Spanglish, Drunken Tagalog. National Currency: Embarrassing childhood videos. National Pastime: Live-Tweeting Buffy Episodes From A Decade Ago." It was, in a way, what he'd dreamed Puerto Rico would be as a child: the Never-Neverland where he wasn't an outsider, where every hybrid facet of his identity fit in, where everything he did met with applause. He promised that each time Twitterico's population approached a new high, he would share a childhood video or a song he'd cut from *In the Heights*. He always knew another one.

As a producer responsible for connecting shows with the public, Jeffrey Seller recognized the power of Lin-Manuel's online presence. "Lin was the first theater artist that saw the value of Twitter in creating his audience," Jeffrey says. "My perception was that he needed something to entertain himself after *In the Heights*. And he likes getting attention. So he could say: 'I can entertain myself with funny, kind tweets. And with every tweet, my fan base grows.'" Twitter offered an extension of the opportunity Lin-Manuel found with his early YouTube uploads promoting *In the Heights* through spoof videos. Now he didn't even need a camera and production crew. Any clever line that occurred to him could instantly reach an audience many times larger than the entire Richard Rodgers Theatre. All he had to do was take out his phone. Having an audience in his pocket, as he put it, provided a constant high. "My three worst addictions are probably coffee, applause, and Twitter, in that order," he confessed—on Twitter.

Tweeting became both a distraction from writing *The Hamilton Mixtape* and a chronicle of its process. For instance, he knew he needed to craft an introduction for Hamilton's close friend the marquis de Lafayette, a gallant French aristocrat who helped the revolutionary forces. "I think Lafayette wants to rap in French now," he tweeted as the Vassar reading approached. "I have to go learn some French. Damnit, Lafayette." (He ended up with a mix of French 101 expressions and lines he remembered from Lancelot du Lac's song "C'est Moi" in *Camelot*, his mom's favorite musical: "Oui oui, mon ami, je m'appelle Lafayette! / The Lancelot of the revolutionary set! / I came from afar just to say 'Bonsoir!' / Tell the King, 'Casse toi!' Who's the best? C'est moi!") And historical tidbits that didn't make it into the musical found a home on Twitter. ("YOU GUYS TODAY'S THE ANNIVERSARY OF HAMILTON'S 'REPORT ON THE SUBJECT OF MANUFACTURES!' IN 1791! Who's celebrating?! . . . Guys?")

On rare occasions, Twitter even provided him with fuel for the show. When a distinguished Hamilton scholar at Yale, Joanne B. Freeman, learned that Lin-Manuel was adapting Chernow's book into a musical, she wanted to make sure that he would draw on Hamilton's own writings, not only a twenty-first-century biographer's account of them. *Hamilton's real words need to be in this*, she recalls thinking. "But I didn't know how to find Lin-Manuel Miranda." As it happened, she was going to celebrate her birthday with a party at the Grange, the estate Hamilton built in uptown Manhattan. A friend of hers tweeted at Lin-Manuel to stop by. He replied to the tweet and showed up at the Grange on 141st Street. Professor Freeman handed him her Library of America edition of Hamilton's writing. "Here are his words," she said. "Put his words into the show."

Lin-Manuel had long been researching Hamilton's writing on his own, searching through the stack of books he brought to lunches with John Kander for language he might incorporate. In Hamilton's very first known letter, the teenager declared his desire to rise beyond the station of a clerk in St. Croix. "I wish there was a war," he wrote to a friend. That sentence struck Lin-Manuel. "What a thing to wish for!" he says. "But war doesn't mean death for him; it means opportunity. He's gotta get out of there. It's the stuff 'I Want' songs are made of!" He decided to feature the sentence in "Aaron Burr, Sir," when Hamilton leads with his ambition: "God, I wish there was a war! / Then we could prove that we're worth more / Than anyone bargained for." Reading Hamilton's correspondence, Lin-Manuel noticed that even when Hamilton and Burr neared their face-off at Wee-hawken, they kept signing their letters to each other "I have the honor to be your obedient servant." That jarring gap between formal politeness and the potential of shooting the correspondent could prove useful for a song later on.

Freeman's scholarship also shaped his approach to a key mechanism in the musical. Lin-Manuel had wondered why Hamilton kept getting involved in duels—why would he agree to fight Burr on the very spot where his son had been shot? Then he read Freeman's book *Affairs of Honor*, which explained the culture of dueling in the early American republic. By studying eighteenth-century accounts of duels, Freeman found that what might have seemed like spontaneous eruptions of violence were actually social rituals that followed a set script. In most cases, the purpose wasn't to kill someone; it was to prove that you were willing to die to defend your honor. Once that had been established with a challenge, often leading to an apology, both parties could generally walk away unscathed, their reputations intact. Hamilton was party to several duels that were resolved long before gunshots. He didn't necessarily have a death wish; he was just adhering to the protocols for an eighteenth-century man of honor.

But how to explain these protocols to a twenty-first-century audience? For the Vassar reading, Lin-Manuel came up with an era-bending mash-up. Even though the style of hip-hop had pulsed in his temples since he was a kid on the Baker bus, the world of drug deals and gang fights that rappers like the Notorious B.I.G. described was as foreign to him as an 1804 duel. ("I'm never going to be the fucking cool, hard hip-hop persona," he says, "because to be able to write, I need to be able to access everything.") Yet he'd come to understand the codes of that world through the hip-hop songs he loved, like Biggie's "Ten Crack Commandments." In a conversational rap, Biggie, less a Moses than a street-corner mentor, spelled out the rules of selling crack: "Number Four: I know you heard this before / Never get high on your own supply." Lin-Manuel decided to write his own "Ten Duel Commandments." ("Number one! The challenge: demand satisfaction. / If they apologize no need for further action.") As he put the social codes that Professor Freeman described into a sequence, he borrowed Biggie's counting structure, rhythm, and even some of the same sky-high sound patterns. ("Five! Duel before the sun is in the sky. / Pick a place to die / Where it's high and dry.") He hoped that mapping a decalogue from crack to duels would make archaic norms feel palpable in the present and trace the perils of hypermasculinity that left both Biggie and Hamilton shot dead.

After he wrote the song, he asked his agent, John Buzzetti, if he could clear the rights to use Biggie's hip-hop sample. "I didn't even know it was a sample," Buzzetti replied. "I thought it was you." Lin-Manuel was surprised. "How did you not know that? It's famous!" he said. Buzzetti snapped back: "Because I'm a musical-theater guy! I know *1776*!"

Lin-Manuel dived into hip-hop and history, but he also kept an eye on the traditions of musical theater. For *In the Heights*, the community template had come from *Fiddler on the Roof*. For *The Hamilton Mixtape*, Lin-Manuel looked at two Andrew Lloyd Webber shows that had begun as concept albums, *Jesus Christ Superstar* and *Evita*—both pop operas about historical figures narrated by their nemeses. Lloyd Webber's score for *Superstar* offered sonic variety by switching up genres; a comic number in a music-hall style for King Herod, for instance, provided a respite from the searing rock intensity of the crucifixion and expressed a little bemused skepticism at Jesus's alleged powers. Lin-Manuel envisioned King George's Beatles-style solo as a comic turn in the King Herod vein, a throwback to an earlier musical mode that could give the audience's ears a break from rap and a way to question the likelihood of the American Revolution succeeding. "You're on your own," King George sings to the newly independent colonies. "Awesome. Wow. / Do you have a clue what happens now?"

Lloyd Webber also kept his listeners' ears engaged by changing the beat between musical numbers. Sung-through scores like *Superstar* and *The Hamilton Mixtape* didn't have spoken scenes to break up the tempo, so rhythmic shifts had to come from the music itself. Those shifts could reinforce the dramatic moment: *Superstar* broke from a steady even meter into a tricky meter called 7/8 time for songs where the crowds surged around Jesus. Lin-Manuel decided to try using 7/8 time for the moment after the show's first duel in which a friend of Hamilton's shoots a general who has insulted George Washington's honor. The ensuing chaos has an unsettled rhythm far from the metronomic regularity of "Ten Duel Commandments." It wasn't easy to compose; the stresses didn't fall in the expected places. Lin-Manuel drafted an email to Sondheim: "Writing raps in 7/8 is breaking my brain!" But he knew the standard Sondheim had set him: "Variety, variety, variety."

Lin-Manuel also studied a pair of Sondheim musicals, *Gypsy* and *Sweeney Todd*. Though a stage mom on the vaudeville circuit and a vengeful barber in Victorian London might seem far afield from the first US treasury secretary, Lin-Manuel saw a structural model for Hamilton's relentlessness: "There's one fucking character and they're a life force and you're either an obstacle or you're a friend but get the fuck out of the way." *Sweeney Todd* offered a model for the ensemble's role too. Sondheim's musical begins with individual members of the chorus taking turns telling the story—"Attend the tale of Sweeney Todd"—until the title character appears to narrate his own entrance. Lin-Manuel decided to do the same for the opening number of *The Hamilton Mixtape*. Instead of Burr delivering the entire song himself, each actor would take a verse, then Hamilton would appear to announce his own name. "I don't know that our opening number could exist without *Sweeney Todd*," Lin-Manuel says.

Right after the Lincoln Center concert, he got a chance to experience a Sondheim show from the inside. Sondheim followed the successful *Sweeney Todd* with *Merrily We Roll Along*, a notorious flop. Adapted by George Furth from a play that told the story of youthful friendship curdling into midlife despair, it moved in reverse chronology, starting with bitter adults and ending with young idealists. The original Broadway production opened to terrible reviews in 1981 and closed after two weeks. But Sondheim's tuneful score, by turns jaunty, playful, and mournful, became well loved through the cast recording. New York City Center's Encores, a concert series of musical revivals, asked Sondheim's later collaborator James Lapine to direct a *Merrily* revival for its 2012 season. When Lapine needed to cast an actor as Charley Kringas, a motormouthed lyricist increasingly angry that his best friend and collaborator has forsaken him for Hollywood, he thought of another young lyricist who had a facility with rapid verse.

Lin-Manuel had seen the announcement for the Encores revival and wondered who would get to play Charley. The character had a bravura turn early in the show with an unhinged patter song about his sellout collaborator, "Franklin Shepard, Inc.," that was about as close to rap as a 1980s musical got. That *Merrily* had been a Broadway failure also held an allure. It tanked, to be sure, but that had freed Sondheim from the burden of trying to live up to expectations. He spent the rest of the decade writing experimental, groundbreaking musicals with Lapine: *Sunday in the Park with George* and *Into the Woods*. Lin-Manuel hoped for a similar freedom. In a way, he reflects, *Bring It On* "kind of was my *Merrily*. It had a young team, and it didn't run as long as it wanted to." When he got an email from Sondheim asking if he might consider playing the role of Charley, he was thrilled. When he received a call from Lapine formally offering him the part, he didn't have to think twice.

He loved being in the rehearsal room with Lapine and Sondheim, and they loved having him. "He's a joyous person," Lapine says. "His energy is so great, and obviously he had the verbal chops to do 'Franklin Shepard, Inc.'" At the end of rehearsals, Sondheim told him, "You really are an actor and a writer." That meant the world to Lin-Manuel. He had enjoyed conversations with Sondheim about *West Side Story* and his early *Hamilton Mixtape* demos, but this was the first time he had been able to see Sondheim at work in the rehearsal room. At one point, Sondheim's longtime orchestrator Jonathan Tunick changed a single chord in the *Merrily* score. Sondheim turned to him in an instant. "He was like, 'Did you think I wouldn't notice?'" Lin-Manuel recalls. "I thought: *That's me and Lac in fifty years.*"

Lin-Manuel marveled at the intricacy of the score. He was used to shows that employed a song and then, later, a reprise, bringing back a familiar melody in a new context. But since *Merrily* moved in reverse order, its reprises came before the initial songs, almost like pre-prises. "There are so many little Easter eggs he plants that you go, 'How did you build backwards and forwards at the same time?'" He wanted to try something like that for *The Hamilton Mixtape*. The trio at the heart of *Merrily* have a refrain that reflects their singular bond: "Here's to us! Who's like us? Damn few." In the show, they first sing it as a reminder to one another after their friendship has become frayed, then, earlier in their lives (but later in the show), they sing it with unalloyed affection. Lin-Manuel assumed *Hamilton*'s narrative would move forward in time for the most part, but he thought a similar refrain could help mark the bond between Hamilton and the first friends he'd made in New York: Hercules Mulligan, the marquis de Lafayette, and the antislavery activist John Laurens.

Sondheim had drawn the "Here's to us" refrain from a toast that circulated among his close friends in college. For his own melody, Lin-Manuel decided to mine his school memories as well. "When I was a teenager and full of dreams, convinced I was going to change the world, what was I writing?" he asked. He found an answer in a high-soaring tune he'd composed for his Hunter a cappella group. "I wanted it to sound like my version of idealism," he said, "and that was singing with my friends as a kid." The lyrics he'd written as a sixteen-year-old—"And if you believe that / I've got a bridge to sell you"—didn't suit a band of revolutionary brothers, so he kept the melody but changed the words: "Raise a glass to freedom / Something they can never take away / No matter what they tell you." Anticipating the future, when their numbers would increase and their children would tell their story, the four men sing, "They'll tell the story of tonight." That would be Hamilton's *Merrily* refrain—anticipating a future that looked back on the past.

—

After the ten-day *Merrily* Encores run in the winter of 2012, Vanessa proposed a vacation. New York offered too many temptations. "We should go to Nevis," she told Lin-Manuel. That was the island in the Caribbean where Hamilton was born. He could do a little research and write while she worked on the beach.

When they arrived, they didn't find much. There was a plaque commemorating Hamilton's birthplace, a little museum of local history, and a small town by the water. Lin-Manuel could see why Hamilton yearned for more opportunity. In the sand, he wrote Hamilton's teenage declaration: *I WISH THERE WAS A WAR.* Then he went to the hotel room to work on the act 1 closer. Looking at the shore, he started to hear the syncopated pulse of a Caribbean dance-hall rhythm.

He and Tommy had decided that even though the Revolutionary War would provide the act 1 climax, the act wouldn't end with victory over the British. Instead, they wanted to propel Hamilton into intermission by showing his unfulfilled ambition. A military triumph marked only the start of his career. Next, he would strive to build a system of government for the newly independent country. The final song of the act would need to take him from the war to President Washington's cabinet, incorporating along the way his new law practice, his six-hour speech at the Constitutional Convention, and the fifty-one *Federalist Papers* he wrote to defend the Constitution.

The act would close not with an answer (the resounding "We won!" at the Battle of Yorktown) but with a question. As in the opening number, Lin-Manuel channeled his own incredulity at Hamilton's drive through the perspective of Burr, the bedazzled onlooker. "Why do you write like you're running out of time?" Burr sings over the dance-hall beat. The ensemble picks up his question: "How do you write like tomorrow won't arrive? / How do you write like you need it to survive? / How do you write ev'ry second you're alive?"

For a writer as prolific as Lin-Manuel, the questions seemed personal. "We're all running out of time," he says. He called the song "Non-Stop."

With the first act mostly filled in, from "Alexander Hamilton" and "Aaron Burr, Sir" at the top to "Dear Theodosia" and "Non-Stop" at the end, Lin-Manuel packed for the Vassar reading in July 2013. He brought his Chernow biography, his trusty Casio keyboard, the collection of Hamilton's writings he'd received from Joanne Freeman, and a skateboard. He was going to room with Tommy and Lac in the college dorms for eight days.

Free from New York City distractions, they could focus on the show. After a decade of working together, the three men had developed "this foundation of incredible faith and trust in each other," Tommy said. "No one here is trying to do anything except evolve the idea and to inspire the other person." They had a nearly wordless shorthand to communicate. At one point in rehearsals when an actor was singing a new number, Tommy looked up at Lin-Manuel. Lin-Manuel nodded. Tommy looked at him as if to say, *Do you really know what I was going to tell you?* Lin-Manuel nodded again. *Okay, then, write it down.* Lin-Manuel did. He was right. "And all I'd done was raise my eyebrows," Tommy says.

For the presentation at the end of the week, the company had another new instrument to play with: the voice of Daveed Diggs. A six-foot-tall rapper from Oakland who'd studied theater at Brown University, Daveed had a rep for technical dexterity, whizzing through bars as the MC for the experimental hip-hop group Clipping. He'd been recruited into the Freestyle Love Supreme crew as an occasional guest artist, and at an FLS gig in New Orleans that winter during Super Bowl week, Tommy Kail told him that Lin-Manuel was writing a rap musical about Alexander Hamilton. "That's a terrible idea," Daveed said. Tommy, undeterred, invited him to join the reading at Vassar. "Are you going to pay me?" Daveed asked. Tommy said he would. Daveed agreed.

Tommy had Daveed in mind for an intriguing double part: Hamilton's friend the marquis de Lafayette in the first act, then his political enemy Thomas Jefferson in the second. A Frenchman, Lafayette starts the show with comically uncertain, elastic English: "I dream of life without a monarchy. / The unrest in France will lead to 'onarchy? / 'Onarchy? How you say, how you say, 'anarchy'? / When I fight, I make the other side panicky!" By the revolutionary battles, however, Lin-Manuel wanted to show that Lafayette had emerged as a military mastermind, expressing himself in commanding, galloping raps: "I'm takin' this horse by the reins makin' redcoats redder with bloodstains. / And I'm never gonna stop until I make 'em drop, burn 'em up and scatter their remains!" For that fast a flow, he needed a virtuosic rapper who could not only speed through Kendrick Lamar–style syllables but keep them intelligible. Enter the Oakland MC. "I could write anything for Daveed and he could rap it," Lin-Manuel exulted.

The idea of differentiating characters through their flow informed his approach to Jefferson too. For much of the 1780s, while Hamilton and Madison were debating the form of the new US Constitution, the author of the Declaration of Independence was abroad in France. Lin-Manuel wanted to show musically that Jefferson came from an earlier generation and didn't know that America had moved on—in the show's conceit, to hip-hop. "So what does he sound like?" the composer mused. "I decided that he sounded like the jazz that becomes hip-hop"—the rollicking bebop and scat of acts like Lambert, Hendricks, and Ross and Gil Scott-Heron. Over the July Fourth weekend, a few weeks before the Vassar reading, at John Buzzetti's house on the Jersey Shore, while everyone else was by the pool, Lin-Manuel sat at the piano trying to stretch his fingers to play jazzy chords with added ninth and eleventh notes. The party went out to dinner; he stayed home to work. Buzzetti brought him back a barbecue chicken pizza while he finished the act 2 opener for Jefferson, "What'd I Miss?"

At the end of July at Vassar, the company performed all of act 1 and four songs from act 2: Jefferson's song, the two Cabinet Battles, and the song about Hamilton's affair. In a small black-box theater, they stood at music stands with Lac on piano. The performance was sold out. Jeffrey Seller, in the audience, was thrilled. "It was a very successful week," he says. "The songs were coming out boom, boom, boom." In its second public presentation, *The Hamilton Mixtape* seemed much farther along than *In the Heights* had been at a similar point. *Heights* had to change its opening number, and even off Broadway, it didn't have the "I Want" song figured out. "Lin-Manuel only wrote one 'I Want' song for *Hamilton*," Jeffrey says. "He only wrote one opening number. That seldom happens." The show was cooking. Sitting next to Andy Blankenbuehler, Jeffrey could sense the choreographer itching to put the numbers in motion.

In the very last row, an actor who didn't have a ticket had squeezed into a folding chair. (His wife was performing in a different project at Vassar that week, so he'd become friends with the ushers.) He was a big fan of Lin-Manuel's work. He'd listened to the *In the Heights* cast album on a Greyhound bus heading to New York City after college, imagining what his life could be, and by the end of the first song, he found himself in tears. When *Bring It On* debuted on Broadway, he got tickets for opening night so he could meet Lin-Manuel. He couldn't wait to see what the songwriter was up to next. He didn't anticipate a polished musical. "When you're experiencing a new work, you expect it to come in fits and starts," he says. Maybe the first draft would get a few songs right.

When the reading began, he couldn't believe it. "Every song was better than the last," he recalls. "It was dense; it was literate; it sounded like the music of our time." The number that particularly moved him, as a Black performer trained in musical theater, was "The Story of Tonight": "It was four men of color on the stage singing about friendship and brotherhood, which was something I'd never experienced." He thought the show was ready for Broadway. He never thought that he would become a part of it; he just appreciated it as an audience member. After the performance, he tweeted at Lin-Manuel: "Good God, you can write. Skillz. Bold, brand new, beautiful work from you today, my brother. Congrats & thanks!"

Three months later, he got an email with the subject line *Octoburr*. There was going to be a reading in Manhattan that October, and Lin-Manuel wanted him to play Aaron Burr.

Leslie Odom Jr. said yes.

Above left, the Miranda family—Luis, Luz, Cita, and baby Lin-Manuel—in 1980 in their graduate housing at New York University. Above right, Lin-Manuel lip-synched "Land of Confusion" by Genesis at the Hunter Elementary School talent show. Below, at his first piano recital, in 1986, at the Washington Heights home of his teacher, Suzzan Craig. (Photos courtesy of the Miranda family.)

Two teachers guided Lin-Manuel into a life in the arts: Barbara Ames, his elementary-school music teacher (top left, in 2022, with Bobby Lopez, another Hunter graduate and Tony-winning composer; photo courtesy of Lin-Manuel Miranda); and Rembert Herbert, his eighth-grade English teacher (above left, in 2008; photo courtesy of Hunter College). As a ninth-grader, Lin-Manuel landed a starring role as the Pirate King in *Pirates of Penzance* (above right, copyright © Jon Kander). As a sophomore at Wesleyan, pictured in a black turtleneck, Lin-Manuel directed his own musical, *In the Heights* (below with his company; photo courtesy of Aileen Payumo).

To develop *In the Heights* after college, Lin-Manuel formed a team of collaborators that he nicknamed "Voltron": above, from left, playwright Quiara Alegría Hudes, music arrangers Alex Lacamoire and Bill Sherman, and director Thomas Kail, at a workshop of the musical in 2005. (Photo courtesy of Alex Lacamoire.) Below, in front of his co-stars Christopher Jackson, Andréa Burns, and Janet Dacal, Lin-Manuel took in the applause on opening night at the Richard Rodgers Theater in 2008. (Jason Kempin/WireImage.)

At the 2008 Tony Awards, the producers of *In the Heights*—above, from left, Jill Furman, Kevin McCollum, and Jeffrey Seller—hoisted up Lin-Manuel after winning the award for Best Musical. (Theo Wargo/WireImage.) That summer, after the Tonys, Lin-Manuel and his girlfriend, Vanessa Nadal, vacationed in Mexico, below, where he read the book he would adapt for his next musical: Ron Chernow's biography of Alexander Hamilton. (Photo by Vanessa Nadal.)

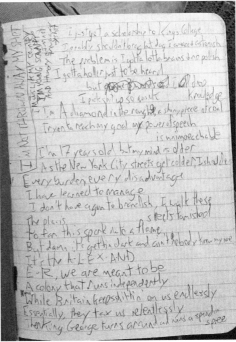

Lin-Manuel and Vanessa were married at the Belvedere Mansion in New York in 2010, above left. (Kelly Shimoda/Redux). Above right, Lin-Manuel's first draft of Alexander Hamilton's song "My Shot," which he performed at Ars Nova in 2011. (Photo courtesy of Lin-Manuel Miranda.) He debuted the first eleven songs of *The Hamilton Mixtape* at Lincoln Center's American Songbook series, below, in 2012. (Brian Harkin/The New York Times/Redux.)

Above, Lin-Manuel and Vanessa welcomed their first child, Sebastian—held by Abuela Mundi—in November 2014, three months before *Hamilton* opened off-Broadway at The Public Theater, where Lin-Manuel shared a dressing room with Leslie Odom, Jr. (Photos courtesy of the Miranda family.) Below, on opening night on Broadway in August 2015, as crowds gathered outside the Richard Rodgers Theater to enter the ticket lottery, he read aloud the first pages of Chernow's biography. (Todd Heisler/The New York Times/Redux.)

Above, for the documentary *Hamilton's America* in 2015, Lin-Manuel discussed the process of writing a historical musical with two of his heroes: Stephen Sondheim and John Weidman. (Photo by Alex Horwitz, courtesy of Adventureland LLC.) Below, he worked on songs for Disney's *Moana* with Samoan-born musician Opetaia Foa'i at Revolver Studios in Waiuku, New Zealand; the animated musical came out in 2016. (Photo by Julie Foa'i.)

After *Hamilton*, Lin-Manuel learned to become a film director; he started shooting Jonathan Larson's autobiographical musical, *Tick, Tick . . . BOOM!* with Andrew Garfield, above center, in March 2020, a week before COVID shut down the production. (Photo by Macall Polay, courtesy of Netflix, Inc.) Below, he discussed his latest project, a musical adaptation of the 1979 movie *The Warriors*, with his co-writer, Eisa Davis, at SiriusXM Studios in 2024. (Santiago Felipe/Getty Images.)

16

THE ROOM WHERE
IT HAPPENS

• •

Who was Aaron Burr? What did he want? Cracking Hamilton's psychology proved far easier than fathoming the man who shot him. Lin-Manuel instinctively understood Hamilton's immigrant ambition, his relentless energy, his drive to write like he was running out of time. But what motivated Burr? Though he came from privilege and Hamilton had grown up in poverty, their lives followed similar tracks. Both became orphans in childhood; both sped through college; both distinguished themselves in the Revolutionary War and began successful careers in law and politics. They were friends and colleagues. Why would one end up killing the other? For Lin-Manuel, writing was a form of acting. He had to become his characters to figure out what they would sing. He hadn't found that inroad to Burr yet.

One evening a year before the Vassar workshop, Lin-Manuel sat on the rooftop patio of his apartment building looking over the Columbia University sports fields at the northern tip of Manhattan. A neighbor walked past, then stopped for a moment. "I hear you're writing a musical about Hamilton," she said. "My husband's a descendant of Aaron Burr."

Antonio Burr turned out to live in the same apartment building as Lin-Manuel and Vanessa. In 2004, for the two hundredth anniversary of the duel, he'd reenacted the scene in Weehawken with a Hamilton descendant. He was a forensic psychologist, and he managed a boathouse at the marina around the corner from the Mirandas' house in Inwood. He offered to take Lin-Manuel for a drink by the water.

Over a glass of wine, Antonio Burr shared his theory of the duel. In his view, Burr wasn't seeking to kill Hamilton. As a psychologist, Antonio thought that Hamilton had become suicidal after his son's death and had basically goaded Burr into shooting him. "My ancestor was the murder weapon!" he insisted.

To Lin-Manuel, it seemed like a valid interpretation. At the very least, it suggested that there was more than one way to understand what might look like a clear-cut killing.

He decided to investigate further. A new book had just come out, a short, sympathetic biography of Burr by H. W. Brands called *The Heartbreak of Aaron Burr*. He got a copy and devoured it in a day. Brands focused on Burr as a loving husband and father, a proponent of women's right to education. Lin-Manuel already knew about Burr's devotion to his daughter; he'd dramatized that affection in "Dear Theodosia." But he learned a detail he hadn't heard before. The woman with whom Burr fell in love was the wife of a British officer. Burr had to wait for her first husband to die before he could marry her. That offered a clue. "You try to get your arms around the character, and then you make discoveries along the way," Lin-Manuel says. "The key was discovering that Hamilton married his wife within two weeks of meeting her, whereas Burr waited *years* for his wife to become a widow." If Hamilton was nonstop, Burr was lying in wait. Lin-Manuel had found his way in. "There's the difference in temperament. My job is to dramatize it."

Hamilton's frenzied pulse came from growing up as an outsider, from seeing his family die around him and resolving to seize any chance he could to get ahead. But Burr had experienced tragedy as well. Both his parents died before he turned two. Why did he hold back? Perhaps because he had something to lose. He had a social position, a prominent name; his father had been the president of Princeton. He needed to wait until he was sure what the right move was. Lin-Manuel understood that, in a way. He'd wondered why he survived when people who loved him had died. He'd wondered what obligations that put on him. If you heard what he called "the ticking clock of mortality" from a young age, that might speed you up or slow you down.

It can be tricky to pin down the genesis of a song. It often remains opaque, almost mystical, even to its composer. Listing influences and cataloging reference points goes only so far. "A plus B doesn't equal *song*," Lin-Manuel likes to say. Ideas might swirl around, lie dormant, then suddenly cohere or slowly morph into a form. He's also fond of quoting Leonard Cohen: "Being a songwriter is like being a nun: you're married to a mystery."

He can confirm that he started with a loop. In his Logic program, he recorded a few bars of a syncopated piano line. It rose and fell, then went back up and down again, shifting its tonality, searching, waiting. He copied and repeated the bars. Then he uploaded the track to his iPod, which could store more music than his iPhone. A friend from Wesleyan was having a birthday party that night in Brooklyn, and as Lin-Manuel walked to the A Train to ride an hour south from 207th Street, he listened to the loop in his headphones. ("I write best when I'm ambulatory," he says.) At Fourteenth Street, he transferred to the L Train. He kept listening.

When the L Train arrived in Brooklyn, the song appeared in his head. He walked out of the station, held the iPod up to his ear so he could hear the loop, and sang the words inside his head into a voice memo on his phone:

Death doesn't discriminate
Between the sinners and the saints,
It takes, and it takes, and it takes,
And we keep living anyway.
We laugh and we cry and we break,
And we make our mistakes.
And if there's a reason I'm still alive . . .
Damn it, I'm willing to wait for it.
I'm willing to wait for it.

He got to the party, wished his friend a happy birthday, and explained that he had to leave. On the train back to Inwood, he finished writing the song. He'd long been thinking about a scene in *Les Misérables* where Inspector Javert puzzles over the preternatural magnanimity of Jean Valjean: "Who is this man? What kind of devil is he?" The relationship between those characters mapped onto his own. "Hamilton is my Valjean, and Burr is my Javert," Lin-Manuel says. Burr tracking Hamilton wasn't the same as a policeman chasing a criminal, but it did involve a kind of psychological pursuit. "Instead of pursuing him for a crime, he's trying to get at the root of who this fucking guy is."

When he got home, he recorded a demo. He put a coy dance-hall beat beneath the piano loop and wrote in a ruminative bass line. When he sang Burr's words, he added a digital reverb to echo the end of each line:

Hamilton faces an endless uphill climb
(climb, climb, climb)
He has something to prove, he has nothing to lose
(lose, lose, lose)
Hamilton's pace is relentless, he wastes no time
(time, time, time)
What is it like in his shoes?

He'd found a more personal connection to Burr too. Even though he often charged forward, writing relentlessly, he'd had to wait years and years to bring *In the Heights* to Broadway. When Tommy told him to turn down the producer who wanted to add drugs and violence, when Jeffrey told him that the show wasn't ready after the O'Neill conference, when he had to rewrite song after song, he'd been willing to wait for it. "With Burr, what I sublimated was the incredible patience it takes to write a musical," he says.

He also knew what it felt like to watch a brilliant friend surpass him. In his senior year at Wesleyan, seeing his classmate Bajir's thesis success, he says, "I was very much Burr watching Hamilton do everything I wanted to do."

Burr's musical soliloquy would establish him as Hamilton's opposite. "Wait for It" provided the counterpoint to "My Shot"—it was a hymn to hesitation instead of an action manifesto. And it set up the eventual tragedy. At the only moment that they switched temperaments, when Hamilton finally hesitated and Burr acted without restraint, the bullet landed in Hamilton's chest.

He sent the demo to Tommy and Lac. Tommy emailed back the sort of thing he often did: "There you go. Keep after it." Lac was more effusive.

He saw possibilities in the musical lines. He could score the reverb echoes for the ensemble's vocals, building harmonies to amplify Burr's hidden thoughts. When Lin-Manuel shared the song with Quiara, she was astounded. She thought he'd come of age as a songwriter. "There's no song like 'Wait for It' in *Heights*," she says. "It's more mature about living in complexity. It's about sticking to instincts that harm you. It's got more fangs, more claws." She calls it "one of the best song's he's written."

Months after Lin-Manuel began writing "Wait for It," Leslie Odom Jr., listening to it in the back row of the Vassar theater, thought whoever got to sing that eight times a week would be a lucky man. Then he got the summons. For this role, Tommy wanted to find an actor who would contrast with Lin-Manuel, as Burr provided a foil for Hamilton. "There are different kinds of people. There's hots and there's cools," Tommy says. "Lin is hot. And certainly not cool. Leslie Odom Jr. is cool." Lin-Manuel brought a bundle of giddy energy into every room he entered, bouncing in a Nintendo T-shirt and baggy jeans with a straggling goatee and a Kangol cap, ready to freestyle. Leslie showed up impeccably groomed and tailored, always prepared, his energy coiled in reserve. Lin-Manuel's voice was unguarded, nasal, fueled as much by passion as technique. Leslie controlled every note in a silky croon, equal parts Sam Cooke and Bobby Brown, with a voice honed in the musical-theater program at Carnegie Mellon. "He runs at a totally different temperature than me," Lin-Manuel said after Leslie agreed to join the cast. "I think it makes for a really exciting contrast onstage."

With Leslie's voice in his head and Burr's character fleshed out in his mind, Lin-Manuel went back through the first act. He wanted to thread Burr's temperamental contrast with Hamilton into each of their encounters, beginning with their very first meeting, when Burr advises the garrulous collegian: "Talk less. Smile more. / Don't let them know what you're against or what you're for." Establishing the Burr-Hamilton dynamic at the start would pay off at the end. "It is the most important relationship in the show," he explained.

Fortunately, he found the perfect place to write. He brought his laptop to Aaron Burr's bedroom.

As with so many of the key sites in the story, Burr's residence toward the end of his life happened to be located in Washington Heights close to where Lin-Manuel grew up. The Founding Fathers weren't far off in Philadelphia or Washington, DC. "They were here," Lin-Manuel marveled. "They were uptown."

The staff at Burr's house welcomed Lin-Manuel; what could be better than a musical to share the site's forgotten stories? Surrounded by history, he sat in the one modern chair in Burr's bedroom wearing a beanie, headphones on, laptop open. One of his college housemates, the filmmaker Alex Horwitz, had begun to make a documentary about the Hamilton project, and that day he brought his camera.

Lin-Manuel was drafting new verses for "My Shot." In his current version, each of Hamilton's friends downed a shot as they explained what they'd do if they got a chance. "So now I'm working on Burr jumping in on this," he told Alex. He looked down at his Word document. "He's going: 'Geniuses, lower your voices. / If you keep out of trouble, then you double your choices. / Shootin' off at the mouth, shootin' from the hip, shootin' the shit . . .' Something shooty, shooty, shooty, shooty, shooty, shooty 'shot'!" He looked up from his laptop. "I haven't figured out how it works yet." He laughed.

Eventually, he settled on a verse for Burr to counsel caution, adding in a reference to Rodgers and Hammerstein's song protesting racism from *South Pacific*, "You've Got to Be Carefully Taught":

> *Geniuses, lower your voices.*
> *You keep out of trouble and you double your choices.*
> *I'm with you, but the situation is fraught.*
> *You've got to be carefully taught:*
> *If you talk, you're going to get shot!*

What, then, would change Burr's mind? How would he pivot from warning Hamilton not to get shot to raising a pistol against Hamilton himself?

To solve this second-act problem, Lin-Manuel holed up at Jeffrey Seller's house in the Hamptons. After the Vassar reading in July 2013, Tommy and Lin-Manuel told Jeffrey that they wanted to start rehearsals for the entire show by the end of the following year. That seemed crazily ambitious to Jeffrey. "You haven't even written act two yet!" he pointed out. The first act had taken five years to complete. How on earth would the second act emerge in only one year? "I know," Lin-Manuel assured him. "I'm going to write it at your house this fall." Jeffrey believed him: "His fervor was palpable."

So in September, Vanessa took Lin-Manuel to Sagaponack. She stayed for a week, then left her husband with their dog to write while she returned to her law firm. "I was just alone in the house with Tobi," he recalls. "She would chase whatever animals off Jeffrey's land while I was doing the math of how to tell this fucking story."

He had an idea. A complicated plot point revolved around Hamilton's plan as treasury secretary to establish federal control over state debt. Jefferson opposed it; in the first Cabinet Battle, he argued that the states should control their own economies (and preserve the system of slavery without interference from the North). Yet at a dinner party in 1790, Jefferson brokered a private deal: If Hamilton supported moving the national capital to the Potomac near Virginia, Madison would rally Virginian votes in Congress to pass Hamilton's debt plan.

That seemed like a lot of gritty policy to convey in a song. But what if Lin-Manuel wrote it from the point of view of someone who wasn't invited to the dinner party? What if the story was told by Aaron Burr? Suddenly, it became a song about power—who had it and who wanted it. "I don't give a shit about the Treasury," Lin-Manuel admits. "I barely understand economics. The whole goal is to show that these guys were all human." Burr would watch as Hamilton entered a room with Jefferson and Madison and he was left alone, outside. "No one else was in the room where it happened," Burr would sing, enviously. "No one really knows how the game is played. / The art of the trade, / How the sausage gets made. / We just assume that it happens. / But no one else is in the room where it happens."

As the son of a political consultant, Lin-Manuel had seen the sausage-making up close. When he was a child, he used to run around Gracie Mansion, the New York City mayor's residence, during the years that Luis worked for Ed Koch. He'd bring his crayons and doodle during meetings in the mayor's office. He knew his father had to make compromises to gain leverage; Koch told Luis, "If you agree with me on six out of every ten things, and then on those other four things you shut your mouth, we'll be in a good place." Lin-Manuel knew, as Hamilton taunts Burr:

You get love for it. You get hate for it.
You get nothing if you wait for it, wait for it.

As the song's tension rose, Hamilton challenged Burr's very core:

God help and forgive me,
I wanna build something that's gonna outlive me.
What do you want, Burr? What do you want, Burr?
If you stand for nothing, Burr, what do you fall for?

It was time for Burr's confession. He didn't have principles. He didn't have a political vision. He simply wanted what Hamilton had. Alone, with the music cut out, he sang his truth: "I wanna be in the room where it happens."

As he repeated his desire, gaining intensity, the music and the chorus built back up behind him: a jazzy swing with a trumpet riff processed to sound like an old record. Lin-Manuel envisioned the song as an homage to Kander and Ebb—both the razzle-dazzle and the political cynicism of their Jazz Age vamps in *Chicago*. The opening number of *Chicago* buttons with two cool beats: "That jazz!" Lin-Manuel gave Burr the same cadence for his final words: "Click-boom!" Once Hamilton stood in the way of Burr's ambition to gain power, the trigger was only a click away.

Back from Sagaponack, Lin-Manuel shared the number with Lac and Tommy. Lac could hear musical colors they hadn't tried yet in the show—a banjo, for instance, to give the chorus a *Chicago*-style vaudeville ring. Tommy had a sense of who the song might really be about. "Lin's desire was always to be where things were being made," he says. "He wanted it desperately, as we all did. He wrote a whole song about it."

When Leslie Odom Jr. heard the new number for the first time, he didn't love it. "I thought it was repetitive," he says. "We were just at music stands going: 'The room where it happens, the room where it happens.'" He was nonplussed. He'd been hoping for a soliloquy with more verbal action, a number that would reveal his character's thoughts through a magnificent cascade of metaphors and wordplay. "I was waiting," he says, "for Burr's 'Satisfied.'"

Nearly everyone involved in *The Hamilton Mixtape* agreed that "Satisfied" was the best number in the show. It rewound the story of Hamilton and Eliza's courtship to retell it from the perspective of Eliza's brilliant older sister, Angelica, who anatomized her own psychology and social position as well as Hamilton's and Eliza's in a dazzling four-minute rap. It was certainly the show's most ambitious musical-theater gambit.

Part of the credit went to Vanessa. At the Lincoln Center concert, the gender division of musical labor pretty much followed Jay-Z and Alicia Keys's roles on "Empire State of Mind": the swaggering, intricate raps went to men; the soulful melodic lines to women. That wasn't unusual for the music industry or for a Miranda musical. *In the Heights* and *Bring It On* had basically adhered to that division too. Back in college, though, Lin-Manuel had written his female characters spectacular raps for *On Borrowed Time*, and he grew up listening to Queen Latifah, Missy Elliott, and Lauryn Hill spit bars. As he worked toward the Vassar reading, Vanessa—a fan of harder rappers like Lil' Kim and Nicki Minaj—gave him an instruction. "This is a rap musical," she told him, "and women should be rapping."

Lin-Manuel heeded her instruction. In "Satisfied," Angelica replays the moment when she first flirted with Hamilton, the two of them bantering about whether either had ever been "satisfied"—in all that term's intellectual, economic, and erotic valences—and kindles their electricity with the alacrity of her rhymes:

> *So so so—so this is what it feels like to match wits*
> *With someone at your level! What the hell is the catch? It's*
> *The feeling of freedom, of seein' the light,*
> *It's Ben Franklin with a key and a kite! You see it, right?*

The sparks fly not only from wits matching and the metaphor of Franklin's lightning strike but from Angelica's rapping prowess, echoing both within the line (*feel/free/see/key*) and at the end of phrases (*light/kite/right*). But at that instant, she sees Eliza smitten, "helpless" over Hamilton, and she introduces him to her sister instead of pursuing her own attraction.

Lin-Manuel drew on all his creative resources to dramatize this choice. The form of Angelica's soliloquy was a wedding toast to her sister and new brother-in-law: "May you always be satisfied." Spiraling piano arpeggios heralded the festive occasion, then turned dissonant as the entire scene spun in reverse, rewinding back to the moment Hamilton met Angelica.

The structure of the number borrowed a trick from Freestyle Love Supreme. As one of their improv games, the group would invite an audience member to tell the story of an experience they wished had turned out differently. Then FLS would improvise a short rap musical from the story—first as it actually happened, then a second time, revisiting the turning point but with a different outcome. They'd even physically undo their motions onstage as though they were actors in a movie that was being rewound. They called the game "Second Chance."

Lin-Manuel had tried a rewind effect before in *Bring It On*. When the Jackson High School cheer squad enters their first national competition, they strive to reach so high that, they sing, "Everyone's gonna stand up and say 'Rewind that.'" With digital-processing effects, the music even spun back a few bars at that moment. But for "Satisfied," he wanted to rewind a whole song, back to the beginning of Eliza's courtship number, "Helpless," to offer Angelica's version. And it would all take place inside Angelica's mind, dilating the instant she raised her glass to the married couple.

To organize Angelica's memories, Lin-Manuel dipped into his own past. In eighth-grade English at Hunter, he'd learned the form of the personal literary essay, the assignment that earned him Dr. Herbert's fateful approbation. He wrote about Stephen King's *It*, employing an introduction, a thesis, three supporting proofs, and a conclusion. Angelica would do the same. For her three proofs that satisfaction will elude her and Hamilton, she raps her realization of "three fundamental truths at the exact same time." The first:

> *I'm a girl in a world in which*
> *My only job is to marry rich.*
> *My father has no sons so I'm the one*
> *Who has to social climb for one,*
> *'Cause I'm the oldest and the wittiest*
> *And the gossip in New York City is insidious.*
> *Alexander is penniless.*
> *Ha! That doesn't mean I want him any less.*

Her rhyming ingenuity (*wittiest/City is/insidious, penniless/any less*) makes its own case for her exceptional prospects even as it reveals the pang of giving up Hamilton as a potential partner. She continues to the second truth (Hamilton is a social climber) and the third (Eliza's trusting kindness is unmatched), racing through intricate rhymes at the speed of thought, then returning to the present moment of the wedding toast and her rueful conclusion: "He will never be satisfied. / I will never be satisfied."

Lin-Manuel's final technique in shaping her memories was forgetfulness. "It was me digesting Ron Chernow's book so it could come out of me as a piece, and conveniently forgetting what didn't serve me," he says. Chernow emphasized Angelica's wit and her flirtatious correspondence with Hamilton; he also mentioned that Angelica was already married when Hamilton met her. Lin-Manuel disregarded that in the service of a dramatic love triangle and disregarded her male siblings too: "I forgot that Angelica and Eliza had brothers."

When Lin-Manuel finished writing the verses, he tweeted: "Beautiful women who can spit FIRE, you're on notice. I just wrote the toughest rhymes of my life for Angelica Schuyler." He told a friend he was worried the song's demands would fall outside a typical actor's skill set. Perhaps they'd need to find a rapper and teach her musical-theater skills instead of the other way around.

Renée Elise Goldsberry didn't want to audition for Angelica. Although she'd starred on Broadway in *Rent* and *The Lion King*, she thought, at forty, that she was too old for the role. She'd just adopted a daughter from Ethiopia and wasn't eager to return to auditioning again—certainly not for a part she wouldn't get. She said no to the casting office. She ignored the messages from her manager. She didn't listen to the demo she'd been sent.

But then, while she waited and waited in a Midtown office to meet someone who'd promised to take gifts from her back to the nurses in Ethiopia, she got one more email from her manager imploring her to reconsider. The part was hers if she would only come to the audition and show she could rap.

She was frustrated about the long wait in the office, so she played the "Satisfied" demo. "My brain exploded," she says. "I said out loud: 'Fuck!' I couldn't believe it existed." She couldn't even process the rap. "I didn't know what he was saying. It just felt like the world had changed."

She finally met her contact, gave him the presents to take to the nurses, and started walking down Fifth Avenue, piecing out the lyrics: "So so so . . ." While she walked, she thought: *I have to learn these words! I have to show up! They expect me to be good!* As she began to make sense of the rap, she loved that it brought in a new perspective, a woman's perspective. "It's part of Lin's genius to care about the women who were Founding Mothers," she says. "You show all the people who are left out of the equation, and you do it by breaking every rule in your musical-theater body. This brilliant woman is going to go through the entire journey in one song that everyone else takes in three hours because she's so smart."

Years later, Lin-Manuel remembered "the feeling of seeing Renée nail the song at her audition." Part of the feeling was relief: "Satisfied" could be performed after all. And part was elation for an actor who could perform it better than he'd imagined. Renée became an obsession among the other actors. "She speaks that fast in real life," a fellow cast member says. "She has that intelligence and grace at all times, and that fun and that humor. The meeting of person and role is complete fire."

Lin-Manuel had been worried that Angelica might not stay a character in the show. "My general rule was: If they're not there for both acts, it's kind of tricky," he says. "Angelica is really present in the courtship, and then she goes off to Europe, but she comes back home when the affair happens. So I have to find ways to keep her popping up in the story." At Tommy's suggestion, he wrote an introductory number, "The Schuyler Sisters," that presented her rapport with Eliza and Peggy like a Destiny's Child trio. For other characters who appeared in only one act, he and Tommy used double-casting to provide a sense of dramatic investment. The audience, having seen Daveed Diggs as Hamilton's friend Lafayette, the speed-rapping Frenchman, in act 1, would get a pleasurable frisson when he arrived back from France as Hamilton's foe, a dandyish Jefferson, at the top of act 2.

Lin-Manuel figured out that a musical reprise would allow the audience to track a character through the show. He wove Angelica's refrain "He will never be satisfied" into "Non-Stop," the frenzied medley that closed the first act, and then, after Hamilton's affair with Maria Reynolds, Angelica returned to rebuke him: "God, I hope you're satisfied." Those reprises helped speed the writing of act 2 along, despite Jeffrey's concern about the timeline. Lin-Manuel had a thrilling sense of creative control: "Oh, I've set up all these pieces and now I can use them!" The counting motif from "Ten Duel Commandments" could also double as a heartbreaking piano scale for Hamilton's son, killed in a duel when he'd barely finished his studies. Eliza's refrain during the Revolutionary War, "Stay Alive," could recur as her anguished cry on her son's deathbed. *I've got it!* Lin-Manuel remembers thinking. *I don't need to reinvent the wheel. I've been setting the runway up for takeoff.*

At times, Lin-Manuel intuited that a phrase would prove important later on, as he did with "I am not throwing away my shot." When Lac was working on the vocal arrangements for "History Has Its Eyes on You," one of Washington's songs in the first act, Lin-Manuel approached him at the piano. He pointed to a phrase that Washington sings to Hamilton as his protégé assumes his first military command: "Let me tell you what I wish I'd known / When I was young and dreamed of glory. / You have no control / Who lives, who dies, who tells your story." The ensemble joined Washington for that last line a cappella, and Lac had to figure out their intricate harmonies. "Really get this right," Lin-Manuel told him. "I'm going to hit 'Who lives, who dies, who tells your story' hard at the end of the show."

"Satisfied" had drawn out one of the show's central themes: How a story is told depends on who's telling it. Angelica's version of meeting Hamilton differed from Eliza's. Hamilton's version of his crucial choices differed from Burr's. Chernow's version of Hamilton—the tragedy of a relentless, hyper-verbal immigrant—differed from the account of the nation's founding that Lin-Manuel had learned at school. And his and Tommy's version of America's flawed origin story, retold by actors of color bursting onstage in pop-music styles, couldn't be further from the stately portraits on the country's monuments.

The show was almost finished, but it still needed a finale. Early on the morning of the day that the cast was supposed to read through the entire show, Vanessa heard her husband at his laptop, sobbing.

"Are you okay?" she asked. "Should I bring you something?" Their dog stood there, whimpering.

"No," Lin-Manuel gasped. "This is how it has to come out!"

He hadn't yet written the finale. It was crunch time. And it was the culmination of the show. "I just have to cry and get to the other side of it," he told Vanessa.

He'd decided to end the show with Eliza. It was a surprise, even to him. In a smoldering solo he'd composed to dramatize her reaction once Hamilton publicized his affair, she'd burned the letters her husband had written to her. "I'm erasing myself from the narrative," she sang. "I hope that you burn." But after Hamilton's death, Lin-Manuel learned from Chernow, she became the guardian of her husband's legacy, defending his reputation against attacks from his political opponents. In her widowhood, which lasted fifty years, she forgave her husband for his errors and dedicated her life to projects that honored him. Eliza was the answer to the question "Who tells your story?"

Waking up before dawn that day, Lin-Manuel turned Chernow's epilogue into his finale. "I would do a sentence, looking at Chernow," he recalls. "I read it; I sob; I write a couplet."

Most moving of all to Lin-Manuel was that, in memory of her husband's growing up without his parents, Eliza paid special attention to orphans. Chernow wrote, "Eliza and other evangelical women cofounded the New York Orphan Asylum society, the first private orphanage in New York." Lin-Manuel started bawling as he adapted Chernow's sentences into Eliza's lyrics: "I establish the first private orphanage."

He felt like he was giving birth to something huge. "Gimme the epidural," he tweeted.

Vanessa watched him, dismayed, while he typed and wept.

At last, he finished. "Done," he tweeted at 9:41 a.m. The finale complete and his equanimity restored, he hurried to the reading to hand the song to the actor playing Eliza.

Phillipa Soo was only two years out of Juilliard. With a radiant voice and an ingenue's openhearted appeal, she'd landed the starring role in *Natasha, Pierre, and the Great Comet of 1812*, an experimental adaptation of Tolstoy's *War and Peace*, right after she graduated. Tommy Kail saw the Chinese-American actor from Illinois as the ardent, naive Natasha during the musical's Ars Nova run and knew he'd found a leading lady.

Tommy called Phillipa and invited her to join a reading of act 2 of *The Hamilton Mixtape*. At Juilliard, a friend had shown her a video of Lin-Manuel performing at the White House. Now she was excited to hear that it was becoming a musical. Tommy asked her to play Eliza. "Cool!" she responded. "Who's that?"

Her response wasn't unusual. Eliza Hamilton didn't occupy a renowned place among America's Founding Mothers, in part because she'd erased herself from the historical narrative. One of Chernow's goals in his biography had been to restore her memory. "I decided when I wrote the book to open and close with Eliza," he says. "Everybody knows about Dolley Madison and Abigail Adams. I want Elizabeth Schuyler Hamilton to be in the pantheon."

The more Phillipa learned about her, the more she was impressed with Eliza's strength and resilience. She slipped easily into the character; it wasn't hard for her to envision herself partnered with a man who wrote like he was running out of time. "Watching Lin in his writing process was very similar in my imagination to Eliza watching her husband," she says.

On the day of the reading, she spotted Lin-Manuel. It was only minutes before they were about to start. "I hear I get another song or something?" she said to him.

"Here, you end the show," he told her, thrusting the song into her hands.

"Why?" she asked, surprised.

"Well, Eliza outlived Hamilton by fifty years!"

Phillipa was flabbergasted. "She did?"

As Phillipa scanned the song, her amazement grew. "I felt what everyone soon would," she says, "that sense of awe and wonderment at this woman." Eliza interviewed soldiers who fought alongside Hamilton; she organized his papers; she raised funds for the Washington Monument; she spoke out against slavery. "You could have done so much more if you only had time," she sings to her dead husband. "And when my time is up, have I done enough? / Will they tell our story?"

Ron Chernow, who was in the audience, didn't know what to expect from the ending. Tommy had mentioned that he would get to see the whole show for the first time, but he hadn't revealed how it would conclude. "There was the duel scene," Ron recalls. "And then, all of a sudden, Phillipa Soo walked out." He was thrilled. "I thought, *Oh my God, Lin came to the same conclusion that I did! He's going to end with the widow!*"

It wasn't only an artistic choice for Ron. He was a widower himself. "I've experienced those sensations in real life," he says. His own wife, Valerie, died of cancer just after he published the Hamilton biography. He dedicated it to her in the words that Alexander used in his final letter to

Eliza: "best of wives and best of women." Seeing Eliza preserve her husband's memory onstage, Ron says, "sent chills down my spine."

It was the end of January 2014. Lin-Manuel had fulfilled his promise to Jeffrey. He had written a draft of act 2. It needed polishing and tightening. Lac had to orchestrate it. Tommy and Andy had to stage it. But they would be ready to start rehearsals by the end of the year.

He was elated and exhausted. He'd hardly slept. He spent the weekend watching the Super Bowl and tweeting musical-theater references about the game. ("Right now, Seattle are the Jets and Denver are the Sharks. They're supposedly equal, but Seattle's getting all the big showstopping numbers.") Then he roused himself. He needed something else big to do.

In March, he flew to New Zealand. He had just been hired to write the songs for a new Disney animated musical set in the Pacific Islands. Vanessa left on a business trip, too, the same morning he departed. At six a.m., she murmured something as she kissed him goodbye. From the airport, he called to make sure he'd heard her correctly.

"Yes," she confirmed. "I'm pregnant."

17

THE PUBLIC THEATER

● ●

*T*he lapping waves of the South Pacific felt far away from Vanessa and their future child. But Lin-Manuel had a job to do. "If you're going to write a musical story," his agent, John Buzzetti, says, "the ultimate is a Disney animated musical." No Broadway show could match the exposure of a globally distributed film. "We knew we had the next stage thing with *Hamilton*," Buzzetti says. "And what I wanted was for him to get a Disney animated movie."

Buzzetti had been trying to get his client a crack at a Disney gig since *In the Heights*. He knew Disney's music producer Tom MacDougall, who'd come to New York in search of songwriting talent. Before MacDougall joined Disney, its animated musical franchise had been revived in the 1980s by young Broadway writers like Alan Menken and Howard Ashman, fresh off *Little Shop of Horrors*, who brought storytelling craft to their songs for *The Little Mermaid* and *Beauty and the Beast* on-screen. Continuing the creative run into the 1990s, Elton John and Randy Newman contributed pop styles to later franchise hits for Disney and its subsidiary Pixar: *The Lion King* and *Toy Story*. One day over lunch in the early 2000s, a Disney animator asked MacDougall, "Who are our Alans and Randys?" MacDougall didn't know. So he went to see some Broadway shows. *Avenue Q* struck him as the right sensibility—fresh, funny, a little cheeky—so he hired its composer, Bobby Lopez, and his wife, lyricist Kristen Anderson-Lopez, to write the songs for *Winnie the Pooh*. A few years later, he tapped them again for *Frozen*, Disney's sisterhood reimagining of the Snow Queen fairy tale. When the film was released in 2013, it took in over one billion dollars at the global box office, and its empowerment anthem, "Let It Go," hit the *Billboard* top ten and won an Oscar.

That same year, MacDougall started to put together the team for Disney's next animated musical, *Moana*. He knew it would draw on Polynesian creation stories about the demigod Maui, who would be voiced by the wrestler turned actor Dwayne "The Rock" Johnson. That meant he needed songwriters who could craft a number suited to The Rock, less a power ballad than speak-singing patter. (As MacDougall put it, "He was not going to sing 'Let It Go.'") Bobby and Kristen were too busy with *Frozen* to take on new songs, but they suggested another graduate of Bobby's alma mater Hunter College High School: Lin-Manuel Miranda. "We recommended Lin a lot," Bobby says. "People would ask us who's great, and he's the person we'd always say, because he would make you look good."

Several other songwriters were in the mix, too, so Lin-Manuel submitted a portfolio of his work to Disney: a few songs from *Heights*, the performance from *Hamilton* at the White House. "Sadly, we don't give breaks to unknowns," MacDougall says. "These movies are very complicated and expensive, so we need to know that people can do it." MacDougall could tell that Lin-Manuel knew how to tell stories through innovative music, but that wasn't what impressed him most. "The thing that really tipped the scale for me," he says, "was the opening number Lin wrote for the Tony Awards."

Ever since Lin-Manuel freestyled his Tony acceptance speech for *In the Heights*, he'd been a go-to rap consultant for the awards broadcast. For the 2011 Tonys, he and Tommy Kail pulled off a stunt: While the ceremony was taking place, they huddled in front of Lin's laptop underneath the stage of the Beacon Theater and wrote a rap verse about each award winner for the host, Neil Patrick Harris, to perform as a surprise conclusion to the night.

Then, in 2013, Lin-Manuel paired up with Tom Kitt, his composing partner from *Bring It On*, to write Neil Patrick Harris an opening number called "Bigger" to celebrate the ceremony's return to a larger stage at Radio City Music Hall. Tom worked out a chorus and melody with plenty of bars for rhyming patter, and Lin-Manuel filled in the measures with lines shouting out the nominated shows:

Now here's the kids from Christmas Story, Annie *and her orphans—*
So many child actors high on Red Bull and endorphins!
They barely come up to your knees, but God, they're singing like MVPs,
And they're the reason this whole season seems to look like Chuck E.
 Cheese!

The rhymes had to line up with the choreography, as Harris would dance with the drag queens from *Kinky Boots*, jump through a hoop in the circus style of *Pippin*, disappear into a magic box onstage, reappear in the back of the house, parade down the aisle with the *Newsies* chorus, and end up onstage again with the cheerleaders from *Bring It On*. "That was constructing a thousand-piece domino puzzle, only to get to do it once," Lin-Manuel says. "And it worked!" After Harris nailed the final beat, hanging like King Kong from a giant Tony statue, a minute-long ovation ensued. "Bigger" won Tom and Lin-Manuel an Emmy Award for their televised music and lyrics.

"The wordplay was so much fun," MacDougall says. "I thought whoever did this could do *Moana* and write something for this Maui character." He arranged a meeting for Lin-Manuel and the film's directors, Ron Clements and John Musker. They'd helmed many a Disney musical together, starting with *The Little Mermaid*. Neither of them knew anything about Lin-Manuel, let alone that he had been obsessed with *The Little Mermaid* since it came out when he was in fourth grade.

But he told them: "I'm here because of you guys, because Ashman and Menken lit my brain up." That passion landed with the Disney team. "A lot of writers say they like Disney movies," MacDougall says. "It's a very different thing to say, 'My absolute favorite movie is *The Little Mermaid*,' and the directors of that movie are the directors of this one."

He got the job. When Buzzetti heard the news, he jumped out of his seat.

The very next day, Disney put Lin-Manuel on a flight to New Zealand, where a giant cultural festival showcasing the music of the Pacific Islands took place every March. The studio was trying to shed its reputation for cultural insensitivity fueled by misrepresentations in films like *Aladdin* and *Pocahontas*. "We don't make documentaries, but we want to be authentic," MacDougall says. For *Moana*, the producers assembled what they called their "Oceanic Story Trust" of experts from different Polynesian cultures to advise on the film. And they hired a celebrated Samoan-born musician, Opetaia Foa'i, as one of the songwriters. "I'd been promoting my culture through music for twenty years," he says, "so if these guys were not for real, I wasn't interested." But when he met the film's directors in Samoa and then again in New Zealand, he felt "they really meant to immerse their heart in the culture."

At the music festival in Auckland, each island had its own stage. Lin-Manuel arrived when the team had begun to watch the Cook Island dancers. They asked for audience volunteers to join a dance competition onstage, and Lin-Manuel, wearing an Ars Nova T-shirt and jeans, his hair growing out for a Hamilton-length ponytail, wound his way up. As the drummers played behind him, he shook his hips. He shimmied his knees. He spun around. He ended with a drop into his signature half-split. He won the competition. Opetaia laughed from the audience. "It blew my mind," he says. "I thought, *Wow, I can work with this guy.*"

Opetaia had arranged a recording studio in Waiuku, a remote town southwest of Auckland. On the drive, Lin-Manuel sat in the back of the van playing DJ. They had a third composer in the van as well: Mark Mancina, who'd helped pop songwriter Phil Collins turn his tunes into a film score for Disney's *Tarzan*. Mark hadn't been quite sure how he'd connect with Lin-Manuel. A classically trained guitarist based in Carmel, California, he didn't grow up listening to hip-hop, and he assumed that rap would be the New Yorker's default genre. But in the van, Lin-Manuel cued up the Beach Boys. "He played a lot of different music, and he knew all the different styles," Mark recalls. "I realized he was an encyclopedia of pop." At that point, he says, he felt "we were going to gel."

In the studio, they started sharing ideas. An opening number for the film needed to establish the ancient wayfinding culture of the Pacific Islanders, who navigated the ocean using only their knowledge of the wind, water, and stars. Part of the story would involve the heroine, Moana (whose name means "ocean" in Maori and other Polynesian languages), learning to sail like her ancestors to restore her island's oceangoing past.

Opetaia brought in a vocal he'd been working on, with a verse in Samoan and a chorus in his father's language, Tokelauan. "Tatou o tagata folau e vala'auina," he sang on a soaring, rhythmic line. Polynesian music often used powerful drums and percussive choral chants; Mark wanted to draw on those traditions and adapt them into the storytelling mode of a film score. He began figuring out chords on the guitar to support the vocal line and clarify its emotional shape. Lin-Manuel looked for a way to contribute too. "At that point, I've done *Bring It On*," he says, "so I'm like, 'Where can I jump into the double Dutch?'"

Opetaia explained what his verse meant: *We are voyagers*. The ocean gods summoned Moana's people to sail. They understood the sea; they looked to the sky; they found a way to make their home in new lands. Lin-Manuel took it all in. He'd written two musicals about characters who left their islands to find a new home. The opening of the Tokelauan chorus, "Aue, aue," sounded like a call to sail in English too: "Away, away!" *The song is great*, he remembers thinking. *I'll write English lyrics to counter Opetaia's lyrics.* He downloaded all of Opetaia's albums on iTunes as reference points.

When the three of them reconvened in Mark's studio back in California, everyone felt inspired. Opetaia picked up a bass. Mark had guitars and recording equipment. Lin-Manuel walked up and down outside the studio, puzzling over the lyrics. On the flight to meet Opetaia, he had read everything he could about wayfinding. Now he was "trying to distill the literal process of wayfinding into metaphor." Opetaia watched him, fascinated. "It was like there was smoke coming out of his head," Opetaia says. "He was totally engrossed." Then he came back inside and sang his words to Opetaia's pulsing melody: "We read the wind and the sky when the sun is high. / We sail the length of the seas on the ocean breeze. / At night, we name every star, we know who we are." For the chorus, he figured out a countermelody to the "Aue, aue" call: "We keep our island in our mind / And when it's time to find home, we know the way!"

Opetaia was delighted. "He got the gist of what I was trying to describe and came in with a genius lyric," he says. They recorded a demo, Opetaia's verse in Samoan first, then Lin-Manuel's in English, then the Tokelauan chorus interwoven with the English countermelody. Mark laid down the chords and the drums to round out the arrangement. When they were done, the Disney producer gave Opetaia a big hug. "I thought he should be hugging Lin!" Opetaia says. "I was so happy we had a track to anchor the movie."

After the initial *Moana* sessions, Lin-Manuel returned to New York. Opetaia and Mark met him there to work on more songs while he finished *The Hamilton Mixtape*. *Moana* had offered a welcome vacation, a South Pacific respite from grappling with American history. Now he needed to get back to the show.

First, though, he somehow found time to write a fifteen-minute musical for *This American Life* ("It was like I was writing a Brick Prison show again") and star in another Encores revival. It was a dream role: playing his hero Jonathan Larson in *Tick, Tick . . . Boom!*. The last time he'd seen it, he was a senior in college, and he'd been devastated by Larson's show about failing to make it as a musical writer. Now, he felt, he could encounter the show from the other side. "At this point, I'm a Tony-winning composer," he says. "I did it, I lived it. I'm Jonathan Larson's wildest dream, and I get to honor him by playing him at this crossroads"—after Larson's first attempt at writing a musical flopped, before he rededicated himself to writing *Rent*. For Jonathan's girlfriend, Lin-Manuel recruited K O, who'd played Usnavi's love interest, Vanessa, opposite him in *Heights*. And for Jonathan's best friend, he brought in his Burr, Leslie Odom Jr.—a chance for them to form a bond before one killed the other every night. "Doing it with my past and present costars, doing it while my wife is pregnant with our first child, felt like riding the roller coaster while it was poised at equilibrium," he says.

Though the Encores show, directed by Oliver Butler, would run only five performances, Lin-Manuel took piano lessons so that he could play the opening pieces as Larson himself had done. He wanted someone who would be patient with him, so he asked Jeffrey Seller for the name of his children's piano teacher. "She was shocked at how shitty my chops were," he laughs. But he was committed to reviving Larson's legacy onstage. The conflict *Tick, Tick* dramatizes—between pursuing a rocky dream of becoming a theater artist or choosing a more stable path, as Jonathan's friend does, in advertising—continued to haunt Lin-Manuel, even with his Tony Award. "I have yet to meet a Tony Award that pays a rent bill," he told a reporter the day before the show opened. "I could go be the friend to the white detective on a TV show and make a shit-ton of money for a few years. Or I could stay home and not be paid to work on *Hamilton* for five years, which is what I've been doing with little odd jobs here or there."

For him, though, playing Larson was not an odd job. For the *New York Times*, he wrote an essay about his debt to the composer. He remembered being seventeen when Meredith took him to see *Rent* for his birthday, and its chronicle of artists struggling in New York to the sounds of contemporary rock gave him permission to start writing about his own life in a musical. He remembered being twenty-one when Aileen took him to see *Tick, Tick* just before he graduated from Wesleyan, and he got a bracing preview of the struggles that would face him as an aspiring composer over the next decade. Now, at thirty-four, he felt gratitude for Larson's model. "Someone else has permission to tell their story because you told yours," he wrote. "Someone else has permission to dream as big as you did. Someone else will struggle to do his best with the time they have." When *Tick, Tick . . . Boom!* opened, the *New York Times* critic said that Lin-Manuel's "funny, anguished and heartbreaking performance throbs with a sense of bone-deep identification."

Then he returned to *Hamilton*. During his sojourn in New Zealand, he'd gotten a reminder that although a musical about the first treasury secretary might excite audiences in New York and the White House, Hamilton's name recognition was limited. One night at the hotel with his Disney collaborators, he offered to show Opetaia some of the songs for the Hamilton project. "He brought out a thick book of music," Opetaia recalls. "I tried to look interested. But I had no idea what *Hamilton* was about. I wanted to talk about *Moana*!"

Responses like Opetaia's weren't lost on Jeffrey Seller, the lead producer. "I was conscious of the fact that we were going to open a new musical about Alexander Hamilton, and there would be no way to sell a lot of tickets in advance," he says. "We'd be starting from scratch."

Jeffrey's solution was to partner with a nonprofit theater, an incubator away from commercial pressures, so the show could develop an audience before a Broadway run. When Lin-Manuel and Tommy told him that they wanted to start rehearsals before the end of 2014, he took them on what they called "the college tour" of New York's nonprofits. After the Lincoln Center concert and the Vassar reading, Jeffrey says, "They were all begging." But only one artistic director welcomed them on his theater's front steps, brimming with excitement.

Oskar Eustis, head of the Public Theater, had earned a reputation as a legendary arts impresario. Built like a genial lion, with a giant mane and a bristling goatee, he continued the Public's tradition of free outdoor Shakespeare in Central Park and added a traveling troupe to take Shakespeare productions to local prisons, libraries, and homeless shelters. If he could make all theater tickets free, he says, he would. Having gained renown as the initial director of Tony Kushner's *Angels in America*, he saw his position as building on the function of theater from classical Greece: an education for democracy, a public forum where all Americans should come to debate ideas, forge community, and see their stories reflected back to them anew.

He had not, previously, been a fan of either Jeffrey or Lin-Manuel. The Public had long developed adventurous musicals that went on to commercial runs on Broadway, all the way back to the theater's founding days with *Hair* and, later, *A Chorus Line*. But every time a Public show went up against one of Jeffrey's productions at the Tony Awards, Jeffrey's show won—most recently in 2008, when Lin-Manuel collected his first prize. "Because *In the Heights* beat out my show *Passing Strange* for Best Musical, I was convinced that Lin-Manuel Miranda was overrated," Oskar says. "But when the White House released the tape of Lin performing, I was immediately one hundred percent hooked. I said, 'This is it. It has to be a musical. And it has to be at the Public Theater.'"

Lin-Manuel agreed. He knew the Public's reputation as an incubator for groundbreaking work. "It's where you go to make new shit," he said. "And I've been wanting to be part of that legacy for a very long time."

The Hamilton Mixtape was slated to begin performances at the Public in January 2015. A workshop of the whole show at the Fifty-Second Street Project in May 2014, with the first act fully staged and the second act performed at music stands, had gone phenomenally well. Lac had orchestrated the numbers for a pit containing a string quartet and a rock band—guitar, keyboard, bass, percussion—to pair lush harmonies with rhythmic drive. Tommy and Andy had staged Angelica's big number, "Satisfied," so the entire show would rewind back to the moment she'd met Hamilton, turning a bravura rap into a complete showstopper. And, to Leslie Odom Jr.'s satisfaction, "The Room Where It Happens" was becoming a second-act knockout. As the ensemble repeated the title phrase, Burr riffed with increasing frenzy, and the music mounted to a giant climax. "Both Andy and Lac asked me for more bars at the end of 'Room,'" Lin-Manuel recalls. "I had four bars and out. Andy said, 'If you give me eight more bars, we can really bring it home.' We built that thing to blow up the Death Star."

Lin-Manuel's producers, however, had notes. Oskar, ever the enthusiast, often began, "If you don't change a word of this show, it will be one of the greatest things the Public has ever produced." Then, after a beat, "But . . ." He frequently pressed Lin-Manuel to clarify the stakes of a scene. For instance, the first Cabinet Battle between Hamilton and Jefferson over the debt plan didn't land with quite the precision and force Oskar hoped for. "The arguments to me felt unsatisfactory," he recalls. "I remember saying to Lin: 'The real contradiction with Jefferson is he's a slaveholder.' Lin got this look in his eye." At the next rehearsal, Hamilton had new bars to rebut Jefferson's claim that the agrarian South shouldn't have to pay other states' debts:

> A civics lesson from a slaver. Hey neighbor.
> Your debts are paid cuz you don't pay for labor.
> "We plant seeds in the South. We create." Yeah, keep ranting.
> We know who's really doing the planting.

Oskar and Lin-Manuel also discussed how Shakespeare might shape the musical's tragic arc. "I was trying to make the tragedy both surprising and inevitable," Lin-Manuel says. "Shakespeare's still the gold standard. Macbeth thinks, 'None of woman born can harm me? I'm fine!' Then along comes old C-section Macduff!"

How to apply that structure to *Hamilton*? Jeffrey and Oskar both worried that the end of the show was trying to contain too many events. The dramatic high point felt like it arrived in Hamilton's version of a Macbeth soliloquy—a solo number called "Hurricane," where he decides, in curiously twisted logic, to defend his good name by writing a pamphlet publicizing his affair with Maria Reynolds. He miscalculates. The Reynolds Pamphlet ruins his reputation, and he's essentially banished from public life and from his wife's bed.

But the show didn't end there. The death of Hamilton's son in a duel, a period of mourning, Eliza's forgiveness of Hamilton's transgressions, his return to politics in the presidential election of 1800 (when he supported his longtime opponent Jefferson over the unprincipled Burr), and his final duel with Burr were all still to come. That sequencing worried Jeffrey Seller. "I remember talking with Oskar: Can we hold the soliloquy in its position and keep going for another twenty minutes?" They experimented with moving "Hurricane" later in the show. "But that's not what the story wanted," Oskar says. "The reason 'Hurricane' is so powerful is because it's not the climax of the show. It's the turning point."

Oskar offered the team a rationale for the show's structure. "I hit on this: The first act is the story of a young man whose personal ambition links up with his country's ambition. Then in 'The Reynolds Pamphlet,' there comes a terrible moment when he tries to use his same tools of writing his way out, and his personal drama becomes separate from the country. He withdraws. But then in the election of 1800, suddenly he has a choice to make in the public sphere again. And for the first time, by choosing Jefferson over Burr, he makes the choice that's not good for his ego but is good for the country. And in making that choice, it kills him." Burr, furious at being kept from the room where it happens, would end up shooting him in a duel: an end both surprising and inevitable.

That account resonated with Lin-Manuel. "One of the secrets of Oskar is that he envisions an even better musical than you do," he said. "And you go, 'Wow—if you see that in my work, I've got to earn it.'"

To earn it, he had to write the one moment he'd been putting off: Hamilton's final thoughts at the duel. He'd been hesitant to explain Hamilton's choice to fire his gun toward the sky instead of shooting at Burr. Oskar wanted him to clarify the decision. "You open with 'I'm not throwing away my shot,' and you end with him throwing away his shot," Oskar pointed out. "You have to explain it!"

Oskar thought that Hamilton was longing for death after failing to keep his son from fighting in a duel. Lin-Manuel was haunted, though, by what happened when he'd tried that theory before, way back in his eleventh-grade history project. He'd offered a clear psychological case for Hamilton longing to end his life after his son died, and he remembered his teacher telling him that his explanation was facile. "That accounted for my resistance to an easy read of what Hamilton's final thoughts were years later," he says.

He had, though, written a song about the moment after Hamilton and Eliza lost their son. That had been difficult too. It took him back to when he was four years old and learned that his best friend, Allie, had drowned. As a child, he kept wondering, *What must her parents be feeling?* Now, as a father-to-be, it seemed almost unfathomable. "I can't possibly know what it's like," he remembers thinking. And then, suddenly, he knew how to write the song. It would be about the impossibility of finding words for the loss.

> *There are moments that the words don't reach.*
> *There is suffering too terrible to name.*
> *You hold your child as tight as you can*
> *And push away the unimaginable.*

The accompaniment had a hushed tone, just a gentle arpeggio pulsing down an F major chord and a spare bass line beneath. At first, he'd thought Burr would narrate. Then he realized it needed to be Angelica. She had seen her sister's union with Hamilton form; she had seen it rupture. Now she would see it tested to the limit and, miraculously, start to heal. After the Hamiltons moved uptown, seeking solace in quiet routines, the song ended with a note of grace: Eliza takes Hamilton's hand. For a moment, at least, they could join in grief. Lin-Manuel wrote "It's Quiet Uptown" in a day, padding around the Public in pajamas and slippers while he remembered his preschool friend. "Truly, the seeds for that song were set when I was four years old," he says.

That fall, just as dance rehearsals were about to start at the Public, the unimaginable happened. Oskar's teenage son, Jack—a beloved, joyous high-schooler—took his own life.

It was shattering, indescribable. No one had words. Everyone offered support. Oskar's best friend, the playwright Tony Kushner, moved in with Oskar and his wife, Laurie, to grieve alongside them.

Lin-Manuel wondered how he could help. "There is nothing you can say. And yet, I had a song about this. So I wrote to him saying, 'If this is useful, then lean on it, and if not, delete this email.'" *There are moments that the words don't reach. There is suffering too terrible to name.* For an artistic director, it was useful. "That demo was all we listened to all week," Oskar says.

The first time Oskar and Laurie left their house was to see a *Hamilton* run-through. "It became our church," Oskar says. "That song became our mourning ritual." When Angelica sang about the loss of a child, they wept together. At the start of the next number, "The Election of 1800," Thomas Jefferson entered with a dry joke: "Can we get back to politics?" Oskar let out a full-bellied laugh. The next day, they'd watch the show again. "It helped to have boundaries on grief," he says. "You can go so deep you can't come out. That structure was crucial for us: We would have three minutes of publicly grieving, and then it would be over with a laugh. It was a return to life."

Signs of life were returning all around them. Vanessa was nine months pregnant. When Lin-Manuel met with his Disney collaborators in New York to work on Moana's "I Want" song, they knew he was on call. He could feel a change in his own outlook as he anticipated fatherhood. "I've been morbid all my life," he told his friend Alex Horwitz for the *Hamilton* documentary. "But for the rest of my life, my heart's going to exist outside my body. You have other reasons to build things besides yourself." He'd seen his sister change when she became a parent. "You're accountable to so much more." As he rehearsed the part of Hamilton now, the line that hit him hardest came in the Battle of Yorktown: "We gotta go, gotta get the job done, / Gotta start a new nation, gotta meet my son!"

In November 2014, Vanessa went into labor. When they arrived at the hospital, she was told that she couldn't go into the birthing center because her midwife hadn't yet arrived. Her normally easygoing and nonconfrontational husband, she says, "turned into Luis," like Bruce Banner becoming the Hulk. Channeling his father, he shouted, "We did not travel this far to be turned away!"

Soon they were holding a healthy baby, Sebastian Miranda. The name came from the Miranda family's Catholic heritage; Sebastian was the chosen saint for Lin-Manuel's confirmation.

Luz and Luis doted on their new grandson. He wore a little onesie that read MY MOMMY PLAYS GRAND THEFT AUTO BETTER THAN YOUR MOMMY. Vanessa's parents, Frank and Diemut Nadal, were on hand to help too. Before the baby arrived, Vanessa and Lin-Manuel had bought a new Washington Heights apartment down the street from the Nadals with a view of the George Washington Bridge through their window. It looked like the set of *In the Heights*. Quiara Alegría Hudes, the *Heights* book writer, lived one floor above. Vanessa and Lin-Manuel stayed with Vanessa's parents while their apartment was being remodeled; two weeks after Sebastian was born, they were finally able to move in. Full rehearsals for *Hamilton* began the next day.

"It's insane to think of what was happening at that moment in Lin's life," John Buzzetti says. "When I think about what the fuck happened: He got *Moana*, he had a baby, and *Hamilton* was opening." Lin-Manuel was emailing demos to the Disney team. He was learning choreography while he finished rewrites at the Public. He was changing diapers at home while Vanessa sang "Dear Theodosia" to their child. "I have a lot of apps open in my brain right now," he told a reporter for the *New Yorker* who was writing a profile of him to coincide with the Public premiere.

To his collaborators, however, he seemed surprisingly unflustered. "We were all firing things at Lin," Ron recalls. "I remember watching him and thinking, *I would have difficulty in that situation*. But he said, 'This is really good: I only have ten things to fix. At this time with *In the Heights*, I had twenty things to fix!'"

One thing Tommy, Ron, and Jeffrey all told him to fix was the name of the show. People outside his generation might not know what a mix-tape was, and that form, so tied to hip-hop, didn't signal the breadth of the show's styles. *Hamilton* it became. The Public mailed out advertisements with the new title emblazoned under a portrait of the man on the ten-dollar bill. Superimposed on his face, the name of the show's final song appeared in all-caps: WHO LIVES / WHO DIES / WHO TELLS / YOUR STORY.

That concluding sentiment received pushback. When Sondheim heard it, he sent Lin-Manuel an email. "The last song feels a little dry and conventionally rueful/uplifting, thesis-like instead of moving with the blood that made you want to write the piece in the first place," he wrote. "I don't think the show is about time and historical reputation. I think it's about something a great deal deeper and broader than that. Give it a little thought."

Oskar Eustis had a similar reaction. "I completely agreed with Mr. Sondheim," he says. "I thought it wasn't deep or resonant enough for a climactic thought."

Lin-Manuel mulled over what they were telling him. "What I try to do with criticism, especially if it's a note from someone as esteemed as Steve or Oskar, is sit with it," he says. "Either they're right, or I'm right, but I haven't earned it yet."

To earn it, he decided, he would need to write that final soliloquy for Hamilton. He would have to respond to the question Oskar had been pressing him to answer: What was Hamilton thinking at the duel? That's what would set up the meaning of the final song.

Yet as rehearsals continued into December, the title character still didn't have his concluding music. On the page of the script where Hamilton died, it said "New Song Under Construction Here." Tommy wasn't concerned. He'd seen Lin-Manuel come through at the last minute many times before. Just before tech rehearsals began, Tommy glanced over at his writer and star. "I feel like it's going to be a New Year's Baby," he said.

On January 1, 2015, Lin-Manuel woke up early. Sebastian, not yet two months old, was sleeping on his chest. Vanessa was asleep too. Tobillo, their dog, lay calmly between them on the bed. All he could hear was his infant son breathing in and out. For once, the spinning world felt still. Silent.

"Silence is the one thing we haven't done in the show," he says he realized. The show was three hours of glorious noise: rap, strings, bass, chorus. But earlier in "My Shot," Hamilton had asked if death was "like a beat without a melody." What if his final moment arrived with no melody, no music at all?

He placed Sebastian gently by Vanessa, put the dog on her leash, and went for a walk. Fort Washington Park stretched out along the Hudson River by their apartment. Across the river in New Jersey lay Weehawken, where Hamilton had faced Burr on another dawn two centuries before. Time seemed suspended in the wintry morning air.

He had been working on a draft of a song that slowed down time as Burr's bullet sped toward Hamilton. Now he decided to toss that draft and try a different sonic approach. The music would cut out, and the only sound would be a kind of "CAT scan of Hamilton's brain." He and Hamilton had both become fathers and were wondering what would outlive them. He started jotting lines in his notebook, a loose sense of assonance carrying him along and broadening his scope.

What if this bullet is my legacy?
Legacy. What is a legacy?
It's planting seeds in a garden you never get to see.
I wrote some notes at the beginning of a song someone will sing for me.
America, you great unfinished symphony,
You sent for me.
You let me make a difference.
A place where even orphan immigrants can leave their fingerprints and
*   rise up.*
I'm running out of time. I'm running and my time's up.
Wise up. Eyes up.

When Lin-Manuel brought the soliloquy to rehearsal, Andy was confused. "Where's the music?" he asked. "There's no music?" He didn't know how to choreograph Hamilton's final moment without a beat to work from. Andy felt completely blocked. He spent that night in agony. The next morning, he waited on the subway platform for the train that would take him to rehearsal. And then, he recalls, "I got the idea that unlocked everything." While Hamilton flashed through his life and legacy as the bullet sped toward him, the ensemble would reprise their choreography from the key moments in his story, sped up into a series of frozen poses. Riding the subway, Andy got so excited as he mapped out each moment that he missed his stop.

When Oskar saw the number, he started to come around to the composer's approach. Lin-Manuel hadn't fully answered the question of why Hamilton threw away his shot, but he'd given the moment significance. "Who tells your story?" had grown into more than a question about Hamilton; it had expanded to become a question for America itself. "It's not just about planting seeds for your own legacy," Oskar recognized. "It's about planting seeds for the country." And then, in the final song, when Eliza becomes the narrator, Oskar says, "It embodied the fact that Hamilton's story isn't his own, that it can be taken over by others." It could be taken over by Wall Street boosters or leaders of the conservative Federalist Society, who'd long claimed Hamilton as their financial progenitor. And it could also become the shared property of immigrants and artists of color, rising up to continue the contested story of America.

Oskar only had one request. "Okay, we're not going to explain exactly how he threw away his shot; we're going to let that resonate," he conceded. "But don't decide to throw away your shot at the start of the soliloquy. Make the soliloquy your attempt to decide what you're going to do."

Lin-Manuel came around too. In his first draft, Hamilton stated his choice from the outset: "I don't run or fire my gun / I let it be." As Lin-Manuel revised the soliloquy, he turned a statement into a question: "Do I run or fire my gun or let it be?," his gun pointed at Burr the whole time. And then, at the very last moment, he raised it to the sky.

"Wait!" Burr shouted as his own pistol fired. It was too late. Hamilton collapsed to the ground. Every night, it seemed like the ending might turn out differently. Every night, Burr hoped that he might avoid tragedy. And yet, every night, Hamilton threw away his shot while Burr took his. It was surprising but inevitable. "It just snapped into place," Oskar says.

On January 20, *Hamilton* held its first preview performance at the Public. Usually, a new show at a nonprofit theater off Broadway needed a movie star in its cast to sell tickets in advance. But thanks to the buzzy workshop that past May and the viral White House video almost six years earlier, word had spread. Before Lac cued the opening downbeat, the entire run at the Public had sold out.

They were still tinkering with the show. "Let's make different mistakes tomorrow," Tommy would tell the company. But even before the show froze, audiences were abuzz. Andrew Lloyd Webber came to a preview and tweeted that *Hamilton* had raised the bar for musicals. The box office list started to resemble a dream for Lin-Manuel: Salman Rushdie, Chelsea Clinton, and Timothy Geithner appeared alongside his elementary-school music teacher Barbara Ames. At one performance, musical-theater royalty Mandy Patinkin and rap royalty Busta Rhymes both showed up. Another night, when Luz announced to some people at intermission that her son had written the show, Paul McCartney turned around and offered his compliments, joking at how surprised he was that it had been so hard for him to score tickets.

For Luis, that moment encapsulated everything that had happened in *Hamilton*'s development since the White House. As he reflected in his memoir, "I was even more astonished that one of the biggest stars in the universe couldn't get tickets to a show where my son—the son of Puerto

Rican migrants—was telling the story of the making of this country. This is the beauty of this country, I thought: a brand-new group of people can come, and their kids can be successful telling the world about the birth of the nation in an entirely new way."

The show was still in previews two weeks before opening night in February; reviews hadn't yet come out. But so many people were calling the Public for tickets that the run had already been extended to March, then to April, then again to May. People kept calling. On the day the final extension was announced, Oskar showed up at the end of rehearsal. Something unprecedented had happened, he said.

"You broke the phones."

18

OPENING NIGHTS

· ·

As opening night approached at the Public, the Jonathan Larson nightmare no longer haunted Lin-Manuel. "I'd gotten through the *Will I live to see it?* fear," he says. "It wasn't the same blood pounding in my chest." Instead, he felt excited. The vacation with Vanessa in Mexico when he first started writing down his idea for Aaron Burr's opening line was six and a half years ago. Now the story he'd envisioned had finally made it to the stage. An off-Broadway audience at the Public would get to see what he'd devoted his thirties to creating.

During rehearsals, since he was onstage for most of the numbers, he'd been able to see the show only in little bits. But he had a secret weapon: His understudy, Javier Muñoz, could step into the lead role for a performance so he would have a chance to watch from the audience. At the conclusion of the rehearsal period, Javier got his shot to play Hamilton. (Lin-Manuel nicknamed his portrayal "Javilton.") "It wasn't until Javi went on for the first time with all the bells and whistles that I could see the work of my collaborators," Lin-Manuel says.

What he saw thrilled him. At the end of the opening number, for instance, Hamilton strode downstage while Burr scurried out of his way, asking, "What's your name, man?" The entire ensemble, clad in ghostly white, arcing a semicircle in the shadows behind him, joined in to sing the response: "*Al-ex-an-der Ha-mil-ton*." Then a spotlight hit Hamilton as the band landed a final chord: *Boom!* Since Lin-Manuel had always faced the audience, he'd never noticed that on the button, the ensemble dropped their heads. Only Hamilton was looking up; everyone else's head was bowed. The show was his requiem. Lin-Manuel burst into tears.

After rehearsals ended, the show would have nearly a month of previews at the Public; Lin-Manuel and his collaborators (whom he dubbed "the Cabinet") had time to make changes before opening night. Having gone through the preview process twice before, with *Heights* and *Bring It On*, Lin-Manuel knew that he'd want to start as soon as possible changing the moments that didn't work. He wasn't sure, though, whether he'd have the stamina to pull off the necessary revisions before the opening. Unlike in *Bring It On*, he was also starring in the show. Unlike either previous musical, he had a newborn child at home. Dark bags under his eyes attested to many sleepless nights. It was January 2015. He had just turned thirty-five.

The first full run-through clocked in at over three hours, longer even than *Les Misérables*. Tommy didn't worry. "The good news is: It works," he told the Cabinet. "The other good news is: We know it's too long." So what to cut? Tommy liked to say that audience attention is a finite resource; they had to decide where to spend it. He set out a principle: Anything that related to an offstage character would get the ax.

First on the chopping block was a second-act rap in which Hamilton eviscerated Washington's successor, John Adams. It contained some of Hamilton's fiercest bars, but since Adams didn't appear in the show, it had to go. The same principle eliminated a poignant reprise of "Dear Theodosia" for Burr after his wife died; the audience never met her, so her elegy couldn't survive. A song for Eliza to prevent her husband from attacking Burr, "Let It Go," also went. (Since a song with the same name from *Frozen* had become a global hit in 2014, it seemed wise not to keep it.) Renée Elise Goldsberry calls Lin-Manuel "a show-and-tell perfectionist"—eager to share his work at each stage and yet committed to revising it. Every time he performed the role of Hamilton, she says, "He slayed, he got a standing ovation, and yet he never stopped working until they grabbed the pencil from his hand."

More changes called, but the show had to freeze when opening night at the Public arrived on February 17. As an opening-night gift, Lin-Manuel gave Tommy a framed napkin inscribed with the director's reminder "MORE THAN ONE SONG A YEAR." Tommy gave him a book of the correspondence between playwright Samuel Beckett and his longtime director, called *No Author Better Served*. Lin-Manuel felt supremely aware that the musical represented a collaborative achievement. "You write for 6 years," he tweeted on February 17. "You surround your work with people who are smarter than you & make it better. Then you get to say: Opening night."

As Aaron Burr, Leslie Odom Jr. walked out into a spotlight on a wooden stage with a scaffolding of bricks and rope and ladders behind him—a nation under construction. Two hours and forty-five hurtling minutes later, as her dead husband let go of her hand, Phillipa Soo's Eliza looked out at the audience and gasped. The lights dimmed.

Then the party erupted in the lobby. The Public had set up statues of Hamilton and Burr facing off in a duel, their pistols raised across the foyer. From attending other opening celebrations at the Public, Lin-Manuel knew what would happen. Oskar Eustis would leap onto the bar, all six foot two of him, and proclaim this the greatest show ever written. ("It's so punk rock," Lin-Manuel says. "He somehow manages to say that about everything he produces. He's a great cheerleader.") But on the night of his own show, Lin-Manuel savored the feeling of getting it out into the world. For him, it was a sense of relief: "It no longer exists only in your brain."

The reviews only fueled the musical's momentum. For the *New York Times*, Ben Brantley extolled "the adrenaline rush of revolution, when men can chant, 'Hey yo, I'm just like my country/I'm young, scrappy and hungry/And I'm not throwing away my shot.' Ambitious, enthusiastic and talented in equal measures," the review concluded, "Mr. Miranda embodies those sentiments in a show that aims impossibly high and hits its target." With a spinning turntable at the center of its stage, *Hamilton* seemed a revolution itself, an unstoppable fusion of America's past and present with the history of musical theater and the sounds of contemporary airwaves. In the *Wall Street Journal*, Terry Teachout called it "the most exciting and significant musical of the past decade."

Everyone seemed to love it. Hillary and Bill Clinton came to the Public and congratulated the cast afterward. Lynne and Dick Cheney were equally enthusiastic. Conservatives could see the show as a celebration of the Founding Fathers and a reinvigoration of the classic bootstrap narrative with a hero who "got a lot farther by working a lot harder / By being a lot smarter / By being a self-starter." Progressives could cheer for artists of color telling America's story in their own protest idioms. At the Battle of Yorktown, the Caribbean-born Hamilton and the French-born Lafayette high-five. "Immigrants," Lafayette says, and Hamilton joins him to finish the line "We get the job done." (That rallying cry drew such a rousing audience response that Lac added a couple of bars afterward so the cheers wouldn't overwhelm the next line.)

Hamilton's capaciousness extended to its musical styles too. Traditionalists could congratulate themselves on spotting references to Shakespeare, Gilbert and Sullivan, and Rodgers and Hammerstein, while hip-hop heads could clock the shout-outs to Biggie and Tupac. The Schuyler sisters' R&B riffs tempered the show's macho energy; Jefferson showed up with jazz; and King George, resplendent in an ermine cape and towering crown, brought down the house with his Beatles-style disdain for the rap revolution. "The great principle of *Hamilton* is: This is the music Lin likes," Oskar says. "He has the courage to say: *Everything I like belongs in the musical*. And that allows all of us to feel ourselves reflected in what Lin wrote."

One day in April, Lin-Manuel arrived at the theater and saw security lined up outside. *Who's here?* he wondered. *Is it the pope?* Backstage, Phillipa Soo nearly smacked into a tall man in a suit wearing a radio earpiece. Occasionally, government dignitaries went to Broadway shows, but one of them visiting an off-Broadway theater with a full retinue was unheard of. And yet after the show, the cast all heard the news: Michelle Obama was in the house. Once the cast changed out of their costumes, the First Lady greeted each of them and announced: "This is the best piece of art that I've ever seen."

With reactions like that, Jeffrey Seller hungered to bring the show to a larger audience. Only three hundred people could see it each night at the Public, and even though the run had been thrice extended, it was entirely sold out. "There was euphoria in the air after opening," he says. "I was eager to go to Broadway." He had lined up the Broadway theater from *In the Heights*, the thirteen-hundred-seat Richard Rodgers. If they opened before the end of April, they would be eligible for the 2015 Tony Awards. It seemed a needless risk to open later and hope the buzz would last until the next awards ceremony in June 2016.

Lin-Manuel and Tommy, however, wanted to wait. If they hurried to open within the Tony-eligibility window, that wouldn't leave time for previews on Broadway so they could make adjustments in a new space. Jeffrey thought the quick transfer could work: "This will be exciting!" He'd done the same thing with *Rent* twenty years earlier—a February opening off Broadway and an April opening on Broadway that led to a Tony victory. But the team would have no time for revisions, no time to test the acoustics and sight lines, no time to let the show settle in. They'd waited six years to get it right. They could wait a few more months. "I don't want to rush this," Tommy told Jeffrey. "I want more time."

That decision affected more than the producers' prospects; it had financial consequences for the cast. Broadway union contracts paid actors a minimum weekly salary of $1,900. At the Public, wages were far lower. "I don't know if there's a better place to work in New York City," Leslie Odom Jr. says, "but after taxes and agents and managers, I was bringing home four hundred dollars a week. As a newly married man, it wasn't going to be easy." His wife was an actor too. He'd passed up a lucrative TV job— "more money than I'd ever been guaranteed for work in my life"—to stick with Burr. He didn't regret it, but delaying the prospect of a living wage on Broadway felt agonizing. Every night during the Public's extended run, he channeled his impatience into Burr's song "Wait for It."

The off-Broadway run concluded in May. At the end of the month, Lin-Manuel returned to Wesleyan University, his alma mater, in Middletown, Connecticut, to receive an honorary degree. He was asked to give the commencement address as well, and he stayed up the night before writing it. He arrived at the podium as sleep-deprived as the graduates. *Hamilton* rewrites loomed in his mind as he thought about what he wanted the students to take away.

His musical, he told them, was about two men who heard the clock of mortality: "The way they chose to live in the face of that knowledge puts them on a collision course from the moment they meet." Hamilton raced forward; Burr bided his time. Graduating from Wesleyan, Lin-Manuel recalled, he'd felt both impulses. He'd seized on a theater major because he could start making things sooner than he could in the film program, and he'd scrambled to put up as many shows as possible during his college time, always conscious that his parents were working seven days a week to cover his tuition. ("My education is their second mortgage and they are *killing* themselves to afford it.") And yet he'd also had to wait the eight years it took to get *Heights* from Wesleyan's student-run theater to Broadway. Although he often followed Hamilton's pace, he didn't discount the need for Burr's patience. "That clock you hear is the sound of your own heart," he concluded. As an exhortation, he repurposed a version of the advice that he'd received as an eighth-grader at Hunter from senior Matt Korahais: "Sink your *teeth* into this life and don't let go."

Unbeknownst to him, his parents were making another sacrifice for his future. They'd finally finished paying off the mortgage on the Inwood house. They'd paid for Cita's and Lin-Manuel's education. Now they wanted to support their son's next show. Jeffrey Seller was trying to raise twelve million dollars to take *Hamilton* to Broadway. "Luz and I wanted to invest, but we didn't have cash lying around," Luis recalled. Their commitment needed to reach a quarter million dollars. So, without telling Lin-Manuel, they mortgaged their house again. They were betting the roof over their heads on his shot at success.

In most cases, it would have been a terrible bet. According to an oft-cited statistic, four out of five Broadway shows fail to recoup their costs. Their investors lose their money. *In the Heights* became financially successful only after it won the Tony Award. Jeffrey had produced shows that won Tonys, and he'd also produced shows that closed in a week. *Hamilton* had just given up its first chance at a Tony nomination by delaying its opening until after the award-eligibility window closed. Enthusiasm at the Public wouldn't necessarily translate to Broadway ticket sales. The Public cultivated a smaller audience for adventurous new work. For a Broadway show, with much higher ticket prices, to take off, it usually needed to attract a wide base of tourists and out-of-town patrons. A celebrity headliner or a title familiar from a popular artist's catalog could offer a boost. *Hamilton* had neither.

Nor did recent precedents offer reassurance. The previous year, a hip-hop musical based on the songs of Tupac Shakur, *Holler if Ya Hear Me*, opened on Broadway. It closed in a month. An even closer comparison, *Bloody Bloody Andrew Jackson*—a clever recasting of the early American president as an emo rock star—earned rave reviews at the Public in 2009, riding a parallel between populist adulation for Jackson and Obama's starstruck path to the presidency. When it moved to Broadway, however, it couldn't attract an audience. It cost only a third of *Hamilton*'s capitalization, but its investors still failed to recover their money.

Hamilton's Broadway run was scheduled to begin previews in July. Tickets became available to purchase in March. On the Sunday morning that the box office started selling *Hamilton* tickets, Jeffrey and Tommy met for breakfast at the Lambs Club in Times Square, three blocks from the Richard Rodgers Theatre. There, they waited to hear their fate.

Ticketmaster's online box office had opened earlier that morning. The sale numbers started to roll in. And in. And in. Someone tweeted Lin-Manuel a picture of the line to buy tickets outside the theater itself. The line ran farther than the camera frame could fit.

Before *Hamilton* even opened on Broadway, its ticket sales reached thirty million dollars. The Mirandas had made a very good bet. "In our gut," Luis wrote in his memoir, "Luz and I knew it was going to be a hit."

Now the *Hamilton* team faced a different problem. Demand for tickets quickly outpaced supply. A show with an appeal rooted in populism—the idea that America's story belonged to everyone—now risked becoming an elite status symbol. In the 1990s, when *Rent* became a cultural phenomenon, Jeffrey wanted to make sure that people like the young artists and bohemians depicted in the musical would still be able to afford seats. He started reserving the front two rows for twenty-dollar tickets, available to whoever showed up first at the box office—though after demand grew so great that self-styled RentHeads camped out on the street to secure their place in line, the discounted seats shifted to a daily lottery. It was the beginning of rush tickets on Broadway. Two decades later, for a show about the man on the ten-dollar bill, Lin-Manuel wanted to adapt the idea. "It can't be twenty dollars," he told Jeffrey. A ten-dollar Hamilton bill should buy a ten-dollar *Hamilton* ticket. "It's gotta be a Ham for a Ham,"

The lottery opened two hours before the first July preview. When he peered out from the balcony above the Richard Rodgers marquee, Lin-Manuel could see a line stretching down Forty-Sixth Street and all the way around the corner of Eighth Avenue. More than seven hundred people had shown up to put their names in the lottery. He realized that most of them were going to go away disappointed. "It was hot, and I didn't want to send six hundred and eighty people angry into the streets of New York," he recalled. "That's bad juju."

He decided to pop down and thank them for coming. "The least I can do is give them a story if I can't give them a ticket," he reflected. In a gray T-shirt and jeans, his hair tucked up in a bun, he surprised the throng in the street. Behind him, on the theater doors, was his silhouette with a finger pointing in the air painted black against a gold background. "Thanks to you, we're probably gonna be here awhile," he shouted. The fans cheered. "So don't be disappointed if you don't win today," he told them. "I love you very much!" He raced back into the theater before the winning names were announced. The lucky few lined up, Hamilton bills in hand.

Inside the Richard Rodgers, Tommy had an idea. "We should do that every day," he told Lin-Manuel. "We've got a bunch of actors here. Just do a little something for the people who show up." It sounded like a fun way to express appreciation. Lin-Manuel started dreaming up possibilities. One night that week, he brought out Alex Lacamoire, who took requests on a handheld melodica, from "Bohemian Rhapsody" to the Super Mario theme song. Another night, he asked Renée Elise Goldsberry to perform George Washington's rap from "Right Hand Man" with Phillipa Soo beatboxing. He brought out Daveed Diggs and switched parts with his costar for the first Cabinet Battle, playing Jefferson opposite Daveed's Hamilton. On Twitter, he teased the three-minute performances with the hashtag Ham4Ham. When fans posted their videos, he retweeted them.

The Ham4Ham shows became a potent mix of street theater, collaborative goodwill, and viral publicity. Hundreds of thousands of people ended up viewing the performance videos on YouTube, far more than could ever have squeezed onto the sidewalk outside the Richard Rodgers, let alone into the theater. With no cast album yet released and hardly any footage of the show available to watch online, the Ham4Ham videos offered most people their only glimpse of what awaited them inside. The videos also connected *Hamilton* to the Broadway community; in addition to showcasing his own company, Lin-Manuel began inviting other casts to perform. Actors from *Fun Home*, *Aladdin*, and *Spring Awakening* made guest appearances. Instead of sucking up all the Broadway air, *Hamilton* became the balloon that lifted its neighbors. And Ham4Ham offered a little wish fulfillment for its creator too. When the understudy for Jean Valjean in *Les Misérables*, playing at the theater next door, agreed to pop over and perform the "Confrontation" duet opposite Lin-Manuel as Javert, Lin-Manuel grinned at the assembled crowd. "Dreams come true," he announced.

Jeffrey was delighted. "Lin has an intuition for reading the emotional current of the public," he says. "He takes that little show and makes it into an act of generosity and an act of audience development and an act of marketing." Lin-Manuel's lifelong desire to enchant an audience synched up with the show's publicity goals. Ham4Ham fueled the frenzy around *Hamilton* and also offered its star a way to channel the hubbub. He could share his own enthusiasm—for his fellow cast members, for the rest of Broadway, even for the work he'd created—with an adoring crowd. Vanessa teased him: "You found *another* audience outside the audience for your show?"

Lin-Manuel got a contractual respite once a week when Javier played Hamilton for a weekend show. During the first week of previews, Javier was scheduled to take the Saturday matinee. Then Jeffrey received word from the head of the National Endowment for the Arts that President Obama was going to bring his daughters to that performance. "What should I do?" Jeffrey asked the NEA director. "Lin won't be on." The director said not to worry. When Lin-Manuel heard that he wasn't going to be the one performing for the president, however, it gave him pause. *Hamilton* got its start when he sang the opening number in front of the Obamas at the White House. "I had a moment of ego," he recalls. But then he thought about it. "Actually, it's great that the president's seeing Javi," he decided. "The show is the star of the show, not me." He'd seen shows that couldn't survive the absence of their leads. Like Hamilton, he wanted to prove that something he built could outlive him. "So I tell Tommy: 'Javi will do the show. I'll take notes.'"

Sitting in the audience awaiting America's first Black president, he felt anxious. "I was most nervous for the president's safety," he says. The legacy of violent backlash against civil rights felt threateningly palpable. His parents, who had lived through the terrifying spate of assassinations in the 1960s, had told him, "Obama's going to get hurt!" All the security at the theater—the police sealing off Forty-Sixth Street, a special canopy for the president's motorcade—offered both a bulwark and a reminder of the ever-present danger. And having to be a spectator at his own show didn't help to calm his nerves. "That's when my control freak comes out," he admits, "when the show's going on, and I'm not onstage to help it." He fidgeted in his seat, afraid.

After the lights had gone down, President Obama and his daughters arrived. As ushers seated them by flashlight two rows behind Lin-Manuel, the audience caught sight of the First Family. There was a huge ovation. Camera phones came out. The show's opening had to hold for all the applause. When Leslie Odom Jr. finally walked onto the stage to begin Burr's number, he received another ovation. By this point, the audience was applauding the occasion. Here they were, watching a show about the formation of America's government with the commander in chief in their midst—a show that reimagined America's leaders as Black and brown stars with the proof of that possibility witnessing the performance. "It was a rock concert of a show," Lin-Manuel recalls.

At intermission, the theater brought down the fire curtain that blocked off the stage from the audience so the president could meet the cast. Up on the stage, he posed for pictures with the actors, who were starstruck. ("We're gonna do a show for Obama!" the Schuyler sisters harmonized in a backstage video before the performance.) The president hailed Javier as "Eminem meets Hamilton." And he told the company that the musical offered a great way to excite young people about civic responsibility; they could learn that all Americans are allowed to tell the story of their country. Then everyone returned to their places for the second act.

At the end of the show, the audience rose, the president included, in a standing ovation. Onstage, Javier was in tears. President Obama was whisked away, but he sent word through his spokesperson that the show had lived up to the hype. "Everything that could have happened for this show has happened, and today is the capstone," Ron Chernow told a *New York Times* reporter. "From the beginning, I've really felt like this show has had 'Obama's America' written all over it."

Since it was a preview performance, Lin-Manuel was still taking notes from the audience. The biggest change to the show that he and Tommy tried to work out before the Broadway opening arose from a number inspired by President Obama. During the 2008 presidential campaign, Obama gave a speech in New Hampshire that encapsulated the hopeful message of his candidacy. "For when we have faced down impossible odds," he declared, "when we've been told we're not ready or that we shouldn't try or that we can't, generations of Americans have responded with a simple creed that sums up the spirit of a people: Yes, we can." He repeated that refrain over and over: "Yes, we can." Watching the speech, the rapper will.i.am, the front man for the Black Eyed Peas, was captivated. He released a "Yes We Can" music video that spliced Obama's speech with popular artists—Common, John Legend, Scarlett Johansson—singing the same words to an uplifting melody.

Lin-Manuel loved the idea of what he calls "musicalizing a speech." For George Washington's Farewell Address in the second act, he decided to try that technique. As Hamilton, who'd drafted the address, he would begin by reading it in prose. And then Chris Jackson, as Washington, would start to sing the words over him. He'd promised Chris an act 2 solo after his second number from *In the Heights* was cut. This moment offered an occasion to honor the actor who considered himself Lin-Manuel's big brother. "George Washington was a stunning leader, as Chris is," Lin-Manuel says, "and Hamilton's job was to help him find words for this moment, as mine is for Chris. And then he can take them and deliver them to a place where I could never go."

At the Public, Chris let Washington's words fly. "We're gonna teach them how to say goodbye," he sang as the president decided not to run for a third term. The problem was that the number contained too many moments before that. Titled "One Last Ride," it tried to cram in Washington's suppression of the Whiskey Rebellion on the Appalachian frontier before getting to his retirement. Lin-Manuel wanted to cut the number down, and he needed to find a way to bridge the first part of the song, when Washington invites Hamilton for a drink, and the conclusion, when Hamilton writes the farewell address.

When Chris showed up for rehearsal one morning in June as the show prepped for Broadway, he was asked to hang out—Lin-Manuel was still working on the song. Then Tommy popped into the composing room. He could tell Lin-Manuel was stuck. He offered an idea.

"Well, there's Washington's thing about the vine and fig tree," he said.

"I don't know what you're talking about," Lin-Manuel said.

"You know, the vine-and-fig-tree thing. From the Bible."

Tommy had grown up outside Washington, DC, near Washington's home at Mount Vernon. His mother worked as an archivist at a historic mansion that belonged to Martha Washington's descendants. He knew Washington liked to quote a biblical verse, Micah 4:4, that promises a space of peace and rest: "They shall sit every man under his vine and under his fig tree; and none shall make them afraid."

Lin-Manuel sat up. "Okay, get out of the room. Goodbye!"

Forty-five minutes later, Lin-Manuel handed the new version of the song to Chris. "As soon as Tommy said the line, I could hear Chris singing it as gospel," he recalls. "I was like, 'This thing's going to write faster than I have chops for!'" Having sung with Chris in *Heights* and Freestyle Love Supreme for more than ten years, he knew how to write for Chris's voice. "I know where the good notes are and where the good leaps are," he says. He built those intervals into Washington's verse.

Lin-Manuel and Chris tried it out. "Why do you have to say goodbye?" Hamilton implored Washington. The president responded:

> *If I say goodbye, the nation learns to move on.*
> *It outlives me when I'm gone.*
> *Like the Scripture says:*
> *"Everyone shall sit under their own vine and fig tree*
> *And no one shall make them afraid."*
> *They'll be safe in the nation we've made.*
> *I want to sit under my own vine and fig tree.*
> *A moment alone in the shade.*
> *At home in this nation we've made.*
> *One last time.*

As Chris sang those lines, reaching high on "fig tree" for the sweet spot in his range, he thought of the news that morning. The night before, in Charleston, South Carolina, a young white man had entered an African-American church, joined a Bible-study session, then opened fire, killing the pastor and eight other people. He had told a friend that he wanted to start a race war. What could it possibly mean to be safe in the nation Washington had made?

When Chris learned he was going to play Washington, his first thought was that the president had been a slaveowner. How could he portray a man who saw people like himself as property? He decided that he wouldn't try to forgive Washington, but he would try to understand him, and perhaps his own presence onstage would offer a counterpoint to the pernicious parts of Washington's legacy.

Now, as he held Lin-Manuel's new lyrics, he lingered on the Bible verse. "The shooting in the South Carolina church framed the entire experience for me in that song," he says. In a musical way, he and Lin-Manuel were going to church, praying for everyone's right to sit under their own vine and fig tree. The song, retitled "One Last Time," built to a call-and-response chorus with the entire ensemble backing Chris. He soared.

"It was way beyond what the historical George Washington deserved," Lin-Manuel says, "but it was every bit what Chris Jackson deserved."

As the Broadway opening approached, the buzz for the show that had been anointed by the president continued to swell. *Vogue* magazine asked the cast to pose for a photo spread in its July issue. "Anytime you write something, you go through so many phases," Lin-Manuel told the *Vogue* reporter. "You go through the I'm a Fraud phase. You go through the I'll Never Finish phase. And every once in a while you think, What if I actually have created what I set out to create, and it's received as such?"

Opening night at the Richard Rodgers arrived: Thursday, August 6. That Monday, Lin-Manuel had woken up unable to move his neck. Stress always accumulated from his shoulders up, and now it paralyzed him. Anti-inflammatory medication got him through Tuesday's preview, but on his doctor's orders, he sat out the Wednesday matinee.

By Thursday, he could move again. For the opening-night Ham4Ham lottery, he planned a one-man show. In pink shorts and a black T-shirt, he strode up the steps outside the theater with Ron Chernow's Hamilton biography in his hand. "I'm going to keep it simple today," he told the cheering crowd. "The whole thing started because I picked up a book and fell in love. And so I'm just going to read you the first five paragraphs of this book. And then to find out the ending, you have to see the show."

He opened Chernow's biography to the prologue about Elizabeth Schuyler Hamilton. He read swiftly until he reached the line "Was it a benign or cruel destiny that had compelled the widow to outlive her husband by half a century?" His voice cracked. He looked aside and sniffed. He made it through the remaining paragraphs, tearing up as he ended with Eliza's murmured words: "I am so tired. It is so long. I want to see Hamilton."

He gulped, his eyes brimming. His voice fluttered as he said, "I hope y'all get to see *Hamilton*," and then he ducked away to the stage door.

When he appeared as Hamilton onstage, the audience gave him a rapturous reception. But that's what opening-night audiences, made up of invited guests, are supposed to do. What mattered were the reviews. *Hamilton* hype had grown so inflated that critics seemed bound to puncture it. When the producers called a press conference to announce the Broadway transfer, the *New York Post* columnist Michael Riedel wrote, "Everyone on Broadway was snickering" at their self-importance. He sounded almost gleeful as he announced: "Let the 'Hamilton' backlash begin!"

The *Post*, though, liked to take a sneering stance. The *New York Times* was the paper that could determine a show's future. As private coaches transported the *Hamilton* company from the theater to the opening-night party at Chelsea Piers, along the Hudson River, the *Times* posted its critic's review.

"Yes," Ben Brantley began, "it really is that good."

The critic went even further. "I am loath to tell people to mortgage their houses and lease their children to acquire tickets to a hit Broadway show," Brantley continued. But *Hamilton*, he conceded, "might just about be worth it."

They were going to have a hit. At the party at Pier Sixty, *The Tonight Show*'s in-house band, the Roots, kicked in to their set. Questlove, the drummer and a celebrated hip-hop chronicler, had already pronounced *Hamilton* "the first authentic hip-hop show." The Roots' MC, Black Thought, called Lin-Manuel onstage—"Give it up for the L Double M!"—and handed him the mic. Beaming and incredulous, he looked out at his friends and family. What could he say?

Questlove gave him a beat. "Uh, six years of labor, these are the fruits: / I'm onstage with the fuckin' Roots!" he freestyled. "This party's gonna go till, like, half past seven, / I'd swear to fucking God, I'd died and went to heaven!"

Over the Hudson, fireworks exploded. Jeffrey had arranged a spectacular display to celebrate their new Broadway smash. The guests cheered as red and white stars burst in the air, broke apart into trails of light, then vanished in the night.

The real rupture was yet to come.

19

SAY GOODBYE

● ●

*D*ear Jeffrey," the letter began. "We love you. We love *HAMILTON*." Though the letter was addressed to the musical's lead producer, Lin-Manuel received a copy as well, a few weeks after the show's Broadway opening. He kept reading. "Many of us came to you separately during our private negotiations but today we stand together, asking you in the humblest and most respectful way that we know how—begging you to reconsider our request to share in the success of this magnificent work."

The letter was signed by every member of the cast except him.

He understood why they'd written the letter. *Hamilton* was becoming a giant moneymaker. Over its first year, the musical was expected to bring in about one hundred million dollars from Broadway ticket sales alone, not counting merchandise, cast-album sales, and future tours. The company members all received a salary of at least $1,900 per week, the union-negotiated base. But they didn't share in the profits. Those went to the producers, the investors, and the creative team. According to calculations by the *New York Times*, Jeffrey Seller and his two other producers would split more than $15 million in the first year. The Public Theater would get $2.5 million. Tommy Kail would receive about $2.3 million. Ron Chernow's annual royalties would total almost $1 million. For his many roles as creator, composer, lyricist, and star, Lin-Manuel was expected to net upwards of $6 million.

To many of the actors, that didn't seem fair. Yes, the producers and investors had put up considerable funds and made the strategic decisions to develop the show, taking a risk without a guaranteed return. Yes, the Cabinet had created every word and note and step onstage. They were entitled to their rewards. But the cast had also contributed to the show's development. They'd given their bodies and voices and energy—risking injury, turning down other jobs, sticking with the show when its future wasn't clear—to try out everything Lin-Manuel and Lac and Tommy and Andy could invent. And in many cases, their innovations went in the show, too; the Schuyler sisters' vocal runs, for instance, came from Lac hearing the actors harmonizing in their dressing room. "There was undeniable genius on the pages we were given at the start," the letter from the cast said. "And once this well-chosen ensemble of artists was assembled, we all witnessed something *else* too: there was a collective emotional intelligence at work."

They had a precedent to cite. The last new musical to become a mega-hit on Broadway, *The Book of Mormon*, had agreed to split a tiny portion of its profits—just 1 percent—among the original cast members. In fact, union contracts for musical workshops often included a provision for profit sharing. But for the *Hamilton* workshops, Jeffrey had opted for a different contract structure, one that paid actors a higher weekly salary up front but precluded a share in the revenue if the show went on to a commercial run. At the time, actors had challenged that contract, but they couldn't reach an agreement. The decision to extend the run at the Public may have exacted a cost too, since it kept the performers at a lower off-Broadway salary. If Jeffrey agreed to share 1 percent of the annual *Hamilton* profits— about $312,000—with the original company, it wouldn't make any of them rich. But it would give them each an extra $10,000 or so a year, enough to help with rent, a medical bill, a gap between jobs when their contracts ran out. "There are no losers in a decision like this," the letter argued. "Please invest in us as we have invested in you. Please allow us and our families to enjoy the fruits of our labor as yours will."

This went beyond finances; a bigger principle seemed to be at stake. "I think we all felt the historic success of the show meant that it had some responsibilities," Leslie Odom Jr. says, "by virtue of the fact that the megaphone was so large, and by virtue of the bodies on which this story was told." Who should profit, some wondered, from a celebrated story of

America performed by a largely Black and brown cast? "We knew its value as entertainment," Leslie says. "We had to ask ourselves, is there more that we're charged to do?"

Though Lin-Manuel agreed with the letter, he felt unnerved to be left off the list of cast signatories. "I was on their side," he says, "but I wasn't included." Somehow, he seemed to have become an outsider in his own show. He understood why the rest of the cast hadn't asked him to put his name down; he wasn't a producer, but his role as both a creator and an actor made him appear to straddle the two sides—part management, part labor. "They did it so they wouldn't put me in a tough spot," Lin-Manuel concedes, "but it othered me inside the building." With the cast of *In the Heights*, he remembers, "it was family, family, family. But now I had the weird sensation of feeling outside my own cast for the first time."

He felt especially disappointed that the cast members had acted as their own negotiators instead of getting a lawyer or manager to approach Jeffrey on their behalf. "The reason we have representatives is so they can have conversations about money, and we can just focus on doing the show," he says. "By not designating a representative, it spilled into the theater. It got very messy."

Jeffrey did not agree to share any profits. Instead, he offered the actors a onetime payment for the difference between their off-Broadway salaries and the Broadway base pay they would have made if *Hamilton* had transferred sooner. They rejected the counteroffer. "This is ground worth standing," Leslie emailed the cast. He'd spoken with actors from *The Book of Mormon* and learned how sustaining a weekly royalty check, however small, could be.

Then one evening, just before the show, Jeffrey had checks for the payment difference delivered to the actors' dressing rooms, along with a note: "This brings to an end this powerful issue that has been weighing on many of us." The actors weren't sure what to do. Was it a peace offering? A trap?

They decided not to accept the checks, and the atmosphere at the Richard Rodgers grew increasingly tense. Lin-Manuel felt torn between Jeffrey and his fellow actors. Jeffrey had believed in him, had championed him, had taken a financial risk on him long before he became a Broadway star. And he knew, from those early *Heights* days, how hard it was to achieve any kind of financial security as an actor and how much uncompensated work went into the development of a show. He hated being caught in the middle. Could he have used his position to press for a resolution? He didn't think so. "I had no way of resolving it because I wasn't in a position of power on either side," he says. "I couldn't see my way out of it."

The conflict felt particularly acute to Lin-Manuel in part because he and Tommy had worked strenuously to develop a creative environment that was free of antagonism. They wanted to show that great art could emerge without conflict. Onstage, they dramatized clashes and toxicity and self-destructiveness, but the process for producing it could be harmonious. They never yelled. They didn't bad-mouth their peers. They teased one another and disagreed and worked through criticism to improve the show, but they kept the energy positive. If someone in the room was dwelling in negativity, a glance from Lin-Manuel was usually enough to turn them around.

But now, none of the strategies he'd developed as a company leader seemed to work. He was used to boosting morale with his indefatigable enthusiasm, leading with joy and creativity, making it feel fun for people to devote endless hours to a show. He loved to inspire the cast with backstage games, freestyle raps, and offstage larks, like the Ham4Ham shows he organized as a treat for fans. "I tried to remind everyone, 'We're on the comet! This happens once every twenty years!'" he says. *Hamilton* broke the record for the highest weekly box office gross of any Broadway show in history—more than three million dollars over only eight performances. The cast recording not only hit the top spot on *Billboard*'s cast-album chart but reached number one on the *rap* chart too. Celebrities from Oprah to Steven Spielberg hailed the show as a masterpiece. But even those benchmarks, Lin-Manuel recognized, didn't solve the problem. "The irony of being in the biggest hit of the twenty-first century and people walking into that building who feel like they're not getting what they deserve felt really bad."

Of course, for many of the other actors, being in an era-defining hit provided all the more reason that they should share in its financial rewards. Some even questioned whether they should continue to participate in Lin-Manuel's Ham4Ham shows. Why offer free labor to advertise a production that didn't seem to recognize their contributions? "I just know that it's hard for me to separate Ham4Ham from the overall theme of compensation for our worth," one actor wrote to the cast. "I feel as if I shouldn't do them, and would love to graciously let Lin know that until this 1% is resolved it's hard to do a Ham4Ham because it isn't vital to the life of the show."

Jeffrey could tell that his author and star was in an untenable position. "It was excruciating for Lin," he says. "I witnessed his distress. I felt guilty and responsible." Still, the negotiations dragged on for seven months.

When the mood became too sour, Lin-Manuel sought refuge elsewhere. Several alumni from *In the Heights* were performing in a Gloria Estefan musical, *On Your Feet*, at the theater next door to *Hamilton*. He'd pop over and hang out with them. Inside the Richard Rodgers, he vented to the friends who'd come with him from the *Heights* company: Chris Jackson and Javier Muñoz, especially, both of whom stepped back from the negotiations out of loyalty to Lin-Manuel. He had another ally: Jonathan Groff, the star from *Spring Awakening* and *Frozen*, who'd taken over the role of King George at the end of the off-Broadway run and therefore didn't have a stake in conflicts over earlier workshop compensation. On Broadway, Lin-Manuel and Jonathan shared a dressing room on the top floor of the theater that became a haven from turmoil outside.

Jonathan made it his mission to keep their dressing room drama-free. They watched silly YouTube videos and sang folk songs they'd learned in elementary school. "I would sit and watch Lin play Nintendo in the way I would watch my brother play when I was five years old," Jonathan says. Together, they could be kids again. They traded *Saved by the Bell* references. They hung a mask of Jonathan's *Frozen* character, Kristoff, over the toilet. When they came offstage in their costumes, they'd giggle to each other: "We're in the play!"

It was a deliberately cultivated space. "During the pressure of the one-percent discussions, Lin was very militant about keeping business outside the stage door," Jonathan recalls. "We never spoke about it. When something tough is happening, he's very careful. That's how I observed him backstage protecting his positivity."

The show itself gave Lin-Manuel his primary outlet. "The most relaxing part of my life in 2015 was the two and a half hours I was onstage," he says. "Playing Hamilton requires all your focus. You get to fall in love, fight a war, have an affair. The act of being present helps a lot. Everything went away when I did the show."

Then, after the final bows, the world returned. When the performance was over, celebrities would come backstage—Joe and Jill Biden one night, Jay-Z and Beyoncé another. Although some actors didn't like to know if a celebrity was going to be in the audience, Lin-Manuel always pored over the VIP list before the show. "He uses their attendance to inspire his performance," Jonathan says. "The day Eminem was there, he was on fucking fire."

At that performance, the rapper who'd inspired many of Hamilton's intricate rhymes watched from the balcony, his arms crossed. Afterward, he asked Lin-Manuel, "What happens when you mess up?"

"I messed up for you three times," Lin-Manuel replied. The answer: He just kept going.

Once the VIPs had signed a giant portrait of Hamilton on the backstage wall, posed for pictures, and said goodbye, the cast would meet fans on the street outside the stage door. Signing autographs might take another hour. The next day, there would be interviews, photo shoots, television appearances, cover stories for *Billboard*, the *Hollywood Reporter*, *Time*, *Rolling Stone*. Endless adulation could go to one's head. That fall, Lin-Manuel received a MacArthur Fellowship, often called the "genius grant"—$625,000 over five years with no restrictions, just the instruction to continue being brilliant. And yet he was also a father, a husband, a son. "He had a baby to go home to and change its diapers and a wife to keep happy," his mother points out. "So I think having a child at the time allowed for him to be grounded."

How did Vanessa experience the whirl of life in the *Hamilton* hurricane? "It was really fucking weird—and wonderful," she says. She was delighted that the world embraced her husband's work. But it was difficult for her to parent an infant with an intense job as a law firm associate while her husband was gone every night and asleep every morning. She worked all day, put Sebastian to bed, then worked again until midnight and went to sleep before Lin-Manuel got home. His family appreciated her realistic influence. "I'm thankful he met Vanessa when he did, before all of this, and that she's not in his world," his sister, Cita, says. "He'll be like, 'I met this famous person!' And she'll be like, 'That's nice, but we need milk!'"

By this point, Cita had taken over managing the finances of her brother's business interests as well as her father's. Lin-Manuel, she says, was generally clueless about money and grateful to have any. Even after *Hamilton* became a hit, he would ask Cita if they could afford for him to take a car service home instead of the subway. "He still walks around in the world like a college kid," she says. His agent, too, noted his indifference to financial matters. "He doesn't give a fuck about the business," Buzzetti says. "He just wants to do the work." On the one hand, that allowed him to stay focused on his art as the business around *Hamilton* started to explode. On the other hand, it made him perceive the profit negotiations primarily through an emotional lens. Vanessa could tell that her husband felt the pain of disappointing people far more than she did. "My nickname is 'Robot' among his friends, because they're all theater people," she says. "I can brush things off in a way that he can't. Lin doesn't have as thick a skin. He feels very badly if something wasn't good enough for everybody."

In the spring of 2016, Leslie Odom Jr. told Lin-Manuel that the cast was going to try appealing to Jeffrey Seller again for a share of the profits. Lin-Manuel implored him to get a lawyer to handle the negotiations instead. A week later, the cast's lawyer announced that the cast and the producers had reached an agreement. The cast would split 1 percent of the Broadway profits and a smaller portion of the profits from touring productions. "They are the ones bringing this show to life," Jeffrey told a *New York Times* reporter. "It was a powerful argument they made; it was gut-wrenching for me, and I took it seriously." In retrospect, he says he regrets not resolving the dispute faster. When the deal came through, his first call was to Lin-Manuel. As Jeffrey recalls, "He almost cried from relief." Three days later, *Hamilton* won the Pulitzer Prize for Drama.

That first year on Broadway had been intensely demanding. The actors who led the negotiations felt that they'd arrived at a place of greater dignity and harmony. "We had a tricky moment," Leslie says, looking back. "We worked through it together as a family. We never dishonored the show. And we never betrayed the artistic bonds and ties we had built."

In June, the 2016 Tony Awards were widely expected to become a *Hamilton* coronation ceremony. The show received a record sixteen nominations, including seven for its actors. Its wins in the musical-theater categories started coming early in the night: Best Costume Design, Best

Lighting Design, Best Orchestrations, Best Choreography, Best Direction. Leslie Odom Jr. won Best Actor in a Musical for playing Aaron Burr (over Lin-Manuel's nomination for playing Hamilton); Renée Elise Goldsberry and Daveed Diggs won in the featured actor categories for playing Angelica and Lafayette/Jefferson. When the *Hamilton* cast performed "Yorktown" for its showcase number, the ensemble's cry at the end—"We won!" "We won!" "We won!" "We won!"—sounded as much like a cheer for the show's skyrocketing awards tally as for the Revolutionary War victory. By the time Barbra Streisand came out, wearing a colonial-style frock coat and a ruffled blouse, to present the Best Musical award, the result seemed almost foreordained. "Thank God I picked the right outfit," she joked just before she announced *Hamilton* the winner.

Yet, the mood wasn't entirely ebullient. In the early hours that Sunday, a gunman had opened fire during Latin Night at a gay nightclub in Orlando, killing forty-nine people—deadlier than any previous mass shooting. "It's a day marked by such tragedy," Lin-Manuel said outside the Tonys, wearing a rainbow flag pin and a silver ribbon in solidarity with the victims, many of whom were Puerto Rican. It was hard to know if celebrating works of art that evening would seem a trivial distraction or if art could offer a recognition of tragedy, even an attempt at healing, however insufficient, in a moment of suffering.

He'd been in an analogous situation before, back in his senior year in college when he was about to open *Basketcase*, his musical about a school shooting, and the terrorist attacks of September 11 took place. He'd put in a note about the content in the program and given the audience a chance to stay or depart. At the Tonys, he knew, the audience likely couldn't leave to avoid a particular number, so he and Tommy decided that the *Hamilton* cast wouldn't bring their prop muskets onstage for the Battle of Yorktown sequence. The actors' empty hands could offer one tiny respite from gun violence that day.

When Lin-Manuel's name was called for Best Original Score, he gave Vanessa a celebratory fist-bump and kissed his mother on her cheek. As he walked up the steps to the microphone, he pulled a folded piece of paper out of his breast pocket. "I'm not freestyling; I'm too old," he told the audience. "I wrote you a sonnet instead."

He started with a quatrain in praise of Vanessa:

My wife's the reason anything gets done;
She nudges me towards promise by degrees;
She is a perfect symphony of one;
Our son is her most beautiful reprise.

Then, continuing the musical motif, he put the process of creation in the context of the nightclub shooting:

We chase the melodies that seem to find us
Until they're finished songs and start to play
While senseless acts of tragedy remind us
That nothing here is promised; not one day.

Broadening his scope, he took *Hamilton* as inspiration that tragedy wouldn't become the enduring note:

This show is proof that history remembers.
We live through times when hate and fear seem stronger.
We rise and fall and light from dying embers,
Remembrances that hope and love last longer.

And then his conclusion burst past the pentameter line to affirm love in all its forms, a poetic response to bigoted violence:

And love is love is love is love is love is love and love
Cannot be killed or swept aside
I sing Vanessa's symphony, Eliza tells her story
Now fill the world with music, love and pride.

By the end of the speech, he wasn't the only one in tears.

Watching the broadcast, the pop star Jennifer Lopez was so moved that she later asked Lin-Manuel to join her on a charity single to benefit the families of the Orlando victims. Their song, "Love Make the World

Go Round," remixed the "love is love" refrain from his Tony sonnet to a dance-hall beat, an affirmation of love in the face of hate. "Those who hate us and fear us cannot keep us down," Lopez sang; Lin-Manuel added a rap verse: "Their malevolence can wait, raise the level of debate, celebrate, elevate."

The single dropped on July 8, the day before Lin-Manuel's final performance as Hamilton on Broadway. Javier Muñoz would take over the role. It was Leslie's and Phillipa's last show, too, the end of their year-long run. Jennifer Lopez came to see them, as did a host of other celebrities—Spike Lee, John Kerry, Jane Fonda, Mariska Hargitay—and legions of fans. At the curtain call, Lin-Manuel shared a bow with the rest of the cast, then Chris grabbed him in a hug and shoved him forward so he could receive his solo ovation. Afterward, in his dressing room, as a ritual farewell to the role, he cut off his Hamilton ponytail.

For many *Hamilton* company members, the highlight of the run came not at a Broadway performance or at the Tonys but on a field trip earlier in March, when President Obama and the First Lady invited them to visit the White House. Michelle Obama wanted to develop a program around education, and Jeffrey Seller had already announced that, in partnership with the Rockefeller Foundation, twenty thousand schoolchildren would get to see *Hamilton* at special matinees for ten dollars each and perform their own songs inspired by American history for the show's cast. The White House would launch the EduHam initiative by hosting DC-area students for workshops with *Hamilton* cast members followed by a command performance of selections from the show in the East Room.

When Lin-Manuel was in high school, his artistic drive had been fueled by writing songs inspired by his heroes, so he was thrilled to involve students in the show and support their creativity. The DC trip also had a pleasing symmetry: He had debuted the very first song he wrote for *Hamilton* in the East Room seven years earlier, and now he would return with his entire company to mark the show's impact. "You know," Tommy joked about his White House performance, "if you'd really bombed that, this would be a very different 2016 for you."

The cast rode down from New York on a bus after their Sunday matinee, singing along to Kendrick Lamar's latest release. The mood was jubilant; although they'd met the president before, they'd never all been invited to his house. For Lin-Manuel, though, it was also a work trip. Between meeting with the students and performing the concert, he planned to shoot an interview with President Obama for the documentary his friend Alex was making about the show, film a couple of Ham4Ham skits for the ticket lottery, do a freestyle rap session with government-themed words supplied by the president, and lobby Congress to address Puerto Rico's worsening financial crisis.

The next morning, when he woke up in his hotel room, he was unable to move his neck. ("The stress has to go somewhere," he says.) Luis, his roommate, blasted "Oh, What a Beautiful Morning" from *Oklahoma!* until his son lumbered out of bed and spread Tiger Balm down his shoulders. He wore a baby-blue blazer and a pair of jeans—a casual choice for which he was mercilessly mocked. Everyone else in the cast looked their spiffiest.

The day started well in the White House lobby with the student workshops. Then the cast went upstairs for a photo shoot with the Obamas, who greeted everyone as they walked in.

Tommy, standing a few people behind Chris Jackson in line, saw President Obama spot the actor who played George Washington.

"Mr. President," President Obama said, putting out his hand.

"Mr. President," Chris replied.

They dapped and hugged each other—the first Black president and the Black first president, in *Hamilton* chronicler Jeremy McCarter's apt phrase.

Oh, thought Tommy, *for the rest of my life, that is* the *memory of this experience for me.*

Tommy moved next to Chris for the group photo, and they stood together in silence, reflecting on the moment. Somehow, *Hamilton* had brought them together in the White House for an image that reframed American history from President Washington to President Obama. "It was as meaningful as anything that has happened in this show," Tommy said the next day, "because it's not possible, except it was, and I saw it."

It was the last year of Obama's presidency. In recognition of the occasion, Lin-Manuel had decided with Tommy and Lac that they would end the concert that afternoon with George Washington's farewell song, "One Last Time."

Chris didn't know the set list until they assembled in the East Room for the sound check. Then he noticed the final song on the program. As he and Lin-Manuel ran it through, he saw the White House staff putting out placards to reserve the seats in the front row. A sign that said POTUS went on a chair five feet in front of him.

Tommy walked up to Chris with a grin. "When you get to the end of the song," Tommy told him, "you might not want to look there."

Lac led the *Hamilton* orchestra as the cast performed their greatest hits: "Alexander Hamilton," "My Shot," "The Schuyler Sisters," "The Room Where It Happens." Then it was time for the final song.

Lin-Manuel, as Hamilton, took the microphone next to his George Washington. Behind Chris, the famous Stuart portrait of the historical George Washington hung on the East Room wall. Seated in front of Chris, President Obama looked up expectantly.

They began the number. "'One last time,'" Chris sang. "'Relax, have a drink with me / One last time. / Let's take a break tonight / And then we'll teach them how to say goodbye.'"

By the end, the song was full gospel. Chris Jackson seemed like he was singing from an exalted place, his voice swooping and soaring, the ensemble echoing each phrase. In front of him, Obama nodded in affirmation.

Lin-Manuel, standing next to Chris, could see tears trickling down his cheek. Chris's face was angled so high that the tears rolled past his ear. "I was thinking of my grandmother," Chris recalls. "She was a deaconess in the church, and she put her hand on my head and my heart and said, 'You're going to do great things.' She could dream in a wide lens, but her dreams could never have seen me in that room."

Just before the final "One last time," Chris glanced at Lin-Manuel and smiled. Lin-Manuel was beaming. Even before Chris finished the final note, the president leaped to his feet, cheering and clapping. The entire room followed.

The Obamas stayed to hug every member of the cast. And the president gave an impromptu speech to close the day.

"That's magic," he said, turning to look at Chris. "It is rare when a piece of art can remind us about what's best in ourselves, and that's what these guys have done. That is a great gift." He looked out at the audience, then back at Chris and Lin-Manuel. "So with that, let me know how to say goodbye."

Most people in the East Room that day expected that when the Obamas said their formal goodbye to the White House, Hillary Clinton would move in as the next president. In July, *Hamilton* performed a special matinee to raise money for the Hillary Victory Fund, with seats going for $2,700 each. Though Lin-Manuel had left the show, he came back to introduce Clinton, his father's former client when she ran for senator from New York. Mentioning that *Hamilton* name-checked the first four presidents, he announced, "Right now, you're going to hear from the forty-fifth president." Clinton picked up the musical cue. "As Washington tells us, history's eyes are on us," she told the donors. "Let's not throw away our shot."

The Clinton campaign looked promising that October when Lin-Manuel fulfilled a childhood dream and hosted *Saturday Night Live*. The day before the show, a tape had leaked of Donald Trump bragging about his ability to grope women; after that admission, his candidacy seemed, to many, sunk for good. That was the mood, at least, on Saturday night at the NBC studio. With his ponytail shorn and his goatee shaved off, Lin-Manuel looked youthful, refreshed. For his opening monologue, he performed a remix of "My Shot," bopping down a hallway decorated with photos of former *SNL* hosts. Then he came across a picture of Trump. Borrowing a line from "The Reynolds Pamphlet" when Hamilton's opponents find out about the treasury secretary's sex scandal, Lin-Manuel sang, "'Well, you're never gonna be president now!'" The studio audience laughed and cheered.

And yet Election Day delivered a different result. "Scared as y'all," Lin-Manuel posted on Twitter after Trump's victory. "But we'll get through it." He thought of his mother's refrain: *This too shall pass.* Someone on Twitter joked that Lin-Manuel was probably moving to Canada. "F*ck that," he replied. "I love this country, and there's more work to do than ever." ("No offense Canada," he added.) Nevertheless, his work had become so closely associated with the Obama White House and its legacy that a headline in the *Boston Globe* asked, "Was the Election a Vote Against 'Hamilton'?"

For Lin-Manuel, the discourse around *Hamilton* felt less pressing than the need to counter Trump's political views. Although the show had become swept up in presidential campaign narratives, he thought its parallels weren't a source of reassurance. Partisan politics had always been combative in America; Burr's failed campaign resulted in him shooting

Hamilton in a duel. The musical dramatized the shifting winds of differ-ent administrations: Hamilton was Washington's right-hand man and then found himself on the outs with the subsequent Adams administration. "That's what the show's about," Lin-Manuel says. "The next guy's presi-dent, and you're worthless."

For the Miranda family, Trump's most pressing outrage came from his demonization of immigrants. "This guy started his election coming down from his palace and saying Mexicans are rapists," Luis fumed. "My wife is half Mexican, and she's a good person, you ass!" Lin-Manuel, as usual, was more temperate, channeling his response into music. Starting ear-lier in November, he'd been releasing tracks from another fantasy project that invited a dream cast of artists to remix songs from the musical: Busta Rhymes writing his own verse for "My Shot"; Kelly Clarkson singing the heartbreak ballad "It's Quiet Uptown"; Queen Latifah spitting Angelica's bars on "Satisfied." (Lin-Manuel called the album *The Hamilton Mixtape*, fulfilling his original vision for the musical.) After the election, he put out a compilation track inspired by the line "Immigrants: We get the job done," where rappers of Somali, Mexican, Pakistani, and Puerto Rican descent delivered verses in English and Spanish about their communities' unher-alded contributions. "This election cycle has brought xenophobia and vil-ification of immigrants back to the forefront of US politics," Lin-Manuel posted alongside the song's lyrics. "This is a musical counterweight."

But then the Trump administration arrived at the show itself. The week after the election, Jeffrey got a call: Mike Pence, the vice president–elect, wanted to see *Hamilton* that night. "Oh, fuck," Jeffrey said to him-self. It felt like a no-win situation. Since the show was sold out, Pence had requested the emergency house seats. Jeffrey knew that if he said no, the story would leak. But he worried that if he gave Pence the seats, the cast wouldn't perform. He knew they felt angry and afraid. He'd held a meeting with the actors the morning after Election Day, and many were in tears. Most were people of color; many, like Jeffrey, were gay. Pence's homophobia was as notorious as Trump's racism.

Then he had an idea. "I thought: *If I'm giving Pence tickets, he's going to have to listen to us.*" He drafted a speech that the cast could deliver to Pence before the show began, expressing their fears about the new administra-tion. Next, he called Tommy to explain what he thought they should do. "I thought, *Well, Tommy's always the voice of reason. He'll say, 'We can't do that, Jeffrey.'*" But Tommy didn't say no. He said, "Let's get Lin on the phone." When they reached Lin-Manuel, his first response was "Call Luis!" He and his dad cut the speech down and argued that it shouldn't come before the performance. "If we have faith in our show to change hearts and minds, let's let it play out," Lin-Manuel said. "Do the speech at the end."

First, though, Jeffrey and Tommy had to meet with the cast. They explained the situation and gave each actor the option not to go on that night. Everyone decided to perform. "Fuck yeah, let's go!" Anthony Ramos shouted. Chris Jackson, who'd arranged to take that performance off, was angry that he couldn't be there too. In his absence, Jeffrey asked Brandon Victor Dixon, a Broadway veteran who'd taken over the role of Aaron Burr, to be the cast spokesperson. He agreed right away. Jeffrey knew that a speech from the stage might attract criticism, but he felt the show needed to speak up. "These are extraordinary times, and we're going to do something extraordinary," he said. "Some people may not agree with it, but I think we have to do it."

That night at the theater, Jeffrey sat next to Tommy, unsure of what would happen. Pence took his seat in the center orchestra to a mix of claps and boos from the audience. The performance began, the atmosphere charged. "Immigrants: We get the job done" received a huge ovation. At the curtain call, Pence headed quickly toward the exit, as dignitaries usually did. But Brandon Victor Dixon hailed him from the stage: "Vice President–Elect Pence, I see you walking out, but I hope you will hear us just a few more moments." At the mention of Pence's name, there were a few boos. "There's nothing to boo here, ladies and gentlemen," Dixon said, raising his arms to calm the response. "We're all here sharing a story of love." Then, as he pulled out a piece of paper from his pocket, he turned back toward Pence. "We have a message for you, sir—we hope that you will hear us out."

Camera phones came out in the audience as Dixon began:

> Vice President–Elect Pence, we welcome you, and we truly thank you for joining us here at *Hamilton: An American Musical*. We really do. We, sir, we are the diverse America who are alarmed and anxious that your new administration will not protect us, our

planet, our children, our parents, or defend us and uphold our in-alienable rights, sir. But we truly hope that this show has inspired you to uphold *our* American values and work on behalf of *all* of us. All of us. Again, we truly thank you for sharing this show, this wonderful American story told by a diverse group of men and women of different colors, creeds and orientations.

By the end of the speech, Pence had left for the lobby, but loud cheers for Dixon's remarks followed him out.

The response was swift. The next morning, Trump posted a series of tweets. "Our wonderful future V.P. Mike Pence was harassed last night at the theater by the cast of Hamilton, cameras blazing. This should not happen!" Eight minutes later: "The cast of Hamilton was very rude last night to a very good man, Mike Pence. Apologize!" Pence himself said he wasn't offended by the speech and that he very much enjoyed the show. But Trump's followers picked up his message. The Broadway company received threats from motorcycle gangs heading down from Albany. That night, at the production of *Hamilton* in Chicago, where a second company had opened in the fall, a Trump supporter started shouting at the cast in the middle of the performance. The show had to heighten security. "It was a scary time," Lin-Manuel recalls.

He got a message from the head of his agent's company that Trump wanted an apology from the *Hamilton* cast for harassing his vice pres-ident. He declined. "Nothing you said happened, and we're not going to apologize for something we didn't do." Looking back, he feels that the entire episode, which generated headlines around the world for days afterward, was something of a setup. "We realized that's the first page in the provocation playbook," he says. "It's a move to send Pence some-where, have him walk out, then go 'The way they treated him!' We were the test case."

During all the furor, Lin-Manuel was in Europe doing a publicity tour for Disney's *Moana*, which opened that Thanksgiving. "I wake up to that shitstorm, and then I have a bunch of *Moana* press to do," he recalls. "I have to go: 'Everything Trump said isn't true. But we made a movie about a young brown woman who saves the world. Can we talk about that?'"

20

FILM SCHOOL

● ●

*T*he Disney team couldn't quite believe that in the middle of the *Hamilton* maelstrom, Lin-Manuel was also finishing the songs for *Moana*. When he'd been hired for the movie back in 2014, people at Disney were still asking who he was. "We started the movie, and then he became the most famous person in the universe," the Disney composer Mark Mancina recalls. "I'm working with Lin on a song, and he goes, 'Mark, wait, I think I just won a Pulitzer Prize!' I thought, *That's the end of Lin. He's not going to write the next three songs.*"

But for Lin-Manuel, working on a new project always excited him. During the *Hamilton* run, if he had a few minutes free between shows, he'd fiddle with a *Moana* lyric in his dressing room. "I remember him on his laptop at his desk, his hair pulled back in a ponytail, with his white blousy shirt and no pants," his dressing-room-mate Jonathan Groff recalls. "There was a manic energy about Lin's room because he always had so much stuff going on." Sometimes, Chris popped into their dressing room, and Lin-Manuel would enlist him to sing the male parts on his Disney demos.

As always, figuring out the "I Want" song for the heroine proved the challenge. "Don't think about 'Let It Go'"—*Frozen*'s giant hit—Lin-Manuel told himself as he sat at the piano. His first attempt was a song called "More." Moana, the daughter of the village chief, was impatient with her home and wanted more than what her island offered. That would spur her to set out on the ocean and discover her ancestors' ancient wayfinding techniques. "I was proud of it," Lin-Manuel says. He sent it to the Disney producers and returned to the world of the American Revolution. Shortly after, he saw he'd missed a call from Bob Iger, the CEO of Disney. "I was planning two Ham4Hams; I was doing my show; I didn't respond," he recalls.

Soon, his agent John Buzzetti was on the line, furious with him. "You've got to call Bob Iger back when he calls you!" he yelled. "You're going to lose this job!" The note Lin-Manuel eventually received from the studio head: "More" wasn't there yet.

For Disney, a pretty good song wasn't sufficient. "Everything in Disney needs to live forever," the composer Bobby Lopez, who cowrote the songs for *Frozen*, says. "That's Disney's operating charter. You're trying to write a classic. There's no such thing as a throwaway song."

Lin-Manuel needed a different approach. So he tried a technique he'd figured out the last time he'd been stuck on an "I Want" song. "I took a page from my *Bring It On* lessons," he says. He returned to his parents' house in Inwood to spend the night in his old bedroom: "It was a good place to reconnect with childhood angst."

Back at the Miranda home, at his old upright piano, he realized that Moana could have a more interesting perspective. What if she loved her home and yet felt different from the people around her, finding herself inexorably drawn to the horizon? "That felt more true to my experience," he says. "I loved my childhood, I loved my neighborhood, I love where I'm from. Yet I had a dream that was so fucking insane, and that's come true beyond my wildest fantasy." He was a Puerto Rican kid growing up at the top of Manhattan; the distance from there to a show-business career seemed impossibly far. To access that feeling of distance, that longing to go beyond the world he knew, he says, "I had to go back to my childhood bedroom and remember when no one would be in my movie, when it all felt like a pipe dream."

The new song poured out that night. Moana tried to fit into her role on the island, a society woven together, but she kept returning to the water. "See the line where the sky meets the sea? It *calls* me," Moana sang. "One day I'll know how far I'll go."

Lin-Manuel asked Phillipa Soo, with her ingenue's voice, to record the demo. Then he played "How Far I'll Go" for Mark Mancina, who was arranging the *Moana* songs and writing the underlying score. Mark thought it was great. He'd been working on a tinkling sound to evoke the play of light on water—an "opalescent quality," he calls it. He added that tinkle to the opening of the demo. Moana's "I Want" song was set.

There were limits, though, to the resonance of Lin-Manuel's childhood as a source for the movie's songs. A goal for the *Moana* team was to represent Pacific Island culture authentically, and their barometer came from Opetaia Foaʻi, the musician born in Samoa. "We realized that Opetaia is the filter," Lin-Manuel says. "Everything that comes out of him is from that part of the world." When Lin-Manuel shared one early demo with a beat that felt intuitive to him, Opetaia responded: "That feels like it comes from an island, but it's not *my* island."

From then on, Lin-Manuel started with a rhythm from Opetaia. One day, in a Disney conference room, they were discussing how to establish the culture of Moana's island. "I'm sort of a romantic when it comes to the South Pacific," Opetaia admits, "so I thought a song could set the scene for our paradise." He began beating out a rhythm on the conference table, vocalizing above the beat. Lin-Manuel ran over from the other side of the room and joined in. Mark picked up a guitar and tried out a few chords over the rhythm. Their improv session soon became "Where You Are," the song that introduces Moana's world, with lyrics drawn from information that Opetaia sent Lin-Manuel about the many uses of coconuts in the Pacific Islands. "I literally stitched Opetaia's improv riffs into the chief's melody," Lin-Manuel says.

The Disney executives loved it. Then the *Moana* screenwriter saw *Hamilton*.

Jared Bush had just finished writing *Zootopia* for Disney when he learned that *Moana* needed a rewrite. Originally, in a version by Maori writer Taika Waititi, Moana had nine brothers who were trapped by a lava god, and she wanted to rescue them, but they doubted that she could pull it off. Then the story changed: Moana no longer had brothers, and her obstacle became an imperiled society that had shifted away from its ancestral seafaring ways. With a boost from her grandmother, Moana ventured out on the ocean, eventually forging a partnership with the demigod Maui to heal a rift in the cosmos and restore her island's fecundity. "We thought of it as a Disney heroine's hero's-journey musical," Jared says.

Jared wanted to learn his songwriter's style, so he went to see Lin-Manuel's new Broadway show. "My brain exploded," he says. "Watching it was like, *Holy shit! We have an unbelievable talent who tells stories in the best way. What he can do is outrageous. We need to set him up to do what he does best.* We weren't doing that."

After the show, he went up to the composer. "We're only using ten percent of your brain!" he exclaimed. "We've got to do more!" He thought perhaps whole sections of *Moana* could become sung-through.

Lin-Manuel's eyes widened. That sounded unrealistic. "You don't need to make *Moana* into *Hamilton*, Jared," he said.

But for Maui's big number, Lin-Manuel did tap into the boastful-patter realm of *Hamilton*'s swaggering warriors. From the *Moana* team, he learned that in Pacific Island origin stories, Maui was credited with creating islands from the sea, introducing fire, and harnessing the sun and the winds. In the team's conception, Maui had grown quite conceited as a result. Was he the kind of guy who'd go around saying "You're welcome"? Lin-Manuel asked the team. "Yeah!" they replied. He had the song.

He knew that Dwayne "The Rock" Johnson would be voicing Maui, so he googled wrestling videos of The Rock. ("I'm a wrestling fan," Lin-Manuel says. "It's theater.") He learned that early in his career, The Rock brought out a ukulele when he was designated the heel. "Everyone would boo, but they'd still love him," Lin-Manuel observed. That charm would allow Maui to brag without becoming entirely unlikable. "Only The Rock could sing 'You're welcome!' to the sky," he says.

He figured out The Rock's highest and lowest notes from the ukulele wrestling videos and mapped out the first two verses to a beat from Opetaia. Maui would school Moana: "What has two thumbs and pulled up the sky / When you were waddling yea high? / This guy!" The directors liked the tone and told Lin-Manuel to keep going. He got excited. Maui could launch into a patter run: "Kid, honestly I could go on and on, / I could explain every natural phenomenon." And then, soon after, Lin-Manuel found himself conducting each speedy phrase of "You're Welcome" for Dwayne Johnson in a Disney recording studio in Florida.

There was one more big number to write: the requisite Disney-villain song. Lin-Manuel had a long history to tap. He'd grown up hearing Ursula, the *Little Mermaid* sea witch, sing a campy vamp to lure poor unfortunate souls to perdition. He knew the arch sneer of Scar's purred plan to become the next Lion King. Even King George's number in *Hamilton* played as a kind of Disney-villain turn, especially in Jonathan Groff's haughty, lurid delivery, with spittle frothing at his lips.

Moana's villain was the giant crab Tamatoa, a monstrous version of *Mermaid*'s Sebastian, hoarding glittery treasures in his undersea lair; Moana had to venture past him in her hero's-journey descent into the underworld. But the crab's menace would be undercut by a comic voice turn from Jemaine Clement, half of the New Zealand parody duo Flight of the Conchords. A dozen years earlier, when Freestyle Love Supreme played the Aspen Comedy Festival, they'd opened for Flight of the Conchords, so Lin-Manuel knew Clement's deadpan style, louche with an undercurrent of sweetness.

His path into the song came from a twist of timing. In January 2016, just as Lin-Manuel needed to draft the crab's number, David Bowie passed away. Lin-Manuel had been obsessed with the British glam rocker as a child, both Bowie's anthemic duet with Freddie Mercury, "Under Pressure," and his otherworldly performance as the Goblin King in the fantasy movie *Labyrinth*, which Lin-Manuel used to watch with his sister. ("I wish the Goblin King would take you away right now," Cita teased her little brother. "And I wouldn't go after you, I'd just marry David Bowie.") On the day of Bowie's death, Chris Jackson went to Lin-Manuel's dressing room and played him an a cappella version of Bowie's vocal track from "Under Pressure." That, Lin-Manuel realized, was the eerie, imperious sound he needed for Tamatoa.

He knew Jemaine Clement could do a spot-on Bowie. In fact, Flight of the Conchords had released a Bowie music-video spoof, "Bowie's in Space," a few years earlier. "I've got to write an homage to Bowie," he told Jonathan Groff in their dressing room. "I don't know if Disney will go for it, but I have to."

Once he'd found the conceit, the lyrics flowed over a cheekily descending bass line. "Tamatoa hasn't always been this glam, I was a drab little crab once, / Now I know I can be happy as a clam, because I'm beautiful, baby!" The jewel-encrusted crustacean dismisses Maui as a "little semi-demi-mini-god," mocks Moana's ancestral call to listen to her heart, and swings to the gospel of bling as he prepares to scarf her down.

When Lin-Manuel brought "Shiny" back to Chris the next day, his stage big brother couldn't believe he'd channeled inspiration into composition so quickly. "I just looked at him like, 'You muthafucka!'" Chris recalls. "He was in the zone, just grabbing stuff out of the air."

Mark Mancina, who turned out to have a background as a Bowie impressionist, added a bridge for the song, echoing Bowie's stretched-out cadence from "Under Pressure." For a spooky undersea arrangement, he played a marimba-like instrument called a flapamba alongside some jittery rattles. The resulting demo spliced together his voice on the bridge with Lin-Manuel's best attempt at Bowie for the verses and chorus. "Neither of us were very good," Mark admits. "I've worked with better singers, but I've never seen a lyricist come up with things like Lin does. He's got that sparkle."

The film opened the day before Thanksgiving 2016, the week after Mike Pence's visit to *Hamilton*. For the *Moana* premiere in Hollywood, Lin-Manuel joined Dwayne Johnson outside the El Capitan theater to sing "You're Welcome" and introduce Auliʻi Cravalho, the Hawaiian high-schooler who made her movie debut as the voice of Moana. Inside the theater, Opetaia Foaʻi appeared onstage with Mark Mancina to perform the ancestors' song "We Know the Way." Instead of a red carpet, Disney rolled out ocean blue.

Moana proved a giant success critically and commercially. It earned the second-highest Thanksgiving-weekend opening on record (after *Frozen*), with $81 million over five days, eventually grossing over $600 million worldwide. Reviews hailed the refreshed Disney formula—an action heroine representing an indigenous culture, unshackled by a love interest, venturing across a digitally animated ocean to heal a crumbling climate. *Moana* came on the heels of Hillary Clinton's electoral defeat, so its portrayal of a world where Moana's strength and succession were assured felt like an appealing fantasy. "You're Welcome" and "Shiny" entered the Disney canon, and "How Far I'll Go" soon landed Lin-Manuel his first Oscar nomination, for Best Original Song.

While *Moana* ruled the box office, *The Hamilton Mixtape* debuted at the top of the *Billboard* 200 chart. It was an unusually high performance for a compilation album, but it arrived on the success of the *Hamilton* cast recording, which remained in the *Billboard* top ten after sixty-three weeks on the charts. The *Mixtape*'s starry roster of cover artists—Usher as Burr, Alicia Keys as Eliza, John Legend as Washington—burnished the image of *Hamilton*'s pop-music cred, and a host of remixes and tracks cut from the Broadway production (the "Adams Administration" rap at last!) offered fans a connection to a show sold out in both New York and Chicago for the foreseeable future.

Lin-Manuel had the top movie in the world, the number-one album on the charts, and the biggest Broadway smash in years. That spring, he even had the number-one book on the *New York Times* bestseller list: a companion volume to *Hamilton*, with chapters on the musical's development by Jeremy McCarter, the former theater critic for *New York* magazine who'd supported the show at the Public, and Lin-Manuel's own annotations to the printed libretto. In the entertainment world, he could do whatever he wanted next.

What he wanted was to make movies. "My choices after *Hamilton* are the film school I never got at Wesleyan," he says.

He didn't actually want to enroll in a university program; he wanted to learn on a set. And the opportunity arose when he received an invitation to star in a *Mary Poppins* sequel directed by Rob Marshall. A dancer and choreographer turned director, Marshall had helmed the last movie musical to win the Oscar for Best Picture: the 2002 adaptation of Kander and Ebb's *Chicago*. Over dinner after a *Hamilton* matinee, Rob gave Lin-Manuel the pitch: He would play Jack the Lamplighter, a successor to Dick Van Dyke's Cockney part in the first film; he'd be number two on the call sheet; and he'd get to sing and dance in London with Emily Blunt, who'd been cast as the magical nanny.

It wasn't a tough sell. Vanessa was eager to experience new cultures. She quit her law firm so she could devote her professional hours to work she valued more: advocating for climate science. Sebastian wasn't yet two, so he wouldn't need to be in school. And although *Mary Poppins* hadn't been one of Lin-Manuel's childhood favorites—he'd cried at "Feed the Birds" and turned off the movie—he was excited at the chance to learn from the lauded director. When the film version of *Chicago* came out, the year after he graduated from college, he and his housemate Sara became obsessed with it. "Rob Marshall made the best movie musical of the modern era," he says. "I wanted to see how he did that."

In the fall of 2016, he and Vanessa moved to an apartment in Notting Hill, their son and their dog in tow. On the set, Lin-Manuel was an eager student. "He definitely was clocking everything I was doing," Rob Marshall recalls. "He would come behind the monitor and want to watch." Even before shooting began, Lin-Manuel learned an important lesson: Rob rehearsed his movies as though they were Broadway shows. Many filmmakers figure out movement and acting choices in front of the camera without any prior rehearsal time. Rob, however, gave his actors weeks to take risks, make mistakes, and let the characters live in their bodies. "The most important thing for me as a director is to protect the actor," Rob says. "I want to give them a sense of safety where they can be bad so that they can become good." He could sense that his lamplighter felt nervous in his first starring film role. But Lin-Manuel learned that Rob always made sure that he got the shot before he moved on. The actors didn't have to worry about getting it right on their own. "That's really empowering," Lin-Manuel says. "You're free to fail, free to try."

Lin-Manuel knew that Rob's openness to the actors didn't stop him from planning; "Rob has the whole movie in his head," he says. But he found that Rob liked to put him in a rehearsal room with the associate choreographers and learn what he could do. Lin-Manuel claims to have two talents besides songwriting: picking up arcade prizes with a claw machine and tossing his hat onto a coatrack. He happened to demonstrate the latter talent in the presence of John DeLuca, Rob's partner. "Can you do that again when Rob's here?" John asked. He could. The trick ended up in the film. "He's making a bespoke role for you," Lin-Manuel says.

Shooting wrapped up in the summer of 2017; Lin-Manuel and his family moved back to New York, and the film went to the animators for postproduction work. Year one of Lin-Manuel's film school was complete. Rob had taught him that he could make a movie musical like a Broadway musical—through rehearsing extensively, creating a supportive environment, tapping the talents of the cast, and relying on collaborators. Vanessa respected his dedication to expanding his craft. "Lin finds a way to learn from every person and every situation he works with," she says.

Year two of Lin-Manuel's film school came from working on the long-awaited screen adaptation of *In the Heights*. It had taken a decade to find a studio that would make the movie. When the show first gained wide renown, after the 2008 Tony Awards, Universal Pictures snatched up the rights, with Lin-Manuel expected to reprise his star turn as Usnavi. "I was so naive with that Universal go-round," he admits. "I didn't know how many lights there were between the green light and when you're actually walking on set." Three years later, in 2011, the movie still hadn't gone into production. Without any big names attached, the studio calculated that the movie's budget had grown too large for its commercial prospects. It relinquished the rights. *Heights* went out to eleven potential buyers. Ten passed. The eleventh was Harvey Weinstein.

In 2016, his company signed on to develop the film, but that hardly improved its prospects. Weinstein demanded a part for Colombian pop star Shakira and wouldn't agree to shoot in Washington Heights. When sexual-harassment allegations against Weinstein were published, in 2017, Quiara, who was writing the screenplay, insisted that they take the film elsewhere. By 2018, they had extricated *Heights* from the Weinstein Company's bankruptcy troubles, but they still needed a studio.

But after *Hamilton* and *Moana*, Lin-Manuel had become a bankable star. Usually, producers had to request meetings with studios; now Hollywood's biggest studios were lining up not only to meet with Lin-Manuel but to court him. Sony put flags from Latin American countries on its windows. Paramount brought out a piragua guy to serve shaved ice in its back lot. Fox announced that it had donated a symbolic $96,000 to a children's cause in Washington Heights.

Lin-Manuel couldn't attend most of the Hollywood meetings. In February 2018, Vanessa gave birth to their second child, Francisco. Having performed in *Hamilton* during much of Sebastian's infancy, Lin-Manuel wanted to stay home with the newborn this time. When a studio invited him to its lot, he teleconferenced in. But one studio, Warner Brothers, begged to host him in person. Its executives even offered to fly him to LA. He declined; he didn't want to travel. The president of Warner Brothers tried something else: Might Lin-Manuel be willing to leave his apartment in Washington Heights and come to the Time Warner Center in Columbus Circle, half an hour downtown? He would. When he arrived at the gleaming office complex, he found the studio president awaiting him in a bodega. Warner Brothers had built a replica of Usnavi's shop, complete with café con leche, music playing, and a chef on hand to make Lin-Manuel breakfast.

It was all rather dazzling, but Lin-Manuel had been burned so many times in the film process already that he felt cautious. He didn't want to ask for too much and find the project stalled yet again over financial concerns. He thought about lowering the budget.

That's when the director Jon M. Chu stepped in. He'd just finished shooting *Crazy Rich Asians* for Warner Brothers—a film that cost $30 million to make and ended up bringing in almost $240 million worldwide. The studio was eager to partner with him on another movie. "Guys, ask for what we need, because we have leverage," Jon told Lin-Manuel and their team. "Don't make the Harvey version. This musical is about dreams! Let's get the resources to shoot our dreams!"

Eventually, Warner Brothers agreed to their terms: a summer-blockbuster release, control over casting, final cut on the film, and a fifty-five-million-dollar budget to shoot on the streets of Washington Heights. "Once we got the film away from Weinstein, I always thought it would be a scrappy indie," Lin-Manuel says. "But Jon said that our movie dreams deserve to be at the scale of Busby Berkeley and *La La Land*. He was pulling me out, saying, 'You can do this!'"

Lin-Manuel had clicked with the director from their first lunch meeting in New York. He and Vanessa had seen one of Jon's movies in the dance series Step Up on an early date, and Lin-Manuel immediately endeared himself to the filmmaker by declaring that he was "a huge fan." When they started talking about their childhoods, they found they'd grown up on the same '80s pop culture: G.I. Joes, ThunderCats, Transformers. They both carried early versions of camcorders around their high schools, navigating the awkwardness of adolescent dynamics through the viewfinder. And both were the children of immigrants—in Jon's case, parents who'd left Taiwan for California—who worked endless hours so the next generation could enjoy more opportunities. With Quiara to oversee the story, Lin-Manuel entrusted Jon with the film: "Take it and run."

At long last, what Lin-Manuel considered year two of his film school could begin in earnest. He and Quiara took Jon on a tour of Washington

Heights: the bodegas, the car services, the hair salons, the best spots for café con leche. As Quiara updated the script (less emphasis on gentrification, more on undocumented immigrants), Jon started to envision the shots. Quiara had shown him the giant Highbridge Pool, a public recreation center off Amsterdam Avenue at 173rd Street. What if they staged "96,000," the ensemble song where everyone imagines what they'd do if they won the lottery, as a massive aquatic dance number, like a classic Hollywood water ballet? What if they filmed the love duet between Nina and Benny like a Fred Astaire fantasy sequence and allowed the characters to somehow dance up the side of an apartment building? "The thing we're doing is making people's dreams on these blocks as big as any Hollywood movie," Jon says. Lin-Manuel was floored. "I would never have thought of that, because I'm too inside the songs," he says. Jon's ideas, he marveled, were "fucking insane."

As the shooting dates approached in the summer of 2019, a question remained: Would Lin-Manuel appear in the movie? He'd received positive notices for *Mary Poppins Returns*, which had come out at Christmas, grossing $360 million worldwide and landing him a Golden Globe nomination for Best Supporting Actor. But at thirty-nine, he felt too old to play Usnavi. He didn't have final say over casting, but he was delighted when the role of Usnavi went to Anthony Ramos, who'd brought his boyish charm and barrio authenticity to *Hamilton*. Watching rehearsals, though, Lin-Manuel sensed impending regret: "I'm going to be kicking myself if I'm not part of this." Quiara nudged him: "If this was just a movie musical starring Latinos, you'd be auditioning." She had an idea. Movies tended to run shorter than stage musicals, so quite a few songs would likely be cut, including "Piragua," the sweetly resilient interlude sung by the shaved-ice vendor. But if there was a name attached to the Piragua Guy, maybe they could justify keeping his number. Back in 2008, Lin-Manuel had made an entire parody web series about the search for the next Piragua Guy. Little did he imagine that the search would lead to him.

For the film, Lin-Manuel decided that he would play the Piragua Guy as his Abuelo Güisin, who had passed away as the musical opened on Broadway. He donned baggy cargo shorts and wore socks pulled high up to his knees. He let his belly hang out and tucked a cowboy novella into his back pocket. "I was cosplaying my grandpa." As a cameo treat, he brought

in his longtime stage brother Chris Jackson to play the Piragua Guy's nem-
esis: the embodiment of corporate ice cream–truck culture, Mister Softee.

When shooting began, Lin-Manuel signed Jon's script and wrote,
"Don't fuck it up." He added a smiley face. He felt grateful and almost over-
awed. He even asked where the casting call for extras was so he could stop
by to thank people for showing up to make his dream a reality. It was hard
to believe that the story he'd begun as a college sophomore was becoming a major Hollywood movie on the very blocks where he'd first imagined it. Jon shot Nina and Benny's first love song, "When You're Home,"
in J. Hood Wright Park, a Washington Heights enclave where Lin-Manuel
and Vanessa strolled on one of their early dates. "It's crazy that we're doing
this song in the park that I wrote the song about!" he said to Jon. He called
his wife to come down to the park, where she could see a childhood vista:
her own abuela's building. Vanessa, not prone to excessive emotion, burst
into tears.

Throughout the shoot, Lin-Manuel eagerly watched Jon and his filmmaking team. "I think of Lin as a sponge where he just soaks up all the
knowledge in the room," Alice Brooks, Jon's longtime director of photography, says. "In retrospect, I realized he was spending that summer to
prepare to go be a director next." Observing their choices on *Heights* offered Lin-Manuel a useful counterpart to the lessons he'd gleaned from
Mary Poppins Returns. "To me, Jon is a composite of Rob Marshall–level
planning, with a checklist of the stuff he wants to get, and openness to
what's happening that day," Lin-Manuel says. On the day they shot Usnavi
and Vanessa's final duet, for example, Jon noticed that the apartment they
were using didn't let in much outside noise. Even though they'd prerecorded the vocals, Jon had an instinct: They could sing the duet live. It
was already a tricky continuous shot to pull off; doing the vocals live on
set would make it harder. "It's not a game-day decision Rob would make,"
Lin-Manuel says. "But Jon called it in the room." That sense of almost freestyle improvisation, that instinct to see what might happen in the shoot
itself, he felt, could serve him well.

The most difficult day of shooting came on a sweltering Monday.
The crew started setting up at 4:30 a.m. They had until sundown to use a
courtyard surrounded by apartment buildings to stage the musical's second-act showstopper "Carnaval del Barrio." It wasn't strictly necessary for

the plot, but it was central to the story's spirit of communal resilience, re-storing a sense of power after the barrio blackout. If they couldn't get the eight-minute-long sequence that day, however, the song would have to be cut from the movie. "It was the greatest pressure I'd felt," Jon says. "It was hot as hell, it had every single character in the movie, and we only had one day." The courtyard could barely even fit the six cameras Jon had brought to capture every angle.

As the song began, everyone felt the pressure. Actors iced themselves. Ankles started to swell. Even the ground radiated heat. But as the ensemble got into the dance, the energy began to rise. The song celebrated Latinidad by saluting the community's places of origin: Mexico, Cuba, the Dominican Republic, Puerto Rico. Each group had its own dance, its own chant, its own flag to raise. Elders danced alongside children. "It becomes gnarly," Jon recalls. "You can feel it. No one's half-assing it." The dance built and built.

From a fire escape balcony, Lin-Manuel, playing Piragüero and chan-neling Abuelo Güisin, shouted, "¡Pa'rriba esa bandera!" (Raise up this flag!)

Anthony as Usnavi joined him: "¡Y cuando yo me muera / Entiérrame en mi tierra!" (And when I die, bury me in my homeland!)

Finally, the entire company erupted in a cheer for their homelands' flags: "¡Alza la bandera!" (Raise the flag!)

They'd done it.

Jon called "Cut!" but no one stopped. They all kept jumping up and down with their flags, chanting "Latinos, Latinos!" and "New York, New York!" There were seventy-five dancers in the courtyard celebrating. Then they looked up at Lin-Manuel on the fire escape above them. He couldn't come down because a camera was blocking his exit.

The chant began: "Lin! Lin! Lin! Lin!"

"He was bawling," Jon says. "He's looking at what he's manifested since Wesleyan: giving people opportunities, characters, jobs."

"Lin! Lin! Lin! Lin!"

"It was like a laser from the moon coming into the courtyard in Wash-ington Heights," Jon says. "Everyone's crying, and it doesn't stop for a long, long time."

At the end of July, Lin-Manuel left the shoot. He and Vanessa were taking their kids to Wales, where he was playing a swashbuckling aeronaut for the HBO adaptation of Philip Pullman's fantasy series *His Dark Materials*. (He was cast because the producer saw him bound onto a stage and thought he resembled the human version of the aeronaut's animal avatar, a rabbit.) He and Vanessa had read the series together when they started dating, and playing a cowboy of the skies, he thought, would offer another opportunity to honor his John Wayne–loving Abuelo Güisin.

On the Friday that the *Heights* shoot wrapped, Alice Brooks, the director of photography, got a call from her agent: "Lin wants you to read a script and meet him on Tuesday." He was ready to direct his first feature film, and he wanted her to be his cinematographer.

In a way, it was an echo of the moment two decades earlier when Lin-Manuel saw Jonathan Larson's *Rent* and realized that he could switch from making movies to writing musicals. Now, having fulfilled his dream of dramatizing his own community's stories and sounds through musicals, he was going to make a movie.

In fact, he was going to make a movie about Jonathan Larson.

21

TICK, TICK

• •

Lin-Manuel was filming *Mary Poppins Returns* in London when he received an email from a producer, Julie Oh, asking if he had any interest in directing a film adaptation of Jonathan Larson's solo show, *Tick, Tick . . . Boom!*. Julie had met Lin-Manuel while he shopped the movie version of *In the Heights* and had been impressed by his filmmaking instincts. "It didn't feel like it was something new he was trying on," she says. "It felt like something he'd hung up for a while as he did musicals." She'd seen him play the role of Jonathan in the 2014 Encores revival and read his piece in the *New York Times* describing his lifelong debt to Larson. "That was the key to everything for me," Julie says, "realizing what Jonathan meant to him." She asked the Larson family how they felt about Lin-Manuel.

As it turned out, they loved him. Back in 2008, when *In the Heights* won the Best Musical Tony Award, the Larsons had been invited to an after-party by the producer Jeffrey Seller, who had also produced *Rent*. "We walked into the party, and it was packed—Lin had half of Puerto Rico there!" Julie Larson, Jonathan's older sister, recalls. "Someone pulled Lin over and said, 'This is Al Larson.' He threw his arms around my dad and started crying. It was so meaningful to us." It didn't matter to the Larsons that he hadn't directed anything beyond YouTube videos since high school. He had something they valued more—a deep respect for Jonathan's legacy and firsthand experience as a composer in his twenties working part-time jobs and struggling for years to get someone to put on his show. "No one else would know how to do it with the same honesty," Julie says, "because he'd been in the same place as my brother."

Once the Larsons were on board, Julie Oh emailed Lin-Manuel. She knew he was, as she says, "the busiest man in the universe" and that he was on set in the United Kingdom. To her surprise, she heard back right away. He'd been preparing for this moment. "If they only let me make one, this is the one I understand."

He'd learned from working with Rob Marshall on *Mary Poppins Returns* that he could develop the film as he would a musical, with readings and workshops and plenty of time for rehearsal before the cameras rolled. He knew that he wanted to build out Larson's universe beyond a monologue to show Greenwich Village in the early 1990s with the host of actors, roommates, musicians, and mentors who populated Larson's bohemian sphere. And following Jon Chu's impulse to give everyday aspirations a Hollywood scale, he wanted to imagine the monologue's songs as fantasy numbers, portraying the theatrical dreams that sustained Larson through the drudgery of his shifts as a waiter in the Moondance Diner.

For the lead role, Lin-Manuel had a casting idea. In London in 2018, he'd seen a revival of *Angels in America* with Andrew Garfield in the lead, braving death and betrayal and supernatural visitations and a recommitment to life over the course of a seven-hour production that later transferred to Broadway and won him the Best Leading Actor in a Play Tony. "I had never seen such a fearless performance onstage in my life," Lin-Manuel recalled. "I knew that I needed that kind of intensity to play Jonathan Larson."

What he didn't know was whether the Spider-Man star could sing. But Lin-Manuel had learned Rob Marshall's principle: Protect the actors. Give them the safety to be bad so they can become good. When Andrew came up to Washington Heights for a secret script read-through workshop, Lin-Manuel said he didn't have to sing if he didn't want to. But a week later, by the end of the workshop (and with the help of a vocal coach), he'd begun trying out the a cappella ditty Jonathan wrote to celebrate his bohemian friends, "BoHo Days." Lin-Manuel gave him the ultimate compliment: He took off a shoe and threw it at him.

In June 2019, with a star in place, Lin-Manuel, Julie Oh, and the screenwriter, *Dear Evan Hansen*'s Steven Levenson, took the project to buyers. It was a giddy Hollywood trip, with studios one-upping one another to land the film. Netflix won the bidding war.

On the drive back to the airport in Los Angeles, Lin-Manuel was excited to tell Steven about a few of the other projects he was working on. He'd released another set of tracks inspired by *Hamilton*, including a new song he'd written with John Kander and a remix of "One Last Time" that featured former president Obama himself reading George Washington's Farewell Address. He was going to rejoin Freestyle Love Supreme for a Broadway run in the fall. And he needed to finish the songs for *Vivo*, a Sony animated movie that he was also starring in; write another set of songs for *Encanto*, a Disney musical he'd helped create; and compose some new numbers for a live-action remake of *The Little Mermaid* that he was writing with Alan Menken. All that was in addition to directing his first feature film.

Steven was curious. "Can I just ask you: What drives you to keep going after *Hamilton*, frankly?"

Lin-Manuel answered right away. "Because I know someday I'm going to die."

It wasn't a glib response. Like Larson, he heard the constant *tick-tick* of mortality. And in a way, he'd accepted it. He'd reached a position where he no longer had to work for money, and his legacy was secure. "*Hamilton* is the first line of my obituary," he says. "I'm never topping it as a cultural event. So then the question becomes: What do you really want to do next?" His answer: "I can only do things out of love. And I like to work on things I'll learn from." A lot of projects fell under that rubric. "In some ways, he's just as relentless as his father," Vanessa says, "though he knows better how to take breaks and relax."

When they started production on *Tick, Tick . . . Boom!*, he didn't seem overwhelmed. "He took what he knew about theater and put it into film," director of photography Alice Brooks says. That meant above all an emphasis on collaboration. Instead of the different departments working separately, he gathered Steven, Alice, the production designer, and his assistant director together with a storyboard artist so they could come up with ideas for each scene. He also adopted Tommy Kail's philosophy that the best idea in the room wins, wherever it comes from. "A lot of first-time directors have a tight grip to prove that they belong," Steven says. "Lin just

had ease and a tremendous sense of self-assurance that came out in allowing other people to do their best work."

He was excited to learn from his collaborators. Early on, Alice began
camera tests to figure out which lenses to use in the shoot. "How involved
do you want to be?" she asked the director. "I know nothing about camera
lenses," he admitted. "But I want to know everything. What would your
process be?" She explained that they'd shoot tests, assess possibilities, and
decide on a lens. When they tried it, he asked her to explain why she preferred one option over another. At the start of the shoot, he sometimes
forgot that *tilt* meant moving the camera up and down, and *pan* meant
moving it left and right. "Let's tilt left," he'd say, and the team would remind him, "No, that's *pan*!" But by the end of the shoot, he'd picked up the
technical language to describe the effect he wanted. "Lin's like a sponge,"
Julie Larson says. "He was learning from Alice, asking questions of everybody, and soaking it all up."

From the start, though, he had a clear vision for the film that guided
his choices. "Lin's incredibly decisive," Steven says. "He gets everyone's
input and then says: 'This is what we're doing.'" He knew Larson's life
well enough that he could trust his gut. When his longtime friend Robin
de Jesús, who'd played Usnavi's cousin Sonny in *Heights*, arrived on set to
play Jonathan's best friend, he wondered if Lin-Manuel would have Alice,
his cinematographer, actually direct the film. Then he saw how the team
worked. The director asked Alice if she could shoot at an angle to convey the cramped, crooked apartment where Jonathan felt trapped or if she
could shoot closer on Andrew's face to align the audience with Jonathan's
point of view. "It was Lin directing," Robin says, "which allowed Alice to
do her job really freakin' well."

One of the sequences Lin-Manuel envisioned took place in a swimming pool where Jonathan found inspiration for a song he needed to write
while he completed his laps. When they went to shoot the scene, they had
a stroke of luck: Andrew turned out to have incredible speed in the pool;
his father was a swim instructor. They crossed the scene off the shot list
with time to spare. Then Lin-Manuel turned to his underwater-camera
operator. "What cool things don't I know that you can do?" he asked.
The operator revealed that he could film upside down. "That's cool!" the

director said. "Let's do it!" Lin-Manuel's tool kit was expanding by the minute. "Directing is fun!" he texted his producer, Julie Oh.

Eight days into the shoot, they began filming outside Jonathan's old apartment on Greenwich Street. Thanks to a video Jonathan had shot of his apartment for insurance purposes just before he died, they were able to re-create his rooms exactly, down to the leaky ceiling, the piles of albums, and the Casio keyboard. It felt almost unbelievable: They were getting paid to make a movie celebrating their artistic hero in the place where he'd lived. "We had the most fun filming ever," Alice recalls. "Lin and I said to each other: 'This is the best day of our lives.'"

The next day, Netflix shut down production.

It was March 12, 2020. There was a global pandemic. No one could film anything. Broadway had shut down too.

It all felt devastating. They'd been making a movie set during the AIDS plague, and now they found themselves in the midst of another plague. People were dying around them. The future was uncertain.

Initially, Netflix told them to expect a two-week hiatus. But the suspension dragged on. Everyone was holed up, kept apart. "We did *Tick, Tick* Zooms," Julie Oh recalls. "We were shell-shocked, faced with the possibility that it could all go away."

—

In those early-pandemic days, as the COVID death toll mounted, Lin-Manuel sheltered in place with his family. In the mornings, he dusted off his substitute-teacher outfit to give his kids a little homeschooling. (Vanessa, who'd recently fused her scientific and legal interests to found a program in cosmetics regulation at Fordham Law School, alternated days with him.) He took their dog for long, socially distanced walks along the Hudson. He Zoomed into *The Tonight Show* to raise money for the Broadway Cares emergency assistance fund. The *Hamilton* companies that had been shut down around the world—New York, London, Chicago, three tours—hosted "The Zoom Where It Happens" to boost morale.

No one knew when live entertainment would return. Movie theaters were closed too. Jon Chu had been working on a cut of the *Heights* film in New York, anticipating its summer release, when the pandemic struck. He had to race back to his family in California before the airports shut down. Warner Brothers pulled the film's release date; yet again, *In the Heights* was on hold.

Hamilton, however, found a different venue. In June 2016, before the original Broadway cast departed, Jeffrey Seller and the producing team had financed a live recording of the show. Disney bought the movie for seventy-five million dollars, planning to release it in theaters in 2021, once the show had run for several years. (Jeffrey shared a portion of the profits from the film sale with the Broadway cast.) But after the pandemic hit, in 2020, the studio head suggested another option. Disney Plus, the studio's streaming service, needed more titles. Revenue had dried up from amusement parks, which no one could visit, and no new productions were being filmed. Attracting subscribers to Disney Plus became the corporate priority.

On the morning of May 12, Lin-Manuel woke up with a jolt. Vanessa noticed his energy ("More than usual," she commented). He couldn't sit still until he'd tweeted the news: "Our Hamilton film. THIS July 3rd. On Disney+."

Starting July 3, instead of having to shell out hundreds of dollars for a Broadway ticket, everyone could see *Hamilton* in their own home. Everyone who had Disney Plus, that is. Over the July Fourth weekend, downloads of the Disney Plus app soared by 74 percent. About 2.6 million people had seen *Hamilton* on Broadway in the nearly five years before the pandemic halted performances. In the weeks before the musical streamed, Disney Plus added three million new subscribers.

As the release date approached, Lin-Manuel felt absolutely giddy at the prospect of watching the show alongside his millions of Twitter followers, live-tweeting each moment. At the appointed hour, 7:00 p.m., he and Vanessa settled their kids with popcorn and Magna-Tiles in front of the TV. For the next two and a half hours, he enjoyed the thrill of seeing the musical unfold and simultaneously getting to share everything he loved about it. Using the hashtag Hamilfilm, he tweeted shout-outs to the cast and crew, anecdotes about backstage shenanigans, stories about writing the songs, and cute reactions from his kids. He reposted favorite fan tweets alongside Vanessa's responses. ("I always boo when Lin kisses someone else onstage," she joked.) At the end of the stream, he felt overwhelmingly gratified. "Thank you for tonight," he posted in a final tweet. "I'm so grateful you just have the whole thing now. With this extraordinary company and crew. It's yours."

The world that received *Hamilton* in July 2020, however, was not the world that had made it the toast of 2016. The show's promise of a multiethnic America fueled by immigrant ingenuity seemed, after four years of the Trump presidency, like an Obama-era fantasy. The Black Lives Matter protests that followed the murder of George Floyd in May brought terms like *systemic racism* out of the academic Left and into popular usage. Amid this racial reckoning, the import of *Hamilton* was up for debate. And as the audience for the musical spilled out beyond the theater into every home that had an internet connection, the conversation expanded as well, with think pieces and social media takes proliferating.

For some commentators, *Hamilton*'s power remained undiminished, perhaps even augmented. It wasn't "just a classic American musical," the culture critic Soraya Nadia McDonald wrote; it could "also act as an antidote to white fear as it reminds the public that Black and brown people—just like *Hamilton*'s titular 'bastard, orphan, son of a whore'—are not throwing away their shot." Others, though, contended that the musical's inclusive casting masked the complicity of all the Founders in establishing the system of racial injustice that the Black Lives Matter movement opposed. The left-wing provocateur Ishmael Reed reposted a piece he'd written when the show premiered, titled "Black Actors Dress Up like Slave Traders . . . and It's Not Halloween." This time, he found a more receptive audience for his critique. The *New York Times* ran a forum in which five critics debated the musical: Did it downplay slavery? Did it sideline its female characters? Did it put a contemporary sheen on white male patriarchy, or did it open America's founding narrative for everyone to claim?

Lin-Manuel didn't take issue with these questions. "All the criticisms are valid," he tweeted. Nor did he think the show's characters should be exempt from judgment. "None of these fuckers were anti-slavery," he says. He'd written a third Cabinet Battle for Hamilton and Jefferson to debate the abolition of the slave trade, then cut it before the show opened; since the Founders hadn't resolved the problem, he thought the number didn't advance the story. "Why would I put it in to make the audience feel good that we've addressed it?" he asks. "I'd rather take the hit." He didn't believe that the musical glorified the Founders; he'd wanted to show them not as monuments but as flawed humans. Nevertheless, for some critics, the act of centering and humanizing the stories of Washington and Jefferson perpetuated a harmful view of American history focused on elite oppressors, especially in a moment when protesters were toppling monuments to slaveholders around the country.

In the agitated atmosphere of the pandemic, the speed of social media commentary and mounting fury under the Trump administration created a volatile environment. Lin-Manuel felt the need to apologize, through *Hamilton*'s official Twitter account, for the show waiting days after George Floyd's killing to speak up in support of protesters, even though he'd issued support through his personal account. "That we have not yet firmly spoken the inarguable truth that Black Lives Matter and denounced systematic racism and white supremacy from our official *Hamilton* channels is a moral failure on our part," he said in a video. "As the writer of the show, I take responsibility and apologize." He acknowledged that *Hamilton* wouldn't exist without the contributions of Black artists, both the generations of hip-hop artists who inspired the musical and the cast and crew who'd brought it to the stage. "While we live in a country where Black people are under attack," he concluded, "it's up to us to do the work to be better allies and have each other's backs."

He'd seen the discourse around the musical shift in an altered environment before. When he took *Hamilton* to Puerto Rico to help the island's economy revive after Hurricane Maria in 2019, he'd anticipated an emotional homecoming. A decade earlier, he'd returned to *In the Heights* to play Usnavi on the first Equity tour to San Juan. (For most Broadway shows, the cost and delay of shipping sets across the ocean made Puerto Rico tours prohibitive.) After his childhood summers estranged from other kids in Vega Alta, he loved coming back to his parents' birthplace as the star of a show about Caribbean immigrants. He felt like "'Lin-Manuel Miranda, the favorite son,'" he says. When he pulled out the Puerto Rican flag at the end of his *In the Heights* Tony speech, he'd earned legions of fans on the island. In San Juan, when the cast brought out their flags in "Carnaval del Barrio," the audience pulled out their own banderas to wave along. Receiving that applause "closed something in me I didn't even know was open," Lin-Manuel later told Oprah.

But in 2019, the story of another Caribbean immigrant making his way in New York found a different reception. In addition to the damage and death toll from the hurricane, Puerto Rico still suffered a colonial legacy of crippling debt, and a financial oversight board appointed by President Obama had imposed unpopular austerity measures—there'd been hundreds of school closures plus tuition hikes and budget cuts at the University of Puerto Rico. Lin-Manuel had originally supported Obama's plan, invoking Hamilton's plea for hurricane relief as he petitioned Congress to pass a debt-restructuring bill. ("I write about Puerto Rico today just as Hamilton wrote about St. Croix in his time," he said in a 2016 opinion piece for the *New York Times*.) It had seemed to him the only way forward with a Republican Congress that wouldn't approve debt relief without an oversight board. "I was trying to do the right thing by the island," he says. "Obviously, I wasn't in support of the fiscal board. I couldn't imagine the closure of schools." Nevertheless, his public statement came to haunt him.

In the fall of 2017, when he visited the University of Puerto Rico, his father's alma mater, and announced that he would play Hamilton in a fundraising production at the campus theater, which *Hamilton* was paying one million dollars to restore, most of the audience cheered. But then a small group of students took the stage. LIN-MANUEL—¡NUESTRAS VIDAS NO SON TU TEATRO! their sign proclaimed (Lin-Manuel—Our Lives Are Not Your Theater!). He didn't feel threatened—his own father had been a frequent protester during his student days—but he regretted that he'd become associated with an austerity policy that he didn't support. "It feels awful to be the face of that," he says. "It wasn't something I understood well enough. I made a mistake, and it's hung around my neck forever. I hate it."

Immediately after Hurricane Maria struck, Lin-Manuel had rallied a starry lineup of Puerto Rican musicians (Luis Fonsi, Jennifer Lopez, Marc Anthony, Rita Moreno) for a benefit single, "Almost Like Praying," that remixed the "Maria" refrain from *West Side Story* with a reggaeton roll call of Puerto Rico's seventy-eight municipalities. He'd helped raise forty-three million dollars for hurricane relief through his father's Hispanic Federation, and all the profits from *Hamilton* in Puerto Rico (eventually totaling fifteen million dollars) would go to the island's arts organizations. Nonetheless, as the opening date approached, employee unions at the university told Lin-Manuel that they would strike if the production went ahead. Workers were facing the loss of tuition benefits for their children, and the publicity around *Hamilton* provided an occasion to gain attention for their cause. As a union show, *Hamilton* couldn't cross a picket line. Though Luis tried to negotiate with the unions, university regulations prohibited police on campus, and facing potential protests without law enforcement nearby felt like too big a risk, especially after the threats the company had received following Mike Pence's visit. Instead of performing in the university theater it had rebuilt, *Hamilton* moved to the governor's theater, Centro de Bellas Artes, where *In the Heights* had played back in 2010.

Luis, who was handling Puerto Rican operations for the tour, didn't blame the unions. "The fiscal crisis, Maria, all the shit this island goes through—people can't calibrate anymore what's the appropriate response to what," he told a filmmaker who was shooting a documentary about his efforts. "And so the appropriate response for many to everything is 'Fuck you!' Because they have been stepped on!" He broke off, almost in tears.

Rather than quelling the controversy, however, the change of venue fueled it. Now *Hamilton* was officially associated with a pro-statehood governor whose administration had drawn ire for suppressing Puerto Rican cultural celebrations in the school curriculum. In a post on *80grados*, a left-leaning journal, the activist Amárilis Pagán Jiménez asked why San Juan should support a show that chronicled "la historia del mismo maldito país que nos tiene bajo un indigno estado colonial" (the history of the same damn country that has us under an unworthy colonial state). The irony wasn't lost on Lin-Manuel. "Boy, is *Hamilton* a bad fit for raising money for Puerto Rico," he says. "It's singing about the financial system that traps Puerto Rico in debt."

Opening night coincided with Hamilton's birthday, January 11. Despite the controversy, the run was sold out. It had attracted publicity far beyond the island. That morning, a CBS television crew surprised Lin-Manuel with a video from his eighth-grade English teacher, Dr. Herbert. In his customary button-up shirt and large glasses, speaking in his gentle southern lilt, he greeted his former student. "I'm sure you didn't imagine when you were in the eighth grade and set some of 'The Chosen' to music that it would lead you where you are today, but congratulations,"

Dr. Herbert said. "I've heard a lot about what you're doing in Puerto Rico, and I wish you well in those endeavors." The former student wiped away tears.

On the website for the San Juan daily paper *El Nuevo Día*, however, comments on a pro-*Hamilton* article were characteristically contentious. Though many people lauded Lin-Manuel for coming to the island and didn't blame him for the education cuts, one commenter said in Spanish that Puerto Ricans who enjoyed *Hamilton* would be "happy colonized subjects applauding like seals at the victory of the independence struggle of the United States."

That night before the show opened, Lin-Manuel wasn't sure if there would be protests. Nor was he sure he'd remember all his lines. He hadn't performed the role for two and a half years. He'd accidentally flooded his dressing room by rinsing off without closing the shower door. He was under attack for causing harm to an island he only wanted to help. "Everything about it sucked," he says.

When the performance began, Lin-Manuel experienced a different sensation, something he'd never encountered before. He made his entrance, singing "'My name is Alexander Hamilton'" as he strode downstage, not knowing how the audience would receive him. There was a roar. Two thousand people rose in a standing ovation that seemed like it would last forever. "It was the first time I *felt* a cheer," he said after the show. "I felt my *hair* move."

Doing the show provided its own balm. During "Hurricane," Hamilton's recollection of the storm that ravaged his childhood island, the hall was hushed. "'In the eye of a hurricane, there is quiet,'" Lin-Manuel sang. ("I feel like I'm going back to Maria when I sing it," he later said.) The musical had become, in a way, about the island's trauma after the disaster.

At the curtain call, Lin-Manuel brought his father onstage. "A lot of people moved a lot of mountains to have us be here in Puerto Rico tonight and to raise as much money as we can for Puerto Rico while we're here," he said to applause. "I'm very proud to say that no one moved more mountains than Vega Alta's own, my father, Luis Miranda."

Luis, wearing a shiny red showman's jacket, embraced his son. In Spanish, he told the cheering audience that he'd taught his children to hold family and country as the most important things in life. Bringing *Hamilton* to Puerto Rico, he said, fulfilled both. "Thank you to my family, that has withstood all this madness, and of course, to my genius son, Lin-Manuel." His son whipped a giant Puerto Rican flag out of his breast pocket and waved it high, tearing up. The crowd exploded.

After the show, however, Lin-Manuel faced a press conference that seemed more like the grilling of a politician. Did he support the austerity board? How did he feel about Trump's plan to divert disaster-relief funds from Puerto Rico to finance the border wall with Mexico? Why had he moved the show away from the university? What did it mean to bring *Hamilton* to Puerto Rico? What entitled him, a New Yorker, to speak on behalf of the island?

"Politics are so anathema to me," he says, looking back. "I've evolved in finding my lane. I'm not here to be mayor; I just want to bring my art here." Performing the role again was a joy, but the interviews and fundraisers afterward wrung him dry. He felt like he was back in Vega Alta as a boy, caught between cultures. On opening night, he told the reporters in Puerto Rico about his musical, "I'm like a little kid with it: I just want you to be proud of what I made."

The following year, as the discourse around *Hamilton* crescendoed with its release on Disney Plus in the summer of 2020, Lin-Manuel no longer had nightly performances to ground him. *Tick, Tick . . . Boom!* was on indefinite hold. He felt isolated in the middle of the pandemic. Social media, which had once provided an adoring audience in his pocket, now seemed increasingly like a space of mockery and attack. ("Why Gen Z Turned on Lin-Manuel Miranda" ran a headline that summer in *Rolling Stone*, which four years earlier had featured him on its cover.) "If you looked at Twitter, every trending topic was *Hamilton*, for good and bad," Lin-Manuel recalls. "I was at home with nothing to do but rage-read. I was drinking from the firehose."

Feeling deluged by the online world, he went back to the therapist he'd seen the summer after he broke up with Meredith. "I was giving myself a lot of agita," he says. "The energy I needed for my family and friends was being sucked out. It was the beginning of the end of my relationship with Twitter."

He reached out to a longtime mentor to find out what to do when the criticism grew too loud. "I don't know how to drown out the negative chatter anymore," he wrote. "Not well enough to get back to my piano, anyway. I know that scrutiny comes with the success of the thing, but god, the scrutiny. Sorry for launching right in, but there's very few people I can talk to about this. I'm struggling with it. Just the weight of all of it."

Stephen Sondheim replied right away. He offered love and sympathy— "and tea, if you want it." His protégé's predicament seemed totally understandable. "I don't know why this hasn't paralyzed you already," he wrote. "I'm sure it's already occurred to you, but the simplest way is the best. Isolate yourself from everything but family and work." Sondheim had suffered the deluge, too, and knew that chatter around the work—both admiring and critical—would never let up. "The only way to deal with it is to stick with your collaborators and write something.

"Preferably," he advised, "a musical."

22

BOOM

••

*L*in-Manuel took Sondheim's advice. He had a musical in the works with Sony Animation, a project he'd started back in 2009 that had followed a similar trajectory as the *Heights* film: One studio acquired it eagerly during the *Heights* wave and then let it languish, but in 2016, after *Hamilton* hit, another studio revived its fortunes. It was a love story about an elderly Cuban musician who plays in the Havana plaza with Vivo, a cuddly and spunky little kinkajou—a South American rainforest mammal—voiced by Lin-Manuel. When the musician dies before he can share his final song with his long-lost love, a singer who'd left for Miami, Vivo sets off to Florida to deliver the music. Quiara Alegría Hudes, writing the screenplay, added a wacky, purple-haired tween based on her own younger sister to aid Vivo in his quest, and Alex Lacamoire, drawing on his Cuban background, was contributing his first film score.

It was a story about the power of music to cross divides, to reunite Caribbeans across the diaspora, and, in a way, compensate for loss. The project, based on a story idea by *High School Musical's* Peter Barsocchini, had come to Lin-Manuel shortly after his Abuelo Güisin passed away: What would you do if you lost your partner, your mentor, your protector? Might a song keep his spirit alive, especially in the voice of an emigrant on the mainland? He'd written the initial songs while he was playing Usnavi, and they continued the mode of *In the Heights*: a catchy opening rap for Vivo to win over the audience; a nostalgic mambo for his Cuban mentor; a 1980s-esque Latin freestyle number to speed Vivo into Miami.

When Quiara introduced Gabi, the irrepressible tween, and told Lin-Manuel that the character followed the beat of her own drum, he heard her rhythm right away. "I got it, I got it," he said, muttering *own drum, ho-hum, unh-unh.* ("Lin is just a walking rhythm seeker," Quiara says.) In ten minutes, he'd come up with a Missy Elliott–style rap for young Gabi: "I bounce to the beat of my own drum! / I'm a wow in a world full of ho-hum!" He added an enthusiastic solo on a recorder that Ms. Ames had given him in elementary school, all his own preteen energy unleashed.

The movie was in good shape, fast-tracked by Sony for a 2020 release before Thanksgiving. Then the pandemic hit. As lockdown continued, the film's future grew less clear. Would it ever come out? Would anyone get to see it? Its creators seemed to be in a parallel position to Vivo and Gabi, who get stuck in the Everglades on their way to Miami, moored on a raft without a clear path ahead. In the script, there was a spoken scene: Gabi shows Vivo her erratic style of drumming, and when he lays on an actual beat, it propels them forward. Lin-Manuel pitched a song instead. "The fate of the movie was uncertain," he later explained. "We were trying to figure out how to keep going from our respective homes." In that mindset, a chorus for Vivo came into his head:

All I can do when the road bends is lean into the curve.
And all I can do when the tank's run dry is see what's in reserve.
And all I can do when the plans break down is stay on my feet.
And all I can do at the end of the day is play on, play on, and keep the
*   beat.*

It was an anthem of resilience, a testament to the power of a beat to keep hope alive. "The lyrics are so resonant of that time," *Vivo* director Kirk DeMicco says. "Our journey mirrored the movie: The road bends with a global pandemic, and we had to keep the beat."

While Lin-Manuel figured out the notes, his son Sebastian came over. "Can I help?" the five-year-old asked. He noodled on the keyboard until he landed on a phrase. It started on the home key, reached up, came back, dipped down, and returned home. "Play that again," his dad requested. The phrase ended up in Vivo and Gabi's song. "Finding that with my son was pretty special," Lin-Manuel reflected.

In addition to *Vivo*, he had another animated musical in development, this one with Disney. Even before *Moana* wrapped, he'd mentioned to the producers that next time, he'd love to be part of creating the story, too—perhaps something closer to home. He told them that he wanted to do "a definitive Latin American Disney musical."

He started talking about possibilities with Jared Bush, the *Moana* screenwriter, and Byron Howard, Jared's directing partner. They kept coming back to questions of family. In an early version of *Moana*, the heroine had nine brothers, but the studio decided that they couldn't devote that much narrative real estate to establishing characters who were going to be left behind as soon as Moana set sail. For the new film, the creators wanted to depict a heroine enmeshed in her family. In a discussion group Disney hosted for Latino employees, participants often shared stories about extended families—an abuela who anchored the household, a *tío* who seemed a little off, one *prima* who outshone another. That aligned with Lin-Manuel's artistic interests; as a contrast to the solos in *Moana*, he wanted to write a big company number to introduce all the family members. "He doesn't make it easy on himself," Jared says. "He's bored if he's not being challenged."

After a research trip to Colombia in 2018, the team decided to set the story there, home to magical-realism writers like Gabriel García Márquez and also the site of La Violencia, a civil war that displaced many families. The conflict wouldn't be specified in the film, but they would explore an abuela who, before the story starts, had escaped violence with her children, lost her husband, and drawn on the miracle of her new home to protect her extended family. When her descendants came of age, they each received a gift of special powers from the *casita*—an enchanted abode that gave the film its name: *Encanto*. The story took off when something went wrong and Mirabel, the heroine, did not get her gift.

The challenge for a film centered on a large family was keeping multiple characters distinct. Jared and Byron liked the idea of defining characters through archetypes—the strong sister, the golden child, the weird uncle. It fell to Lin-Manuel to distinguish each character with a musical style. "We had so much exposition to get out!" Charise Castro Smith, a Cuban-American playwright who was brought on as a second screenwriter, recalls. "Lin, help us out, man!" He welcomed the challenge. "We had a lot of characters with a lot of gifts, and it was going to be tough for an audience to keep them straight," Lin-Manuel explained. "I said, 'Let me write Mirabel's introduction of her family.' Let her clearly lay out 'Here's Abuela, here are her kids, here are their kids, and here's me.'" It was a version of Usnavi's opening rap in *Heights*, this time with a female MC to guide the audience through her part of the world: "The home of the Family Madrigal / Where all the people are fantastical and magical."

In 2019, "The Family Madrigal" went into an initial screening—basically a series of black-and-white storyboard images with voices recorded by Charise and Jared on their phones and, for the rest of the score, temporary songs to hold the place of the numbers that would come. Jared liked to tease Lin-Manuel by writing terrible temp songs—"Fake lyrics that are awful, just to make him mad, before we have real music and lyrics."

Before the rest of the real music and lyrics could arrive, COVID struck. Everyone went home. Lin-Manuel kept working, though. He'd had an intuition that the strong sister, Luisa, should sing to a reggaeton beat. He imagined her song as what he called "a love-letter-slash-apology" to his own older sister, Cita, who'd been saddled with much more responsibility than he had. She was the one his parents asked to assemble his He-Man play set on Christmas Eve. She was the one who managed their father's businesses. She'd even taken over Lin-Manuel's business, freeing him up to write music. "Give it to your sister, your sister's older, / Give her all the heavy things we can't shoulder," he wrote. And yet, playing with the archetype, he imagined a crack in her indestructible image. What if, inside, she suffered from "pressure like a tick, tick, tick 'til it's ready to blow"? (As an homage to his sister's '80s musical tastes, he scored the *tick* to a repeated eighth-note pattern he borrowed from "The Lovecats" by the Cure.) That pressure felt acute to him, too, as he juggled all his projects, stuck at home, facing increased scrutiny from the world, barely able to guide his kids through their math lesson. "There's a reason I was writing a song called 'Surface Pressure' that year," he says.

Cita acknowledges her role as the responsible one among the Mirandas, taking care of their businesses' accounting and financial planning. "I like numbers," she says. "Give me a bank statement to reconcile!" Although her efforts aren't usually heralded, she claims not to mind. "I like doing a lot of the work, keeping the plates spinning so they can do what they need to do," she says. "I'm in the background. That's my comfort zone." She knows her brother's "eyes glaze over" when financial issues arise. Nevertheless, she says, "Sometimes I guess I'm surprised that he has an idea of all the stuff I do. It's nice."

When Lin-Manuel sent his demo for "Surface Pressure" to Jared and Charise, they realized they had to rethink their approach to the character. Luisa was more than just the strong sister. "Before he wrote that song, Luisa didn't have much nuance," Jared says. "He added a lot of weight and yearning. He cracked into her to show you this person's in trouble. Charise and I went back through the entire script to look at her differently." With its reggaeton beat and '80s motif, the song also changed the sound of the film. Lin-Manuel had brought on a music producer, Mike Elizondo, who'd developed tracks for Eminem and Dr. Dre. "When I got his demo for 'Surface Pressure,' I was like, 'Whoa, this is different than anything I've heard Disney do,'" Mike recalls. "Lin inspired me to feel we didn't have to treat this as a Disney production. We could add drumbeats that we don't usually consider part of Disney's catalog."

That sense of departing from a classic Disney sound grew even stronger on the next demo Lin-Manuel submitted—the one about the weird uncle. During the pandemic, the team met for weekly Zooms on Friday nights. Before one session, Jared and Charise had sent over some script pages, a scene where the members of the family traded gossip about the uncle, circulating ever-juicier stories to describe his creepiness. On the Zoom, Lin-Manuel took in the tone. "It feels like a spooky *montuno,*" he said. He turned to his keyboard, next to his computer, and played three rising notes in a low octave: *dun-dun-DUN.*

"Yes, that's what it is!" Jared reacted at once. He recalls, "As the writer-director, that's when you think: *Get the fuck off the call and let him get it done.* Some light bulb went off in his brain—go!"

Within a week, Lin-Manuel sent a demo. As soon as he heard it, Jared understood something about a text exchange they'd had earlier in the pandemic. Originally in the script, the creepy uncle's name was Oscar. But the legal team told them that two Oscar Madrigals lived in the region of Colombia where they set the story, so they had to pick a different name. Worried about finding the right alternative, Jared woke up at five a.m. the next day and texted Lin-Manuel a few possibilities. "Anything in here you love or hate: 1. Arlo 2. Anko 3. Andre 4. Emo 5. Bruno 6. Marco."

Lin-Manuel texted back: "Love Bruno."

Now, listening to the demo, Jared knew why. The *montuno* pattern kicked it off, rising to the downbeat: *dun-dun-DUN*. And then the chorus began: "We don't talk about Bruno, no, no, no! / We don't talk about Bruno . . ." Bruno had the family's denial built into his name.

Lin-Manuel had designed the gossipy group number so the audience could hear from several of the dozen family members who didn't get their own songs. Each verse offered a different person's account of Bruno's prophetic menace: He'd cursed this one's wedding day; he'd said another's beloved would never be hers. Then, for the song's finale, all the characters' verses overlapped in a frenzied medley following the same chord progression in a range of individual cadences. "It was fuhuucking complicated," Lin-Manuel tweeted after finishing the song. He'd used a pure musical-theater technique for an act 1 closer, interweaving all the characters' motifs, like in "One Day More" from *Les Misérables* and "Non-Stop" from *Hamilton*, building tension to a climactic tipping point. In this case, Mirabel's prying into the secret of Bruno would cause the *casita* to crack, shattering the family order that her abuela had clung to and, ultimately, opening the possibility of a new way to see the family. Hearing the composer sing all ten parts on the demo, one of the actors said, was like "Lin-Manuel on steroids."

When Mike Elizondo got the demo, he loved the hook. "Instantly you know this is super-catchy," the music producer says. "The chorus pulls you in: Who's Bruno? What's going on?" He latched onto the sense of ominous mystery in the song. "We can get spooky on this one," he realized. Working out of his home studio in Nashville, he layered in eerie sonic elements. Then, to build drama, in each verse he cut out an element—removing the piano for one character; muting the drums for another. A syncopated, loping bass line drove all the characters' verses, so Mike doubled it on an 808 bass, a popular hip-hop instrument that derived a more contemporary sound from tweaking a drum machine. "I added in the low end, turning it into something that has ties to hip-hop but keeps that *montuno* part," he says. "I was taking Lin's ideas and going: Here's the fully realized version of it."

Lin-Manuel's biggest departure from his own style came in a song he wrote for the final act, when Mirabel's abuela realizes that she has to let go of her fixed image of her relatives and allow them to be themselves. By this point in the film's development, he'd seen some of the animators' work and noticed their use of a butterfly motif, taking inspiration from García Márquez's novels. "It was a metaphor for the family transforming," Charise, one of the screenwriters, says. "Lin took that metaphor and ran with it." What about a song, he proposed, that featured two caterpillars who love each other but have to let each other go in order to become the next version of themselves? He said he wanted it "to sound like a song that has always existed—a kind of Colombian folk song." And he wanted to write it in Spanish. *Caterpillar* wasn't nearly as beautiful a word as *oruguita*.

As usual, he found a personal path into the song's theme. It would be narrated from the perspective of an observer who assures the young *oruguitas* that if they endure the pain of separation, they will find themselves changed for the better. He thought back to the difficulty of parting from his high-school sweetheart midway through college. "In a lot of ways, I am the narrator," he told a reporter, "looking at myself at age 19 like, 'Buddy, it's OK. There's good stuff on the other side of the painful part.'"

He also had a model in his life of a doting abuela, devoted to her family, displaced from her past, who had to let go of her home. Just before he joined the Disney team for the Colombia research trip, his beloved Abuela Mundi passed away. Mundi's favorite songs were old-fashioned Spanish-language boleros, songs that seemed almost out of time. For *Heights*, Lin-Manuel had tried to write a bolero that Abuela Claudia would listen to on her record player. He got only as far as the first verse. In *Encanto*, the actor who'd played Abuela Claudia onstage and in the film, Olga Merediz, would provide the singing voice for Mirabel's abuela. Lin-Manuel had another chance to compose the type of song that his abuela might have known.

He wrote "Dos Oruguitas" simply, in C major, an unadorned vocal accompanied by a piano line that gently descended each measure. He listened to folk-song models like "Cielito Lindo" and "Guantanamera." He used a Spanish thesaurus to locate the right words and checked the grammar with his father. To his surprise, he found himself dreaming in Spanish— something he hadn't done since he was a child visiting his grandparents. The result didn't sound like anything he'd written before: "Ay, oruguitas, no se aguanten más. / Hay que crecer aparte y volver, / Hacia andelante seguirás." (Ay, oruguitas, don't you hold on too tight. / Both of you know it's your time to grow, / To fall apart, to reunite.)

The composer's real test came when Vanessa heard the demo. She sometimes sent him back to the drawing board, as she had when he shared his first draft of Eliza's song "Helpless" in *Hamilton*. Other times, she simply acknowledged a draft without reacting. This time, she cried. "Goddamn it, this is your best song!" she told him. "You asshole, I have a headache now!" When Jared listened to the song, he found himself in tears too. "I've never heard a demo from Lin that felt that intimate, that revealing, that vulnerable," he says. "It was so simple. It's a flavor I've never heard from Lin, ever." Olga Merediz, singing "Dos Oruguitas" and thinking back to the young man she knew in *Heights*, says: "I'm looking at him in awe of what he's become. He had to live up to the name his father gave him, Lin-Manuel Miranda. Now he's grown into that name."

The number Lin-Manuel wrote for Isabella, the golden child, when she discovers that her powers extend beyond the pretty adornment everyone expects of her was called, fittingly, "What Else Can I Do?"

———

In the fall of 2020, six months into the pandemic, *Tick, Tick . . . Boom!* became one of the first films to go back into production. COVID protocols were strict. Like the rest of the crew, Lin-Manuel needed to wear a face shield and a KN95 mask. He was tested three times a week. Lin-Manuel's assistant director, Mariela Comitini, knew when his ideas were flowing because he stuck out his tongue, but now she couldn't tell. She and Lin-Manuel liked to sing and dance around the set, giving each other hugs and high fives. "No touching," the COVID compliance officer would remind them. However inconvenient, precautions were necessary. The death toll had dipped over the summer, but in the fall, it started to climb even higher. "Pre-vaccine, it was terrifying to shoot," the cinematographer Alice Brooks recalls.

The biggest challenge came from the film's showstopper scene, an homage to Stephen Sondheim. Jonathan Larson, like Lin-Manuel, was a giant Sondheim fan. He'd gotten to play two of his songs for Sondheim at a musical-theater workshop, and when Sondheim praised one of them, he phoned his sister to crow, ecstatic. Sondheim had invited him to sit in on rehearsals for the new musical he was developing in the mid-1980s, *Into the Woods*, and even called Jonathan to discuss what wasn't working in the show.

Perhaps not surprisingly, when Jonathan toiled away waiting tables in the Moondance Diner, he dreamed of composing something with the impact of a Sondheim score. In fact, he wrote a song about Sunday brunch at the diner in the style of "Sunday," the act 1 finale of *Sunday in the Park with George*, Sondheim's musical about an artist. Instead of Georges Seurat assembling figures on a Parisian riverside for a pointillist composition "by the blue purple yellow red water," Jonathan sang about wrangling customers "in the blue silver chromium diner." On Broadway, Sondheim's number was a giant ensemble piece that united all the characters in the musical for a stunning choral tableau, re-creating Seurat's painting. Jonathan's was an homage sung alone at the piano on a small, empty stage. He didn't live to see his songs get the Broadway treatment.

But what if a movie could fulfill the fantasy that Jonathan never realized in his lifetime? Lin-Manuel had an idea: Instead of shooting "Sunday" as a solo number, he could enter Jonathan's imagination and populate the Moondance Diner with Jonathan's dream chorus. The actors who inspired Jonathan—and the actors who continued his legacy—could magically congregate to sing his vision of becoming an artist.

Lin-Manuel pulled out his contact list. He wanted Joel Grey, the original Emcee in *Cabaret*. He wanted André De Shields, the original Wizard in *The Wiz*. He wanted the stars of *Phantom*, of *Rent*, of *Fun Home*, of *Hamilton*. And of course, he had to have Bernadette Peters, who'd played the artist's muse in the original *Sunday in the Park with George*. Once Peters said yes, the rest of the cast fell into place. He called them "the Legends."

It was an audacious vision. Lin-Manuel describes it as "an enormous Avengers for musical theater." He might not have had the chutzpah to attempt it, he says, if not for the director Jon Chu "telling me a million times on *Heights*: 'Yes, the story is small, but the dreams are big.'" He could play out Larson's diner dream on a blockbuster scale.

His specific inspiration came from Rob Marshall's film of *Chicago*; the legendary Chita Rivera—one of the original *Chicago* stars on Broadway—made a brief cameo appearance on-screen. "I remember the pandemonium that unleashed in the Ziegfeld Theater when we saw Chita Rivera," Lin-Manuel says. "My motto became: I want twenty Chita Riveras!"

Getting twenty Chita Riveras on set during the pre-vaccine phase of the pandemic wasn't easy. "Our main goal was to make sure we didn't kill anybody," Mariela says. When they'd storyboarded the scene before the shutdown, they imagined all twenty actors moving freely around the diner. Now everyone would have to stay six feet apart. Some of the actors weren't comfortable appearing unmasked with other people in the room, even if everyone was quarantined and tested. "It became this football play," Mariela says. "We broke people into teams." They would shoot five people at a time, all spaced at a distance. Then their visual effects artists would tile the different shots into one composite image that made it look as though all the Legends were appearing together.

The one Chita Rivera they couldn't get was Chita Rivera herself. Two weeks before the shoot, they learned that she'd had an injury. "It was devastating for all of us," the producer Julie Oh recalls. "Lin told me: 'One way or another, Chita Rivera will be in this scene.' He pointed to a table and said, 'We're going to leave that seat empty—like for Elijah at the seder, but for Chita.'"

While they were planning the scene, Jonathan Larson's sister took Lin-Manuel and Alice Brooks aside. As Alice recalls, Julie told them that she didn't think the idea of having Broadway legends was enough to pull off "Sunday." There needed to be one more layer. "I challenge you guys to think of what other magical, dreamlike element could come into play," she said.

They thought about it. In their rehearsal space, the production designer had a model of the Moondance Diner set that they were using to map the choreography. Lin-Manuel pulled down the front wall of the diner so they could look inside.

"What if it's as simple as that?" he asked. The frame of the diner looked like a theater. At the climax of "Sunday," Jonathan could magically push down the wall of the diner and find himself on his dream stage conducting his fantasy cast.

Lin-Manuel had one more surprise for Julie. As the camera pulled out for the final shot of the diner, he told the visual effects team to add Jonathan Larson's name on the top, as though the diner had become a theater marquee dedicated to him. Then the entire image would shade into pointillist dots of color like *Un dimanche après-midi*, Georges Seurat's painting in *Sunday in the Park*. When Julie saw the footage, it took her a little while to realize that her brother's signature was there. "Oh my God!" she said when she spotted it. "He finally got his name on a marquee."

Although Julie appreciated the film as a love letter to her brother, she was glad that it didn't present "a whitewashed version of Saint Johnny." Larson was often playful, affectionate, generous; he could also be obsessive, insecure, self-absorbed. The script reflected both sides. Lin-Manuel had interviewed many of Larson's friends, who gave him an insight: "Jonathan was a pain in the ass, but that's because he wasn't doing what he was supposed to be doing." When he wondered why he was working in a diner instead of having his show produced, his idealism would curdle into bitterness. But in a rehearsal with friends, he was delightful. "I recognized that in myself," Lin-Manuel says. "It became a note I gave the actors: If you're in the room with him, that's his happy time."

But what Julie found refreshingly honest in the portrayal of her brother, others found annoying. Andrew Weisblum, the editor who worked on a first cut of the film, didn't sympathize with the main character. "He just looks like a selfish dick," Andrew says. Jonathan brushes off his loving girlfriend because he's obsessing over a song for his upcoming workshop, and he complains about people who sell out to his HIV-positive best friend who's gotten an advertising job to pay for health insurance. "The way he deals with his girlfriend and his best friend—what's his actual suffering?" Andrew asks. "That he can't become an artist? Does that really compare?" The challenge, he discussed with Lin-Manuel, was to "get at what was most universal about the character: somebody choosing to pursue their dreams before it's too late."

Andrew left the film midway for another project, but his successor, Myron Kerstein, who'd edited *In the Heights*, encountered the same problem. "Jonathan Larson's character was over-the-top neurotic, and he treated his girlfriend like shit," Myron says. "I was like, 'I hate this guy!'" Myron wasn't alone. As he remembers, "When we first screened the movie, the test audience really turned on us: 'How dare you make a movie about this white guy, and why the fuck do I care?'" Myron was afraid they'd never get the audience to root for Larson, but to his surprise, Lin-Manuel didn't appear ruffled. "He equated screenings with previews for Broadway," Myron recalls. "He was like, 'This is what you do. You screen and you tinker.'"

Both editors suggested that a different frame for the movie might change the audience's response. Although Broadway insiders knew the story of Larson's untimely death just before his first musical opened, others didn't realize the implied end to his artistic struggle. Lin-Manuel wanted to make a movie about Jonathan's life, not his death, but, the editors argued, audiences needed to learn about his death in order to appreciate his life. They added in archival footage of the cast of *Rent* dedicating their performances to Jonathan—a glimpse of the world he created but never got to see. At first, the footage went at the end of the film as a coda, then they moved it to the beginning so viewers would root for Jonathan to race against the ticking clock.

Myron moved in down the block from Lin-Manuel so they could edit together during the pandemic. The director found that editing was his favorite part of the process; playing with rhythm, surprise, tension, and release felt like writing a song. The editor was glad to find a fellow craftsperson. "Lin understood that it's a process," Myron says. "Being an artist isn't about making something that day and it's a masterpiece. It's about making something over time, reworking, rewriting, making it better." While Myron tinkered with a scene, Lin-Manuel would go to his keyboard and work on a number for *Encanto*. (The heroine's "I Want" song, as always, was taking him draft after draft to get right. He'd just had a new idea: A *bambuco* waltz he'd heard in Colombia could give Mirabel her own beat.) Myron would show Lin-Manuel his cut, then they'd tinker some more. When they had a version they liked, they showed it to Vanessa. "She's one of the smartest people I've ever met," Myron says. "She's honest too. If you were onto something, she'd give a nod."

Myron also argued for reshooting some scenes. The musical numbers in Jonathan's imagination worked well, but Myron thought the film needed a scene "where the common man can relate to this guy." He wanted to see Jonathan taking out the trash in the diner and having the bag burst open. He wanted to see Jonathan having fun with his girlfriend before neglecting her to prep for his workshop. Lin-Manuel had a few reshoots in mind too. Chita Rivera was available at last. Her empty seat awaited.

Netflix gave them three more days for reshoots. It was June 2021, eight months after production restarted. Actors could finally get vaccinated and appear together on the set.

There was one more cameo that Lin-Manuel wanted to include. In the turning-point song, "Why," Jonathan thinks back on the moments he fell in love with theater—singing in a talent show at age nine, getting a part in his high-school production of *West Side Story* at age sixteen—to remember why he wants to spend his life in such a fleeting pursuit. "I had the exact same emotional pressure points," Lin-Manuel says. "I wasn't nine, but I was twelve when we did the sixth-grade play. Between *Bye Bye Birdie* and Bernardo, that was the most incredible experience I had in elementary school. And then in high school, I directed *West Side Story*." For Jonathan's number, he decided to intercut flashbacks to childhood memories of those formative performances. (In the rough cut of the film, he even used grainy VHS footage from his Hunter productions.) He wanted to shoot the flashback scenes at Hunter, but COVID prevented that, so he asked his designers to build a replica of the Hunter auditorium on the film's Brooklyn soundstage. He set up child actors to stand in for younger versions of Jonathan and his friend Michael. And then, for the role of Jonathan's elementary-school teacher, he brought in his own personal legend.

Barbara Ames had hardly left her house in two years. She had asthma, so she stayed away from respiratory risks. She was now elderly, with spinal problems that made it difficult for her to walk. She had long ago retired from teaching music at Hunter. Nevertheless, when her former pupil called, she made her way to the film studio in East Williamsburg. "The first day was my first COVID test ever!" she recalls. On the second day, she had her costume fitted. On the third day, she received her own trailer with her name on the outside.

When it was time for her scene, she went to the soundstage. It looked just like the Hunter auditorium where she'd directed a sixth-grade Lin-Manuel Miranda as Bernardo in *West Side Story*, down to the red curtain. "My scene was to lead the fourth-graders across the stage," she says. "I led them across, sort of limping." When she reached the other side of the stage, Lin-Manuel wrapped her in a giant hug. "Here's this person giving me such gifts," she says. "I'm getting old, but Lin put me in *Tick, Tick . . . Boom!*. I have a credit that says 'Music Teacher: Barbara Ames'!"

On Twitter, Lin-Manuel posted a clip of the scene. "Thank you, Miss Ames," he wrote. "You changed my life."

Lin-Manuel screened *Tick, Tick . . . Boom!* for Sondheim before it was released by Netflix in November 2021, before the American Film Institute listed it as one of its ten best films of the year, before Oscar nominations arrived for Andrew Garfield's acting and Andrew Weisblum's and Myron Kerstein's editing. Lin-Manuel wanted Sondheim's opinion, but he also wanted to show the composer that he was a character in the movie himself. Portrayed by Bradley Whitford with a squint, a growl, and a deep heart, he appeared in a re-creation of the songwriters' workshop where Jonathan shared a few of his numbers, earning Sondheim's treasured acclaim. In a later scene, Sondheim slipped into the back row of a workshop performance of Jonathan's sci-fi musical. He didn't stick around, but he left Jonathan a voicemail praising the work.

Sondheim appreciated the portrayal, but he didn't think the language of the voicemail that Whitford had recorded was what he would have told Larson. He asked Lin-Manuel if he could record the message in his own voice, sharing something closer to what he might have said. Soon, the producer Julie Oh received a voice file in her email. "Is this real?" she asked. "What surreal world are we in that we're getting messages from Sondheim?" She asked Lin-Manuel if they could get away with putting Sondheim's voice in the movie or if audiences would notice the shift from Whitford. He assured her that they wouldn't.

So in the final film, the character of Jonathan comes home to the real Sondheim's voice on his answering machine. "I didn't get a chance to speak with you after the reading, but I just wanted to say it was really good. Congratulations," Sondheim said. "I'd love to get together and talk to you about it if you have any interest. No pressure. The main thing, though, is that it's first-rate work and has a future, and so do you. I'll call you later with some thoughts if that's okay. Meanwhile, be proud."

Larson had been the beneficiary of Sondheim's mentorship just as Lin-Manuel had. Sondheim himself had been mentored as a young man by Oscar Hammerstein II, who encouraged him, gave him writing challenges, offered rigorous feedback, steered him through career choices, and took him seriously as an artist. It turned out that Sondheim had mentored legions of young composers, reviewing their work, giving advice, bestowing praise. Many of them reached out to Lin-Manuel after *Tick, Tick . . . Boom!* came out, sharing stories about his kindness and generosity. Lin-Manuel dropped Sondheim a note mentioning the mentorship anecdotes: "Hope your ears have been ringing in all the best ways with the release of the film.

And thanks for the rewrite on the phone machine, it made all the difference."

Sondheim, now ninety-one, wrote back: "Thanks for the nice boost to my spirits, Lin. It's an aspect of my life I'm proud of. I feel as if I've repaid (partially, at least) what I owe Oscar."

The next week, he died.

Because of the studios' pandemic rescheduling, Lin-Manuel ended up with four movies coming out within six months in 2021. "There was so much of him everywhere," Myron marvels. "I can't believe that he was developing and writing music for *Vivo*, and then writing stuff for *Encanto*, and then shooting his own movie, and then promoting *In the Heights*. He was like, 'Are people going to get sick of me? I don't even know if *I* want that much of me!'"

The first film to appear was *In the Heights*, in June—thirteen years after the film-adaptation process began, twenty-one years after Lin-Manuel staged the initial version. Test screenings for *Heights* had been rapturous. Warner Brothers told the editors that no film had scored higher with test audiences in the history of the studio. Jon Chu was looking forward to a giant release with the cultural reach that his previous film, *Crazy Rich Asians*, had enjoyed around the world; a big box office would provide an incentive for studios to create more movies with Latino talent. The film premiered in Washington Heights itself, at the United Palace theater around the corner from the primary shooting location. The neighborhood turned out. Reviews were glowing. It felt like a party.

Across the country, however, the box office fizzled. *In the Heights* cost $55 million to make and millions more for Warner Brothers to market. *Variety* estimated that it needed to gross around $110 million to cover its costs. On its opening weekend, it drew only $11.4 million. "It was a really shocking moment," John Buzzetti recalls. "It's nothing we don't know in this business, but to look at the numbers and see: There are no stars in the movie, there are a lot of black and brown people in it, and moviegoers won't give it a shot."

Jon Chu felt that the studio had undercut the movie's debut. Warner Brothers' parent company, AT&T, had made the decision to release all

2021 films on HBO Max, its streaming service, at the same time they appeared in theaters. "Having it come out on streaming takes the air out," Jon says. "If you want people to go to a theater, you have to provoke them to go." Other Warner Brothers releases that year had big openings despite appearing on the streaming service simultaneously, but those were mostly action sequels with a large, established audience. Lin-Manuel took a little comfort in the fact that no movie musical performed well at the box office that year, including Steven Spielberg's remake of *West Side Story*. It cost twice what *Heights* did but brought in even less in its first weekend. "I forgave myself," Lin-Manuel says. "You didn't fuck it up; the audiences just weren't there."

Rather than analyzing the film's cinematic success, the media conversation around *Heights* turned to its casting. Discussions about Latino representation had changed since *Heights* appeared on Broadway and even in the years since the film was cast. The Black Lives Matter protests in 2020 had sparked discussions in Latino communities about colorism, the legacies of industries like film and television that historically privileged lighter-skinned Latino talent. Although the performances in *Heights* were generally lauded, some critics questioned the absence of dark-skinned Afro-Latino leads in a film set in Upper Manhattan, with its large Dominican population.

Publicity interviews with the *Heights* stars turned increasingly to one issue: Why weren't there dark-skinned Latino actors in the leading roles? Lin-Manuel wasn't surprised at the question. "I knew it was coming," he says. "It was a conversation in the Latino community in the wake of 2020. We're not bystanders here. I knew we had great Afro-Latino casts coming with *Vivo* and *Encanto*. But the fact that there isn't a dark-skinned Dominican lead in *Heights* is a fair point."

His agent didn't want him to say anything. Jon Chu wanted to give his own response. He felt disappointed by the conversation; he saw the movie as a celebration of the community with people of color at the helm throughout. "Jon, don't say *shit*," Lin-Manuel told him. "I'm accountable to this community. I'm going to be part of this community for as long as I make things." He hadn't cast the movie, but he knew that he was the face of the result, and that it was up to him to speak.

Jon respected that response. He'd expected Lin-Manuel to shut the conversation down. "Instead, when we talked about it," he recalls, "Lin said: 'Let's react the way we'd want someone to react to us, and just listen. Win or lose.'" That resonated with Jon. "What it showed was that at the expense of our own movie, we were going to live up to the ideals of what we were presenting: Everyone has a voice, and everyone deserves to be heard."

The Monday after the film came out, Lin-Manuel posted a statement on Twitter. "I started writing *In the Heights* because I didn't feel seen," he began. "And over the past 20 years all I wanted was for us—ALL of us—to feel seen." He acknowledged the discussion around Afro-Latino representation. "I can hear the hurt and frustration over colorism, of feeling still unseen in the feedback," he wrote. "In trying to paint a mosaic of this community, we fell short. I'm truly sorry." He concluded: "Thanks for your honest feedback. I promise to do better in my future projects, and I'm dedicated to the learning and evolving we all have to do to make sure we are honoring our diverse and vibrant community."

Behind the scenes, Vanessa could tell that it was a hard experience for her husband. "I don't think it was difficult because of the criticism," she says. "I think it was difficult because it was his baby, and he wrote it with the goal of increasing Latino representation. He and Quiara fought for lots of different body types. It hurts because it was something they were striving for. I feel like if it had been cast after 2020, the studio would have accommodated their vision."

When Lin-Manuel Zoomed into *The Daily Show* two days later, the host, Trevor Noah, said he felt defensive on his behalf. "I was like, 'Lin does so much! We have Black people singing on Broadway! Why are you doing this to Lin? Why are you tearing down one of our own?'" He asked how Lin-Manuel approached the criticism. "You have to acknowledge it and let it in," Lin-Manuel replied. "I'm happy to take the learning from it and bring that to the next one, and also hold space to be proud of this thing we made that's been half my life." In response, Noah shared what one of his writers had told him: "I don't think anybody is angered at Lin because they think he did something. I think it's because they know he's the one person who will listen."

Cultural success is hard to engineer and hard to predict. *Vivo* had been slated to come out in theaters in 2021, but instead, Sony licensed it to

Netflix for a streaming release. When it appeared that August, twelve years after Lin-Manuel began writing its songs, it received generally favorable reviews and became the most-watched Netflix movie that month. In September, it was the second-most-watched movie on Netflix. By October, it had dropped off the list entirely.

Encanto, by contrast, opened well in theaters at Thanksgiving, taking in $40 million. It was a moderate box office success, eventually reaching $256 million globally, but not on the scale of *Moana* or *Frozen*. Yet when it launched on Disney Plus at Christmas, its viewership took off. It became by far the most-streamed movie of the year in 2022, and in 2023 was streamed more than any other movie except *Moana*.

The *Encanto* soundtrack also became a viral sensation. TikTok, which had turned against Lin-Manuel in 2020, now embraced his songs as users posted their own versions of the Family Madrigal's solos and group numbers. To nearly everyone's surprise, "We Don't Talk About Bruno," the interlocking ensemble bop that seemed most embedded in the film's complicated family structure, became the breakout hit—the biggest Disney song *ever*, according to *Billboard*'s tally, holding the number-one spot for five weeks. Was it the funky groove? The catchy chorus? The playfully dramatic rendering of a family's secrets? A post-"Despacito" appetite for Latin crossover tunes? A new rubric for calculating the charts that took music streaming services like Spotify into account? In fact, all eight songs that Lin-Manuel wrote for *Encanto* charted on the *Billboard* Hot 100. At the end of 2022, *Billboard* named him the top songwriter of the year.

That level of recognition could prove dizzying, but after living through the *Hamilton* wave, Lin-Manuel felt somewhat protected. "I could write three other *Encanto*s, and I will still never top that recognition tsunami," he says. "I have to get away from topping. That way madness lies." Instead, he decided, "I'm just going to make cool, weird shit."

Oh, and he also agreed to write the songs for an upcoming *Lion King* prequel, directed by the Oscar winner Barry Jenkins. Why? The answer was easy: "I'm going to learn a lot."

EPILOGUE

• •

*D*uring the three years that I researched and wrote this book, Lin-Manuel was also writing his origin story, of a sort, back in the basement of the Drama Book Shop. For his first stage musical after *Hamilton*, he wanted to explore something totally different—no hip-hop version of Abraham Lincoln, much as people asked him. He had already become, arguably, the preeminent musical storyteller of the twenty-first century, creating globally beloved narratives through song in film, animation, and theater, the heir to Sondheim and Lloyd Webber, Schwartz and Menken, the rare Broadway artist who, because of his rise on the charts and power as an entertainer, could be mentioned alongside pop stars. It would have been understandable to coast on a world-topping hit or feel paralyzed by the pressure to repeat its success. But his continual appetite for learning, for adding another tool to his kit, buoyed him along a new current. His engine, he says, "is what won't leave me alone."

Following that persistent tug, he found himself back in his childhood—back, in fact, in his childhood nightmares. When he was four, with his parents at work and Abuela Mundi not quite clocking his English-language entertainment tastes, he'd watched a stylized action movie from 1979, *The Warriors*. The film tracks the titular gang from its home turf in Coney Island to a peace summit in the Bronx; when the leader of the truce is shot, the Warriors are wrongly blamed for his death and have to fight their way back home over one long night as every other crew in the city tries to hunt them down. It's a lurid, propulsive vision of the city as a perilous nocturnal playground with violent terrors lurking at each jittery subway stop. "*The Warriors* have all my fears wrapped up in one movie," Lin-Manuel says. "The fear of being lost, the fear of being accused of something I didn't do, the fear of not being able to get back home alive." He decided to turn the movie into a musical.

The process reprised all his best practices. Part of his interest lay in blending his love of musical storytelling and his fascination with making action movies, which he'd wanted to do since his days popping fake blood capsules on his grandparents' roof. "How do you make an action musical?" he asks. "The Rumble in *West Side Story* is the only scary sequence we have, and there's no singing." Sondheim had told his high-school cast, in fact, how Robbins cut the lyrics in the prologue that set up the musical's gang warfare and replaced them with choreography. Lin-Manuel set his own bar high: He wanted to release his adaptation of *The Warriors* as a concept album before it became a stage show, as he had initially planned to do with *Hamilton*. There would be no choreography to convey the action; the songs would have to do all the punching, chasing, and shooting work.

The songs would also need to convey New York City as a musical map, tracking the Warriors' journey from the Bronx summit down through Manhattan to Brooklyn as they battled different gangs. The film had distinguished neighborhoods and encounters through visual design; the album would have to achieve those shifts through sonic variety. The year *The Warriors* came out was also a banner year for hip-hop, when the Sugarhill Gang released "Rapper's Delight." Hip-hop itself, in some tellings, emerged from a gang truce like the one in *The Warriors*, as Bronx crews shifted from street clashes to rap battles. Excavating the styles of the city in 1979 could, in a sense, offer a hip-hop origin story, conjuring the world into which, a year later, Lin-Manuel was born.

With a project that united personal urgency with a broader cultural narrative, he brought on a collaborator who could complement his skills, a friend and fellow hip-hop theater compatriot. When Lin-Manuel discovered *Bizarre Ride II the Pharcyde* as a lovelorn seventh-grader in 1992, Eisa Davis was hanging with the Pharcyde in Los Angeles as a hip-hop journalist fresh out of Harvard. She was also a classically trained pianist, a Pulitzer-finalist playwright, a composer, performer, and an early advocate of the Hip-Hop Theater Festival, which premiered *Angela's Mixtape*, her autobiographical play about finding her artistic voice as the niece of the activist Angela Davis. A longtime friend of Quiara's, she got to know Lin-Manuel when she starred in *Passing Strange* the season it ran alongside *In the Heights*. "I wanted to write with someone smarter and cooler than me," Lin-Manuel said. "I thought Eisa would keep me honest." At a party for his forty-second birthday, he told her that he'd love to discuss a project. "Did I just win the lottery?" she wondered afterward.

Over coffee at the Drama Book Shop at the start of 2022, he asked if she'd heard of the movie *The Warriors*. Though she'd never seen it, she knew it had become a cult film that hip-hop artists like to sample. (Particularly popular were the truce leader's thundering refrain *"Can you dig it?"* and the villain's creepy taunt, accompanied by the sound of clinking beer bottles: "Warriors, come out to *play-ay*!") When she watched the movie, at his suggestion, she understood how Lin-Manuel would have been drawn as a child to the survival aspect of not knowing whether you could make it home. "Actually, my first response was: 'You want to make this a musical? Why not a video game?'"

Lin-Manuel explained that it had, in fact, been adapted into a game by the makers of Grand Theft Auto and that he had an idea for a different adaptation: He wanted to flip the gender of the Warriors and make them an all-female gang. "The idea came around the time that GamerGate was happening," he says, "when terminally online assholes were like, 'Women shouldn't be in games; here's her address'—doxing women because they fucking felt like it. That's what the villain does to the Warriors; he shoots the truce leader and is like, 'They did it. Good luck getting back home.' So having women fighting their way home felt more interesting at every step. I'd come off a year and a half of *Hamilton* surrounded by dudes. *Heights* and *Bring It On* were full of women's voices, and I wanted to get back to that."

Eisa was curious, if skeptical. "Is that shift something that has to happen or is it just an artificial move?" she asked. She thought they'd first have to research the struggles that women faced in gangs in the 1970s. While Lin-Manuel appreciated her skepticism (he concedes he has "no critical distance from the story"), she grasped that the flip was "the floodgate that opened him up creatively." She agreed to go through the movie and outline possible song spots, like Lin-Manuel and Tommy had done with Chernow's Hamilton biography. As she researched the historical period, they started to make each other playlists of New York genres so they could evoke what Eisa calls "the music that hip-hop would sample." Eisa was impressed with "how voracious Lin is as a listener," excited by jazz-funk composer Roy Ayers, spoken-word pioneer Gil Scott-Heron, and the female punk band ESG.

Writing, for Lin-Manuel, is a form of acting, melding research and empathy. So a year after his first meeting with Eisa, they retraced the Warriors' odyssey from Van Cortlandt Park in the Bronx thirty-odd miles south to the Coney Island boardwalk. Eisa didn't want to use phones for navigation as they walked and rode the subway. "You have to confront your fears," she told Lin-Manuel. "Let's get lost! Let's feel it!" He saw the trip differently. "By the time we got to Coney, it was night," he recalls. "She's like, 'We have to walk to the ocean!' And I'm like, 'But it's dark!'"

That dynamic of hope tempering anxiety came to define much of their artistic partnership. For Eisa, raised in an Oakland family dedicated to movements for social justice, *The Warriors* offered the possibility of peace, a dream that New York's embattled populations could unite in solidarity and mutual aid, even if the movie started by shattering that promise. For Lin-Manuel, the movie was about the "gut-level dread" that had haunted him since preschool: "Is the person I care about going to make it home?" Eisa wanted to ensure that they held on to both, "getting at those fears, and getting at my dream of what the city can be."

They worked together in the basement of the bookshop, then on weeklong retreats upstate. The songs bubbled up. "Eisa's incredibly remarkable," Lin-Manuel says. "And she's an easy hang." Experiencing his creative energy up close, Eisa jotted in her notebook: "Lin is an octopus brain on a pogo stick." She also found his enthusiasm matched with generosity. Through the Miranda Family Fellowship, he sponsored dozens of students from underrepresented communities who wanted careers in the performing arts, and he created a directory of artists of color to help theaters hire more inclusively. Feeling that he needed to pick up Sondheim's mantle of musical theater's "encourager-in-chief," he'd begun to mentor many younger composers. (Shaina Taub remembers the notes she requested from him for *Suffs*, her Broadway-bound musical: "He gives feedback in such a spirit of positivity. He wrote me two incredible emails, one for each act, talking to me composer to composer, and he said, 'I'm going to give you a bunch of notes, but if it feels wrong to you, you're right; it's *your* show.' No one had said that to me before.")

"His rudder is true," Eisa says. "How is he so healthy?" Sure, Lin-Manuel had anxieties, but they didn't inhibit him; they fueled his work. Eisa credits Vanessa, who'd become global marketing counsel for Estée Lauder, with keeping him levelheaded. "You better come correct with Vanessa," she says. "All the bullshit that comes with fame, it's all stripped away immediately. If there was any moment that he might have lost his mind, she made sure that it didn't happen." (Vanessa gives the credit to Lin-Manuel's mother: "He's the child of a therapist. He was schooled early on in how to process things and move forward.")

By 2024, they had a full set of demos for their *Warriors* as a sung-through concept album. Lin-Manuel began as the songwriter with Eisa as the book writer, but she contributed so many musical and lyrical ideas that they decided, in her phrase, to "Lennon-McCartney it" and simply share credit. They both tapped the sounds of their childhoods. Eisa hearkened back to her elementary-school posse's playground chant "Ah-she-ca! Ah-ah-she-ca!" for an a cappella cipher session when the women of the Warriors introduce themselves. ("I'm Cochise, oh please, you know my style / I'm always ready with the verses and I'm versatile!") Lin-Manuel lifted an eerie descending bass line from *Nightmare in D Major*, his first high-school musical, for one of the rival gangs' themes.

They also pushed each other in new directions. Eisa suggested that the villain wail a heavy-metal tune; Lin responded with a screaming anthem of gleeful nihilism in an '80s pop-culture idiom. ("Wow, Little Ms. Pac-Man is tryin' to skip town / I am the ghost and I'm hunting them *down*!") For a gang that presents a nonthreatening facade, Lin-Manuel turned a ditty he'd written for his younger son into glorious '90s boy-band harmonies with a concluding verse that even ventured into K-pop. ("The idea is not to keep it locked in the 1970s," Eisa says, "the way *Hamilton* is not locked in the 1770s.") The *Nightmare* bass line ended up in an electronic dance music bop after Eisa proposed an homage to queer ballroom culture. ("I was like, 'We have to have a gay gang—this is fucking New York City!'") They added tastes of ska, rockabilly, Mexican folk song. They wrote in shifting tempos that burst into higher speeds for chase scenes, percussion that battered for fights, and a bass heartbeat that petered out for a gut-wrenching demise. Their goal, Eisa says, was to give "a sense of propulsion to the Warriors on their journey" that could come from "a rich tapestry of musical subcultures that are all in New York."

Excited though they felt about their demos, they wanted to test whether astute listeners would feel the same; being willing to revise is a key part of the process. "What I always want to get at is: Here's what I meant; what did you get?" Lin-Manuel says. "I'm trying to shorten the gap." They invited a bunch of friends to a listening party—Tommy and Lac; fellow playwrights and composers Quiara, Shaina, *The Great Comet*'s Dave Malloy, and *Hadestown*'s Anaïs Mitchell; plus the producers of the original *Warriors* film. Busta Rhymes showed up at the end of the party. According to Lin-Manuel, "There was mostly cheerleading, but there were a couple of places where the playwrights told us that they were confused. That was very helpful for clarifying motivations." The villain needed more of an explanation, so Lin-Manuel and Eisa texted each other lyrical possibilities and then fused their favorites.

Lin-Manuel had long recruited the most talented collaborators he could find to execute his musical impulses. Now his contacts included a much more extensive list than when he first turned his nightmares into a musical at Hunter. And unlike the starry list of contributors to the *Hamilton Mixtape* compilation album, most of whom sent in their tracks, Lin-Manuel says, "Eisa and I made a rule: We wanted to be *in the room* with these amazing artists." As an executive producer, he brought on the rapper Nas, who agreed to perform a verse Lin-Manuel had written for the gang from Queens, Nas's home borough. It was unusual for a rapper to deliver someone else's bars, but with Nas on board, other hip-hop heavyweights signed on too: Ghostface Killah and RZA for Staten Island, Busta for Brooklyn, Cam'ron for Manhattan. ("Uh-oh, Manhattan's on the scene / When you say 'New York,' we're *actually* what you mean.")

These rappers likely wouldn't agree to do eight shows a week on Broadway, but for a concept album, they could show up to a recording session. To kick off the opening track that summons all the gangs to the peace meeting, the deceased Bronx rapper Big Pun's son, Chris Rivers, performed Lin-Manuel's homage to his father's dazzlingly complex across-the-bar rhymes. In the spirit of Eisa's hope for communal rebirth, he rapped a rebuttal to the devastation of Robert Moses–style urban renewal: "The car horn honks / Across the Cross-Bronx / And what the Bronx wants / Is not a combative retaliatory response / It's a renaissance!"

Some writers buckle under the anxiety of influence, fearful that they can't measure up to their forebears, but Lin-Manuel celebrates his influences and seeks wisdom from his heroes. Also on his call list was the composer of one of the original musical-theater concept albums. Over breakfast, he told Andrew Lloyd Webber: "I'm finally doing my *Jesus Christ Superstar*. Any advice?" The senior composer replied: "Yes. Get live musicians." Eisa wanted to work with a house band, too, so she and Lin-Manuel spent two weeks in Nashville, where their producer, bassist Mike Elizondo, put together an all-star group that included Paul McCartney's drummer.

Even having worked on *Encanto* and *The Hamilton Mixtape*, Mike was astonished at the new album's breadth of genres, from metal to ballroom. "Lin's a sponge, man," Mike says. "He's always thirsting for new things. He can hear music and just put it into his blender and make it come out something that's distinct to him." It wasn't only that *Warriors* blended styles, Mike explains. It was that Lin-Manuel could fuse the rhythmic ingenuity of rap with the emotional pull of melody to tell a coherent dramatic story. "No one does it better than him."

Of course, as the last recording day approached, Lin-Manuel hadn't yet finished the finale. "He needs the coals under his feet," Eisa says. "I was joking: 'I sent you everything it's supposed to be—the words, the chords. You just need to turn it into the song. Come on, homey!' Lin's like, 'Yeah, I'm not nervous, it'll come out.'" That night after dinner, he mentioned that he had a splinter in his foot. She said she could help him extract it. She succeeded. "He's like, 'Oh my God, it's like the fable: You got the thorn out of my paw! Now I can write the final song!'" The next day at five a.m., he texted her: "It's coming!" The song poured out in a rush of tears and typing, like Eliza's finale in *Hamilton*. But his computer fritzed and his Logic program wouldn't record what he'd written. "Fuck it, let's go to the studio," he announced. "I'll teach the band what I'm hearing."

Eisa remembers Lin-Manuel jumping around the studio, singing a phrase, asking the guitarist to play the melody from an earlier track, mixing together the motifs they'd built up. "It becomes this huge gumbo of returning themes," she says. She and Lin-Manuel popped into the recording booth to lay down the final vocals themselves, a return to the Warriors' exultant "Ah-she-ca!" chant. "I'm sobbing as we come to the end," she re-calls. "I've never had a collaboration like this."

There were more thrills to come: Recording the Nuyorican crew's salsa number with Marc Anthony and his band over an all-night session in Miami; landing Jamaican dance-hall sensation Shenseea as the radio DJ who narrates the story; getting a Dropbox file with the truce leader's vocals recorded by none other than Ms. Lauryn Hill. ("Nobody's wastin' nobody / You are brothers and sisters now / And everywhere you go / You are home free!") For the Warriors, they cast women they loved from the theater world, including three former Elizas, who knew how to gel as an ensemble, harmonize beautifully, and reveal a tougher edge as they took back the night.

Lin-Manuel and Eisa decided that they wouldn't worry about how to stage the musical just yet. (In his view, it's always better to start by mak-ing something rather than merely thinking about making the ideal thing.) "We came around to the idea that the album is its own meal," Lin-Manuel says. "You have to sit down and listen to it, feast on it." They welcomed the freedom of the recording studio to layer vocals, play with distortion, add spray-can and subway-track sound effects—"ear-candy moments," as Mike calls them. "Lin got to flex in the studio and really push the bound-aries and learn some techniques he'd never gotten to explore in his music," Mike says. "He's a true collaborator. He's great at taking in other people's advice, realizing another person's strengths, and just leaning on them."

That sense of collective strength and discovery powers the *Warriors* fi-nale. Home on the Coney Island beach but still hounded by the villain who is blaming them for the murder he committed, the Warriors face him down at last. His crew scatters while theirs stands together, their bond sealed in a tight quadruple rhyme: "We're the Warriors, and our story is / In our loyalty, that's where the glory is." It's hard not to hear Lin-Manuel's story in that declaration as well: a faith in the power of collaborative music-making to handle any fear, a relish in the glory of an unexpected sonic connection.

"It's very exciting, and there's a little dread too," he told me the day before he and Eisa announced the album. When *Warriors* was released in October 2024, a few critics objected to adapting a grimy gang epic into musical-theater fantasy, but most agreed with the *Guardian*, which, in a five-star review, lauded the album's "blistering, kaleidoscopic" soundscape, at turns suspenseful, funny, thunderous, and poignant. In 2025, Lin-Manuel and Eisa could turn to the possibilities of the musical in the theater.

As I listened to the album, I thought of the little boy at the piano recital realizing that music could transform an audience's attention, a boy hungry to write and perform, not yet knowing how to find the chords or summon the words, eager to absorb the models that would give him permission to create. I thought of the sensitive child overwhelmed with emotion, haunted by the loss of a loved one, slowly learning that his vulnerability could become a superpower. I thought of the high-schooler burning to make things, frustrated that his friends didn't also want to sacrifice their weekends and vacations, devastated when they wouldn't play his attempt at an original tune, figuring out how to inspire other students around a shared vision. I thought of the college student discovering that he could forge art out of everything that mattered to him, bringing all his inspirations into play with a story that lifted his whole community. And I thought of the professional constantly revising, welcoming collaborators into the room to make something he couldn't on his own, finding joy in the process, meeting the historical moment, seeking ever more ways to learn and grow. What was most remarkable was that even as Lin-Manuel became the grown-up master of the modern musical, he held on to his childlike self, with a sparkling desire to entertain, an openness to what scares and thrills him, a delight in playful creation.

In *Warriors*, I could hear through-lines, almost like reprises, from Lin-Manuel's earlier work: the jubilant portrait of the city as a jumble of immigrant cultures in *Heights*; the galvanizing drama of revolutionary promise mixed with tragedy in *Hamilton*; the opportunities for women as action heroes and MCs in *Bring It On*, *Moana*, and *Encanto*; the persistent questions of mortality and legacy in *Tick, Tick . . . Boom!*. But there was also a sense of expansiveness, of freedom in creation—the confidence to write from his deepest self, for any voice, in any genre. "That's what's fun about seeing him make his new work with Eisa," Quiara says. "It doesn't feel beholden. He's going to create what he wants to create."

The final line on the *Warriors* album is a shout that echoes with reverb, accumulating resonance across the decades for Lin-Manuel's world and his art:

This is the sound of something being born.

ACKNOWLEDGMENTS

If I hadn't already been convinced of the power of collaboration by learning about Lin-Manuel Miranda's career, the process of writing this book would have taught me. It wouldn't exist without the extraordinary generosity and keen conviction of James Shapiro, who gave me the idea to write it in the first place, discussed its possibilities over many a delightful brunch, offered characteristically insightful feedback on every chapter, and introduced me to his own wonderful agent, Anne Edelstein. Anne understood the project from the start and, with her enthusiastic combination of literary insight and publishing savvy, brought it to just the right editor: Bob Bender at Simon & Schuster, who championed the book and encouraged me through the early chapters. When Bob retired, I was fortunate that as astute and supportive an editor as Mindy Marqués Gonzalez adopted the project. With skilled assistance from Johanna Li and eagle-eyed copyediting from Tracy Roe, Mindy guided me to completion through the perfect blend of appreciation and perceptive criticism.

I'm immensely grateful for Lin-Manuel Miranda's vulnerability in allowing me to delve into every corner of his artistic life, agreeing to sit for a dozen interviews in the midst of a zillion other endeavors, unearthing his student videos and scripts for me to peruse, opening his network of friends and collaborators, and fielding innumerable questions with patience and good humor. Owen Panettieri, his longtime associate, facilitated connections with many luminaries who populate the Mirandaverse and handled the logistics of this project with unwavering kindness and professionalism. Luz Towns-Miranda and Luis A. Miranda Jr. welcomed me into their home and shared a treasure trove of photos and papers from their son's childhood. Luis also introduced me to his relatives in Puerto Rico—Rodolfo Concepcíon, Yamilla Miranda, Elvin Miranda, and Rosita Arroyo—who gave me a tour of the neighborhood where Lin-Manuel and Cita visited their grandparents. In addition to talking with me multiple times, Lin-Manuel, Owen, Luz, Luis, Cita, and, especially, Vanessa Nadal took the time to review earlier drafts for factual accuracy, for which I am most appreciative.

At Galería Lin-Manuel Miranda in Vega Alta, Thaïs Ortiz shared her knowledge and passion while also acting as a helpful translator. My college pal David Davidson, who sang in Lin-Manuel's high-school a cappella group, kindly connected me with the rest of Fat Joe and the Boys, as well as Clayton's Friends, and he set up a tour of Hunter College High School with Lin-Manuel's childhood best friend, Dan SanGermano, who now chairs the Hunter art department. Meredith Summerville, a college classmate of mine, generously let me pore over her collection of Hunter memorabilia, including Lin-Manuel's high-school project on the Burr-Hamilton duel, as well as his first draft of *In the Heights*. At Wesleyan University, Professor Rashida Z. Shaw McMahon arranged a virtual campus tour with an exemplary theater student, By Martinez-Castaneda. Lin-Manuel's college housemate Alex Horwitz, director of the indispensable documentary *Hamilton's America*, graciously shared all of his interview transcripts in addition to several illuminating mementos from Wesleyan.

I feel tremendous gratitude to the 150 people who were willing to be interviewed for this book; their names appear at the start of the notes. I'm also grateful to the many people who connected me with archival materials—photos, programs, mixtapes, school newspapers, scripts, audio recordings, videos—often venturing into storage lockers and parents' basements to track them down. My heartfelt thanks to Barbara Ames, Billy and Diane Baker, Catherine Young, James Green-Armytage, Erica Rosenfeld Halverson, Amy Eliza Greenstadt, Rachel Axler, Robert Sosin, Siobhan Lockhart, David Rosen, Steve Hofstetter, Alex Sarlin, Arthur Lewis, Dan Gonen, Eric Fleisig-Greene, Sophie Oberfield, Una LaMarche, Elizabeth Kandel, Jon Kandel, Lona Kaplan-Werner, Campbelle Austin, Katie Takayanagi, M. Graham Smith, Micah Allen, Jeff Zorabedian, Matthew Lerner, William Stowe, Neil Patrick Stewart, Alex Lacamoire, Stephanie Leah Evans, Andrew Fried, Nicole Pusateri, Tania Carrasquillo Hernández, Julie Larson, and especially the expert sleuthing and support of Poly Gianniba. My thanks as well to Wesleyan University Special Collections and Archives, Lincoln Center for the Performing Arts Archives, and the Theater on Film and Tape Archive at the New York Public Library for the Performing Arts. Jeremy McCarter's adroit essays in *Hamilton: The Revolution* and *In the Heights: Finding Home*, accompanying Lin-Manuel's annotated lyrics, are essential starting points for any research, as are the deliciously candid interviews on Gillian Pensavalle's podcast *The Hamilcast*.

I could not have pursued this project without the exceptional generosity of Ronni Lacroute, a patron of the arts as magnanimous in her courage as in her largesse. Thanks as well to a remarkable gift from the canny, visionary Nathan Cogan, I was able to collaborate with excellent student researchers and teaching assistants: Melory Mirashrafi, Kiana Anderson, Abigail Edwards, and Madison Willis. I appreciated the invitation from several colleagues to share preliminary versions of my research on their campuses: Priti Joshi at the University of Puget Sound, Kevin Dettmar at Pomona College, Sarah Wagner-McCoy at Reed College, Rebecca Lingafelter at Lewis and Clark College, and Ayanna Thompson at Arizona State University. David Haglund at the *New Yorker*, Lauren N. Williams at the *Atlantic*, and Sharon Marcus and Ben Platt at *Public Books* provided incisive editing on earlier articles that informed this project.

At a crucial moment, Portland State University offered me a new academic home where many colleagues have supported my work through their expertise, generosity, and institutional knowledge, among them Marie Lo, Bishupal Limbu, Elisabeth Ceppi, Josh Epstein, Joel Bettridge, Jonathan Walker, Kathi Inman Berens, Robyn Crummer, Michael Clark, Paul Collins, Karin Magaldi, Solomon Weisbard, Sarah Dougher, Catherine McNeur, Annie Lindgren, Todd Rosenstiel, and Sarah Schwarz. I'm grateful to the students in my seminars on *Hamilton* and the American musical for sharpening my thinking, sparking my curiosity, and sustaining my faith in the future of creativity. More than two decades ago, Yale professor Joanne B. Freeman introduced me to the age of Hamilton and Jefferson and the pleasures of primary-source research; she's been an encouraging guide ever since.

Writing can be isolating, but I felt lucky to pursue this project in the company of friends who pushed my ideas and renewed my energy over walks, lunches, phone calls, and cross-country visits: Nick Buccola, Rachel Norman, David Sumner, Rachel Schley, Pat Cottrell, Alicia Jo Rabins, Rebecca Clarren, Daniel Littlewood, Alex Liebman, Frances Brown, Stephen

Fishbach, Anna Ziegler, Eric Calderwood, Michael Schachter, Elizabeth Tavares, and Lisa Rosenbaum. Whenever I came to New York City, Marcella and Jason Manoharan opened their beautiful home to me with unmatched warmth. Gernot Wagner and Siripanth Nippita also let my family stay in their lovely apartment for a key visit.

I'm deeply indebted to those who read the entire manuscript as I drafted it. My beloved aunt Jude Pollack responded with an open heart and reminded me to look for the humanity in every character. My ever-loving, ever-supportive parents, Debby Pollack and Barry Pelzner, and my extraordinarily caring in-laws, Lois and Rick Rosenbaum, kept their eyes trained on what was most important, as they do in so much of my life. My dear sister, Emma Pelzner, brought good judgment and a sense of humor to puncture my pretensions, as usual. Lindsey Mantoan, a loyal friend and musical-theater maestro, not only cheered and refined each chapter but also guided me in cutting down the first draft when it ended up twice the desired length and talked me through each stage of the writing process on our Tryon Creek walks. Anna Keesey sprinkled her literary magic on my fledgling sentences, and Harper McClure offered me editorial notes with a wisdom many times her years.

Most of all, I'm grateful to Laura Rosenbaum, who's never stopped believing in this book or its author. She models love and thoughtfulness, conscientious hard work, intellectual rigor, and a sense of play, adventure, inquisitiveness, and care for our children and me every day.

Noah and Maya, you have endured this project with your customary humor, curiosity, and ethical sense. I remember years ago when you rallied your friends to put on an original *Hamilton*–Harry Potter mash-up in your elementary-school library. ("The broom where it happens . . . ") I can't wait to see what you learn to do next.

NOTES

All quotes except as noted below come from interviews conducted by the author with the following sources, listed according to the sequence of Lin-Manuel Miranda's career (with some overlap between sections):

Lin-Manuel Miranda: 2/18/22, 9/9/22, 9/12/22, 12/19/22, 1/9/23, 2/15/23, 3/15/23, 6/21/23, 9/20/23, 6/24/24, 7/31/24, 9/9/24.

Family: Luz Towns-Miranda, 3/9/22, 9/12/22, 9/20/23, 5/16/24; Luis A. Miranda Jr., 1/12/19, 10/2/20, 6/13/22, 3/27/23; Luz Miranda-Crespo, 3/15/22, 3/31/23; Yamilla Miranda, 3/10/23; Rodolfo Concepción, 3/10/23; Vanessa Nadal, 3/15/22, 9/20/23, 1/10/25.

Hunter College Elementary and High School: Barbara Ames, 6/27/22; Rembert Herbert, 6/29/22; Michael Stratechuk, 8/12/22; Satinder Jawanda, 9/2/22; Campbelle Austin, 11/7/23; Gina Nocera McCort, 2/10/23; Billy and Diane Baker, 6/7/22; Dan SanGermano, 8/2/22; Arthur Lewis, 7/18/22; Luke Stein, 7/28/22; James Green-Armytage, 2/10/23; Emily Pinkowitz, 2/13/23; Clare Newman, 7/18/24; Alex Sarlin, 2/8/23; Rob Sosin, 9/8/23; Matt Korahais, 11/30/23; Siobhan Lockhart, 1/30/23; David Rosen, 12/11/23; Chris Hayes, 7/26/22; Andrew Gursky, 8/1/22; Paul Jacobs, 8/11/22; Adam Rauscher, 8/15/22, 7/26/23; Aaron Leopold, 8/17/22; Rachel Axler, 9/5/23; Isaac Hurwitz, 9/6/22; Loren Hammonds, 11/4/22; Antonia Grilikhes-Lasky, 2/1/23; Lona Kaplan-Werner, 6/26/23; Meredith Summerville, 7/15/22, 8/4/22, 6/18/24, 7/2/24, 8/14/24; David Davidson, 5/6/22, 7/1/22; Mark Roaquin, 7/25/22; Dan Gonen, 3/22/23; Dane Martinez, 2/17/23; Rebecca Podolsky, 2/6/23; Elia Monte-Brown, 9/28/23; Una LaMarche, 6/22/23; Michael Frazer, 5/23/22; Eric Fleisig-Greene, 2/1/23; Sophie Oberfield, 11/19/22; Abigail Weintraub, 1/6/23,

1/30/23; Vanessa Nadal, 3/15/22, 9/20/23, 1/10/25; Laura Weidman Powers, 11/30/22; John Weidman, 10/21/22.

Wesleyan University: Josh Gleich, 7/6/23, 7/10/23; Jake Cohen, 7/18/23; Dani Snyder-Young, 8/1/22, 8/10/22; Sarah Krainin, 8/19/22; Sara Elisa Miller, 6/30/22, 7/29/22; Owen Panettieri, 7/21/22; Sabina Neugebauer, 4/13/23; Katie Takayanagi, 5/9/23; Dawn Papacena, 2/3/23; Leana Amáez, 4/25/23; Ralphie Santiago, 5/7/23; Julio Pabón, 4/18/23; M. Graham Smith, 6/7/22, 6/14/22, 7/6/23; Josh Hecht, 5/19/23; Emily Wilson-Tobin, 7/12/23; Siobhan Lockhart, 1/30/23; Antonia Grilikhes-Lasky, 2/1/23; Abigail Weintraub, 1/6/23, 1/30/23; Alex Horwitz, 7/26/22, 7/27/22; Murray Horwitz, 6/27/23; Micah Allen, 10/5/22; Jeff Zorabedian, 6/22/23; Una LaMarche, 6/22/23; Aileen Payumo, 8/29/22, 10/3/22; Lauren Bloom Hanover, 6/10/22; Bill Sherman, 3/16/22, 3/17/22; John Adler, 2/8/23; Matthew Lerner, 6/13/23; Jesse Soursourian, 6/20/23; Bajir Cannon, 10/17/22; Karl Scheibe, 7/12/23; William Stowe, 3/13/23; Rashida Z. Shaw McMahon, 1/27/23; By Martinez-Castaneda, 9/28/23.

In the Heights: Thomas Kail, 4/14/22, 9/12/23; Anthony Veneziale, 5/20/22; Neil Patrick Stewart, 8/15/22; Bill Sherman, 3/16/22, 3/17/22; Jill Furman, 7/20/22; Kevin McCollum, 7/21/22; Jeffrey Seller, 7/29/22, 9/13/22, 11/15/22, 12/20/22; Alex Lacamoire, 5/5/22, 10/17/22; Quiara Alegría Hudes, 12/5/22, 12/7/22; Andy Blankenbuehler, 8/13/22, 8/19/22; Christopher Jackson, 1/5/23; Janet Dacal, 8/9/22; Andréa Burns, 8/11/22; Robin de Jesús, 8/9/22, 8/16/22; Javier Muñoz, 3/26/23; Karen Olivo, 7/26/22; Mandy Gonzalez, 7/15/22; Olga Merediz, 7/28/22; Stephanie Klemons, 1/12/24; Kurt Crowley, 1/8/24; Andrew Fried, 8/17/23; Scott Sanders, 1/25/23; Jon M. Chu, 8/22/22; Alice Brooks, 10/22/22; Myron Kerstein, 11/4/22.

Freestyle Love Supreme: Anthony Veneziale, 5/20/22; Chris "Shockwave" Sullivan, 4/25/22; Bill Sherman, 3/16/22, 3/17/22; Arthur Lewis, 7/18/22; Christopher Jackson, 1/5/23; Thomas Kail, 4/14/22, 9/12/23; Jill Furman, 7/20/22; Utkarsh Ambudkar, 8/13/22; Andrew Bancroft, 4/27/22; Andrew Fried, 8/17/23.

Bring It On: Andy Blankenbuehler, 8/13/22, 8/19/22; Tom Kitt, 7/1/22; Amanda Green, 7/27/22; Jeff Whitty, 7/20/22; Alex Lacamoire, 5/5/22, 10/17/22; Kurt Crowley, 1/8/24; Adrienne Warren, 6/14/24.

Hamilton: Ron Chernow, 8/17/22; Jeffrey Seller, 7/29/22, 9/13/22, 11/15/22, 12/20/22; Jill Furman, 7/20/22; Oskar Eustis, 11/11/22, 12/2/22; Thomas Kail, 4/14/22, 9/12/23; Alex Lacamoire, 5/5/22, 10/17/22; Andy Blankenbuehler, 8/13/22, 8/19/22; Stephanie Klemons, 1/12/24; Kurt Crowley, 1/8/24; Christopher Jackson, 1/5/23; Leslie Odom Jr., 10/26/22; Renée Elise Goldsberry, 12/8/22; Phillipa Soo, 11/14/22; Jonathan Groff, 1/6/23; Javier Muñoz, 3/26/23; Joanne Freeman, 4/23/19; Annette Gordon-Reed, 4/24/19; Alex Horwitz, 7/26/22, 7/27/22; Gillian Pensavalle, 4/27/22; Martha Southgate, 9/14/23.

Disney: Tom MacDougall, 1/27/23; Opetaia Foaʻi, 10/25/22; Mark Mancina, 9/6/22; Jared Bush, 8/10/22; Rob Marshall, 8/18/22; Charise Castro Smith, 5/2/23; Germaine Franco, 10/21/22; Olga Merediz, 7/28/22; Mike Elizondo, 9/6/22, 12/13/24.

Tick, Tick . . . Boom!: Julie Oh, 8/31/22; Julie Larson, 9/2/22; Steven Levenson, 7/25/22; Alice Brooks, 10/22/22; Andrew Weisblum, 1/27/23; Myron Kerstein, 11/4/22; Mariela Comitini, 1/10/24; Bill Sherman, 3/16/22, 3/17/22; Alex Lacamoire, 5/5/22, 10/17/22; Kurt Crowley, 1/8/24; Robin de Jesús, 8/9/22, 8/16/22; Christopher Jackson, 1/5/23; Janet Dacal, 8/9/22; Agustina San Martin, 10/3/22.

Additional projects: Stephen Schwartz, 6/29/22; Robert Lopez, 4/27/23; John Kander, 7/13/22; Kyle Jarrow, 7/12/23; Kristoffer Diaz, 5/5/23; Kirk DeMicco, 8/1/22; James Lapine, 1/27/23; Oliver Butler, 1/23/23; Ira Glass, 1/26/23; Robyn Semien, 6/12/23; Michael Mayer, 1/31/24; Michael Starobin, 7/3/23; Alan Menken, 8/18/22; Andrew Lloyd Webber, 2/1/23; Shaina Taub, 12/6/24; Eisa Davis, 11/28/23, 5/31/24; John Buzzetti, 2/6/24.

All lyrics except as noted below are quoted from Lin-Manuel Miranda, Quiara Alegría Hudes, and Jeremy McCarter, *In the Heights: Finding Home* (New York: Random House, 2021); *Bring It On: The Musical,* music by Tom

Kitt and Lin-Manuel Miranda, lyrics by Amanda Green and Lin-Manuel Miranda (Milwaukee, WI: Hal Leonard, 2012); Lin-Manuel Miranda and Jeremy McCarter, *Hamilton: The Revolution* (New York: Grand Central Publishing, 2016); and, for *Moana, Vivo,* and *Encanto,* from *The Lin-Manuel Miranda Collection* (Milwaukee, WI: Hal Leonard, 2022).

Prologue

1   *its most-streamed title*: Alison Durkee, "'Hamilton' Boosts a Struggling Disney as Broadcast Dominated Streaming Platforms In July," *Forbes*, August 10, 2020.

1   *the most-streamed movie in the world*: "Streaming Unwrapped: Streaming Viewership Goes to the Library in 2023," Nielson, January 2024.

2   *2022 songwriter of the year*: Xander Zellner, "Lin-Manuel Miranda Is the Top Hot 100 Songwriter of 2022: The Year in Charts," *Billboard*, December 1, 2022.

3   *suggested I check out the guy*: Daniel Pollack-Pelzner, "American Playwrights Try to Reinvent the History Play," *New Yorker,* August 9, 2016.

3   *I covered the 2017 opening*: Daniel Pollack-Pelzner, "How Will 'Hamilton' Play in England?," *New Yorker,* December 16, 2017, and Daniel Pollack-Pelzner, "The Surprising Timeliness of *Hamilton* in London," *New Yorker,* January 6, 2018.

3   *I traveled to Puerto Rico*: Daniel Pollack-Pelzner, "The Mixed Reception of the *Hamilton* Premiere in Puerto Rico," *Atlantic*, January 18, 2019.

3   *I wrote about his contributions*: Daniel Pollack-Pelzner, "Lin-Manuel Meets 'Moana,'" *Public Books,* December 2, 2016, and Daniel Pollack-Pelzner, "'Mary Poppins,' and a Nanny's Shameful Flirting with Blackface," *New York Times,* January 28, 2019.

3   *a born genius*: See, for instance, Rembert Browne, "Genius: A Conversation with 'Hamilton' Maestro Lin-Manuel Miranda," *Grantland*, September 29, 2015, and Jeff MacGregor, "Meet Lin-Manuel Miranda, the Genius Behind 'Hamilton,' Broadway's Newest Hit," *Smithsonian*, November 12, 2015.

5   *artistic genius is a team sport*: I'm indebted to Frances Z. Brown for this formulation.

1: *The Top of the World*

9   *songs like "Camptown Races"*: Program from a piano recital by students of Suzzan Craig, Lin-Manuel's piano teacher, courtesy of Luz Towns-Miranda.

10   *"Music became a route to applause"*: Lin-Manuel Miranda, opening keynote at the Association of Performing Arts Presenters Conference, New York City, March 18, 2013.

11 *"Your feelings are as real"*: Alvyn M. Freed, *T.A. for Tots* (Jalmar Press, 1973), 92–93.

12 *Jewish and Irish immigrants*: For the history of immigrants in Inwood and northern Manhattan, see Robert W. Snyder, *Crossing Broadway: Washington Heights and the Promise of New York City* (Ithaca, NY: Cornell University Press, 2015).

13 *Cita and her brother played a game*: Juan A. Ramírez, "Lin-Manuel Miranda, Eisa Davis, and Mike Elizondo Talk Assembling Their Wildly Ambitious, Deliciously Theatrical New Hip-Hop Concept Album, *Warriors*," *Vogue*, October 18, 2024.

13 *Born in a hill town*: This biographical sketch of Luis A. Miranda Jr. draws on the documentary *Siempre, Luis,* directed by John James (HBO, 2020), and Luis A. Miranda Jr. and Richard Wolffe, *Relentless: My Story of the Latino Spirit That Is Transforming America* (New York: Hachette Books, 2024).

13 *"Koch loved him"*: *Siempre, Luis.*

14 *"The Garbage Pail Kids are in town"*: Lin-Manuel posted this childhood recording on his SoundCloud.

15 *"We were a struggling middle-class family"*: Miranda and Wolffe, *Relentless,* 162.

15 *"I could do no wrong"*: David Low, "Scaling the Heights," *Wesleyan Alumni Magazine,* June 20, 2007.

15 *She'd pick him up*: Lin-Manuel Miranda, "Lin-Manuel Miranda: Scaling the Heights," Broadway.com, January 9, 2007, https://www.broadway.com/buzz/6213/lin-manuel-miranda-scaling-the-heights/. He posted about Now and Laters with Mundi on Twitter, June 26, 2018.

15 *selective public school*: For the history of Hunter College Elementary School and its admission policies, see Elizabeth Stone, *The Hunter College Campus Schools for the Gifted: The Challenge of Equity and Excellence* (New York: Teachers College Press, 1992).

15 *sharing his crayons*: Lin-Manuel tells this anecdote in his Hunter College High School commencement speech, June 26, 2008; video posted on Facebook by John Shang.

15 *"Inside of me is a volcano"*: Lin-Manuel Miranda, "Gross Is Great!," a poem he wrote as a first-grader for a school collection, *Turning Grass and Hay into Emeralds and Gold,* Hunter College Elementary School, courtesy of Luz Towns-Miranda.

16 *On an elementary-school standardized test*: California Achievement Test for Lin-Manuel Miranda, Hunter College Elementary School, grade three, courtesy of Luz Towns-Miranda.

16 *"I am a very bad poet"*: Lin-Manuel Miranda, "Weird Poem," courtesy of Luz Towns-Miranda.

17 *"Nana Roja Para Mi Hijo Lin Manuel"*: Lin-Manuel posted a copy of the poem that José Manuel Torres Santiago inscribed to him on Twitter, March 3, 2016.

For English translations, I'm indebted to comparative literature professor Rachel Norman.

18   *"In my neighborhood"*: "Eleven Things We Learned from Lin-Manuel Miranda's Desert Island Discs," *Desert Island Discs,* podcast, BBC, October 11, 2019.

19   *"Land of Confusion"*: "Digital #Ham4Ham 2/24/16—Lin's Stage Debut, Land of Confusion," *Hamilton,* February 24, 2016, YouTube, https://www.youtube .com/watch?v=lydVr7muHXc.

20   *"When there's trouble"*: *We Are Freestyle Love Supreme,* directed by Andrew Fried, 2020.

20   *Hip-hop had been born in the Bronx*: For histories of hip-hop, see Jeff Chang, *Can't Stop Won't Stop: A History of the Hip-Hop Generation* (New York: Picador, 2005); Shea Serrano, *The Rap Year Book* (New York: Abrams, 2015); Jonathan Abrams, *The Come Up: An Oral History of the Rise of Hip-Hop* (New York: Crown, 2022).

20   *another big sibling*: Lin-Manuel Miranda, *The Hamilton Mixtape,* Lincoln Center American Songbook Series, January 11, 2012, filmed for Lincoln Center Archives.

21   *"after some initial nervousness"*: Lin-Manuel's fourth-grade report card from Ms. Gottling, courtesy of Luz Towns-Miranda.

21   Romeo and Juliet *narrative*: Lin-Manuel's sixth-grade report card from Ms. Fogler, which mentions "DMC Meets 24601," courtesy of Luz Towns-Miranda.

21   *"It rocked my world"*: Julie Bloom, "Lin-Manuel Miranda on 'Mary Poppins Returns' and Movie Musicals," *New York Times,* November 2, 2018.

21   *dancing to the* Footloose *soundtrack*: "Young Lin-Manuel Miranda: *Footloose,*" Usnavi, posted April 18, 2011, YouTube, https://youtu.be/kEdiwkQ13dk.

21   *"I was never the brightest student"*: Miranda, Hunter College High School commencement speech.

22   *"Nos jodimos todos ahora"*: Lin-Manuel Miranda, Twitter, December 28, 2017.

24   *he sang one of the Phantom's big solos*: Erica Rosenfeld Halverson and Alek Lev, hosts, *Arts Educators Save the World,* podcast, interview with Lin-Manuel Miranda, August 29, 2022.

24   *"Life is all right in America"*: Lin-Manuel Miranda and Emily Pinkowitz, "America," *Four Plus Six by Six,* Hunter College Elementary School, 1992, video courtesy of Barbara Ames.

2: Brick Prison

26   *rounds of admissions tests*: For the history of Hunter's admissions policies, see Stone, *The Hunter College Campus Schools for the Gifted.* For a criticism of Hunter's claim to meritocratic admissions written by one of Lin-Manuel's classmates, see Chris Hayes, *The Twilight of the Elites: America After Meritocracy* (New York: Crown, 2013).

27 *"I Ran with Roses"*: Lin-Manuel Miranda, opening keynote at the Association of Performing Arts Presenters Conference, New York City, March 18, 2013.

28 *For a unit on* Macbeth: Lin-Manuel posted the *Macbeth* video on Twitter, December 29, 2017.

29 *"That lousy Hasidim"*: Miranda, Association of Performing Arts Presenters Conference.

29 *"Lin-Manuel—This is an excellent"*: Lin-Manuel quotes Dr. Herbert's note in his letter nominating Dr. Herbert for the 2011 Kennedy Center/Stephen Sondheim Inspirational Teacher Awards; Dr. Herbert was one of the winners.

30 *"It was the first time"*: Miranda, Association of Performing Arts Presenters Conference.

30 *"Dr. Herbert essentially called me out"*: Miranda, letter nominating Dr. Herbert for the 2011 Kennedy Center/Stephen Sondheim Inspirational Teacher Award.

30 *Cynthia Nixon was an alum*: Amy Eliza Greenstadt, correspondence with the author, March 24, 2023. For Nixon's appearances, see Marc Acito, "Cynthia Nixon Talks Making Broadway History While Still in College and Her Theatrical Obsession," *Playbill*, October 4, 2014.

30 *two future filmmakers*: The filmmakers were Mora Stephens and Cas Nozkowski; the television producer was Siobhan Lockhart; the theater professor was Matt Korahais; the dancer was Rebecca Alson-Milkman; the comedy writer was Rachel Axler.

31 Swingline 457: Thanks to Siobhan Lockhart for sharing the script of Rob Sosin's *Swingline 457*.

33 *On a Saturday*: "Thank You, Dr. Herbert," Usnavi, posted May 20, 2012, YouTube, https://youtu.be/ieQJH1BlNIU.

33 *too fancy*: Jesse Thorn, host, *Bullseye with Jesse Thorn*, podcast, interview with Lin-Manuel Miranda, November 25, 2019.

33 The Pushcart War: "Young Lin-Manuel Miranda . . . *The Pushcart War*," Usnavi, posted May 20, 2012, YouTube, https://youtu.be/L6T8TCM1t3w.

34 *Lin-Manuel devoured*: Robert Rodriguez, *Rebel Without a Crew* (New York: Plume, 1996).

36 *"I had this horrible feeling"*: Lin-Manuel Miranda, correspondence with Aaron Leopold, courtesy of Aaron Leopold.

39 *"It wasn't until this song"*: Lin-Manuel Miranda, *The Hamilton Mixtape*, Lincoln Center American Songbook Series, January 11, 2012, filmed for Lincoln Center Archives.

40 *"Well, hello, my name is Lin"*: *Fresh Air with Terry Gross*, podcast, interview with Lin-Manuel Miranda, January 3, 2017.

41 *she crouched down*: *The Pirates of Penzance*, Hunter College High School DVD, 1995, courtesy of Rachel Axler.

41 *"ON stage"*: Lin-Manuel Miranda, note on Meredith Summerville's poster for *The Pirates of Penzance*, February 1995, courtesy of Meredith Summerville.

41 *"All for the Best"*: Macauley Peterson, who played Jesus, posted a video of the performance: "*Godspell*, the Musical: 'All for the Best' (with Lin-Manuel Miranda)," Macauley Peterson, posted August 27, 2011, YouTube, https://youtu.be/Mgb1w37Z_tM.

41 *"LIN ENUNCIATE"*: Meredith Summerville notebook for *Godspell*, courtesy of Meredith Summerville.

42 *an unexpected slap*: *Godspell*, video recording, Hunter College High School, 1996, courtesy of Lin-Manuel Miranda.

43 *"Rent rocked my conception"*: Lin-Manuel Miranda, "Pursuing the Muse Against the Clock," *New York Times*, June 19, 2014.

43 *"It felt like"*: *Bullseye with Jesse Thorn*, Miranda interview.

44 *"Mark lives for his work"*: Jonathan Larson, "Goodbye Love," *Rent* (New York: Melcher Media, 1997), 121.

44 *"That's when Jonathan Larson"*: Lin-Manuel Miranda, "When the Truth Pops Out," *Moth*, June 30, 2021.

44 *"No one had ever told me"*: *Fresh Air with Terry Gross*, Miranda interview.

46 *"You probably do not remember me"*: All script quotes come from Lin-Manuel Miranda, *Nightmare in D Major*, Hunter College High School, 1997, recording courtesy of Arthur Lewis.

48 *Chris's production*: *Nightmare in D Major*, Hunter College High School, Brick Prison, VHS, 1997, courtesy of Eric Fleisig-Greene.

3: *Dream Show*

49 *"Rep will be your life"*: Meredith Summerville, notes for directing *A Chorus Line*, Hunter College High School, December 1996, courtesy of Meredith Summerville.

51 *"Dueling is a sin"*: Lin-Manuel Miranda, Burr-Hamilton duel shooting script, April 10, 1996, courtesy of Meredith Summerville.

51 *"He thought that"*: The history teacher, Irv Steinfink, offered a different recollection when he was interviewed after the musical *Hamilton* became a hit. "Every student chose a research paper to work on for the semester on whatever topic they wish," Steinfink told a *Newsweek* reporter. "When I came to Lin, he hadn't yet a clue, so I told him to think for a while and come to me later. He approached me at my desk and still was blank, so I recommended him the Burr-Hamilton duel. He lit up and agreed and, in the end, submitted a wonderful term paper, A-plus." Zach Schonfeld, "The High-School Teacher Who Introduced Lin-Manuel Miranda to Alexander Hamilton," *Newsweek*, June 13, 2016.

54 *at lunchtime in room 210*: This account draws extensively on a Facebook post

by David Davidson, November 16, 2021, which Lin-Manuel Miranda calls the most accurate description of Sondheim's visit, as well as ten additional author interviews.

55   *"That's the first thing"*: David Axelrod, *The Axe Files*, podcast, Lin-Manuel Miranda interview, October 3, 2016.

55   *"I was a kid"*: Mike Birbiglia, *Working It Out*, podcast, Lin-Manuel Miranda interview, October 21, 2024.

56   *"watching a mortally wounded animal"*: Ben Brantley, "The Lure of Gang Violence to a Latin Beat," *New York Times*, January 30, 1998.

56   The Capeman *closed*: Larry Rohter, "Paul Simon's 'Capeman' Stalks Another Chance," *New York Times*, August 11, 2010.

57   *"Well, I'm only just thirteen"*: All script quotes come from Lin-Manuel Miranda's script for *7 Minutes in Heaven* and the Hunter College High School, Brick Prison, digital recording, 1998, courtesy of Lin-Manuel Miranda.

58   *"It's the first song I wrote that sounds like me"*: Lin-Manuel Miranda, opening keynote at the Association of Performing Arts Presenters Conference, New York City, March 18, 2013.

61   *Jeanine Basinger*: Sam Wasson, "The Professor of Hollywood," *Hollywood Reporter*, December 10, 2015.

4: *La Casa*

62   *old Saturn wagon*: Lin-Manuel wrote a rap about each of his first three years at Wesleyan that he performed for the Wesleyan Alumni Association annual meeting on May 26, 2012. He discussed his college listening tastes on the podcast *New York Times Popcast* on September 25, 2015.

63   *"We are occupied"*: Dani Snyder, "Dani Snyder Brings Jesus to Wesleyan," *Wesleyan Argus*, February 26, 1999.

64   *On the Wesleyan stage*: "Young Lin-Manuel Miranda: *Jesus Christ Superstar*," Usnavi, posted June 7, 2011, YouTube, https://youtu.be/oVy4jOf9Umo.

64   *"I was like, 'Who is this freshman'"*: *Partners*, podcast, Lin-Manuel Miranda and Thomas Kail interview, April 3, 2022.

66   *Gilberto Concepción de Gracia*: See Gerald J. Meyer, "Pedro Albizu Campos, Gilberto Concepción de Gracia, and Vito Marcantonio's Collaboration in the Cause of Puerto Rico's Independence," *Centro Journal* 23, no. 1 (Spring 2011): 87–123.

66   *Latin Explosion*: For context on the music industry refashioning Spanish-language stars for crossover appeal, see Leila Cobo, *Decoding "Despacito": An Oral History of Latin Music* (New York: Vintage, 2021).

67   *"Benny Blanco from the Bronx"*: Lin-Manuel Miranda, Twitter, August 11, 2011.

68   *"baby doll"*: Lin-Manuel Miranda, *In the Heights*, Wesleyan cast recording, April 2000; Wesleyan script courtesy of Meredith Summerville.

68   *"Never give your heart away"*: *In the Heights*, Wesleyan recording.

69   *In the notebook for his astronomy class*: Lin-Manuel posted the sketch on Twitter, March 7, 2019.

70   *his own best friend*: The friend, Dan SanGermano, says: "I remember seeing Lincoln in early incarnations of *In the Heights* and going, *Oh, that's me!* I came out to Lin in our senior year of high school. He was one of the first people I told. For me, it was a big monumental moment of sharing with my best friend. I was flattered that he took that into his world. I was surprised. I didn't know he was working on this character."

70   *"My salty tears"*: Lin-Manuel Miranda inscription, *In the Heights* Wesleyan script, courtesy of Meredith Summerville.

71   *an audition notice*: Luis Miranda posted the audition notice on Twitter, February 27, 2016.

73   *He developed a nervous tic*: Lin-Manuel Miranda told a version of this story in his University of Pennsylvania commencement address, May 16, 2016.

5: *Basket Case*

76   *Alex, who'd drawn the poster*: *In the Heights* and *Basketcase* posters courtesy of Alex Horwitz.

78   *Lin-Manuel planned to drive*: Lin-Manuel shared his experience on 9/11 in his commencement address at Wesleyan University, May 24, 2015.

79   *"This is, in many ways"*: Lin-Manuel Miranda, director's note, *Basketcase*, Wesleyan University, September 2001, program courtesy of Micah Allen.

80   *"Come see"*: Pepe Ahn, email titled "THIS WEEKEND at the '92!!!," October 2, 2001, courtesy of Matthew Lerner.

80   *He wanted to write a strong role*: Pepe Ahn, "'On Borrowed Time' Reinvents Theater Experience," *Wesleyan Argus*, February 22, 2002.

81   *"That's sloppy, Lin"*: Lin-Manuel Miranda, "Lyrics: An Examination of Musical Theater Writing Through *On Borrowed Time*," thesis, Wesleyan University, 2002. All further thesis quotes come from this source.

83   *their first time downtown*: Lin-Manuel Miranda, "Pursuing the Muse Against the Clock," *New York Times*, June 19, 2024.

83   *"It was a sneak preview"*: Ibid.

83   *"work-in-progress"*: Lin-Manuel Miranda, email titled "My note for the program," February 13, 2002, courtesy of Matthew Lerner.

83   *he'd attempted a cappella harmonies*: Musical descriptions come from Lin-Manuel Miranda, *On Borrowed Time* cast album, February 2002, courtesy of Matthew Lerner.

86   *Bajir adapted*: Nicole Hsiang, "'Loveliest and Saddest Landscape' Reinvents Theater, an Old Classic," *Wesleyan Argus*, March 29, 2002.

6: *The Drama Book Shop*

88   *"Two thoughts occur to me"*: Lin-Manuel Miranda, "Scaling the Heights," Broadway.com, January 9, 2007, https://www.broadway.com/buzz/6213/lin -manuel-miranda-scaling-the-heights/.

90   *"I am Usnavi"*: Thanks to Neil Patrick Stewart for providing access to early *Heights* recordings from the Drama Book Shop.

90   *they jointly recited*: Lin-Manuel Miranda and Jeremy McCarter, *Hamilton: The Revolution* (New York: Grand Central Publishing, 2016), 22.

94   *"What if she's pregnant"*: Lin-Manuel told a version of this story in his University of Pennsylvania commencement address, May 16, 2016.

95   *"I'm graduating from college"*: Lin-Manuel Miranda, Hunter College High School commencement speech, June 26, 2008.

96   *Luis had seen how hard*: Luis A. Miranda Jr. and Richard Wolffe, *Relentless: My Story of the Latino Spirit That Is Transforming America* (New York: Hachette Books, 2024), 22.

96   *"For better or worse"*: *Siempre, Luis,* directed by John James (HBO, 2020).

96   *"I'll never live up"*: Miranda and Hudes, *In the Heights: Finding Home*, 45.

97   *"Dear baby"*: Luis A. Miranda Jr., email to Lin-Manuel Miranda, October 29, 2002, courtesy of Luis A. Miranda Jr.

7: *Voltron*

103   *she felt out of place*: This section draws on interviews conducted by the author while researching the article "Quiara Alegría Hudes Rewrites the American Landscape," *New Yorker*, April 15, 2018.

105   *"Like a drunk Chita Rivera"*: Lin-Manuel Miranda and Quiara Alegría Hudes, *In the Heights* (Milwaukee, WI: Applause Books, 2013), 30.

105   *"the watermelon of my heart"*: Ibid., 15.

106   *"I pop in the cassette"*: *In the Heights: El Sueñito*, podcast, Alex Lacamoire interview, June 2, 2021.

108   *"Research and empathy"*: Rhonda Abrams, "Tips from *Hamilton*'s Miranda," *USA Today*, March 14, 2018.

108   *"I want to change the landscape of American Musical Theatre"*: Lin-Manuel Miranda, application for the Jonathan Larson Performing Arts Foundation Award, 2003.

8: *The O'Neill*

111   *"We're always here"*: Lin-Manuel Miranda, "On My Shoulders," *In the Heights*, July 2005, courtesy of Alex Lacamoire.

112   *For the final shows, held in the barn*: This description draws on Jeremy McCarter's helpful scene-setting in *In the Heights: Finding Home*, 43.

114 *pop into the basement*: For a visual chronicle of this origin story, see the documentary *We Are Freestyle Love Supreme*, directed by Andrew Fried, 2020.

115 *"Foundations of Freestyle"*: Ibid.

115 *"Maya Angelou"*: This example of Lin-Manuel's freestyle was filmed for a Pivot TV show a few years later; see "Freestyle Love Supreme—Maya Angelou Clip," Pivot, posted October 21, 2014, YouTube, https://youtu.be /yClaU0cHDqM.

116 Whose Line Is It Anyway? *meets the Wu-Tang Clan*: E. H. Reiter, "Anthony Veneziale Talks About How the Love of Improv and Hip-Hop Became Freestyle Love Supreme," BroadwayWorld.com, June 30, 2022.

116 *"a bunch of fresh-faced"*: Lin-Manuel Miranda posted this review on Twitter, August 16, 2018.

117 *"Yo. If I won the lotto tomorrow"*: Lin-Manuel Miranda, "96,000," *In the Heights*, July 2005, courtesy of Alex Lacamoire.

118 *she listed salsa and hip-hop*: Lois Smith Brady, "Vows: Vanessa Nadal and Lin Miranda," *New York Times*, September 10, 2010.

119 *They salsaed*: Vanessa also told her version of this story as part of a Freestyle Love Supreme show at the party the night before her wedding; see "Lin Manuel & Vanessa's Pre Wedding BBQ," posted February 7, 2016, YouTube, https://youtu.be/Rm2uMmj0LQM.

119 *"Stop talking to me"*: Miranda and Hudes, *In the Heights*: *Finding Home*, 100, n. 1.

119 *the sentiment he felt as a child*: Ibid., n. 3.

9: *Off Broadway*

123 *the legends of* Fiddler on the Roof: Alisa Solomon provides a better-researched version of this legend in *Wonder of Wonders*: *A Cultural History of Fiddler on the Roof* (New York: Picador, 2013), 138–39.

129 *The set looked like Lin-Manuel's childhood view*: This description of the production at 37 Arts draws on the author's viewing of *In the Heights* at the Theater on Film and Tape Archive, New York Public Library for the Performing Arts, September 22, 2023.

130 *a Biggie-style slant rhyme*: Miranda and Hudes, *In the Heights*: *Finding Home*, 6, n. 1.

131 *Charles Isherwood's review*: Charles Isherwood, "From the Corner Bodega, the Music of Everyday Life," *New York Times*, February 9, 2007.

131 *David Rooney's review*: David Rooney, "In the Heights," *Variety*, February 8, 2007.

131 *"a musical that owes more to Big Pun"*: Jeremy McCarter, "Something's Coming," *New York*, February 14, 2007.

132 *less than 6 percent*: Karen Hauser, "The Demographics of the Broadway

Audience, 2008–2009," Broadway League, September 2009, https://static01
.nyt.com/packages/pdf/arts/NY2008-09revised.pdf.

132   *four out of five Broadway shows*: Joshua Rogers, "Invest in the Next 'Hamilton'? Broadway's Odds Look Like Silicon Valley's," *Forbes*, May 31, 2016.

10: *Broadway*

133   The Making of a Musical: Richard Altman with Mervyn Kaufman, *The Making of a Musical: Fiddler on the Roof* (New York: Crown, 1971).

134   *a bagful of little buttons*: Jeremy McCarter recounts this anecdote in *In the
Heights: Finding Home*, 71.

134   *The film crew*: The film crew was making the documentary *In the Heights:
Chasing Broadway Dreams*, directed by Paul Bozymowski, 2009. This scene
ended up being cut from the film, but it was posted online: "In the Heights,
Cut Sequence: Finding 96,000," posted June 13, 2021, YouTube, https://you
tu.be/_O_bD1xDO-8. All quotes in this scene come from this clip.

135   *"Sometimes you throw out good stuff"*: David Axelrod, *The Axe Files,* podcast,
Lin-Manuel Miranda interview, October 3, 2016.

137   *"Just breathe"*: Lin-Manuel Miranda, "Breathe," *In the Heights*, June 2007, recording courtesy of Alex Lacamoire.

137   *"I was painfully aware"*: *The Hamilcast*, podcast, Lin-Manuel Miranda interview, October 16, 2017.

138   *"Will I be"*: "Heights Cool Musical Too . . . Bet on It!," Usnavi, September 28,
2007, YouTube, https://www.youtube.com/watch?v=ep0tpRqaZ4Y.

138   *"You can come home to your a-bu-ela"*: "In the Heights . . . Abuela," Usnavi,
December 23, 2007, YouTube, https://youtu.be/bGoU1HBmNOQ.

139   *One night in January 2008*: This scene appears in *In the Heights: Chasing
Broadway Dreams*, directed by Paul Bozymowski, 2009. All quotes in this
scene come from the documentary.

140   *"I thank you for everything"*: Ibid.

140   *"I feel like it's commencement"*: Ibid.

140   *"The whole thing is to keep your head down"*: Ibid.

140   *"the first musical of the Barack Obama era"*: Richard Zoglin, "Life After *Rent*,"
Time, February 29, 2008.

140   *his dressing room*: Lin-Manuel gave Broadway.com a tour of his dressing room
at the Rodgers; see "Backstage at 'In the Heights' with Lin-Manuel Miranda,"
Broadwaycom, posted February 19, 2011, YouTube, https://youtu.be/en214
VS52qE.

141   *"Dreams come true, bitches"*: *In the Heights: Chasing Broadway Dreams*.

141   *"It's like prom night"*: Ibid.

141   *"Lin, I'm so sorry"*: "Luis Miranda and Family in Conversation with *The View*'s
Ana Navarro," Ninety-Second Street Y, May 6, 2024.

141   *"Eat 'em up"*: Lin-Manuel itemized his preshow ritual in an email to the *Heights* cast and subsequently posted it on Twitter on April 27, 2018.

141   *The applause started*: *In the Heights*: *Chasing Broadway Dreams* concludes with footage of the opening night performance and curtain call. All quotes in this scene come from the documentary.

142   *"not inconsiderable flaws"*: Isherwood, "From the Corner Bodega."

142   *"It has been lamented in certain circles"*: Charles Isherwood, "The View from Uptown: American Dreaming to a Latin Beat," *New York Times*, March 10, 2008.

142   *"Oh my God"*: *In the Heights*: *Chasing Broadway Dreams*.

144   *Hispanic attendance on Broadway*: Karen Hauser, "The Demographics of the Broadway Audience, 2008–2009," Broadway League.

144   *half the box office potential*: The week of April 20, 2008, for example, *In the Heights* earned $466,664 out of a potential gross of $925,549. See "Grosses, *In the Heights*," Playbill.com, https://playbill.com/production/gross/p3?production=00000150-aea2-d936-a7fd-eef6db330003.

145   *According to the* New York Times: Campbell Robertson, "Sunday in the Dark with Tony?," *New York Times*, June 13, 2008.

145   *"We have to be in* white mode*"*: *Siempre, Luis,* directed by John James (HBO, 2020).

147   *"I'll never forget"*: Frank DiGiacomo, "Lin-Manuel Miranda on His Lifelong Oscars Obsession and Why the Show Still Matters," *Hollywood Reporter*, February 20, 2017.

148   *grossing over one million dollars*: "Grosses," Playbill.com.

11: *The White House*

149   *he googled it*: Lin-Manuel Miranda interview for *Hamilton's America*, directed by Alex Horwitz (PBS, 2016), May 6, 2016; transcript courtesy of Alex Horwitz.

149   *at the Borders bookstore*: Ibid., January 11, 2014.

149   *By the time Hamilton turned fourteen*: Ron Chernow, *Alexander Hamilton* (New York: Penguin, 2004), 26.

150   *"Hamilton did not know it"*: Ibid., 37.

150   *make himself into a new man*: Ibid., 40. Chernow wrote that Hamilton "chose a psychological strategy adopted by many orphans and immigrants: he decided to cut himself off from his past and forge a new identity."

150   I know this guy: Miranda interview, *Hamilton's America*, January 11, 2014.

150   *recognized such an insatiable drive*: Chernow wrote that Hamilton's "relentless drive, his wretched feelings of shame and degradation, and his precocious self-sufficiency combined to produce a young man with an insatiable craving for success"; see Chernow, *Alexander Hamilton*, 40.

150　*he told Jeremy McCarter*: Lin-Manuel Miranda and Jeremy McCarter, *Hamilton: The Revolution* (New York: Grand Central Publishing, 2016), 10–11.

154　*"Hiya Daddy"*: Una LaMarche, email to Gara LaMarche, October 7, 2008, courtesy of Una LaMarche.

156　*his father got a call from David Axelrod*: Luis A. Miranda Jr. and Richard Wolffe, *Relentless: My Story of the Latino Spirit That Is Transforming America* (New York: Hachette Books, 2024), 171.

156　*Axelrod remembered Luis telling him*: David Axelrod, *The Axe Files,* podcast, Lin-Manuel Miranda interview, October 3, 2016.

156　*One of the first events*: "President and Mrs. Obama Open the White House Poetry Jam (1 of 8)," Obama White House, posted May 20, 2009, YouTube, https://youtu.be/cUfekqAJHeI.

156　*"An Evening of Music, Poetry, and the Spoken Word"*: Ibid.

156　*worked as solos*: Lin-Manuel solicited advice for solos he could perform from *In the Heights* in a Facebook post on April 24, 2009, that he reposted on Twitter on April 24, 2017.

156　*his first cabinet nominee*: President Barack Obama, "Remarks by the President in Nomination of Secretary of the Treasury," White House, January 10, 2013.

156　*He passed along the lyrics*: Miranda and Wolffe, *Relentless*, 171.

157　*He brought Lac a lyric sheet*: Alex Lacamoire described the process of arranging "Alexander Hamilton" in an interview with Laura Heywood; see "Alex Lacamoire on 'Hamilton,'" BUILD series, posted May 31, 2016, YouTube, https://youtu.be/Ux5CGsi6DAc.

157　*shared a van with James Earl Jones*: Blake Ross, "Lin-Manuel Goes Crazy for HOUSE and Hamilton," Playbill.com, September 21, 2009.

157　*"Um, I'm, I'm thrilled"*: "Lin-Manuel Miranda Performs at the White House Poetry Jam (8 of 8)," Obama White House, May 12, 2009, YouTube, https://youtu.be/WNFf7nMIGnE. Unless otherwise noted, all quotations and descriptions of the May 12, 2009, performance come from this video.

157　*"That's too scary"*: Adam Grant, *Taken for Granted*, podcast, "Lin-Manuel Daydreams, and His Dad Gets Things Done," June 29, 2021.

157　*"I was like, 'Okay'"*: Ibid.

159　*"Where is Timothy Geithner"*: Ross, "Lin-Manuel Goes Crazy."

12: *Working*

160　*he waited by his phone*: "Interview with Songwriter Lin-Manuel Miranda," WorkingTheMusical, June 3, 2011, YouTube, https://youtu.be/zP711T6OEUs.

161　*"We talked about"*: "Working: An Interview with Lin-Manuel Miranda," Old Globe, March 18, 2009, YouTube, https://youtu.be/Y8vdMDq_Rf0.

161　*He thought of his own Abuela Mundi*: Lin-Manuel Miranda, Twitter, February 3, 2018.

162 *"You should, because we stole it from you"*: "Joseph Stein and Lin-Manuel Miranda," Dramatists Guild Foundation, July 31, 2019, YouTube, https://youtu.be/BWknUMMbNrk.

162 *came up with their own spoof*: *Legally Brown: The Search for the Next Piragua Guy*, Usnavi, September 4, 2008, YouTube, https://youtu.be/K2yoyjJtKWg.

162 *"a surprising medical condition"*: "*Legally Brown* Exclusive: Hunter's Condition," Usnavi, September 17, 2008, YouTube, https://youtu.be/wn2aM7UxKag.

164 *"Boy, you'll be doing me a favor"*: All quotations from Sondheim come from Lin-Manuel's recollection in this interview as well as his address at Sondheim's memorial.

164 *"the hardest bilingual crossword puzzle"*: Patricia Cohen, "Same City, New Story," *New York Times*, March 11, 2009.

164 *moved to tears*: Luis A. Miranda Jr. and Richard Wolffe, *Relentless: My Story of the Latino Spirit That Is Transforming America* (New York: Hachette Books, 2024), 30–31.

165 *"I feel pretty"*: Stephen Sondheim, *Finishing the Hat: Collected Lyrics (1954–1981)* (New York: Knopf, 2010), 47.

165 *"A boy like that"*: Ibid., 52.

166 *Laurents heard complaints*: Patrick Healy, "Some 'West Side' Lyrics Are Returned to English," *New York Times*, August 26, 2009.

167 *"It was he who persuaded me"*: Sondheim, *Finishing the Hat*, 26.

13: *Bring It On*

171 *he imagined Burr rapping these lines*: Lin-Manuel, Twitter, August 16, 2016.

173 *"The answers to your questions"*: Stephen Sondheim, email to Lin-Manuel Miranda, November 27, 2009, courtesy of Lin-Manuel Miranda.

174 *"I just want to be Rubén Blades"*: Lin-Manuel Miranda, Twitter, December 7, 2011.

174 *a note from Kander*: "Backstage at 'In the Heights' with Lin-Manuel Miranda," Broadwaycom, February 19, 2011, YouTube, https://youtu.be/en214VS52qE.

174 *made him weep*: Lin-Manuel recorded his reaction to returning home in a Facebook post on December 20, 2009, and reposted it on Twitter, December 20, 2017.

174 *Universal Pictures had acquired the rights*: Michael Fleming, "Universal Gets 'In the Heights' Rights," *Variety*, November 6, 2008.

175 *three-hundred-person flash mob*: "'In the Heights' Flash Mob for Lin-Manuel Miranda—City Walk—Los Angeles," Flash Mob America, June 28, 2010, YouTube https://youtu.be/Klf8IBrXFWY.

175 *"Happier Than the Morning Sun"*: "Happier Than the Morning Sun . . . Lin's

Wedding Surprise," Usnavi, posted September 5, 2012, YouTube, https://youtu.be/kfqozP4LZT8.

175 *"To Life"*: All quotes from this performance come from "To Life: Vanessa's Wedding Surprise," Usnavi, posted September 8, 2010, YouTube, https://youtu.be/KgZ4ZTTfKO8.

176 *"the bride looked like a young Elizabeth Taylor"*: Lois Smith Brady, "Vows: Vanessa Nadal and Lin Miranda," *New York Times*, September 10, 2010.

176 *sales had tapered off*: See "Grosses, *In the Heights*," Playbill.com, https://playbill.com/production/gross/p3?production=00000150-aea2-d936-a7fd-eef6db330003.

177 *"What is* Bring It On*"*: Stephen Sondheim, email to Lin-Manuel Miranda, January 25, 2011, courtesy of Lin-Manuel Miranda.

178 *"Something that's a little scary"*: "*Playbill* Exclusive: 'Bring It On''s Miranda, Kitt and Green Sample Their Musical Wares," *Playbill*, posted July 2, 2012, YouTube, https://youtu.be/gRJAhvej5-o.

178 *"I knew that we had to drop"*: Ibid.

179 koo-kada-KAH-kada-koo-KAH-koo-KAH: "Lin-Manuel Miranda Shares the Secrets to Making Great Art," Lin-Manuel Miranda interview, Chicago Humanities Festival, September 23, 2016.

181 *"Version 5.67"*: Amanda Green, "Herkie Time: Amanda Green on Her Dream Collaboration for the High-Flying New Musical *Bring It On*," Broadway.com, July 24, 2012.

182 *Broadway debut of a whopping thirty actors*: Steven McElroy, "Broadway, Broadway, Here We Are! (Clap!)," *New York Times*, August 15, 2012.

182 *Reviews lauded*: See, for example, Charles Isherwood, "High School Rivalry, with a Leg Up," *New York Times*, August 1, 2012, and Scott Brown, "The Unexpected Charms of *Bring It On: The Musical*," *New York*, August 1, 2012.

182 *Ticket sales, however, never took off*: See "Grosses, *Bring It On: The Musical*," Playbill.com, https://playbill.com/production/gross?production=00000150-aea8-d936-a7fd-eefc733a0002.

182 *"We write musicals"*: "Lin-Manuel Miranda Shares the Secrets."

14: *American Songbook*

185 *"I was trying to prove my thesis"*: "Lin-Manuel Miranda Breaks Down His Biggest Songs, from *Hamilton* to *Moana*," Rotten Tomatoes, July 3, 2020, YouTube, https://youtu.be/Urp9MjHLP0s.

185 *"We all suffer from verbosity"*: Stephen Sondheim, email to Lin-Manuel Miranda, October 5, 2011, courtesy of Lin-Manuel Miranda.

185 *"I am not throwing away my shot"*: All quotations from this performance come from "My Shot First Draft," a demo that Lin-Manuel posted to his SoundCloud.

185 *"Eminem meets Sweeney Todd"*: Lin-Manuel Miranda, "*Hamilton* Equity Principal Auditions," BroadwayWorld.com, March 12, 2015.

186 *He tripped up*: Lin-Manuel Miranda and Jeremy McCarter, *Hamilton: The Revolution* (New York: Grand Central Publishing, 2016), 21.

186 *shout-outs to the greatest MCs*: "Lin-Manuel Miranda Breaks Down His Biggest Songs."

187 *"I wanted it to feel like his words are reverberating"*: Ibid.

187 *the most autobiographical line*: Miranda and McCarter, *Hamilton: The Revolution*, 28, n. 12.

187 *"I'm trying to make it the densest couplets"*: "Lin-Manuel Miranda Breaks Down His Biggest Songs."

187 *"felt the room lean"*: Gordon Cox, "'Hamilton' Star Lin-Manuel Miranda Is Ready for His Next Coup," *Variety*, September 27, 2016.

188 *"You could feel the hair"*: Hannah Ellis-Peterson, "'This Isn't Colour-Blind Casting': Hamilton Makes Its Politically Charged West End Debut," *Guardian*, December 20, 2017.

188 *"When we were upstairs afterwards"*: The West Wing Weekly, podcast, "*Hamilton* Special," Lin-Manuel Miranda and Thomas Kail interview, April 3, 2018.

188 *"That went well"*: Thomas Kail interview for *Hamilton's America*, directed by Alex Horwitz (PBS, 2016), March 18, 2016; transcript courtesy of Alex Horwitz.

189 *"What's interesting to you"*: The West Wing Weekly, "*Hamilton* Special."

189 *"Do you recommend writing"*: Miranda and McCarter, *Hamilton: The Revolution*, 173.

189 *"Absolutely"*: Ibid.

189 *Chernow's account described her*: Ron Chernow, *Alexander Hamilton* (New York: Penguin, 2004), 133.

190 *a perfect song*: "Countdown by Beyonce is the most perfect song ever written, and influences EVERYTHING," Lin-Manuel Miranda, Twitter, September 24, 2015.

191 *"Wilkommen, Bienvenue, Welcome"*: Lin-Manuel Miranda, Twitter, November 21, 2011.

191 *a little stray puppy*: Lin-Manuel Miranda, Twitter, November 22, 2018.

192 *"We were always much more compelled"*: Kail interview, *Hamilton's America*, March 18, 2016.

193 *"eliminate distance between then and now"*: Ibid.

193 *"the people who can pull off hip-hop"*: Lin-Manuel Miranda interview for *Hamilton's America*, directed by Alex Horwitz (PBS, 2016), January 11, 2014; transcript courtesy of Alex Horwitz.

194 *Lin-Manuel bounded onstage*: All descriptions and quotes from Lin-Manuel Miranda, *The Hamilton Mixtape*, Lincoln Center American Songbook Series, January 11, 2012, filmed for Lincoln Center Archives.

195 *Eminem's 8 Mile*: Miranda interview, *Hamilton's America*, May 6, 2016.

197   *"It was just like our first piano recital"*: Lin-Manuel Miranda, Twitter, January 13, 2012.

197   *"What it is, is hot"*: Stephen Holden, "Putting the Hip-Hop in History as Founding Fathers Rap," *New York Times*, January 12, 2012.

197   *Kevin and Jeffrey had split up*: Patrick Healy, "Producing Partnership Between 'Rent' and 'Avenue Q' Comes to an End," *New York Times*, January 6, 2012.

198   *"Though I've expressed to each of you"*: Jeffrey Seller, email to Lin-Manuel Miranda and Thomas Kail, May 2, 2012, courtesy of Jeffrey Seller.

15: *Non-Stop*

200   *"It sounds like a dude talking"*: *New York Times Popcast*, podcast, Lin-Manuel Miranda interview, September 25, 2015.

201   sir, sure, pure: The Instagram account @lin_manuel_out_of_context posted a photo of a page from Lin-Manuel's notebook with a list he'd written of rhymes for Burr, July 20, 2023.

202   *"with as much rapidity"*: Ron Chernow, *Alexander Hamilton* (New York: Penguin, 2004), 47.

202   *"the rhyme was too good to pass up"*: Lin-Manuel Miranda and Jeremy McCarter, *Hamilton: The Revolution* (New York: Grand Central Publishing, 2016), 23, n. 3.

202   *"Wherever I go, I know he goes"*: Stephen Sondheim, *Finishing the Hat: Collected Lyrics (1954–1981)* (New York: Knopf, 2010), 69.

202   *"Surprising a pro"*: Ibid., 71.

203   *"the God MC Sondheezy"*: Lin-Manuel Miranda, Twitter, February 4, 2015.

203   *"I wish I could bottle that laugh"*: Ibid.

203   *"A Westchester Farmer"*: Chernow, *Alexander Hamilton*, 57–59.

204   *Lin-Manuel cherished a tribute to Big Pun*: Lin-Manuel Miranda, Twitter, November 5, 2016.

204   *"getting my Bach on"*: Miranda and McCarter, *Hamilton: The Revolution*, 47.

205   *"Add homonyms ad hominem"*: Lin-Manuel Miranda, Twitter, July 23, 2013.

205   *"Feliz Usnavidad"*: Lin-Manuel Miranda, Twitter, December 24, 2011.

205   *"Sovereign State of Twitterico"*: Lin-Manuel Miranda, Twitter, October 31, 2011.

205   *"Population: 13,862"*: Lin-Manuel Miranda, Twitter, January 2, 2012.

205   *"My three worst addictions"*: Lin-Manuel Miranda, Twitter, September 24, 2014.

206   *"I think Lafayette wants to rap in French now"*: Lin-Manuel Miranda, Twitter, May 2, 2013.

206   *"YOU GUYS TODAY'S THE ANNIVERSARY"*: Lin-Manuel Miranda, Twitter, December 5, 2013.

206   *A friend of hers tweeted at Lin-Manuel*: Honor Sachs, Twitter, April 28, 2012.

206   *"I wish there was a war"*: Alexander Hamilton, *The Essential Hamilton: Letters and Other Writings*, ed. Joanne B. Freeman (New York: Library of America, 2017), 3.

207 *"I have the honor to be your obedient servant"*: For instance, Aaron Burr to Alexander Hamilton, June 18, 1804, ibid., 353.

207 Affairs of Honor: Joanne B. Freeman, *Affairs of Honor: National Politics in the New Republic* (New Haven, CT: Yale University Press, 2002); Miranda and McCarter, *Hamilton: The Revolution*, 99, n. 1.

209 *"There's one fucking character"*: Rembert Browne, "Genius: A Conversation with 'Hamilton' Maestro Lin-Manuel Miranda," *Grantland*, September 29, 2015.

209 *"Attend the tale of Sweeney Todd"*: Sondheim, *Finishing the Hat*, 333.

209 *wondered who would get to play Charley*: Pat Cerasaro, "Lin-Manuel Miranda Talks *Bring It On, Merrily, Heights, Hamilton* & More," BroadwayWorld.com, November 3, 2011.

210 *"Here's to us! Who's like us"*: Sondheim, *Finishing the Hat*, 394.

211 *a toast that circulated*: Meryle Secrest, *Stephen Sondheim: A Life* (New York: Vintage, 2011), 90, 316.

211 *"When I was a teenager and full of dreams"*: *The Hamilcast*, podcast, Lin-Manuel Miranda interview, October 16, 2017.

211 *"And if you believe that"*: Ibid.

211 I WISH THERE WAS A WAR: Lin-Manuel Miranda posted a photo of his sand inscription on Twitter, February 19, 2015.

212 *close not with an answer*: Tommy Kail told Jeremy McCarter, "You have to end an act with a dramatic question"; see *Hamilton: The Revolution*, 124.

212 *He brought his Chernow*: Lin-Manuel Miranda, Twitter, July 20, 2013.

212 *"this foundation of incredible faith"*: Ruthie Fierberg, "*Hamilton* Director Tommy Kail Talks the Show's Earliest Days of Development," *Playbill*, June 10, 2016.

213 *"That's a terrible idea"*: Daveed Diggs, "The Undefeated Presents: Hamilton In-Depth," DisneyPlus.com, 2020.

213 *"I could write anything for Daveed"*: Lin-Manuel Miranda interview for *Hamilton's America*, directed by Alex Horwitz (PBS, 2016), May 6, 2016; transcript courtesy of Alex Horwitz.

213 *"So what does he sound like"*: Ibid.

213 *ninth and eleventh notes*: Lin-Manuel Miranda, Twitter, July 3, 2018.

214 *"Good God, you can write"*: Leslie Odom Jr., Twitter, July 27, 2013.

16: *The Room Where It Happens*

216 The Heartbreak of Aaron Burr: H. W. Brands, *The Heartbreak of Aaron Burr* (New York: Anchor Books, 2012).

216 *he learned a detail*: Lin-Manuel Miranda and Jeremy McCarter, *Hamilton: The Revolution* (New York: Grand Central Publishing, 2016), 87, n. 3.

216 *"the ticking clock of mortality"*: Lin-Manuel Miranda, commencement address at Wesleyan University, May 24, 2015.

217   *"Being a songwriter"*: Steve Appleford, "Leonard Cohen Offers Rare Peek into His Process at 'Popular Problems' Preview," *Rolling Stone*, September 11, 2014.

217   *he started with a loop*: Miranda and McCarter, *Hamilton: The Revolution*, 91, n. 3. He also describes his composition of "Wait for It" on a 2020 episode of *Song Exploder*: "Lin-Manuel Miranda—Wait for It," episode 2, created by Hrishikesh Hirway, on Netflix, which includes Lin-Manuel's original voice memo along with Thomas Kail's and Alex Lacamoire's reactions.

219   *"He runs at a totally different temperature than me"*: Lin-Manuel Miranda interview for *Hamilton's America*, directed by Alex Horwitz (PBS, 2016), August 2, 2014; transcript courtesy of Alex Horwitz.

219   *"It is the most important relationship in the show"*: Miranda, *Hamilton's America*.

220   *"They were here"*: Miranda interview, *Hamilton's America*, January 11, 2014.

220   *"So now I'm working on Burr"*: Miranda, *Hamilton's America*.

220   *"Geniuses, lower your voices"*: Miranda and McCarter, *Hamilton: The Revolution*, 27, n. 9.

221   *"If you agree with me"*: Siempre, Luis.

222   *an homage to Kander and Ebb*: "'The Room Where It Happens' Is a Love Letter to 'All That Jazz'—Lin-Manuel Miranda and John Kander," *Late Show with Stephen Colbert*, April 5, 2023, YouTube, https://youtu.be/epQdnqubTA0.

224   *For her three proofs*: Miranda and McCarter, *Hamilton: The Revolution*, 82, n. 7.

225   *"Beautiful women who can spit FIRE"*: Lin-Manuel Miranda, Twitter, December 19, 2012.

226   *"the feeling of seeing Renée nail the song"*: Lin-Manuel Miranda, Twitter, November 26, 2018.

228   *"Eliza and other evangelical women"*: Ron Chernow, *Alexander Hamilton* (New York: Penguin, 2004), 728.

228   *"Gimme the epidural"*: Lin-Manuel Miranda, Twitter, January 29, 2014.

228   *"Done"*: Lin-Manuel Miranda, Twitter, January 30, 2014.

230   *"best of wives and best of women"*: Chernow, *Alexander Hamilton*, xi.

17: *The Public Theater*

232   *he and Tommy Kail pulled off a stunt*: "Writing the Closing Number—Backstage at the Tonys," Usnavi, June 13, 2011, YouTube, https://youtu.be/4CR-sAit8LE.

232   *Tom worked out a chorus*: Lin-Manuel Miranda, "Bigger!," SoundCloud.

234   *"Oceanic Story Trust"*: Joanna Robinson, "How Pacific Islanders Helped Disney's *Moana* Find Its Way," *Vanity Fair*, November 16, 2016.

234   *a dance competition*: Disney's special features include video clips of the dance competition: "They Know the Way: Making the Music of *Moana*," Special Features, April 6, 2021, YouTube, https://youtu.be/93ocEn2ZpH0.

236   *"I have yet to meet a Tony Award"*: "What a Way to Spend a Day: Lin-Manuel

Miranda, Karen Olivo, and Leslie Odom Jr. on Living Inside Jonathan Larson's *Tick, Tick . . . Boom!,*" *Theater Mania,* June 24, 2014.

237 *"Someone else has permission"*: Lin-Manuel Miranda, "Pursuing the Muse Against the Clock," *New York Times,* June 19, 2014.

237 *"funny, anguished and heartbreaking"*: Charles Isherwood, "A Creator and His Doubts," *New York Times,* June 26, 2014.

238 *"It's where you go to make new shit"*: Adam Green, "Inside the High-Drama Life of *Hamilton* Impresario Oskar Eustis," *Vogue,* February 24, 2016.

239 *"If you don't change a word"*: Lin-Manuel Miranda, "Lin-Manuel Miranda on the Public Theater that Oskar Eustis Built," *Variety,* October 3, 2017.

240 *"One of the secrets of Oskar"*: Green, "Inside the High-Drama Life."

241 *"I can't possibly know what it's like"*: *The Hamilcast,* podcast, Lin-Manuel Miranda interview, October 16, 2017.

241 *Oskar's teenage son, Jack*: Michael Paulson, "'Hamilton' and Heartache: Living the Unimaginable," *New York Times,* October 13, 2016.

241 *moved in with Oskar*: Green, "Inside the High-Drama Life."

241 *"There is nothing you can say"*: Paulson, "'Hamilton' and Heartache."

242 *"I've been morbid all my life"*: Lin-Manuel Miranda interview for *Hamilton's America,* directed by Alex Horwitz (PBS, 2016), August 2, 2014; transcript courtesy of Alex Horwitz.

242 MY MOMMY PLAYS GRAND THEFT AUTO: Lin-Manuel Miranda posted a photo (where Grand Theft Auto is abbreviated GTA) on Twitter, November 19, 2014.

243 *"I have a lot of apps open"*: Rebecca Mead, "All About the Hamiltons," *New Yorker,* February 2, 2015.

243 *"The last song feels a little dry"*: Miranda interview, *Hamilton's America,* August 2, 2014.

244 *"New Song Under Construction Here"*: Mead, "All About the Hamiltons."

244 *"I feel like it's going to be a New Year's Baby"*: Lin-Manuel Miranda and Jeremy McCarter, *Hamilton: The Revolution* (New York: Grand Central Publishing, 2016), 273, n. 3.

244 *On January 1, 2015*: Ibid. and Mead, "All About the Hamiltons."

245 *"I got the idea that unlocked everything"*: Alyssa Brandt, "The Man Who Put the Groove in *Hamilton,*" *Cincinnati,* May 3, 2016.

246 *"I don't run"*: Miranda and McCarter, *Hamilton: The Revolution,* 270–71.

246 *"Let's make different mistakes tomorrow"*: Lin-Manuel Miranda, Twitter, January 20, 2015.

246 *tweeted that* Hamilton *had raised the bar*: Andrew Lloyd Webber, Twitter, February 2, 2015.

246 *Paul McCartney turned around*: Luis A. Miranda Jr. and Richard Wolffe, *Relentless: My Story of the Latino Spirit That Is Transforming America* (New York: Hachette Books, 2024), 171–72.

246 *"I was even more astonished"*: Ibid.

247   *the run had already been extended*: Michael Gioia, "Despite Buzz of a Broadway Transfer, *Hamilton* Announces Another Off-Broadway Extension," *Playbill*, February 4, 2015.

247   *"You broke the phones"*: Lin-Manuel Miranda, Twitter, February 4, 2015.

18: *Opening Nights*

248   *"Javilton"*: Lin-Manuel Miranda, Twitter, October 19, 2014.

249   *Lin-Manuel burst into tears*: Adam Green, "Lin-Manuel Miranda's Groundbreaking Hip-Hop Musical, *Hamilton*, Hits Broadway," *Vogue*, June 24, 2015.

249   *"MORE THAN ONE SONG A YEAR"*: Lin-Manuel Miranda, Twitter, September 17, 2017.

250   *"You write for 6 years"*: Lin-Manuel Miranda, Twitter, February 17, 2015.

250   *The Public had set up statues*: Rebecca Mead, "All About the Hamiltons," *New Yorker*, February 2, 2015.

250   *"the adrenaline rush of revolution"*: Ben Brantley, "Review: In 'Hamilton,' Lin-Manuel Miranda Forges Democracy Through Rap," *New York Times*, February 17, 2015.

250   *"the most exciting and significant musical of the past decade"*: Terry Teachout, "'Hamilton' Review: A Star-Spangled Success," *Wall Street Journal*, February 19, 2015.

250   *Hillary and Bill Clinton came*: Jennifer Schuessler, "'Hamilton' Puts Politics Onstage and Politicians in Attendance," *New York Times*, March 27, 2015.

251   *Lac added a couple of bars*: Lin-Manuel Miranda and Jeremy McCarter, *Hamilton: The Revolution* (New York: Grand Central Publishing, 2016), 121, n. 1.

251   *"This is the best piece of art"*: Phillipa Soo, "*Hamilton* Star: Michelle Obama Gave Me 'the Best Compliment I Have Ever Received,'" *Time*, January 9, 2017.

252   *minimum weekly salary of $1,900*: Michael Paulson, "'Hamilton' Producers and Actors Reach Deal on Sharing Profits," *New York Times*, April 15, 2016.

252   *"The way they chose"*: Lin-Manuel Miranda, commencement address at Wesleyan University, May 24, 2015.

253   *"Luz and I wanted to invest"*: Luis A. Miranda Jr. and Richard Wolffe, *Relentless: My Story of the Latino Spirit That Is Transforming America* (New York: Hachette Books, 2024), 172.

253   *It closed in a month*: Gordon Cox, "Tupac Shakur Musical 'Holler if Ya Hear Me' Flops on Broadway," *Variety*, July 14, 2014.

254   *its investors still failed to recover*: Patrick Healy, "'Bloody Bloody Andrew Jackson' to Close," *New York Times*, December 1, 2010.

254   *Someone tweeted Lin-Manuel a picture*: Lin-Manuel Miranda, Twitter, March 8, 2015.

254   *sales reached thirty million dollars*: Andrew Gans and Michael Gioia, "*Hamilton* Opens with Multi-Million-Dollar Advance," *Playbill*, August 7, 2015.

254 *"In our gut"*: Miranda and Wolffe, *Relentless*, 172.

254 *"It was hot"*: National Endowment for the Arts, podcast, Lin-Manuel Miranda interview, May 6, 2016.

255 *"The least I can do"*: Ibid.

255 *"Thanks to you"*: "#Ham4Ham: Behind the Scenes at the First Ticket Lottery for Broadway's *Hamilton*," Theatermania, July 14, 2015, YouTube, https://youtu.be/umsumZ0POeY.

255 *"We should do that every day"*: Miranda interview, National Endowment for the Arts.

256 *"Dreams come true"*: "A #Ham4Ham Confrontation on 46th Street," *Hamilton*, August 15, 2015, YouTube, https://youtu.be/ASlkb6CLJng.

256 *"You found* another *audience"*: *The West Wing Weekly*, podcast, "Hamilton Special," Lin-Manuel Miranda and Thomas Kail interview, April 3, 2018.

257 *"We're gonna do a show for Obama"*: Renée Elise Goldsberry, Twitter, July 18, 2015.

257 *"Eminem meets Hamilton"*: Jennifer Schuessler, "Starring on Broadway, Obama and Alexander Hamilton," *New York Times*, July 18, 2015.

257 he sent word through his spokesperson: Olivia Clement, "President Obama Offers His Review of *Hamilton*," *Playbill*, July 19, 2015.

257 *"Everything that could have happened"*: Schuessler, "Starring on Broadway."

258 *"For when we have faced down impossible odds"*: Barack Obama, New Hampshire primary speech, transcript published in *New York Times*, January 8, 2008.

258 *"Yes We Can" music video*: "Yes We Can Obama Song by will.i.am," will.i.am, February 2, 2008, YouTube, https://youtu.be/2fZHou18Cdk.

259 *Washington liked to quote*: George Tsakiridis, "Vine and Fig Tree," George Washington Presidential Library, Mount Vernon, Virginia.

259 *He had told a friend*: Ralph Ellis, Greg Botelho, and Ed Payne, "Charleston Church Shooter Hears Victim's Kin Say, 'I Forgive You,'" CNN, June 19, 2015.

260 *his first thought*: Chris Jackson interview for *Hamilton's America*, directed by Alex Horwitz (PBS, 2016), March 10, 2016; transcript courtesy of Alex Horwitz.

260 *"Anytime you write something"*: Green, "Lin-Manuel Miranda's Groundbreaking Hip-Hop Musical."

260 *"I'm going to keep it simple today"*: "Hamilton August 6, 2015 #Ham4Ham Pre-Show," Joe Gambino, August 6, 2015, YouTube, https://youtu.be/aToj9Jrbkeo.

260 *"Was it a benign or cruel destiny"*: Ron Chernow, *Alexander Hamilton* (New York: Penguin, 2004), 1.

261 *"I am so tired"*: Ibid., 2.

261 *"I hope y'all get to see Hamilton"*: "Hamilton August 6, 2015, #Ham4Ham Pre-Show."

261 *"Everyone on Broadway was snickering"*: Michael Riedel, "Pompous 'Hamilton' Already Eyes Tony—for Next Year," *New York Post*, February 24, 2015.

261   *"it really is that good"*: Ben Brantley, "Review: 'Hamilton,' Young Rebels Changing History and Theater," *New York Times*, August 6, 2015.

261   *"the first authentic hip-hop show"*: Chris Hayes, "'Hamilton' Creator Lin-Manuel Miranda, Questlove and Black Thought on the Runaway Broadway Hit, Its Political Relevance and Super-Fan Barack Obama," *Billboard*, July 30, 2015.

261   *"Uh, six years of labor"*: Miranda, *Hamilton's America*.

262   *The guests cheered*: Lin-Manuel Miranda, Twitter, August 7, 2015.

19: *Say Goodbye*

263   *"Dear Jeffrey"*: Richard Morgan, "How *Hamilton*'s Cast Got Broadway's Best Deal," Bloomberg.com, September 28, 2016.

263   *According to calculations by the* New York Times: Michael Paulson and David Gelles, "'Hamilton' Inc.: The Path to a Billion-Dollar Broadway Show," *New York Times*, June 8, 2016.

264   *agreed to split a tiny portion of its profits*: Michael Paulson, "'Hamilton' Producers and Actors Reach Deal on Sharing Profits," *New York Times*, April 15, 2016.

265   *Jeffrey did not agree*: Morgan, "How *Hamilton*'s Cast Got Broadway's Best Deal."

265   *"This is ground worth standing"*: Ibid.

265   *"This brings to an end"*: Ibid.

266   Hamilton *broke the record*: Caitlin Huston, "'Hamilton' Breaks All-Time Broadway Box Office Record," *Broadway News*, November 27, 2017.

266   *The cast recording not only hit*: "*Hamilton* Broadway Cast Album to Hit #1 on *Billboard* Rap Chart," *Playbill*, November 16, 2015.

266   *Celebrities from Oprah to Steven Spielberg*: Maya Robinson and Nate Jones, "Browse the Backstage *Hamilton* Cutout That Celebrities Sign When They See the Show," *Vulture*, January 12, 2016.

266   *"I just know that it's hard for me"*: Morgan, "How *Hamilton*'s Cast Got Broadway's Best Deal."

268   *"What happens when you mess up"*: The Breakfast Club, podcast, Lin-Manuel Miranda interview, October 18, 2017.

268   *MacArthur Fellowship*: Robert Viagas, "Lin-Manuel Miranda Among MacArthur 'Genius' Grant Winners," *Playbill*, September 29, 2015.

269   *"They are the ones"*: Michael Sokolove, "The C.E.O. of 'Hamilton' Inc.," *New York Times*, April 5, 2016.

269   Hamilton *won the Pulitzer Prize*: Gordon Cox and Brent Lang, "'Hamilton' Wins Pulitzer Prize for Drama," *Variety*, April 18, 2016.

269   *The show received a record*: Michael Paulson, "'Hamilton' Makes History with 16 Tony Nominations," *New York Times*, May 3, 2016.

270　*"Thank God I picked the right outfit"*: Lauren Le Vine, "Barbra Streisand Dresses for *Hamilton* at Her First Tonys in 46 Years," *Vanity Fair*, June 13, 2016.

270　*a gunman had opened fire*: Steven W. Thrasher, "Latino Community Mourns Pulse Shooting Victims: '90% Were Hispanic,'" *Guardian*, June 14, 2016.

270　*deadlier than any previous mass shooting*: Eyder Peralta, "Putting 'Deadliest Mass Shooting In U.S. History' into Some Historical Context," NPR, June 13, 2016.

270　*"It's a day marked by such tragedy"*: "Red Carpet: Lin-Manuel Miranda (2016)," Tony Awards, June 12, 2016, YouTube, https://youtu.be/EFgewhjEoeQ.

270　*wearing a rainbow flag pin and a silver ribbon*: Theresa Avila, "Celebrities at the 2016 Tony Awards Wore a Silver Ribbon to Show Solidarity with Victims of the Orlando Mass Shooting," *Cut*, June 13, 2016.

270　*wouldn't bring their prop muskets*: Katie Reilly, "The *Hamilton* Cast Will Drop Muskets from Their Tony's Performance After the Orlando Shooting," *Time*, June 12, 2016.

271　*she later asked Lin-Manuel*: "Jennifer Lopez: I 'Stalked' Lin-Manuel Miranda into Singing with Me," *Today*, July 11, 2016, YouTube, https://youtu.be/OM jcbi7Y0kM.

272　*a host of other celebrities*: Joshua Barone, "Lin-Manuel Miranda's Final Bows in 'Hamilton' on Broadway," *New York Times*, July 10, 2016; Rembert Browne, "Here's What It Was Like at Lin-Manuel Miranda's Final *Hamilton* Performance," *Vulture*, July 11, 2016.

272　*he cut off his Hamilton ponytail*: Lin-Manuel Miranda, Twitter, July 9, 2016.

272　*"You know"*: Thomas Kail interview for *Hamilton's America*, directed by Alex Horwitz (PBS, 2016), March 18, 2016; transcript courtesy of Alex Horwitz.

273　*"Oh, What a Beautiful Morning"*: Lin-Manuel Miranda, Twitter, March 14, 2016.

273　*"Mr. President"*: Kail interview, *Hamilton's America*, March 18, 2016.

273　*the first Black president and the Black first president*: Lin-Manuel Miranda and Jeremy McCarter, *Hamilton: The Revolution* (New York: Grand Central Publishing, 2016), 284.

273　*for the rest of my life*: Kail interview, *Hamilton's America*, March 18, 2016.

274　*the final song*: All details and quotes from this performance come from this video: "'One Last Time'—Hamilton at the White House #ObamaLegacy," *Hamilton*, January 10, 2017, YouTube, https://youtu.be/uV4UpCq2azs.

275　*"Right now, you're going to hear from the forty-fifth president"*: Matt Flegenheimer, "$2,700 for Hillary Clinton at 'Hamilton'? That Would Be Enough," *New York Times*, July 12, 2016.

275　*"As Washington tells us"*: Ibid.

275　*"'Well, you're never gonna be president now'"*: "Lin-Manuel Miranda Monologue–SNL," *Saturday Night Live*, October 8, 2016, YouTube, https://youtu.be/AsupmN90wBk.

275 *"Scared as y'all"*: Lin-Manuel Miranda, Twitter, November 8, 2016.

275 *This too shall pass*: Lin-Manuel Miranda, Twitter, November 9, 2016.

275 *"F*ck that"*: Lin-Manuel Miranda, Twitter, November 8, 2016.

275 *"Was the Election a Vote Against 'Hamilton'"*: Niall Ferguson, "Was the Election a Vote Against 'Hamilton'?," *Boston Globe*, November 14, 2016.

276 *"This election cycle"*: Lin-Manuel Miranda comment on "Immigrants (We Get the Job Done)," *The Hamilton Mixtape*, Genius.com.

277 *Pence took his seat*: Adam Hetrick, "Vice President-Elect Mike Pence Greeted with Boos and a Speech at *Hamilton*," *Playbill*, November 18, 2016.

277 *"Vice President–Elect Pence"*: *Hamilton* posted a video of Brandon Victor Dixon's speech on Twitter, November 18, 2016.

278 *"Our wonderful future V.P."*: Eric Bradner, "Pence: 'I Wasn't Offended' by Message of 'Hamilton' Cast," CNN, November 20, 2016.

278 *a Trump supporter started shouting*: Alan Henry, "Trump Supporter Shouts Profanities and Interrupts *Hamilton* in Chicago," BroadwayWorld.com, November 20, 2016.

20: *Film School*

279 *"Don't think about 'Let It Go'"*: "Lin-Manuel Miranda Dishes 'Moana,' 'Hamilton,' and Possibly Joining EGOT Club with Oscar Win," Gold Derby, November 20, 2016, YouTube, https://youtu.be/uSib1PziwxQ.

283 *"I wish the Goblin King"*: Lin-Manuel Miranda, Twitter, January 11, 2016.

283 *He knew Jemaine Clement*: Kara Warner, "How Lin-Manuel Miranda Pays Tribute to David Bowie with 'Moana' Song 'Shiny,'" *People*, November 24, 2016.

283 *"Tamatoa hasn't always been this glam"*: Lin-Manuel Miranda, "Shiny—Demo," *Moana* original motion picture soundtrack, 2016.

284 *For the* Moana *premiere*: "'You're Welcome' Live by Dwayne Johnson and Lin-Manuel Miranda at *Moana* World Premiere," The Rock, November 15, 2016, YouTube, https://youtu.be/8C9-3-emJxU.

284 *the second-highest Thanksgiving-weekend opening*: Brooks Barnes, "'Moana' Has the Second Best Thanksgiving Weekend Opening of All Time," *New York Times*, November 27, 2016.

284 *eventually grossing over $600 million*: *Moana* grosses from BoxOfficeMojo .com.

284 *Reviews hailed*: See, for instance, Brian Truitt, "'Moana' Really Sings as a Respite from the Usual Princess Story," *USA Today*, November 9, 2016; Peter Travers, "Disney's Animated Polynesian Musical Is a Feminist Delight," *Rolling Stone*, November 23, 2016.

284 The Hamilton Mixtape *debuted*: Keith Caulfield, "'The Hamilton Mixtape' Debuts at No. 1 on *Billboard* 200 Albums Chart," *Billboard*, December 11, 2016.

284 *the number-one book*: Alexandra Alter, "'Hamilton: The Revolution' Races Out of Bookstores, Echoing the Musical's Success," *New York Times*, May 3, 2016.

287 *Universal Pictures snatched up the rights*: Michael Fleming, "Universal Gets 'In the Heights' Rights," *Variety*, November 6, 2008.

287 *his company signed on*: Dave McNary, "The Weinstein Company Boards Lin-Manuel Miranda's 'In the Heights' Movie," *Variety*, May 31, 2016.

287 *sexual-harassment allegations*: Jodi Kantor and Megan Twohey, "Harvey Weinstein Paid Off Sexual Harassment Accusers for Decades," *New York Times*, October 5, 2017.

288 Crazy Rich Asians: *Crazy Rich Asians* grosses from BoxOfficeMojo.com.

288 *in Jon's case, parents who'd left Taiwan*: Jon M. Chu and Jeremy McCarter, *Viewfinder* (New York: Random House, 2024).

289 *Quiara had shown him the giant Highbridge Pool*: Jackson McHenry, "How *In the Heights* Pulled Off the Big Swimming-Pool Scene," *Vulture*, June 10, 2021.

289 *grossing $360 million*: *Mary Poppins Returns* grosses from BoxOfficeMojo.com.

290 *"Don't fuck it up"*: Lin-Manuel Miranda, Twitter, June 3, 2019.

292 *He was cast*: Jesse Thorn, host, *Bullseye with Jesse Thorn*, podcast, interview with Lin-Manuel Miranda, November 25, 2019.

292 *He and Vanessa had read the series*: Sinead Garvan, "Lin-Manuel Miranda: 'I Fell in Love to His Dark Materials,'" BBC, November 2, 2019.

292 *another opportunity to honor*: Benjamin Lindsay, "Lin-Manuel Miranda's His Dark Materials Mustache Was His Idea," *Vulture*, November 25, 2019.

21: *Tick, Tick*

294 *"If they only let me make one"*: Kristen Chuba, "Lin-Manuel Miranda, Andrew Garfield Call 'Tick, Tick . . . Boom!' a 'Love Letter to Jon Larson,'" *Hollywood Reporter*, November 11, 2021.

294 *"I had never seen such a fearless performance"*: Lyra Hale, "Lin-Manuel Miranda and Andrew Garfield Talk 'Tick, Tick . . . Boom'—and Prove Their Bromance Is Real," *Remezcla*, November 17, 2021.

294 *He took off a shoe*: Michael Ordoña, "Andrew Garfield, Oscar Isaac and More Reveal Their Most Daunting Experiences on Set," *Los Angeles Times*, December 18, 2021.

296 *"What cool things don't I know"*: "How Lin-Manuel Miranda Made *Tick, Tick . . . Boom!*—Netflix," Still Watching Netflix, December 8, 2021, YouTube, https://youtu.be/7MLv2xbl36k.

297 *"The Zoom Where It Happens"*: "The Zoom Where It Happens," *Hamilton*, April 7, 2020, YouTube, https://youtu.be/HCK_1ydMhiE.

298 *Jeffrey shared a portion*: Michael Paulson, "'Hamilton' Is Coming to the Small Screen. This Is How It Got There," *New York Times*, June 25, 2020.

298 *Attracting subscribers to Disney Plus*: Brooks Barnes, "Disney, Staggered by Pandemic, Sees a Streaming Boom," *New York Times*, August 4, 2020.

298 *"More than usual"*: Vanessa Nadal, Twitter, May 12, 2020.

298 *"Our Hamilton film"*: Lin-Manuel Miranda, Twitter, May 12, 2020.

298 *downloads of the Disney Plus app*: Todd Spangler, "'Hamilton' Drives Up Disney Plus App Downloads 74% over the Weekend in U.S.," *Variety*, July 6, 2020.

298 *Disney Plus added*: Joan E. Solomon, "Disney Plus Hits 60.5 Million Subscribers, Helped by Hamilton Bump," CNET, August 4, 2020.

298 *with popcorn and Magna-Tiles*: Lin-Manuel Miranda, Twitter, July 3, 2020.

298 *"I always boo"*: Vanessa Nadal, Twitter, July 3, 2020.

299 *"Thank you for tonight"*: Lin-Manuel Miranda, Twitter, July 3, 2020.

299 *brought terms like* systemic racism: See, for instance, Justin Worland, "America's Long Overdue Awakening to Systemic Racism," *Time*, June 11, 2020.

299 *"just a classic American musical"*: Soraya Nadia McDonald, "Five Years Ago, 'Hamilton' Turned a Revolution into a Revelation—What Now?," *Andscape*, June 30, 2020.

299 *"Black Actors Dress Up"*: Ishmael Reed, "'Hamilton: The Musical:' Black Actors Dress Up like Slave Traders . . . and It's Not Halloween," *CounterPunch*, August 21, 2015.

299 New York Times *ran a forum*: Stephanie Goodman, "Debating 'Hamilton' as It Shifts from Stage to Screen," *New York Times*, July 10, 2020.

299 *"All the criticisms are valid"*: Lin-Manuel Miranda, Twitter, July 6, 2020.

300 *Nevertheless, for some critics*: See, for instance, Cate Young, "'Hamilton' Felt Revolutionary in 2015—but It Strikes a Different Chord Today," *Today*, July 7, 2020.

300 *"That we have not yet firmly spoken"*: Hamilton, Twitter, May 30, 2020.

300 *When he took* Hamilton *to Puerto Rico*: Portions of this section were first published in Daniel Pollack-Pelzner, "The Mixed Reception of the *Hamilton* Premiere in Puerto Rico," *Atlantic*, January 18, 2019.

300 *"closed something in me"*: Ruthie Fierberg, "Lin-Manuel Miranda Can't Help but Cry During This Interview with Oprah About *Hamilton* in Puerto Rico," *Playbill*, March 7, 2018.

301 *"I write about Puerto Rico today"*: Lin-Manuel Miranda, "Give Puerto Rico Its Chance to Thrive," *New York Times*, March 28, 2016.

301 NUESTRAS VIDAS: *Siempre, Luis.*

302 *"The fiscal crisis"*: Ibid.

302 *"la historia del mismo"*: Amárilis Pagán Jiménez, "Hamilton, la UPR y Puerto Rico," *80grados*, December 23, 2018.

302 *"I'm sure you didn't imagine"*: Jessica Kegu, "Message from Lin-Manuel Miranda's 8th Grade Teacher Brings 'Hamilton' Star to Tears," CBS, January 11, 2019.

303   *"happy colonized subjects"*: Mariela Fullana Acosta, "Emocionante el Inicio de 'Hamilton' en Puerto Rico," *El Nuevo Día,* January 11, 2019.

304   *"Why Gen Z Turned on Lin-Manuel Miranda"*: E. J. Dickson, "Why Gen Z Turned on Lin-Manuel Miranda," *Rolling Stone,* August 4, 2020.

305   *"I don't know how to drown out"*: Lin-Manuel Miranda, email to Stephen Sondheim, courtesy of Lin-Manuel Miranda.

305   *"and tea, if you want it"*: Stephen Sondheim, email to Lin-Manuel Miranda, courtesy of Lin-Manuel Miranda.

22: *Boom*

306   *another studio revived its fortunes*: Mike Fleming Jr., "Sony Animation Sets Lin-Manuel Miranda's 'Vivo' for 2020 Bow," *Deadline,* December 14, 2016.

307   *fast-tracked by Sony*: Patrick Hopes, "'Vivo,' Lin-Manuel Miranda's Animated Movie, Shifts Release Dates," *Deadline,* January 26, 2018.

307   *"The fate of the movie"*: Lin-Manuel Miranda, Twitter, August 10, 2021.

307   *"Can I help"*: Ibid.

308   *"a definitive Latin American Disney musical"*: John Hazelton, "'Encanto' Filmmakers Talk Working with Lin-Manuel Miranda to Create 'A Definitive Latin American Disney Musical,'" *Screen Daily,* January 17, 2022.

308   *"We had a lot of characters"*: Disney Music, podcast, "Disney for Scores: Lin-Manuel Miranda and Germaine Franco," December 16, 2021.

309   *"a love-letter-slash-apology"*: Christina Radish, "Lin-Manuel Miranda on Writing the Songs in 'Encanto' and Working with One of His Musical Heroes on 'The Little Mermaid,'" *Collider,* November 24, 2021.

309   *he borrowed from "The Lovecats"*: Disney Music, "Disney for Scores."

311   *"Anything in here you love"*: Jared Bush, Twitter, January 30, 2022.

311   *"It was fuhuucking complicated"*: Lin-Manuel Miranda, Twitter, May 15, 2020.

311   *"Lin-Manuel on steroids"*: Ashley Spencer, "We're Going to Talk About 'Bruno,' Yes, Yes, Yes," *New York Times,* January 13, 2022.

312   *"to sound like a song"*: Disney Music, "Disney for Scores."

312   *"In a lot of ways, I am the narrator"*: Michael Ordoña, "Lin-Manuel Miranda's Complex Quest for Simplicity with 'Dos Oruguitas' from 'Encanto,'" *Los Angeles Times,* March 8, 2022.

312   *Abuela Mundi passed away*: Lorena Blas, "Lin-Manuel Miranda Grieving After Death of His Beloved 'Abuela,'" *USA Today,* December 26, 2017.

312   *He got only as far*: Disney Music, "Disney for Scores."

312   *He listened to folk-song models*: Chris Lee, "Lin-Manuel Miranda on the Hardest Song He Wrote for *Encanto*," *Vulture,* January 31, 2022.

314   *"by the blue purple yellow red water"*: Stephen Sondheim, "Sunday," *Look, I Made a Hat* (New York: Knopf, 2011), 32.

314   *"in the blue silver chromium diner"*: Jonathan Larson, "Sunday," *Tick, Tick . . . Boom!*, original footage courtesy of Julie Larson.

314   *Jonathan's dream chorus*: "How Lin-Manuel Miranda Made *Tick, Tick . . . Boom!*—Netflix," Still Watching Netflix, December 8, 2021, YouTube, https://youtu.be/7MLv2xbl36k.

317   *He'd just had a new idea*: *Disney Music*, "Disney for Scores."

318   *"Thank you, Miss Ames"*: Lin-Manuel Miranda, Twitter, November 22, 2021.

319   *"I didn't get a chance"*: Stephen Sondheim voice message, courtesy of Lin-Manuel Miranda.

319   *"Hope your ears have been ringing"*: Lin-Manuel Miranda, email to Stephen Sondheim, courtesy of Lin-Manuel Miranda.

319   *"Thanks for the nice boost"*: Stephen Sondheim, email to Lin-Manuel Miranda, courtesy of Lin-Manuel Miranda.

320   *Reviews were glowing*: See, for instance, Leah Greenblatt, "*In the Heights* Review: Lin-Manuel Miranda's Vibrant Musical Dazzles on Screen," *Entertainment Weekly*, May 21, 2021; Mick LaSalle, "Jon M. Chu's Joyful 'In the Heights' Marks Return of Big Dreams, Large Screens," *San Francisco Chronicle*, May 23, 2021; Ty Burr, "'In the Heights' Reaches the Top," *Boston Globe*, June 10, 2022.

320   *Variety estimated*: Rebecca Rubin, "HBO Max Isn't to Blame After 'In the Heights' Fizzles at the Box Office," *Variety*, June 14, 2021.

320   *it drew only*: Rebecca Rubin, "Box Office: 'In the Heights' Disappoints with $11 Million Opening Weekend," *Variety*, June 13, 2021.

321   *Other Warner Brothers releases*: Rubin, "HBO Max Isn't to Blame."

321   *brought in even less*: Anthony D'Alessandro, "'West Side Story' Isn't Kicking Up with $10M+ Opening," *Deadline*, December 12, 2021.

321   *some critics questioned*: See, for instance, Frances Negrón-Muntaner, "The Generic Latinidad of 'In the Heights,'" *New Yorker*, June 21, 2021.

321   *Why weren't there dark-skinned Latino actors*: Felice León, "Let's Talk About *In the Heights* and the Erasure of Dark-Skinned Afro-Latinx Folks," *Root*, June 9, 2021.

322   *"I started writing"*: Lin-Manuel Miranda, Twitter, June 14, 2021.

322   *"I was like"*: "Lin-Manuel Miranda—'In the Heights: Finding Home' and Importance of Representation," *Daily Show*, June 16, 2021.

322   *Sony licensed it to Netflix*: Anthony D'Alessandro, "Sony Animation's Lin-Manuel Miranda Musical Pic 'Vivo' Headed to Netflix," *Deadline*, April 26, 2021.

323   *became the most-watched Netflix movie*: Samuel Spencer, "Top 10 Most-Watched Netflix Movies in August 2021," *Newsweek*, August 27, 2021.

323   *second-most-watched movie*: Samuel Spencer, "Top 10 Most-Watched Netflix Movies in September 2021," *Newsweek*, September 30, 2021.

323   *dropped off the list*: Samuel Spencer, "Top 10 Most-Watched Netflix Movies in October 2021," *Newsweek*, October 29, 2021.

323   *opened well in theaters*: "Weekend Box Office: *Encanto* Enchants Thanksgiving with $40M 5-Day Debut," Boxoffice Pro, November 28, 2021.

323   *eventually reaching $256 million globally*: *Encanto* grosses from BoxOffice Mojo.com.

323   *the most-streamed movie*: "Nielsen Pins 'Encanto' at Top of Very Animated Most-Streamed List for 2022," *Animation*, January 26, 2023.

323   *streamed more than any other movie except* Moana: Mike Blair, "These Are the Top 10 Most Streamed Movies of 2023," *CultureSlate*, February 1, 2024.

323   *the biggest Disney song* ever: Andrew Unterberger, "'We Don't Talk About Bruno' from 'Encanto' Now Tops *Billboard*'s Greatest of All Time Disney Songs Chart Ranking," *Billboard*, April 6, 2022.

323   *A new rubric for calculating the charts*: Chris Molanphy, "'We Don't Talk About Bruno' Didn't Get to No. 1 Just Because It's Catchy," *Slate*, February 4, 2022.

323   *all eight songs*: Rachel Labonte, "Every Encanto Song Is on the *Billboard* Hot 100 Charts," *Screen Rant*, February 8, 2022.

323   *the top songwriter of the year*: Xander Zellner, "Lin-Manuel Miranda Is the Top Hot 100 Songwriter of 2022," *Billboard*, December 1, 2022.

Epilogue

327   *"I wanted to write with someone smarter"*: Maria Sherman, "Lin-Manuel Miranda and Eisa Davis on Their 'Warriors' Musical Concept Album with Lauryn Hill," Associated Press, September 18, 2024.

329   *"I'm Cochise"*: All *Warriors* lyrics quoted from Lin-Manuel Miranda and Eisa Davis, *Warriors*, Atlantic Records, 2024.

332   *a few critics objected to*: Carl Wilson, "Lin-Manuel Miranda's *Warriors* Musical Pulls Too Many Punches," *Slate*, October 18, 2024; Craig Jenkins, "*Warriors* Come Out and Grate," *Vulture*, October 22, 2024.

332   *a five-star review*: Chris Wiegand, "Lin-Manuel Miranda and Eisa Davis Come Out to Play with Firecracker Musical," *Guardian*, October 17, 2024.

COPYRIGHT AND PERMISSION ACKNOWLEDGMENTS

BREATHE
INÚTIL
96,000
PACIENCIA Y FE
WHEN YOU'RE HOME
CARNAVAL DEL BARRIO
ATENCIÓN
FINALE
Words and Music by LIN-MANUEL
MIRANDA

WHAT I WAS BORN TO DO
Words and Music by LIN-MANUEL
MIRANDA, THOMAS KITT, and
AMANDA GREEN

ONE PERFECT MOMENT
Words and Music by LIN-MANUEL
MIRANDA, THOMAS KITT and
AMANDA GREEN

DO YOUR OWN THING
CROSS THE LINE
Words and Music by LIN-MANUEL
MIRANDA

FRIDAY NIGHT JACKSON
Words and Music by LIN-MANUEL
MIRANDA, AMANDA GREEN and
THOMAS KITT

I GOT YOU
Words and Music by LIN-MANUEL
MIRANDA, AMANDA GREEN and
THOMAS KITT

ALEXANDER HAMILTON
AARON BURR, SIR
THE STORY OF TONIGHT
FARMER REFUTED
YOU'LL BE BACK
RIGHT HAND MAN
HELPLESS
SATISFIED

INDEX